The Function of Emotions

Heather C. Lench
Editor

The Function of Emotions

When and Why Emotions Help Us

 Springer

Editor
Heather C. Lench
Department of Psychological and Brain Sciences
Texas A&M University
College Station, TX, USA

ISBN 978-3-319-77618-7   ISBN 978-3-319-77619-4   (eBook)
https://doi.org/10.1007/978-3-319-77619-4

Library of Congress Control Number: 2018938555

Printed on acid-free paper

This Springer imprint is published by the registered company Springer International Publishing AG part of Springer Nature.
The registered company address is: Gewerbestrasse 11, 6330 Cham, Switzerland

Special thanks to the Emotion Science Laboratory Group, who were continuously passionate about the idea that emotions must do something. Especially Zari Carpenter, whose conscientiousness and compassion helped foster the collaboration necessary, and whose comments for authors and fact checking helped develop this book. Thanks to the Virtue, Happiness, and Meaning of Life Working Group sponsored by the John Templeton Foundation for comments on the ideas and scope of this book.

Synopsis

This book poses and answers the question: What do emotions do for us? This question is centuries old, but only recently has behavioral and neurological study of emotion progressed to the point that we can start to answer. Emotions do not just make us feel good or bad. Findings have revealed that they change the way that we think, feel, and behave in powerful ways. The changes wrought by emotion have real-world implications for whether or not we succeed in attaining our goals, for our relationships with others, and for our well-being and life satisfaction. This book draws on current work in psychology, management, education, and neuroscience to address the functions of emotion in everyday life. The authors discuss a range of emotional experiences and their functions, including fear, love, sadness, boredom, awe, and pride.

Contents

Contributors

Dong An Department of Philosophy, Texas A&M University, College Station, TX, USA

Cassandra L. Baldwin Department of Psychological and Brain Sciences, Texas A&M University, College Station, TX, USA

Zari Koebel Carpenter Department of Psychological and Brain Sciences, Texas A&M University, College Station, TX, USA

Alice Chirico Department of Psychology, Catholic University of the Sacred Heart, Milan, Italy

James Danckert Department of Psychology, University of Waterloo, Waterloo, ON, Canada

Alexander F. Danvers Institute for the Study of Human Flourishing, University of Oklahoma, Norman, OK, USA

Elizabeth L. Davis Department of Psychology, University of California, Riverside, Riverside, CA, USA

John Eastwood Department of Psychology, York University, Toronto, ON, Canada

Tsachi Ein-Dor The Baruch Ivcher School of Psychology, The Interdisciplinary Center (IDC) Herzliya, Herzliya, Israel

Katie E. Garrison Department of Psychological and Brain Sciences, Texas A&M University, College Station, TX, USA

Gilad Hirschberger The Baruch Ivcher School of Psychology, The Interdisciplinary Center (IDC) Herzliya, Herzliya, Israel

David Huron Center for Cognitive and Brain Sciences, Ohio State University, Columbus, OH, USA

Melissa M. Karnaze Department of Psychology and Social Behavior, University of California, Irvine, Irvine, CA, USA

Heather C. Lench Department of Psychological and Brain Sciences, Texas A&M University, College Station, TX, USA

Linda J. Levine Department of Psychology and Social Behavior, University of California, Irvine, Irvine, CA, USA

Norman P. Li School of Social Sciences, Singapore Management University, Singapore, Singapore

Jhotisha Mugon Department of Psychology, University of Waterloo, Waterloo, ON, Canada

Makenzie J. O'Neil Department of Psychology, Arizona State University, Tempe, AZ, USA

Parisa Parsafar Department of Psychology, University of California, Riverside, Riverside, CA, USA

Ira J. Roseman Department of Psychology, Rutgers University, Camden, NJ, USA

Michelle N. Shiota Department of Psychology, Arizona State University, Tempe, AZ, USA

Justin Storbeck Queens College, CUNY, Flushing, NY, USA

The Graduate Center, CUNY, New York, NY, USA

Andriy Struk Department of Psychology, University of Waterloo, Waterloo, ON, Canada

Lisa A. Williams School of Psychology, University of New South Wales, Sydney, NSW, Australia

Jordan Wylie The Graduate Center, CUNY, New York, NY, USA

David B. Yaden Department of Psychology, University of Pennsylvania, Philadelphia, PA, USA

Jose C. Yong School of Social Sciences, Singapore Management University, Singapore, Singapore

List of Figures

List of Tables

Chapter 1
What Do Emotions Do for Us?

Heather C. Lench and Zari Koebel Carpenter

> And then it dawned on him that he and the man with him weren't talking about the same thing. For while he himself spoke from the depths of long days of brooding upon his personal distress, and the image he tried to impart had been slowly shaped and proved in the fires of passion and regret, this meant nothing to the man to whom he was speaking, who pictured a conventional emotion, a grief that is traded on the marketplace, mass-produced.
>
> – Albert Camus, *The Plague,* 1991

This book poses and answers the question: What do emotions do for us? This question is centuries old, but only recently has behavioral and neurological study of emotion progressed to the point that we can start to answer. Scientific study of emotions has been a relatively recent development, in part because of the sentiment conveyed in the quote above from Camus. Emotions feel so deeply personal, and so related to our values and hopes, that it is almost impossible to convey their meaning to others in ways that can be understood. As soon as we apply a label to the emotion, it seems to lessen the experience itself. Yet the strength of the scientific study of emotion rests in the ability of researchers to approach the topic with methodological rigor – they must define what emotions are, what causes them, and how to elicit and measure them. Applying the scientific method to the study of emotion has allowed researchers who study human behavior to examine the consequences of emotions for people. The findings help us to understand emotions in daily life and in mental health disorders, as well as how to think about emotion to improve our lives.

These studies have revealed that emotions change the way that we think, feel, and behave in powerful ways. The changes wrought by emotion have real-world implications for whether or not we succeed in attaining our goals, for our relationships

H. C. Lench (✉) · Z. K. Carpenter
Department of Psychological and Brain Sciences, Texas A&M University,
College Station, TX, USA
e-mail: hlench@tamu.edu

© Springer International Publishing AG, part of Springer Nature 2018
H. C. Lench (ed.), *The Function of Emotions*,
https://doi.org/10.1007/978-3-319-77619-4_1

with others, and for our well-being and life satisfaction. This book draws on current work in psychology, management, education, and neuroscience to address the functions of emotion in everyday life. The experts who contributed each chapter discuss the many ways that emotions affect us – everything from helping us accomplish our goals, to fostering caretaking of others, to driving us to rethink our life and priorities. This introduction provides an orientation to the reader about the major concepts and issues in this field of study.

A New Perspective on Emotion

Emotions have traditionally been viewed as sources of trouble and irrationality – overwhelming us and causing us to behave in ways that cause harm to ourselves or others. This perspective seems to have resulted in a widespread distrust of emotional responses and the view that emotion and intelligence are mutually exclusive (Oatley, 2004). The character Spock in Star Trek exemplifies this view – he strives to eliminate all emotional experience in order to be as analytic as possible. Studies have corroborated these views, showing examples of emotions overwhelming people's attempts to control their judgments or behavior (Hofmann, Friese, & Strack, 2009; Loewenstein, 1996). Findings such as these led Daniel Kahneman, who received the Nobel Prize for his research on human irrationality, to identify emotional processes as primary determinants of irrational decisions. He argues that analytic processes must regulate or override these processes if people are to make rational and informed decisions (2003).

The bad reputation of emotions is particularly prevalent for negative emotions. People appear to recognize the value of happiness and believe that happiness can have benefits. In fact, people report that being happy is incredibly important to their lives and often list attaining happiness as a life goal (Diener, 2000). In contrast, negative states are often targeted during studies and interventions as states to be managed or regulated rather than experienced (Erber & Erber, 2000; Taylor, 1991). One particularly compelling investigation found that people will pay money to avoid experiencing negative emotions (Lau, White, & Schnall, 2013).

But this traditional view of emotions as states that should be regulated or avoided is beginning to change due to a flood of new findings demonstrating the benefits of varied, and negative, emotional experiences. This book brings together recent research in this area that addresses the value of emotions by identifying what emotions do that benefits people. Each chapter addresses the function and value of particular emotions and discusses the impact of the emotion on our lives. The sections below present two key points that are critical to frame this discussion – the definition of emotion and a framework for modern theories of functional emotions.

Defining Emotion

The first, most basic, question for any discussion of the effects of emotion is what do we mean when we talk about an "emotion"? The term is used for everything from the appetitive response to the sight of a tasty treat to the complex nostalgia we experience when graduating. Although all of the experiences covered by the term "emotion" involve an internal response, they also vary in the complexity, nuance, controllability, and cognitive evaluation involved in the response. In this book, the authors were asked to focus on the functions of discrete emotions, so that is our focus here. Emotions are considered discrete if they have been identified as separable from other states. For example, happiness is considered a discrete emotion because it represents a category of responses that can be identified and separated from other emotions, such as anger or sadness or love.

The definition of emotion once contained the statement that emotions are relatively brief responses compared to other more long-lasting states, such as mood (Russell, 2003). This sometimes led to the assumption that emotions were ephemeral – there-and-then-gone, fleeting states (Lench, Bench, & Perez, 2017). Of course, this does not fit with our experiences, when the joy of a success or the crushing grief of a severe loss affects us for weeks at a time. Recent empirical findings have revealed that emotions can last anywhere from a few moments to a few days and that the duration of the emotion really depends on the type of emotion felt and the circumstances that the emotion is felt in. For example, people typically reexperience an emotion or continue to feel an emotion when they ruminate about past events or when the surrounding context makes an event salient (Levine, Lench, Kaplan, & Safer, 2012; Verduyn, Van Mechelen, & Tuerlinckx, 2011). A recent breakup can still have a strong impact on people's feelings when Valentine's Day makes relationships and love salient (Lench, Safer, & Levine, 2011). So emotions are not defined by how long they last.

Instead, the hallmark feature of emotion appears to be that they are directed toward a specific object or event. Although debate continues, there is emerging consensus that the key defining feature is that emotions are responses to events or circumstances – they are "about" something (Eich, Kihlstrom, Bower, Forgas, & Niedenthal, 2000; Kaplan, Levine, Lench, & Safer, 2016; Lench, Bench, Darbor, & Moore, 2015; Verduyn et al., 2011). They are intentional states, in the philosophical sense, meaning they are directed toward the environment. People do not just feel happy or angry – they feel joy about a recent meaningful success or they feel angry about an insult. Thus discrete emotions include those states that are separable and identifiable responses to specific events or conditions. These responses can include emotions that are positive or negative and intense or mild, such as anger, joy, boredom, pride, and love.

Functional Accounts of Emotion

There are many functional accounts of emotion – enough to fill their own book discussing the theories and the distinctions among them. Here, however, the details of the particular accounts are set aside to instead focus on the shared assumptions that represent the foundational aspects of a functional approach to emotion (e.g., Arnold, 1960; Averill, 1983; Ekman, 1992; Frijda, 1987; Lerner & Keltner, 2001). It is these shared assumptions that guide the authors of the chapters in this text and which shape the majority of research in this area.

Most functional accounts of emotion appeal directly or indirectly to natural selection as the mechanism through which different emotions emerged in humans. The basic idea is that discrete emotions, such as anger, sadness, and joy, helped our ancestors in ways that promoted their mating and reproduction. This argument hinges on two related claims (Lench et al., 2015):

1. Emotions are elicited by particular events and situations that represented adaptive problems during evolutionary history.
2. Emotions are organized responses to those problems that helped resolve the event or situation (Mauss, Levenson, McCarter, Wilhelm, & Gross, 2005; Pinker, 1997).

Each author discusses, to the extent that evidence is available, the situations that elicit the emotion, the responses that occur during the emotion, and when and why those responses could be functional. Being functional from an evolutionary perspective, of course, does not mean that the emotion is "good" for us as individuals. Feeling angry at and attacking a spouse is clearly not a "good" response and is likely to have many negative effects for everyone involved.

From an evolutionary perspective, functional means that the emotion helps to resolve the problem that elicited it. A claim that anger is functional means that anger (with an urge to attack) helps to resolve the problem that elicited the anger (an obstacle or insult). According to functional accounts, one function of anger is to intimidate others so that future insults will not occur. In human evolutionary history, this would have helped protect the interests and resources of those who experienced and expressed anger over insults. If these conditions can be demonstrated – that anger intimidates others and lessens the likelihood of future insults – then researchers would consider anger to be functional. The same applies to other emotions. However, it is important to keep in mind that whether or not the particular response is helpful to the individual experiencing the emotion will depend on the particular situation in which the emotion is experienced. Just because an emotion can be considered functional in an evolutionary sense does not necessarily mean that it is always helpful to a person experiencing it.

The Importance of Function

Researchers who study human behavior and emotion find the framework of functionality to be particularly useful in setting and driving empirical work on what emotions are and what they do. This frame lets scientists build hypotheses and then test those hypotheses in studies of emotion. If, for example, anger is theorized to function to intimidate others into compliance, then a researcher can design a study that makes some people angry and others not angry and assess whether angry people are more intimidating in contentious exchanges. If this is supported, the scientist can then look for mechanisms – why people are intimidated by anger and what angry people do that promotes compliance in others. Is it the facial expression? The vocal tone and pitch? Body posture? Word choice? Studies can be designed to alter these factors and assess their importance in the process. Thus, thinking about functions of emotion provides a framework for scientific investigation and discovery.

Understanding the functions of emotion is also inherently interesting to us as people. Simply, emotion connects us to humanity. People around the world and at every age experience emotion. The cultural prescriptions and proscriptions for emotion vary among cultures, of course, but the shared elements of emotion rooted in our evolutionary history help to connect us. Many students of psychology experience a moment of insight when they first learn about *schadenfreude* – a German word representing the experience of pleasure at someone else's misfortune. There is no similar word in the English language, and yet almost everyone immediately and intuitively understands this experience and has felt it at some point. Similarly, learning about the functions of emotion can provide a richness to experience and a connection to humanity. We observe similar shifts with appreciation of artistic expression. Pablo Picasso's painting, *Guernica*, is a large, black-and-white painting of what appears to be a chaotic scene involving a bull, a horse, and people who appear to be suffering. While the painting is striking in itself, understanding the history that surrounded the painting provides a depth of understanding not possible without this bigger picture. *Guernica* was painted in response to the needless 1937 bombing and destruction of a town in northern Spain by the Nazi regime (Weisberg, 2004). The destruction of this small town came to represent the millions of innocent people resisting and being destroyed by fascism. Understanding this context provides not only insight into the actions of the figures in the painting but also a connection with the humanity of those who lost their lives. Understanding the evolutionary context and function of emotion can provide a similar depth of appreciation for our own experiences, as well as the experiences of others.

If emotions are considered to be functional, that also means that people can improve their ability to identify the emotion that they are experiencing and make informed choices about whether or not the emotion will be useful in a particular situation. Thus, learning about the functions of emotion can make people better "users" of emotion. There are often cultural proscriptions against expressing anger, for example, with recommendations to manage, repress, or suppress the experience. But studies have shown that, in some situations, anger can be useful and help people attain their goals. In one investigation, participants watched videos of a politican expressing either anger or sadness (Tiedens, 2001). People had more positive attitudes toward the politican who expressed anger compared to sadness and also viewed the angry politican as a better leader and said they were more likely to vote for the angry politican. This is very useful information for decision makers who must respond publicly in often difficult circumstances. Expressing anger can increase the confidence of followers and result in better outcomes. Clearly, understanding the function of anger and appropriately channeling anger can have benefits and advantages. Understanding the functions of emotion can therefore enhance our ability to use emotions in daily life and to recognize the value of even difficult or negative emotions.

An Invitation to Consider Emotions

This book invites you to consider emotions as the subject of scientific inquiry, to learn about the ways that emotions affect us and can often be useful for us. Science cannot, of course, fully capture the beauty and power of emotional experiences or express the importance of each experience as it is felt. Instead, science provides powerful tools to understand and measure the effects of emotions on us and provides a framework to think about how best to incorporate emotions into our lives. Understanding how emotions work can help people recognize and harness the power of emotions in ways that can improve well-being and success.

References

Arnold, M. B. (1960). *Emotion and personality*. New York, NY: Columbia University Press.

Averill, J. R. (1983). Studies on anger and aggression: Implications for theories of emotion. *American Psychologist, 38*, 1145–1160.

Camus, A. (1991). *The plague*. New York, NY: Vintage Books. (Original work published 1947).

Diener, E. (2000). Subjective well-being: The science of happiness and a proposal for a national index. *American Psychologist, 55*, 34–43.

Eich, E., Kihlstrom, J. F., Bower, G. H., Forgas, J. P., & Niedenthal, P. M. (Eds.). (2000). *Cognition and emotion*. New York, NY: Oxford University Press.

Ekman, P. (1992). Are there basic emotions? *Psychological Review, 99*, 550–553.

Erber, R., & Erber, M. W. (2000). The self-regulation of moods: Second thoughts on the importance of happiness in everyday life. *Psychological Inquiry, 11*, 142–148.

Frijda, N. H. (1987). Emotion, cognitive structure, and action tendency. *Cognition and Emotion, 1*, 115–143.

Hofmann, W., Friese, M., & Strack, F. (2009). Impulse and self-control from a dual-systems perspective. *Perspectives on Psychological Science, 4*, 162–176.

Kahneman, D. (2003). A perspective on judgment and choice: Mapping bounded rationality. *American Psychologist, 58*, 697–720.

Kaplan, R. L., Levine, L. J., Lench, H. C., & Safer, M. A. (2016). Forgetting feelings: Opposite biases in reports of the intensity of past emotion and mood. *Emotion, 16*, 309–319.

Lau, H. P. B., White, M. P., & Schnall, S. (2013). Quantifying the value of emotions using a willingness to pay approach. *Journal of Happiness Studies, 14*, 1543–1561.

Lench, H. C., Bench, S. W., Darbor, K. E., & Moore, M. (2015). A functionalist manifesto: Goal-related emotions from an evolutionary perspective. *Emotion Review, 7*, 90–98.

Lench, H. C., Bench, S. W., & Perez, K. A. (2017). Building a house of sentiment on sand: Epistemologial issues with contempt. *Behavioral and Brain Sciences, 40*, 33–34.

Lench, H. C., Safer, M. A., & Levine, L. J. (2011). Focalism and the underestimation of future emotion: When it's worse than imagined. *Emotion, 11*, 278–285.

Lerner, J. S., & Keltner, D. (2001). Fear, anger, and risk. *Journal of Personality and Social Psychology, 81*, 146–159.

Levine, L. J., Lench, H. C., Kaplan, R. L., & Safer, M. A. (2012). Accuracy and artifact: Reexamining the intensity bias in affective forecasting. *Journal of Personality and Social Psychology, 103*, 584–605.

Loewenstein, G. (1996). Out of control: Visceral influences on behavior. *Organizational Behavior and Human Decision Processes, 65*, 272–292.

Mauss, I. B., Levenson, R. W., McCarter, L., Wilhelm, F. H., & Gross, J. J. (2005). The tie that binds? Coherence among emotion experience, behavior, and physiology. *Emotion, 5*, 175–190.

Oatley, K. (2004). *Emotions: A brief history*. Malden, MA: Blackwell Publishing.

Pinker, S. (1997). *How the mind works*. New York, NY: Norton.

Russell, J. A. (2003). Core affect and the psychological construction of emotion. *Psychological Review, 110*, 145–172.

Taylor, S. E. (1991). Asymmetrical effects of positive and negative events: The mobilization-minimization hypothesis. *Psychological Bulletin, 110*, 67–85.

Tiedens, L. Z. (2001). Anger and advancement versus sadness and subjugation: The effect of negative emotion expressions on social status conferral. *Journal of Personality and Social Psychology, 80*, 86–94.

Verduyn, P., Van Mechelen, I., & Tuerlinckx, F. (2011). The relation between event processing and the duration of emotional experience. *Emotion, 11*, 20–28.

Weisberg, R. W. (2004). On structure in the creative process: A quantitative case-study of the creation of Picasso's Guernica. *Empirical Studies of the Arts, 22*, 23–54.

Chapter 2
Fear and Anxiety

Parisa Parsafar and Elizabeth L. Davis

Abstract Fear and anxiety *feel* different. The different lexical labels attached to these discrete emotions reflect a subjective understanding of their distinction. But emotions are more than just feelings, and this chapter journeys far beyond the subjective experiences of fear versus anxiety. The processes these different emotions evoke are supported by distinct neural substrates and carry divergent consequences for behavior, cognition, and subsequent emotional responding. Their distinction matters. This chapter draws from theoretical and recent experimental work using cutting-edge research methodologies to describe what makes fear different from anxiety and how they uniquely influence different forms of psychopathology.

Detecting an immediate threat, like hearing footsteps behind you while walking through a dark alley, can mobilize a rapid state of alertness, automatic defensive or escape behaviors (e.g., the urge to attack or run), and the conscious experience of fear. When the specter of threat is no longer present (e.g., the sound turns out to be the echo of your own footsteps), the fear subsides. A state of anxious alertness can remain, however, accompanied by hypervigilance to notice any new, potential, or continued threat (e.g., cautiously listening for any additional sounds). As illustrated by this example, fear and anxiety are closely related threat-relevant emotions that share similar features, and both evolved to serve a protective, harm-avoidance function. Yet despite their overlap, there is compelling empirical support for their distinction (Craske, 2003; Sylvers, Lilienfeld, & Prairie, 2011). This chapter presents an overview of recent scientific findings that show how fear and anxiety are similar, yet also vastly different.

This chapter describes the contemporary definitions and purported functions of fear and anxiety and reviews recent neurophysiological and behavioral evidence that support their conceptual distinction. Of particular use to researchers across disciplines, the chapter highlights cutting-edge paradigms that can be employed across

P. Parsafar · E. L. Davis (✉)
Department of Psychology, University of California, Riverside, Riverside, CA, USA
e-mail: elizabeth.davis@ucr.edu

© Springer International Publishing AG, part of Springer Nature 2018
H. C. Lench (ed.), *The Function of Emotions*,
https://doi.org/10.1007/978-3-319-77619-4_2

animal, adult, and developmental research models that allow investigations of fear and anxiety response profiles across varying threat contexts. The chapter then reviews the ontogeny of normative fear and anxiety responses – many of which are shaped by developing cognitive and social processes – to contrast these patterns with the disordered fear and anxiety response patterns that are present in psychopathology. The chapter concludes by identifying several broad, open questions for emotion researchers to answer that will advance our understanding of differences and similarities across state, trait, and psychopathological manifestations of fear and anxiety.

Defining Fear and Anxiety

Fear and anxiety are both emotions that are evoked by the initial perception of threat when the certainty of harm is not yet known. What differentiates these two emotions is the cascade of appraisals that occur after the detection of threat – the imminence of the threat, the distance (physical or psychological) from the perceived threat, and the severity of possible harm (see Table 2.1). Whereas fear is a response to a specific, identifiable, proximate stressor and the perception of immediate and predictable substantial harm, anxiety results from appraising an unpredictable threat – one that poses a low probability of actual harm (Rachman, 1998) or is so vague or ambiguous as to not have a clear source (e.g., a sense of foreboding; Öhman, 2008). Thus, fear can be conceptualized as a response to an "actual," predictable threat (e.g., a predator encountered on a hiking trail), but anxiety is a response to a "potential," unpredictable threat (e.g., rustling sounds just off the trail that could either be made by a predator or a harmless animal, nimh.nih.gov, n.d.; Öhman, 2008).

Animal models of defensive behavior support this distinction between fear and anxiety based on the imminence or distance from the threat and the severity of harm. In lab-based paradigms, a defensive state evoked in response to immediate or imminent contact with a predator is linked to a "fear" response in rats, whereas the

Table 2.1 Characteristics of threat across fear and anxiety

	Imminence/ distance	Predict- ability	Severity	Elicitor	Prob- ability	Encounter	Threat
Fear	Immediate/ proximal	Predictable consequence	Severe harm	Specific, identifiable	High prob- ability of harm	Post- stimulus	Actual
Anxiety	Distant	Unpre- dictable consequence	Less severe harm	Vague or ambiguous, undiffer- entiated no clear source	Low prob- ability of harm	Pre- stimulus	Potential

defensive state evoked either in a location where previous contact with a predator occurred or when a predator is present but distant is described as "anxiety" (Davis, Walker, Miles, & Grillon, 2010). Similarly, in fear-conditioning paradigms, rats who receive a greater number of shocks are more likely to demonstrate a fear response when they return to a locale where they were previously shocked than rats who receive a low number of shocks – indicating that fear responses are linked to the severity of harm (Poulos et al., 2016). Thus, fear and anxiety can be defined as distinct emotional states that are characterized by different appraisals of threat features (e.g., actual vs. potential threat; low vs. high severity of harm; Grillon, Baas, Cornwell, & Johnson, 2006).

The Functions of Fear and Anxiety

From an evolutionary perspective, fear and anxiety both protect against harm, yet they lead to notably different response patterns. Fear prompts active defensive reactions (via the sympathetically mediated fight or flight response) that promote targeted escape and avoidance behaviors and subsides in the absence or cessation of the eliciting threat (de Jongh, Groenink, van der Gugten, & Olivier, 2003). Anxiety, however, is associated with less active coping methods and can persist or sustain for much longer periods of time (de Jongh et al., 2003; Dias, Banerjee, Goodman, & Ressler, 2013).

   Fear functions to mobilize resources for immediate action (Muris, 2010), prompts "primitive" escape and avoidance behaviors (Nesse & Ellsworth, 2009), serves a protective purpose from immediate harm, and promotes survival (Plutchik, 2003). Studies using fear-conditioning paradigms have revealed that people will demonstrate fear, such as a startle response, when they encounter a conditioned stimulus that consistently precedes a harmful outcome (Beckers, Krypotos, Boddez, Effting, & Kindt, 2013). Neuroimaging work using virtual threats demonstrates that areas of the midbrain, including the periaqueductal gray, that support automatic and reflexive, "primitive" escape behaviors become more strongly activated as a pain-inflicting predator comes closer. This contrasts with greater distance from the predator (and potential pain), which is associated with more dominant activation in the ventromedial prefrontal cortex, an area implicated in preparing and avoidance behaviors (Mobbs et al., 2007). Fear is thus adaptive because it enables escape from harm.

   Anxiety also functions to promote survival but does so via processes involved in anticipating and preparing for an unexpected, potentially harmful situation (Muris, 2010). For example, the sustained alertness and hypervigilance to interpret cues as threatening that is characteristic of anxiety serves a precocious threat-detection purpose, allowing for advanced preparation to deal with or completely avoid a potential threat (Bateson, Brilot, & Nettle, 2011). Epidemiological work demonstrates that having low levels of anxiety may actually increase risk for mortality. In a nationally representative sample of adults in Norway, a U-shaped association between anxiety and mortality emerged. Although both low and high anxiety were associated with increased mortality risk across a 3–6-year period, the risk was greatest for people with the lowest self-reported anxiety (Mykletun et al., 2009). The authors suggest that lower levels of anxiety may reduce the likelihood that people will seek help from others and increase the likelihood of engaging in risky behaviors in adulthood. Indeed, higher trait anxiety in adolescence is associated with a lower likelihood of accidental death in early adulthood (Lee, Wadsworth, & Hotopf, 2006), which suggests that anxiety may serve as a protective function by promoting avoidance of potentially harmful situations. Thus, a broad literature provides evidence for the adaptive features of fear in supporting rapid escape behaviors and anxiety in prompting avoidance of harm. Both emotions enhance survival via different patterns of responding to threat.

The Neurophysiology and Behavior of Fear and Anxiety

The behavioral patterns most typical of fear (e.g., startle, freezing, escape) and anxiety (e.g., avoidance) are rooted in overlapping yet dissociable neuroanatomical substrates activated in response to detection of predictable (fear) and unpredictable (anxiety) threats (Davis et al., 2010). In an extensive review, Davis et al. (2010) present findings from both animal and human studies that implicate overlapping amygdala networks in fear and anxiety. The central and lateral amygdala has long been considered the fear "center" of the brain, sending signals that facilitate automatic defensive responses (LeDoux, 1990; Phelps, 2006). Detection of an immediate, present threat in the case of a fearful situation activates the amygdala, which is associated with *automatic* defensive actions like startle and freezing behaviors. Immediate threat, such as a tone reliably paired with impending shock, is associated with activation of the medial division of the central nucleus of the amygdala (CeA_M), which sends signals to both the hypothalamus and brain stem to initiate processes that support automatic responses (e.g., startle).

In contrast, experiences of unpredictable or distant threat, such as contexts where shocks previously occurred, or exposure to darkness, are associated with activation of the extended amygdala, believed to underlie more controlled anxiety threat reactions. Lateral activation of the central nucleus of the amygdala (CeA_L) facilitates the release of corticotrophin-releasing factors (CRF) that signal to the bed nucleus of the stria terminalis (BNST). From here, outputs are sent to the hypothalamus and the brain stem. The influence of CRF on the BNST is particularly implicated in anxiety, providing neurophysiological support for a distinction between fear and anxiety substrates. Activity of the BNST is responsible for increased hypervigilance during anticipatory periods of unpredictable danger (e.g., anxiety, Somerville, Whalen, & Kelley, 2010). For example, increased BNST activation is evident among spider phobics during *anticipation* of the presentation of phobic compared to non-phobic stimuli, but not in controls, supporting the role of the BNST in anxiety (Straube, Mentzel, & Miltner, 2007).

Previous work with phobic patients demonstrates not only activation of the amygdala and BNST but also implicates activation of the insula, anterior cingulate cortex, and periaqueductal gray in fear responses (Öhman & Soares, 1994). The anterior insula (aINS) is also believed to underlie unpredictable threat responses and is implicated in interoceptive awareness and anticipatory responses (Craig, 2009; Gorka, Klumpp et al., 2017). It integrates information about appraisals of the salience of external stimuli and bodily responses by passing on interoceptive information to the anterior cingulate cortex, a neural substrate involved in attentional deployment, evaluation, and planning processes (Paulus & Stein, 2006). A hyperreactive aINS during the experience of unpredictable threat in individuals with anxiety disorders may influence experiences of extreme, exaggerated distress (Nitschke, Sarinopoulos, Mackiewicz, & Schaefer, & Davidson, 2006) that interferes with the ability to recognize differences between current and potential physical states (Paulus & Stein, 2006). The worry and avoidance behaviors that are characteristic of anxiety may be a result of the mismatch between physical states and external experience and a hyperreactive aINS (Paulus & Stein, 2006). For example, expecting negative outcomes to occur can result in heightened physiological reactivity that is decoupled from the objective characteristics of the environment. Various cognitive efforts to minimize the discomfort produced by this mismatch are thus not directed toward a specific eliciting target (because nothing actually happened) and can result in generalized worry (cognitive symptoms). Similarly, behavioral efforts (e.g., avoidance) may allow for disengagement from the uncomfortable physiological response (Paulus & Stein, 2006).

Ultimately, however, the fear and anxiety pathways show considerable concordance across their connections and result in activation of the same downstream regions. Although previously believed to be more distinct, in Davis and colleagues' model (2010), the CeA$_M$ is inhibited in part through feedback from the BNST, thus facilitating a shift from fear to anxiety responding. This feedback suggests that the CeA and BNST are part of an overlapping and unified network that works together to transition responses from experiences of fear to anxiety – a theory which is garnering substantial attention (e.g., Shackman & Fox, 2016) and supports the supposition that disordered anxiety stems from deficits in fear responding.

Paradigms like the Neutral, Predictable, Unpredictable (e.g., NPU) threat test (Schmitz & Grillon, 2012) can usefully separate fear (e.g., predictable threat) and anxiety (e.g., unpredictable threat) contexts and have gained in popularity. In a prototypical paradigm, participants are compared across three conditions, a neutral safe condition (N), a predictable threat condition (P – fear context) in which a cue is reliably paired with an aversive experience, and an unpredictable threat condition (U – anxiety context) in which the aversive experience is not consistently indicated by a cue. Freezing or startle behaviors in response to an immediate, present threat are characteristic of fear, whereas avoidance in unpredictable, lower threat conditions is characteristic of an anxious response (Öhman, 2008). In these paradigms, the aversive experience is typically evoked by electric shocks and verbal threats, which produce a more robust response than puffs of air (Davis et al., 2010).

Grillon et al. (2006) used a virtual reality NPU procedure to capture people's responses in fear and anxiety contexts. They found that startle responses were much stronger in situations in which harm was reliably predicted by a cue (e.g., a light always precedes the onset of a shock) than in situations where harm might occur (unpredictable electric shocks), supporting the notion that startle responses are more characteristic of fear. In contrast, in the same study, unpredictable shock was related to greater avoidance of locations where shocks previously occurred. Thus, whereas fear-potentiated *startles* are elicited in response to specific danger cues (e.g., presentation of a cue like lights that reliably predict immediate harm via shock), people are more likely to *avoid* specific contexts where harm previously occurred, particularly if the harm is not linked to an obvious elicitor, like in anxiety.

Insights About Normative Fear and Anxiety from Developmental Science

As Muris (2010) points out, whether children's normative responses to typical fear and anxiety elicitors reflect the same processes that underlie the fear and anxiety responses of disordered children is under-explored. According to clinical conceptualizations motivated by DSM criteria, fear that is disproportionate to the actual threat posed by a concrete elicitor (American Psychiatric Association, 2013; Muris, 2010) reflects abnormal phobic reactions, whereas anxiety reflects disorders characterized by worries, precocious caution, and a sense of foreboding with no specific elicitor. Findings from developmental work document the ontogeny of fear and anxiety elicitors that reflect these clinical definitions – helping to separate normative and nonnormative fear and anxiety responses.

The progression of normative fear elicitors corresponds to problems that children face at different maturational stages, beginning with those that concern physical harm/danger and are most evolutionarily relevant to survival (Muris, 2010). For example, loud noises and the presence of strangers elicit fear in infancy, when children face developmental challenges including biological regulation, attachment with social partners, and object permanence. Across toddlerhood and early childhood, as children make gains in locomotion, autonomy, and cognitive capacities, fears of animals, the dark, storms, and imaginary monsters are reported. During middle childhood, children's abilities to infer causation increase, and fears of death and bodily harm by more modern threats, such as shootings, AIDS, being hit by a car, and war, become more common (Burnham, 2005). Fears of concrete harm-related stimuli begin to decrease around 10–12 years of age (Muris, Merckelbach, Gadet, & Moulaert, 2000) and decline rapidly across adolescence (Michiel, Drewes, Goedhart, Siebelink, & Treffers, 2004).

The fears of early childhood appear to differ in kind from those of later childhood and adolescence. Typical fear elicitors in later developmental stages reflect changes in cognitive processes and social and cultural influences (e.g., worries about gangs) as children become more autonomous, establish their identities, and experience changes in their social structures and interpersonal relationships. During these maturational stages, psychological fears (e.g., social evaluation) that are more abstract and representative of hypothetical (e.g., car accident, being kidnapped, sexual assault, contracting an illness) situations – thus requiring greater cognitive sophistication – or fears tied to specific social contexts (e.g., giving a speech, meeting new people, changing clothes in front of others) become more prevalent (Muris, 2010).

Anxiety can also be developmentally typical (e.g., worries about looks and physical appearance during late childhood and adolescence). Undifferentiated worries are a cognitive characteristic of anxiety disorder and are relatively infrequent in early childhood but increase throughout middle and late childhood (7–12 years, Muris et al., 2000). Like fears, worries also adhere to a typical progression that reflects a child's maturational stage – and sociocognitive sophistication in particular (Michiel et al., 2004). Across childhood, worries and concerns about separation from a caregiver are common but decline rapidly with increasing autonomy. However, social evaluative and performance-related worries that are not tied to a specific elicitor (e.g., general concerns about competence, need for reassurance, self-consciousness, worries over performance or behaviors) increase from late childhood across adolescence, when peer relationships become prominent and social settings expand.

Thus, certain fears and anxieties are common in childhood and, depending on developmental stage, can be normative. When fears or anxieties occur outside of the typical stage or context, this can serve as an indicator of abnormal responding. For example, children's social contexts require greater autonomy across development, so separation anxiety that persists into adolescence and adulthood would interfere with the ability to engage in age-normative activities (e.g., stay out with friends, be home alone, hold a steady job) and thus signals an atypical response.

Abnormal Fear and Anxiety: Implications for Mental Health

Recent contributions from a broad clinical literature and the use of hierarchical modeling techniques have helped to reconceptualize internalizing disorders into two main factors – those characterized by distress and misery and those characterized by fear (Clark & Watson, 2006; Eaton et al., 2013). Fear disorders include specific phobias, social phobia, separation anxiety, panic disorder, and agoraphobia, which can be broadly characterized by abnormal, exaggerated defensive responses to specific, identifiable elicitors that would normally be perceived to pose a low probability of harm. In contrast, generalized anxiety disorder (GAD), post-traumatic stress disorder (PTSD), and depression are "distress disorders" that broadly reflect abnormal distress responses that are not tied to a specific elicitor, are associated with heightened and sustained distress, and generalize across contexts (Prenoveau et al., 2010; Waters, Bradley, & Mogg, 2014). Therefore, fear disorders are more strongly linked to fear, whereas distress/misery disorders are more strongly linked to anxiety.

Research on attention helps explain differences between normal cognitive processing patterns in fear and abnormal processing patterns in abnormal fear (and fear disorder). Fear is linked to specific detection biases with visual attention. Using visual search tasks in which participants are asked to detect a fear-relevant target (e.g., snakes, spiders) among irrelevant distractor images (e.g., flowers, caterpillars), LoBue and DeLoache (2008) have shown that adults and children are quicker to detect threat-relevant stimuli than threat-irrelevant stimuli. Furthermore, watching a frightening film clip was shown to facilitate more rapid detection of threatening material (LoBue, 2014). This work suggests that normal fear facilitates rapid attentional deployment to threat-relevant information.

People with fear-related disorders, however, demonstrate an even greater threat-detection effect. Phobic individuals (e.g., people with a phobia of spiders) are faster at detecting phobic stimuli (spiders) than non-phobic threat-relevant stimuli (e.g., snakes, Öhman, 2008; Öhman, Flykt, & Esteves, 2001) and demonstrate slower reaction times to detect threat-irrelevant targets among phobic distractors (Rinck, Reinecke, Ellwart, Heuer, & Becker, 2005). Moreover, an occasional random phobic distractor captures attention long enough to slow down detection times for neutral targets (Miltner, Kriechel, Hecht, Trippe, & Weiss, 2004). Thus, fear-related disorders facilitate the rapid threat-orienting process and simultaneously slow attentional disengagement from fear-relevant stimuli (Öhman, 2008). Patterns of attention-orienting speeds and latencies to disengage attention from threats may thus be one avenue toward differentiation between normal and abnormal fear responding.

Investigations of attentional focus across anxiety disorders have provided further support for their decomposition into fear versus distress/misery disorders. Biased attention toward threatening information, which is a selective preference to attend to ambiguous, threat-relevant information from the environment (e.g., threat vigilance or overgeneralization), has been documented in people with distress-related anxiety disorders like GAD. Attention biases away from threat (e.g., threat avoidance), however, have been documented among people with fear-based disorders like specific phobias (for a review, see Waters et al., 2014). These distinctions are consistent with fear prompting escape and avoidance (e.g., turning away from threat), whereas anxiety prompts an undifferentiated hypervigilance (e.g., turning toward threat).

Behavioral startle work using the NPU paradigms described above further demonstrates an exaggerated defensive response in fear-related anxiety but not distress disorders. People with fear-related anxiety disorders show heightened startle potentiation, demonstrating an abnormal fear response, to unpredictable threats (Gorka,

Lieberman, Shankman, & Phan, 2017) and presentation of clinically relevant fear-related images (McTeague & Lang, 2012), whereas this response is not documented among those with distress-related disorder. Similarly, compared to adolescents with distress disorders and to healthy controls, adolescents with fear disorders demonstrate greater startle responses during periods of relative safety and low harm (Waters et al., 2014). Furthermore, a recent intervention demonstrated that individuals with fear-based disorders show a significant reduction in startle responses to unpredictable threats after treatment intervention, and this reduction corresponded to decreases in fear symptoms. Thus, defensive startle in response to a potential, unpredictable threat situation distinguishes fear-based disorder from distress/misery disorders.

The underlying pattern of fear responses in low-threat contexts that is characteristic of fear-related disorder has been examined in the developmental literature as well. By controlling the threat context (e.g., degree of controllability, level of threat, degree of uncertainty/novelty, type of threat) and examining associations with dispositional characteristics and different patterns of fear reactions (Buss, Davidson, Kalin, & Goldsmith, 2004; Buss, 2011; Buss et al., 2013; Buss, Davis, Ram, & Coccia, 2017), Buss and colleagues identified a subset of temperamentally fearful children who showed extreme fearfulness in low-threat contexts. These children demonstrate greater physiological reactivity to stress (shorter PEP, higher basal cortisol and lower baseline RSA, less RSA suppression to challenge) and are at the greatest developmental risk for developing social anxiety, a fear disorder. Trait-level fear (e.g., fearful temperament) is thus linked to later development of fear-based anxiety (social phobia, Chronis-Tuscano et al., 2009; Perez-Edgar et al., 2010) when behavioral freezing responses and physiological profiles are considered.

Early temperamental fear in toddlerhood can also precede attentional threat biases and anxiety symptoms. For example, a longitudinal study (Perez-Edgar et al., 2011) found that greater temperamental fear and wariness at age 5 preceded age 7 social withdrawal symptoms only for children who demonstrated a bias to attend to threatening angry faces. Temperamental fear and wariness did not, however, predict social withdrawal symptoms for children with an attentional bias away from threat. There were no direct associations between early fear and wariness or attentional biases. Thus, temperamental fear – a dispositional factor – and patterns of attention biases may help to further clarify development of different disorders. Developmental findings thus complement results with adults using NPU paradigms but underscore the need for future work to integrate information across numerous facets of a fear response (e.g., freezing behaviors and physiological profiles) to identify disorder risk groups based on profiles of response patterns and trait-level characteristics.

Response patterns across distress disorders vary notably from those associated with fear-related disorders. In contrast to the exaggerated fear response in low-threat/unpredictable contexts documented by individuals with fear-related disorders, people with distress disorders display a diminished startle response to fear-based imagery (McTeague & Lang, 2012), and adolescents with distress disorders show a similar pattern of diminished response to context conditioning cues (Waters et al., 2014). Early evidence from animal models suggests that chronic threat experiences (e.g., greater intensities, longer duration, more regular) can damage defensive fear systems, possibly accounting for reduced escape-related defensive tendencies in distress disorders. Rats exposed to brief intruder stress showed heightened arousal and defensive behaviors compared to rats exposed to longer periods of stress. Symptoms of distress in rats exposed longer to an intruder were maintained even after the intruder was removed (Chalmers, Hohf, & Levine, 1974). Similarly, McTeague and Lang (2012) showed that accumulated threat experiences may alter the connectivity of defensive fear circuits and propose that training individuals to reexperience typical reflexive responses may be a fruitful part of intervention work for people with distress disorders (McTeague & Lang, 2012). Epidemiological work also shows that fear disorders often precede distress disorders, which suggest that abnormal fear responses may contribute to distress disorders over time (Roest et al., 2017).

Deficits in the ability to discriminate true threats from non-threats may play a role in distress disorders. For example, Lissek et al. (2014) utilized a fear-conditioning paradigm to examine whether overgeneralization of fear responses to cues that resemble a danger cue is evident in distress disorders (GAD specifically). Individuals with and without GAD were presented with cues that differed in size (the cues were rings of different sizes). The largest rings represented danger cues and the smallest represented safety cues. Compared to controls, people with GAD demonstrated less differentiation and discrimination among the cues of varying sizes, supporting an overgeneralization of fear to safety cues in GAD. Although hypervigilance is a hallmark characteristic of GAD, people with this disorder pay less attention to discrimination cues and use less information in their threat interpretations. In line with this reasoning, a recent study found that improving individuals' perceptual discrimination ability reduced fear generalization to cues that were similar to but different from a danger cue (Ginat-Frolich, Klein, Katz, & Schechner, 2017).

Although anxiety and fear share a similar harm-avoidance feature and are both threat-relevant emotions, the above review presents findings from a broad empirical literature that supports their discreteness. Neuroimaging research supports overlapping yet distinctive neuroanatomical substrates and accompanying reflexive behaviors that helps to distinguish these two emotions. The ontogeny of fear and anxiety elicitors supports the role of cognitive maturational processes in helping to distinguish between them. Comparisons of attention processing across fear- and anxiety-related disorders support the notion of diverse deficits in coping patterns (e.g., diverting attention away from threat, escape/avoidance vs. attention toward threat and hypervigilance) that helps to distinguish them. Developmental research has shed light on individual difference contexts that help to characterize individuals based on subtypes at risk for fear-based disorder. Abnormal responses (e.g., startle) to NPU cue conditioning paradigms have provided a useful tool for modeling fear-based disorders, whereas context conditioning has allowed for a model of more sustained fear disorders characterized by distress/misery (Grillon, 2002). Finally, an understanding of differences and similarities between typical response patterns across fear and anxiety or fear- and distress-related disorders has helped to improve intervention targets, promoting novel intervention methods. Findings from these studies have all helped to clarify differences between fear and anxiety and their respective disorders.

Unresolved Questions

The literature on fear and anxiety is extensive and reflects a scientific understanding that is perhaps the most developed of all the emotions. Despite these breakthroughs, there are several avenues of fear and anxiety research that could use greater empirical attention and clarity. First, a substantial number of empirical studies examining differences across fear and anxiety rely on behavioral responses from individuals with anxiety disorders, individuals with high trait-level inhibition, or individuals with high dispositional anxiety as a proxy for studying state anxiety. Similarly, fear is often assessed via self- and other-reports of behavioral avoidance, which can be characteristic of both fear and anxiety (Sylvers et al., 2011). Assessments of dispositional fear (e.g., temperament) also often encompass composites of fear reactions, reticence, and wariness or withdrawal from novel situations in general (Kagan & Fox, 2006). Thus, whether the typical experience of state fear and anxiety is equivalent to the experiences of people with fear- and distress-related disorders or people with greater dispositional levels of fear and anxiety remains an open question and raises some methodological concerns as to whether measurements of each reflect distinct constructs. Some work has demonstrated that fear prompts greater attention orienting to threat-relevant information in general, but individuals with fear-based disorders demonstrate an even faster response. This suggests differences in response patterns across state and disordered fear reactions that indicate these experiences are not necessarily equivalent. An expansion of this work aimed at understanding the nuances and research methodologies that can more clearly separate state, trait, and disordered fear and anxiety responses would greatly improve understanding of response patterns that pose a risk for disorder.

Second, emotions involve not just a subjective feeling but a cascade of responses across multiple systems including behaviors, cognitive processes, expressions, and psychophysiology. The work aimed at integrating and comparing fear and anxiety responses across multiple levels of analysis is in its infancy. Developmental approaches highlight the importance of integrating information from multiple levels of analysis in the study of fear and anxiety and their respective disorders. Moving beyond the use of composites to explain individual differences to focus on profiles of response patterns across systems and varying threat contexts can illuminate nuanced individual subtypes with a greater ability to detect and predict trajectories toward fear or distress disorders (Buss & McDoniel, 2016).

Third, few empirical studies have shown support for convergence across emotion indices to help distinguish between related but discrete emotional experiences (e.g., fear compared to anxiety). There is, however, some work to suggest that convergence across emotion-related processes is indicative of disordered responses. For example, Schaefer, Larson, Davidson, and Coan (2014) recently compared behavioral, physiological, and affective correlates of normal (non-phobic) and non-normal (phobic) fear in a snake-viewing paradigm and found that phobic participants showed greater convergence across indices of emotion. Phobic participants demonstrated more extreme pupil dilation as well as electrodermal responses (e.g., fight or flight responses) that coincided with more intense self-reported fear than non-phobic participants. Thus, investigations integrating examination of responses across levels of analysis can greatly help to improve understanding of normative vs. nonnormative responses profiles.

Finally, this same work demonstrates that emotion correlates coincided with greater activation across more neural networks, including activation in the prefrontal cortex (Schaefer et al., 2014), a region implicated in emotion regulation. The effectiveness with which people regulate emotion carries substantial consequences for mental health. Yet, not all emotion regulation strategies are equal in their effectiveness or appropriateness – this varies by the discrete emotion context, characteristics of disorder, and individual difference factors that make implementation of a strategy more or less difficult to do. For example, an emerging literature suggests that the effectiveness of a given emotion regulation strategy depends on features of the negative emotional context like how controllable a situation is (Troy, Shallcross, & Mauss, 2013). Because fear is associated with a predictable, identifiable threat, the strategies that can effectively manage it should differ from strategies aimed at managing anxiety and unpredictable, diffuse threats. Similarly, neuroimaging work provides evidence that distress disorders like GAD are less associated with exaggerated fear responses and might be undergirded by difficulties with fear regulation (Greenberg, Carlson, Cha, Hajcak, & Mujica-Parodi, 2013). Different emotion regulation strategies might be better for managing dysregulation across fear compared to distress disorders. Thus, many open questions remain as to whether fear and anxiety should be regulated differently or how emotional regulatory processes might link profiles of fear and anxiety responding to distress and fear disorder. Understanding when a given emotion regulation strategy can be effective for people based on their profiles of fear or anxiety responses and dispositional characteristics can pinpoint which strategies to coach to help people manage different threat contexts. Extending this work requires integrative research using multi-method and longitudinal designs but can transform the potency of preventative programs and intervention outcomes. In sum, integrating information from multiple levels of analysis represents a new frontier in emotion science that will improve understanding of the distinctions between fear and anxiety, the psychopathological disorders they correspond to, and the most effective strategies to manage them across individuals and contexts.

References

American Psychiatric Association. (2013). *Diagnostic and statistical manual of mental disorders* (5th ed.). Arlington, VA: American Psychiatric Publishing.

Bateson, M., Brilot, B., & Nettle, D. (2011). Anxiety: An evolutionary approach. *The Canadian Journal of Psychiatry, 56*, 707–715.

Beckers, T., Krypotos, A. M., Boddez, Y., Effting, M., & Kindt, M. (2013). What's wrong with fear conditioning? *Biological Psychology, 92*, 90–96.

Burnham, J. J. (2005). Fears of children in the United States: An examination of the American Fear Survey Schedule with 20 new contemporary fear items. *Measurement and Evaluation in Counseling and Development, 38*, 78–91.

Buss, K. A. (2011). Which fearful toddlers should we worry about? Context, fear regulation, and anxiety risk. *Developmental Psychology, 47*, 804–819.

Buss, K. A., Davidson, R. J., Kalin, N. H., & Goldsmith, H. H. (2004). Context-specific freezing and associated physiological reactivity as a dysregulated fear response. *Developmental Psychology, 40*, 583–594.

Buss, K. A., Davis, E. L., Kiel, E. J., Brooker, R. J., Beekman, C., & Early, M. C. (2013). Dysregulated fear predicts social wariness and social anxiety symptoms during kindergarten. *Journal of Clinical Child & Adolescent Psychology, 42*, 603–616.

Buss, K. A., Davis, E. L., Ram, N., & Coccia, M. (2017, March). Dysregulated fear, social inhibition, and respiratory sinus arrhythmia: A replication and extension. *Child Development*. Online first version retrieved from http://onlinelibrary.wiley.com/doi/10.1111/cdev.12774/full

Buss, K. A., & McDoniel, M. E. (2016). Improving the prediction of risk for anxiety development in temperamentally fearful children. *Current Directions in Psychological Science, 25*, 14–20.

Chalmers, D. V., Hohf, J. C., & Levine, S. (1974). The effects of prior aversive stimulation on the behavioral and physiological responses to intense acoustic stimuli in the rat. *Physiology & Behavior, 12*, 711–717.

Chronis-Tuscano, A., Degnan, K. A., Pine, D. S., Perez-Edgar, K., Henderson, H. A., Diaz, Y., … Fox, N. A. (2009). Stable early maternal report of behavioral inhibition predicts lifetime social anxiety disorder in adolescence. *Journal of the American Academy of Child & Adolescent Psychiatry, 48*, 928–935.

Clark, L. A., & Watson, D. (2006). Distress and fear disorders: An alternative empirically based taxonomy of the "mood" and "anxiety" disorders. *The British Journal of Psychiatry, 189*, 481–483.

Craig, A. D. (2009). How do you feel-now? The anterior insula and human awareness. *Nature Reviews Neuroscience, 10*, 59–70.

Craske, M. G. (2003). *Origins of phobias and anxiety disorders. Why more women than men?* Oxford, UK: Elsevier.

Davis, M., Walker, D. L., & Grillon, C. (2010). Phasic vs. sustained fear in rats and humans: Role of the extended amygdala in fear vs. anxiety. *Neuropsychopharmacology, 35*, 105–135.

de Jongh, R., Groenink, L., van der Gugten, J., & Olivier, B. (2003). Light-enhanced and fear-potentiated startle: Temporal characteristics and effects of α-helical corticotrophin-releasing hormone. *Biological Psychiatry, 54*, 1041–1048.

Dias, B. G., Banerjee, S. B., Goodman, J. V., & Ressler, K. J. (2013). Towards new approaches to disorders of fear and anxiety. *Current Opinion in Neurobiology, 23*, 346–352.

Eaton, N. R., Krueger, R. F., Markon, K. E., Keyes, K. M., Skodol, A. E., Wall, M., … Grant, B. F. (2013). The structure and predictive validity of the internalizing disorders. *Journal of Abnormal Psychology, 122*, 86–92.

Ginat-Frolich, R., Klein, Z., Katz, O., & Shechner, T. (2017). A novel perceptual discrimination training task: Reducing fear overgeneralization in the context of fear learning. *Behaviour Research and Therapy, 93*, 29–37.

Gorka, S., Klumpp, H., Ajilore, O., Francis, J., Craske, M., Langenecker, S., … Phan, K. L. (2017). Startle reactivity to unpredictable threat as a psychophysiological treatment target for fear-based anxiety disorders. *Biological Psychiatry, 81*, S134.

Gorka, S. M., Lieberman, L., Shankman, S. A., & Phan, K. L. (2017). Startle potentiation to uncertain threat as a psychophysiological indicator of fear-based psychopathology: An examination across multiple internalizing disorders. *Journal of Abnormal Psychology, 126*, 8–18.

Greenberg, T., Carlson, J. M., Cha, J., Hajcak, G., & Mujica-Parodi, L. R. (2013). Ventromedial prefrontal cortex reactivity is altered in generalized anxiety disorder during fear generalization. *Depression and Anxiety, 30*, 242–250.

Grillon, C. (2002). Startle reactivity and anxiety disorders: Aversive conditioning, context, and neurobiology. *Biological Psychiatry, 52*, 958–975.

Grillon, C., Baas, J. M., Cornwell, B., & Johnson, L. (2006). Context conditioning and behavioral avoidance in a virtual reality environment: Effect of predictability. *Biological Psychiatry, 60*, 752–759.

Kagan, J., & Fox, N. A. (2006). Biology, culture, and temperamental biases. In N. Eisenberg, W. Damon, & R. M. Lerner (Eds.), *Handbook of child psychology: Social, emotional, and personality development* (pp. 167–225). Hoboken, NJ: Wiley.

LeDoux, J. E. (1990). Fear pathways in the brain: Implications for a theory of the emotional brain. In P. F. Brain, S. Parmigiani, R. J. Blanchard, & D. Mainardi (Eds.), *Fear and defense* (pp. 163–177). London: Harwood.

Lee, W. E., Wadsworth, M. E. J., & Hotopf, M. (2006). The protective role of trait anxiety: A longitudinal cohort study. *Psychological Medicine, 36*, 345–351.

Lissek, S., Kaczkurkin, A. N., Rabin, S., Geraci, M., Pine, D. S., & Grillon, C. (2014). Generalized anxiety disorder is associated with overgeneralization of classically conditioned fear. *Biological Psychiatry, 75*, 909–915.

LoBue, V. (2014). Deconstructing the snake: The relative roles of perception, cognition, and emotion on threat detection. *Emotion, 14*, 701–711.

LoBue, V., & DeLoache, J. S. (2008). Detecting the snake in the grass: Attention to fear-relevant stimuli by adults and young children. *Psychological Science, 19*, 284–289.

McTeague, L. M., & Lang, P. J. (2012). The anxiety spectrum and the reflex physiology of defense: From circumscribed fear to broad distress. *Depression and Anxiety, 29*, 264–281.

Michiel, W. P., Drewes, M. J., Goedhart, A. W., Siebelink, B. M., & Treffers, P. D. A. (2004). A developmental analysis of self-reported fears in late childhood through mid-adolescence: Social-evaluative fears on the rise? *Journal of Child Psychology and Psychiatry, 45*, 481–495.

Miltner, W. H., Krieschel, S., Hecht, H., Trippe, R., & Weiss, T. (2004). Eye movements and behavioral responses to threatening and nonthreatening stimuli during visual search in phobic and nonphobic subjects. *Emotion, 4*, 323–339.

Mobbs, D., Petrovic, P., Marchant, J. L., Hassabis, D., Weiskopf, N., Seymour, B., … Frith, C. D. (2007). When fear is near: Threat imminence elicits prefrontal-periaqueductal gray shifts in humans. *Science, 317*, 1079–1083.

Muris, P. (2010). *Normal and abnormal fear and anxiety in children and adolescents*. Burlington, MA: Elsevier.

Muris, P., Merckelbach, H., Gadet, B., & Moulaert, V. (2000). Fears, worries, and scary dreams in 4- to 12-year-old children: Their content, developmental pattern, and origins. *Journal of Clinical Child and Adolescent Psychology, 29*, 43–52.

Mykletun, A., Bjerkeset, O., Øverland, S., Prince, M., Dewey, M., & Stewart, R. (2009). Levels of anxiety and depression as predictors of mortality: The HUNT study. *The British Journal of Psychiatry, 195*, 118–125.

National Institute of Mental Health (n.d.). Retrieved from https://www.nimh.nih.gov/research-priorities/rdoc/constructs/negative-valence-systems.shtml

Nesse, R. M., & Ellsworth, P. C. (2009). Evolution, emotions, and emotional disorders. *American Psychologist, 64*, 129–139.

Nitschke, J. B., Sarinopoulos, I., Mackiewicz, K. L., Schaefer, H. S., & Davidson, R. J. (2006). Functional neuroanatomy of aversion and its anticipation. *NeuroImage, 29*, 106–116.

Öhman, A. (2008). Fear and anxiety: Overlaps and dissociations. In M. Lewis, J. M. Haviland-Jones, & L. F. Barrett (Eds.), *Handbook of emotions* (pp. 709–729). New York, NY: Guilford Press.

Öhman, A., Flykt, A., & Esteves, F. (2001). Emotion drives attention: Detecting the snake in the grass. *Journal of Experimental Psychology: General, 130*, 466–478.

Öhman, A., & Soares, J. J. (1994). "Unconscious anxiety": Phobic responses to masked stimuli. *Journal of Abnormal Psychology, 103*, 231–240.

Paulus, M. P., & Stein, M. B. (2006). An insular view of anxiety. *Biological Psychiatry, 60*, 383–387.

Pérez-Edgar, K., Bar-Haim, Y., McDermott, J. M., Chronis-Tuscano, A., Pine, D. S., & Fox, N. A. (2010). Attention biases to threat and behavioral inhibition in early childhood shape adolescent social withdrawal. *Emotion, 10*, 349–357.

Pérez-Edgar, K., Reeb-Sutherland, B. C., McDermott, J. M., White, L. K., Henderson, H. A., Degnan, K. A., … Fox, N. A. (2011). Attention biases to threat link behavioral inhibition to social withdrawal over time in very young children. *Journal of Abnormal Child Psychology, 39*, 885–895.

Phelps, E. A. (2006). Emotion and cognition: Insights from studies of the human amygdala. *Annual Review of Psychology, 57*, 27–53.

Plutchik, R. (2003). *Emotions and life: Perspectives from psychology, biology, and evolution.* Washington, DC: American Psychological Association.

Poulos, A. M., Mehta, N., Lu, B., Amir, D., Livingston, B., Santarelli, A., … Fanselow, M. S. (2016). Conditioning-and time-dependent increases in context fear and generalization. *Learning & Memory, 23*, 379–385.

Prenoveau, J. M., Zinbarg, R. E., Craske, M. G., Mineka, S., Griffith, J. W., & Epstein, A. M. (2010). Testing a hierarchical model of anxiety and depression in adolescents: A tri-level model. *Journal of Anxiety Disorders, 24*, 334–344.

Rachman, S. (1998). *Anxiety.* East Sussex, UK: Psychology Press.

Rinck, M., Reinecke, A., Ellwart, T., Heuer, K., & Becker, E. S. (2005). Speeded detection and increased distraction in fear of spiders: Evidence from eye movements. *Journal of Abnormal Psychology, 114*, 235–248.

Roest, A. M., de Jonge, P., Lim, C. W. W., Stein, D. J., Al-Hamzawi, A., Alonso, J., … Ciutan, M. (2017). Fear and distress disorders as predictors of heart disease: A temporal perspective. *Journal of Psychosomatic Research, 96*, 67–75.

Schaefer, H. S., Larson, C. L., Davidson, R. J., & Coan, J. A. (2014). Brain, body, and cognition: Neural, physiological and self-report correlates of phobic and normative fear. *Biological Psychology, 98*, 59–69.

Schmitz, A., & Grillon, C. (2012). Assessing fear and anxiety in humans using the threat of predictable and unpredictable aversive events (the NPU-threat test). *Nature Protocols, 7*, 527–532.

Shackman, A. J., & Fox, A. S. (2016). Contributions of the central extended amygdala to fear and anxiety. *Journal of Neuroscience, 36*, 8050–8063.

Somerville, L. H., Whalen, P. J., & Kelley, W. M. (2010). Human bed nucleus of the stria terminalis indexes hypervigilant threat monitoring. *Biological Psychiatry, 68*, 416–424.

Straube, T., Mentzel, H. J., & Miltner, W. H. (2007). Waiting for spiders: Brain activation during anticipatory anxiety in spider phobics. *NeuroImage, 37*, 1427–1436.

Sylvers, P., Lilienfeld, S. O., & LaPrairie, J. L. (2011). Differences between trait fear and trait anxiety: Implications for psychopathology. *Clinical Psychology Review, 31*, 122–137.

Troy, A. S., Shallcross, A. J., & Mauss, I. B. (2013). A person-by-situation approach to emotion regulation: Cognitive reappraisal can either help or hurt, depending on the context. *Psychological Science, 24*, 2505–2514.

Waters, A. M., Bradley, B. P., & Mogg, K. (2014). Biased attention to threat in pediatric anxiety disorders (generalized anxiety disorder, social phobia, specific phobia, separation anxiety disorder) as a function of "distress" versus "fear" diagnostic categorization. *Psychological Medicine, 44*, 607–616.

Chapter 3
On Sentinels and Rapid Responders: The Adaptive Functions of Emotion Dysregulation

Tsachi Ein-Dor and Gilad Hirschberger

Abstract Feeling good, enjoying positive relationships with others, and looking on the brighter side of life represent a mode of living that most people aspire to. Our emotion system, however, was not designed to provide us with such a blissful existence, but rather it is primarily concerned with keeping us safe and alive. The current chapter takes a critical look at the emotion regulation literature and suggests that in this literature positivity and adaptiveness are often mistaken for one and the same. Specifically, the chapter takes an attachment and social defense theory perspective to show that some individuals, primarily those who are insecurely attached, suffer from a multitude of emotional and relational problems at the individual level. When examining their functioning at the group level, however, it becomes clear that these individuals play an indispensable role in keeping themselves and their group members out of harm's way. The chapter concludes that emotion dysregulation, albeit not pleasant, may be highly adaptive.

The human response to sudden life-threatening violence such as a terror attack is not uniform; some respond with screaming and shouting, while others display a seemingly more controlled and level-headed response (Ein-Dor & Hirschberger, 2016; Mawson, 2012; Perry, 1994). Do these different behaviors actually reflect the difference between adaptive and maladaptive and regulated and dysregulated responses, or is there adaptive value even in responses that seem out of control? The emotion regulation literature recognizes that emotions need to be expressed, not only regulated, and that regulation should take place only when emotions are incongruent with goals (Gross, 2015). Much of the literature, however, still seems to hold a one-size-fits-all understanding of emotion regulation whereby some forms of regulation are better than others and that "good" emotion regulation is the antidote

T. Ein-Dor (✉) · G. Hirschberger
The Baruch Ivcher School of Psychology, The Interdisciplinary Center (IDC) Herzliya, Herzliya, Israel
e-mail: teindor@idc.ac.il

© Springer International Publishing AG, part of Springer Nature 2018
H. C. Lench (ed.), *The Function of Emotions*,
https://doi.org/10.1007/978-3-319-77619-4_3

to a plethora of personal, interpersonal, and social problems. For instance, in the conflict resolution literature, emotions such as anger and hatred are considered destructive emotions that must be successfully regulated for peaceful resolution to take place (Čehajić-Clancy, Goldenberg, Gross, & Halperin, 2016). There seems to be little consideration of the possibility that these emotions may be adaptive in protecting groups from naively expecting peace from a disingenuous adversary. Further, this literature seems to implicitly hold a master-slave understanding of the relationship between cognition and emotion, implying that optimal functioning entails the triumph of reason over passion (Solomon, 2000). If emotions are portrayed as a savage force that must be controlled, it is no wonder that recent reviews of emotion regulation maintain that people should be "active regulators not passive victims of their emotions" (Goldenberg, Halperin, van Zomeren, & Gross, 2016). These perceptions of emotions, and particularly of negative emotions as negative forces that must be actively resisted, persist in spite of a growing recognition of the adaptive function of negative emotions (Coifman, Flynn, & Pinto, 2016) and the understanding that emotion regulation is a complex phenomenon that depends on context and culture (Gross, 2013).

This chapter addresses these issues from the perspective of attachment theory (Bowlby, 1973) and social defense theory (Ein-Dor, Mikulincer, Doron et al., 2010; Ein-Dor & Hirschberger, 2016) to demonstrate how emotion regulation strategies that have been deemed maladaptive and harmful may in fact be highly adaptive and essential strategies to cope with specific threats and challenges in specific situations. Thus, notions of good, bad, adaptive, and maladaptive are often presented in the literature in simplistic and absolute terms. A more nuanced view of emotion and emotion regulation may reveal that while some regulation strategies carry a heavy price in some domains, they are highly adaptive, essential, and irreplaceable in others.

Attachment Theory and Emotion

One way to contend with the diversity of responses to affective phenomenon is to consider individual differences. Attachment theory (Bowlby, 1973, 1980, 1982) has proved to be one avenue of research that is particularly suited to study individual differences in affect regulation. The attachment behavioral system evolved to respond to threat (Ein-Dor & Hirschberger, 2016). It is a system that compliments basic fight-or-flight responses that are individual in nature by adding a mechanism for the solicitation of help from others. Because at the individual level the human ability to effectively deal with threat is limited (Chapman & Chapman, 2000), humans rely on their superior cognitive abilities that enable them to deal with existential threats at the group level. When facing danger, humans can band together and effectively deal with the threat using cooperation and the strength of numbers.

According to attachment theory, the ability to deal with threat and adversity is an inborn psycho-evolutionary mechanism that is shaped throughout development as a function of interactions with close others (Ainsworth, Blehar, Waters, & Wall, 1978; Bowlby, 1979). The default of the attachment system is a sense of security that is obtained and enhanced through interactions with close others who are responsive and sensitive to one's needs. However, this optimal fit between child and parenting style is not always present. Although all babies have the potential to feel secure, some develop secondary attachment strategies as a result of less-than-optimal inter- actions with close others and the recognition that normal proximity seeking is not possible. These secondary strategies can be conceptualized as two orthogonal dimensions of attachment insecurity – anxiety and avoidance that reflect either a hyperactivation or deactivation of the attachment system – strategies that overutilize or underutilize the solicitation of other people's help (Mikulincer & Shaver, 2003).

People who develop in an environment that is only sporadically responsive to their needs, and does so in an insensitive manner, learn over time that only when the alarm button is pressed repeatedly will other people take notice and provide assis- tance. Such individuals, characterized as *anxiously attached*, adopt cognitive work- ing models that reflect preoccupation with issues of neglect and abandonment. Their behavior is clingy and controlling (Davis, Shaver, & Vernon, 2003), they show over- dependence on relationship partners as a source of protection (Shaver & Hazan, 1993), and they perceive themselves to have difficulties regulating their emotions (Mikulincer & Shaver, 2003). These self-perceptions are corroborated by evidence that individuals high on attachment anxiety display emotion overregulation (Quirin, Pruessner, & Kuhl, 2008) to the extent that their regulation attempts may even back- fire and increase rather than reduce the expression of emotion (Ben-Naim, Hirschberger, Ein-Dor, & Mikulincer, 2013).

Other individuals may develop in an environment that shows a consistent pattern of unresponsiveness to the individual's needs. Under such conditions, people learn that the alarm button (i.e., the activation of the attachment system) does not work. Summoning help does not seem to influence the likelihood that their needs will be met, and they often find themselves alone having to resolve their own problems without the assistance of their attachment figures. Over time, these individuals learn to strategically deactivate their attachment system, they inhibit support-seeking behaviors (Ein-Dor, Verbeke, Mokry, & Vrtička, in press), and they are resolved to learn how to fend for themselves and to require as little help from others as possible (Mikulincer & Shaver, 2003). Highly avoidant individuals also tend to avoid and suppress emotions to limit their exposure to aversive states (Fraley & Shaver, 1997).

The Classic Attachment Perspective on Affect Regulation

From an emotion regulation perspective, both attachment avoidance and attachment anxiety reflect impairments in emotion regulation, and this failure to regulate emo- tions should be manifest in social, emotional, and interpersonal problems that these individuals experience. Research supports this perspective and indicates that attach- ment anxiety is associated with an intensification of adverse emotional states and difficulties in downregulating emotions. For example, anxiously attached individuals experience higher levels of explicit and implicit death anxiety that they cannot effectively downregulate (Mikulincer & Florian, 2000; Mikulincer, Florian, Birnbaum, & Malishkowitz, 2002; Mikulincer, Florian, & Tolmacz, 1990), they are often flooded with angry feelings (Buunk, 1997; Calamari & Pini, 2003; Dutton et al., 1994), and they ruminate on these angry feelings, showing sadness and despair following conflicts (Mikulincer, 1998). Because of the impairment in the downregulation of negative emotions and the persistence of distress, people high on attachment anxiety experience an unmanageable stream of negative thoughts and feelings, which contributes to cognitive disorganization and fuels chronic worries and distress. Attachment anxiety also intensifies fear-related responses to even minimal signs of threats, exaggerates the catastrophic implications of threats, and encourages rumination on threats and their imagined consequences (Ein-Dor, Mikulincer, Doron, & Shaver, 2010). Social neuroscience research corroborates these findings and shows that when people high on attachment anxiety are confronted with negative social information, their right amygdala is highly activated, which indicates heightened emotional arousal (Vrtička, Bondolfi, Sander, & Vuilleumier, 2012).

Attachment avoidance, on the other hand, is organized around deactivating strategies of affect regulation, which involve deemphasizing threats and attempting to cope with them alone, without seeking help or support from other people (e.g., Kobak, Cole, Ferenz-Gillies, & Fleming, 1993; Shaver & Mikulincer, 2002). Avoidant people also deny attachment needs and suppress attachment-related thoughts and emotions (Mikulincer & Shaver, 2003). These tendencies hinder the social-based emotion regulation that secure people often deploy (Coan, 2008; Sroufe, Egeland, Carlson, & Collins, 2004): a secure person is often motivated to alleviate his or her distress by seeking actual or symbolic proximity to significant others. People high on attachment avoidance tend to forgo this tendency and to maintain a defensive façade of security and composure while managing cognitive and emotional avoidance and dealing with threats without seeking help from others (Shaver & Mikulincer, 2002). To independently overcome life's many challenges, they tend to block access to emotions and to cope with stress by ignoring, suppressing, or denying it (e.g., Dozier & Kobak, 1992). These deactivation strategies may be effective in regulating mild levels of stress (e.g., Ein-Dor, Doron, Solomon, Mikulincer, & Shaver, 2010), but they leave suppressed distress unresolved nonetheless. When faced with prolonged and demanding stressful experiences that require active confrontation with a problem and the mobilization of external sources of support, suppressed distress may impair avoidant people's ability to deal with inevitable adversities. In these cases, avoidant people may feel an inadequacy to effectively cope with distress and may display a marked decline in functioning (Horowitz, 1982). In support of this perspective, social neuroscience research shows that when people high on attachment avoidance are confronted with negative social information, their prefrontal and anterior cingulate are highly activated, which indicates effortful control of emotions (Vrtička et al., 2012). Interestingly, these regions were not activated when avoidant people employed suppression techniques for regulating emotions as opposed to reappraisal strategies, which implies that suppression is more effective than reappraisal for people high in attachment avoidance (Vrtička et al., 2012), a finding evident in psychophysiological research as well (Ben-Naim et al., 2013).

Contemporary theory and research on emotion regulation considers attachment insecurity (anxiety and/or avoidance) as maladaptive and as characterized by emotion dysregulation that is linked with an array of psychopathologies (Mikulincer & Shaver, 2012; Sroufe, Duggal, Weinfield, & Carlson, 2000) and serves as fertile ground for mental and physical disorders (Ein-Dor & Doron, 2015; Ein-Dor, Viglin, & Doron, 2016). For example, attachment insecurities are linked with depression (e.g., Catanzaro & Wei, 2010), general anxiety disorder (e.g., Marganska, Gallagher, & Miranda, 2013), obsessive-compulsive disorder (e.g., Doron, Moulding, Kyrios, Nedeljkovic, & Mikulincer, 2009), post-traumatic stress disorder (e.g., Ein-Dor, Doron, et al., 2010), eating disorders (e.g., Illing, Tasca, Balfour, & Bissada, 2010), and suicide ideation (e.g., Davaji, Valizadeh, & Nikamal, 2010). Attachment insecurity is also related to many personality disorders (Crawford et al., 2007; Meyer & Pilkonis, 2005). For example, people high on attachment anxiety have a higher prevalence of dependent, histrionic, and borderline personality disorders, which are manifested in identity confusion, anxiety, emotional liability, cognitive distortions, submissiveness, self-harm, and suspiciousness. These have been labeled the *emotion dysregulation* component of personality disorders (Livesley, 1991). Avoidant individuals are also at risk for psychopathologies that differ from those of anxious individuals and are in line with their tendency to avoid emotions or suppress them. They have a higher prevalence of schizoid and avoidant personality disorders, which consist of restricted expression of emotions, problems with intimacy, and social avoidance. These tendencies have been dubbed the *inhibitedness* component of personality disorders (Livesley, 1991).

A Social Defense Theory Perspective

The classic attachment model has amassed an impressive body of research to support the link between attachment insecurity and affect dysregulation. The current chapter challenges this perspective. It contends that, although attachment insecurities are undoubtedly related to affect regulation strategies that are costly and seemingly maladaptive at the individual level, it would be incorrect to deem these strategies impairments. Specifically, what appears as dysregulation at the individual level confers clear advantages at the group level. From this perspective, there are no inherently good or bad emotion regulation strategies. Rather, emotion expression and regulation are complex systems that respond to various needs and challenges. Observing these processes from a new angle may reveal that what seems to be dysregulation from one angle may in fact be a highly complex and adaptive response system from another.

Research on social defense theory (SDT; Ein-Dor & Hirschberger, 2016; Ein-Dor, Mikulincer, et al., 2010) – an extension of attachment theory – suggests that the emotion regulation strategies employed by people high in attachment insecurity (anxiety and/or avoidance) are not maladaptive or irregular but serve an important function. According to social defense theory, the current understanding of the function of different attachment styles is limited because most research on attachment focuses on individual differences in relational-related domains, in which the advantages of secure individuals are apparent (e.g., Mikulincer & Shaver, 2007; Mikulincer, Shaver, & Pereg, 2003; Simpson & Rholes, 2015). SDT argues that each of the three major attachment dispositions – security, anxiety, and avoidance – confer unique advantages for the individual and for his or her social environment that are adaptive and increase the likelihood of surviving perilous events.

Advantages and Disadvantages of Secure Individuals' Defensive Reactions

Attachment research has indicated that secure people tend to lead team efforts and promote the success of their social group by collaborating with others in times of need because they are calm and emotionally regulated. For example, secure individuals endorse greater prosocial and task-oriented leadership motivations and lower self-enhancing and self-reliance motivations than their more insecure counterparts (Davidovitz, Mikulincer, Shaver, Izsak, & Popper, 2007; Hinojosa, Davis-McCauley, Randolph-Seng, & Gardner, 2014). Secure leaders are also appraised by their followers as demonstrating higher efficacy in emotion-focused situations and task-focused ones (Davidovitz et al., 2007). As teammates they cope by being problem-focused and not emotion-focused and so work more effectively with other group members when solving problems and facing challenges (e.g., Molero, Moriano, & Shaver, 2013; Rom & Mikulincer, 2003). These advantages are believed to be the manifestation of a sense of security that was developed in past supportive experiences with attachment figures (Mikulincer & Shaver, 2007) that reflect core beliefs regarding the safeness of the world and the trustworthiness of the people in it. Holding such optimistic, comforting mental representations promote self-regulatory reappraisals of threats and negative emotions, which help secure people outperform insecure individuals in many situations (Mikulincer & Shaver, 2007).

The sense of security, composure, and calmness enjoyed by securely attached individuals is not always adaptive, however, and at times may even compromise actual physical security. In times of acute danger, a chronic sense of security may be maladaptive if it impairs the detection of threats and slows down rapid, effective responses. Studies of responses to acute physical danger indicate that many individuals in time of high threat rather than engaging in self-protection seek affiliation: "while mass panic (and/or violence) and self-preservation are often assumed to be the natural response to physical danger and perceived entrapment… the typical response to a variety of threats and disasters is not to flee but to seek the proximity of familiar persons and places" (Mawson, 2012, p. 233). This tendency to seek proximity to others is characteristic of secure individuals (Mikulincer, Shaver, Sapir-Lavid, & Avihou-Kanza, 2009; Waters & Waters, 2006), and under certain conditions, this tendency may exacerbate rather than reduce the threat. Adopting a schema of security about the self, others, and the world may, therefore, incur two prominent disadvantages: (a) delayed perception of danger and (b) slower employment of effective defensive behaviors in response to threats and danger.

Research based on police reports of reactions to a fire in a large coastal resort on the Isle of Man in 1973 examined the disadvantages of proximity seeking at times of acute distress and found that people who reported being close to family members were less likely to react to early signs of danger such as noises and shouts. Rather, they tended to react only after witnessing unambiguous cues of danger such as smoke, flames, and people running with fire extinguishers (Sime, 1983, 1985). These relatively late reactions suggest a loss of precious time in successfully managing the situation. Other studies of survivor behavior during perilous events have also indicated that people who reported being calmer and close to family members were slower to perceive that they were in danger than people who were alone or who felt highly distressed in the situation (Aguirre, Wenger, & Vigo, 1998; Köster, Seitz, Treml, Hartmann, & Klein, 2011). Similar observations were made in other reports of natural disasters indicating that "people tended to turn to and protect loved ones rather than flee from the threat" (Form & Nosow, 1958, p. 26) and that "traditional family ties often keep individual members in the danger zone until it is too late" (Hill & Hansen, 1962, p. 217). According to SDT, the tendency to suspend reactions until the presence of clear signs of threat, to fail to notice earlier and more subtle cues of danger, and to prioritize affiliation over self-protection is characteristic of securely attached people (Ein-Dor & Hirschberger, 2016; Ein-Dor, Mikulincer, et al., 2010).

These field studies of survival in times of acute threat are corroborated in recent SDT laboratory research, which also indicates that security with respect to attachment may be linked with nonoptimal reactions in times of danger. For example, to experimentally assess the possible disadvantages of secure people's emotion regulation strategies under threat, Ein-Dor and colleagues (Ein-Dor, Perry-Paldi, Merrin, Efrati, & Hirschberger, 2017) used a behavioral design with high ecological validity in which they recorded participants' responses to a real-life event that is ambiguous in nature: While participants were allegedly alone in a house, performing an engaging task in the living room, a fire alarm went off in the kitchen that was accompanied by a burning smell and smoke – cues of a possible kitchen fire. They monitored participants' reactions to these threatening stimuli and specifically examined whether they called for help, escaped the apartment, or entered the kitchen to locate the source of the threat. They found that whereas secure people tended to continue working on the engaging task (locating a pickpocket in online surveillance footage), insecure people tended to take effective action by calling for help or by heading for the kitchen to handle the fire.

This research and others indicate that while securely attached individuals show optimal performance in some tasks wherein their emotion regulation strategies come into play, such as in leadership and the coordination of group activities, in other tasks these exact emotional responses become a liability. The highly regulated and calm response of securely attached individuals has the downside of being slow to perceive actual threats, and when they do become aware of threat, their response is often suboptimal because of their calmness and their tendency to stay close to people around them. On a daily basis, these tendencies are relatively benign, but in times of acute danger, ignoring signs of threat, minimizing the threat, an inclination to continue with ongoing tasks, and seeking proximity to others may have serious implications for their survival. SDT suggests that in emergency situations, calmness and emotional stability may not be the optimal strategy, and then high attachment avoidance or anxiety that are usually considered maladaptive may confer under these conditions highly adaptive advantages that may increase the chances of survival for them and for the people around them.

Advantages of Anxiously Attached Individuals: The Upregulation of Emotion

People high on attachment anxiety often appraise their own functioning in groups as faulty and are judged by others as falling short in their ability to effectively lead team efforts (Davidovitz et al., 2007). They seem to take work less seriously than their secure counterparts and make fewer contributions to a team. This contribution is often of poorer quality because they are engulfed in stress, ruminate on negative outcomes, and focus on emotions instead of on the problems and their solutions (Rom & Mikulincer, 2003). Despite these shortcomings, the hypervigilant strategies that anxious people adopt when dealing with threats and their tendency to upregulate their emotions may nevertheless promote their survival and benefit others in their social surrounding in specific circumstances. Because anxiously attached individuals are chronically stressed, they vigilantly monitor the environment for threats, and upon detection of danger, they alert others, seek support by actively calling on others for help, and display overt signs of extreme distress that in other cases would seem an overreaction (Cassidy & Kobak, 1988; Feeney & Noller, 1990). Ein-Dor, Mikulincer, Doron and colleagues (2010) named these behavioral and emotional tendencies *sentinel behavior*.

According to SDT, sentinel behavior stems from a self-schema that guides anxious people's responses in times of need. It comprises default action tendencies that cause people high on attachment anxiety "(a) to remain vigilant [and stressed] with respect to possible threats, especially in unfamiliar or ambiguous situations; (b) to react quickly and strongly to early, perhaps unclear cues of danger (e.g., unusual noises, shuffling feet, shouts); (c) to alert others about the imminent danger; (d) if others are not immediately supportive, to heighten efforts to get them to provide support; and (e) to minimize distance from others when coping with a threat" (Ein-Dor, Mikulincer, & Shaver, 2011a, p. 2).

The benefits of sentinel behavior are apparent in many species of animals. For example, African elephants (Soltis, King, Douglas-Hamilton, Vollrath, & Savage, 2014), chimpanzees (e.g., Schel, Townsend, Machanda, Zuberbühler, & Slocombe, 2013), and many types of birds (Evans, Evans, & Marler, 1993) produce shrill alarm calls when they detect a potential threat such as the approach of a predator. Humans may also benefit from the hyperactivating strategies of people high on anxiety in similar ways as these strategies seem to function as an alarm system that benefits the entire group.

The first evidence in favor of this notion reveals the association between attachment anxiety and heightened accessibility to core components of the sentinel schema – being stressed and vigilant, noticing danger quicker than others, and warning them about the danger (Ein-Dor et al., 2011a). For example, when participants were asked to write a story about a TAT-like (Thematic Apperception Test; Murray, 1943) card with a scary scenario, those higher on attachment anxiety composed stories with more sentinel-related narratives. After reading a story about a person who behaved in a sentinel manner, participants who scored higher on attachment anxiety were more likely to appraise the target's personality dispositions with greater accuracy.

Attachment anxiety was later linked with actual sentinel-related behavior in response to emergencies (Ein-Dor, Mikulincer, & Shaver, 2011b). In one research, the behavior of small groups of three was observed in an experimentally manipulated threatening situation: a room progressively filling up with nontoxic smoke from what seemed like a malfunctioning computer. In line with SDT, groups higher on attachment anxiety detected the presence of smoke quicker than less anxious groups. Specifically, a one-point increase in anxiety was linked with an 11.5-s decrease in detection time. In addition, the person with the highest score on anxiety, who was also the most stressed, detected the presence of smoke in the room more often than predicted by chance alone (Ein-Dor et al., 2011a). In another study that examined responses to an experimentally manipulated kitchen fire, participants who scored higher on attachment anxiety were more likely to call the experimenter upon hearing the fire alarm in the kitchen (Ein-Dor, Perry-Paldi, et al., in press). In complementary self-report research, participants were asked to report the first action that they would be likely to take in various threat scenarios (Ein-Dor & Perry-Paldi, 2014). Results indicated that individuals high on attachment anxiety were high in self-reports of sentinel (e.g., yelling) and fear-related behaviors (e.g., running away) that increased as a function of the dangerousness of the situation and the clarity of the threat.

People high on attachment anxiety do not only alert others of an impending threat by vocalizing, they often go out of their way to deliver a warning message (Ein-Dor & Orgad, 2012). Using software designed for this experiment, participants were led to believe that they accidently activated a Trojan horse that completely erased the experimenter's hard drive and possibly the campus server. Participants were then asked to alert the computer technicians about the hazard. On their way, the experimenters created four behavioral obstacles to try to delay participants from delivering the warning message (e.g., a confederate who asked the participant to help her complete a short questionnaire). In line with SDT, results indicated that high attachment anxiety was linked with fewer delays on the way to deliver the message.

The sentinel abilities of anxiously attached individuals are not only adaptive in emergency situations, but confer to these individuals a unique set of skills such as high perceptivity and detection skills. People high on attachment anxiety are more accurate in reading their partners' true thoughts and feelings in situations that pose a threat to the relationship (Simpson, Ickes, & Grich, 1999; Simpson et al., 2011). They also show superior performance in telling truthful from untruthful statements shown in video clips (Ein-Dor & Perry, 2014). This enhanced lie detection ability comes in handy at times when others are deliberately trying to conceal their intentions. For instance, in one study semiprofessional poker players completed a self-report questionnaire measuring attachment dispositions and then participated in a poker tournament during which their behavior was monitored. The results of this study indicated that people higher on attachment anxiety were more accurate in detecting deceitful statements made by other players and that players higher on anxiety won an overall greater amount of money during the tournament. Not surprisingly, the amount of money earned was directly related to participants' ability to call their opponents' bluffs (Ein-Dor & Perry, 2014). Anxious individuals are not only better lie detectors, they are also better liars (Ein-Dor, Perry-Paldi, Zohar-Cohen, Efrati, & Hirschberger, 2017). This may not seem to be an advantage, but research indicates that lying is commonplace among humans and that being able to get away with a lie has adaptive advantages (Ein-Dor, Perry-Paldi, Zohar-Cohen et al., 2017). Finally, research indicates that people high in attachment anxiety are not only more accurate at detecting threats but are also more accurate in their response to these threats. In a realistic shooting paradigm wherein participants needed to quickly distinguish between hostiles and bystanders, anxious individuals showed superior performance and did not merely shoot more rounds but shot more accurately (Ein-Dor, Perry-Paldi, & Hirschberger, in press). Taken together, research provides support for the SDT contention that the typical upregulation of emotion seen among people high in attachment anxiety is advantageous in certain environments and circumstances and that most importantly these regulation strategies may promote, and not hinder, individual and group survival.

Advantages of Avoidantly Attached Individuals: The Downregulation of Emotion

People high on attachment avoidance tend to relegate appraisals of threat and downgrade emotions, sensations of pain, and vulnerability (e.g., Fraley & Shaver, 1997). Therefore, they are usually less vigilant to signs of danger and tend to recognize the extent of threat later than others (Ein-Dor & Hirschberger, 2016; Ein-Dor,

Mikulincer, et al., 2010). They tend to appraise team cohesion as more fractured than others and are often appraised by others as less apt to lead because of their apparent detachment (Davidovitz et al., 2007). They do not tend to collaborate with others, and, as a consequence, they do not perform well as teammates (Rom & Mikulincer, 2003). In emergency situations, they are compulsively self-reliant (Bowlby, 1973) and tend to take self-protective actions that promote their own interests (Feeney & Collins, 2001), a reaction tendency that Ein-Dor, Mikulincer, Doron and colleagues (2010) dubbed *rapid fight-or-flight behavior*. As a result, while anxious individuals alert others to threat and secure individuals focus their attention on the whereabouts of significant others around them, without focusing quickly enough on how to evade the progressive threat, avoidant people are especially apt to find a way to effectively deal with the threat.

The shallow emotional state and the asocial tendencies of people high on avoidance may seem to be discordant with the needs of the group, but they might actually help people around them escape danger. Suppose that an avoidant person is in a shopping mall engrossed by flames. To save herself or himself, he or she will quickly evaluate the best course of action – either to escape or to quickly extinguish the fire. The relative emotional calm of avoidant individuals enables them to execute these behaviors with little delay, while others might be in a state of panic. Although avoidant individuals' primary focus is on themselves with little regard for others, their effective actions may not only increase their own chances of survival but may inadvertently save others who follow their lead. Research on real emergency situations indicates that the sight of people running from danger can motivate the escape of others around them and unintentionally save lives (e.g., Mawson, 2012). In extreme situations, such as a battlefield, these behavioral cues may determine collective behavior. For instance, one observation from the battlefields of World War II was that "It can be laid down as a general rule that nothing is more likely to collapse a line of infantry than the sight of a few of its number in full and unexplained flight to the rear.... One or two or more men made a sudden run to the rear which others in the vicinity did not understand.... In every case the testimony of all witnesses clearly [indicated] that those who started the run ... had a legitimate or at least a reasonable excuse for the action" (Marshall, 1947, pp. 145–146). These observations gain experimental support from research that shows that, when facing an experimentally manipulated emergency situation – fire in an apartment lobby – the ostensibly asocial escape of highly avoidant individuals motivated the escape of other members even in the absence of an alarm call (Ein-Dor, Perry-Paldi, et al., in press). Aside from promoting the motivation for escape, people who flee before others must clear an escape route of possible obstacles and by doing so pave a clear way to safety for those who follow. Taken together, people high on avoidance tend to downregulate their emotions to the point of hindering their interpersonal relations, but this emotion regulation strategy is highly adaptive in emergency situations and may increase their own and their group members' chances of survival.

According to SDT, the asocial behavior of avoidant individuals stems from a rapid fight-or-flight schema that comprises the following action tendencies: "(a) minimize the importance of threatening stimuli; (b) when danger is clearly imminent, take quick self-protective action, either by escaping the situation or by taking action against the danger; and (c) at such times, do not worry about coordinating one's efforts with those of other people" (Ein-Dor et al., 2011a, p. 3).

The relationship between attachment avoidance and the core cognitive schema of rapid fight-or-flight was first documented in research wherein participants were asked to read short descriptions of behaviors in threatening situations. After reading a story about a person who behaved in accordance with the rapid fight-or-flight script, participants high on attachment avoidance generated more inferences about the person's behaviors and thoughts than people low on avoidance (Ein-Dor et al., 2011a).

Attachment avoidance was later linked with actual rapid fight-or-flight behavior in times of threat (Ein-Dor et al., 2011b). Specifically, in this research a room consisting of small groups of participants progressively filled up with smoke. In line with the main tenants of SDT, groups higher on attachment avoidance (higher average score) were quicker to escape the room than more secure groups and were appraised by judges as more effective in dealing with the situation. In another study, when faced with an experimentally manipulated kitchen fire and/or a fire in an apartment lobby, people high in attachment avoidance were quicker to assess the risk of the events and were quicker to take effective action (handling the fire or escaping the scene) (Ein-Dor, Perry-Paldi, et al., in press). When asked to report on their behavior, participants high on attachment avoidance tend to report rapid-responder (e.g., attacking; which relates to fight responses), fear-related (e.g., running away; which relates to flight reactions), and anxiety-related (e.g., risk assessment) reactions (Ein-Dor & Perry-Paldi, 2014). Taken together, research supports the SDT notion that attachment-related avoidance is associated with rapid fight-or-flight cognitions and behaviors and that these behaviors have clear adaptive benefits for individuals and groups in emergency situations.

Attachment, Threat, and the Effectiveness of Heterogeneous Groups

Over the course of evolution, humans lived in relatively small groups or tribes of kin and often faced various threats and perils. As individuals, however, humans were at a significant disadvantage compared to other animals: they have a fragile body, which hinders their ability to effectively fight threats, and they evolved to walk on two legs, which limits their ability to effectively escape threats. They have poor eyesight, poor hearing, and a poor sense of smell. They cannot fly and have no tail to hang from or claws to fight back or climb trees. Humans should be no match for any of nature's many predators. Yet, not only have humans survived and prevailed, they have ascended to the top of the animal kingdom and unquestionably dominate the planet. How did such an ostensibly puny creature attain such remarkable evolutionary success? Humans survived due to their superior cognitive faculties, by utilizing the strength of numbers, and by facing danger as a group (Ein-Dor &

Hirschberger, 2016). According to SDT, this success is not just a matter of sheer numbers, but of the unique characteristics of human groups. Specifically, to survive, human groups require several abilities that one person can never hope to have: heightened vigilance to threats and danger, quick responses to threats once they are detected, and calm and calculated collective efforts to overcome the threats. An effective response to threats could only be achieved by combining efforts of people with different attachment dispositions. According to SDT, each of the three major styles of attachment– security, anxiety, and avoidance – have unique adaptive advantages that promote survival, and the combination of different attachment styles in a group offsets the limitations of each individual disposition. Heterogeneous groups with respect to attachment dispositions should be more sensitive to early signs of threat by utilizing the sentinel abilities of anxious members, act quickly in response to threats without much deliberation by utilizing the rapid fight-or-flight abilities of avoidant members, and manage complex group-level tasks by utilizing the leadership and social-oriented abilities of secure members. Accordingly, a group comprising all three styles of attachment patterns may benefit from the combined abilities of each disposition and counterweigh the shortcomings of each individual disposition. Therefore, such groups might be superior to other groups in dealing with threats and survival problems.

In support of this proposition, heterogeneous groups with respect to attachment patterns were appraised by external judges as dealing more effectively with a room gradually filling up with smoke than more homogenous groups (Ein-Dor et al., 2011b). In a recently completed dissertation, the effectiveness of heterogeneous groups with respect to attachment patterns was examined among professional soccer teams (Refaeli, 2017). Players from 15 professional teams in Israel filled out attachment questionnaires before the beginning of the soccer season, and then the performance of the groups was monitored using the official scores. Results indicated that heterogeneity with respect to avoidance scores (i.e., avoidant and secure people in the team) was linked to accumulating more league points, whereas heterogeneity with respect to anxiety scores (i.e., anxious and secure people in the team) was related to fewer opponent goals. Thus, the individualistic, self-reliant, and composed tendencies of avoidant individuals helped the team score more points, whereas the hypervigilant and aroused tendencies of anxious individuals helped protect the team against the threat posed by the opponent team.

Heterogeneity in attachment patterns was also found to promote the success of work teams. Specifically, teams' heterogeneity in attachment anxiety and avoidance scores was related to better academic grades (Lavy, Bareli, & Ein-Dor, 2015). This latter finding was moderated by the teams' level of cohesion, however. Heterogeneity was linked with better performance only among teams that were able to create a high sense of cohesion, by providing a safe and accepting environment. When teams were not cohesive, however, heterogeneity could be a double-edged sword. In such cases, individuals with either anxiety or avoidance dispositions could present a social challenge to groups' dynamics: People high on attachment anxiety because of their hyperactivation tendencies are clingy, needy, vexed, and fearful and are constantly seeking approval of others, sometimes by being intrusive (Smith, Murphy, &

Coats, 1999). People high on attachment avoidance might neglect the needs of others and keep their distance from others, which may hinder effective communication within the group (Rom & Mikulincer, 2003; Smith et al., 1999). These tendencies may cause conflicts between team members and reduce teams' socioemotional functioning (Pelled, Eisenhardt, & Xin, 1999), although teams' objective performance might still be high.

The research on social defense theory stands as a case example of how simplistic notions of emotion and emotion regulation may be overlooking the possible adaptive functions of what may seem at first sight to be maladaptive. Attachment insecurity carries many personal and interpersonal costs. Anxious and avoidant individuals suffer from more psychopathologies, they have more relationship-related problems, and their overall well-being is lower than that of their secure counterparts (Cassidy & Shaver, 2008). Why did such seemingly maladaptive tendencies persist over the long course of evolution? When examining attachment insecurity from a different angle and understanding that attachment is not about relationships, but about survival (Ein-Dor & Hirschberger, 2016), the necessity of attachment insecurity for the very survival of individuals and groups becomes abundantly clear.

The conclusions drawn from attachment theory and social defense theory can be extended to the entire emotion and emotion regulation literature. When negative emotions persist, are they necessarily maladaptive? Should we actively engage in regulating seemingly destructive emotions such as anger, hatred, and despair, or should we first examine whether these emotions are conveying an important message that we should at least consider? The literature on emotions in conflict (Halperin, 2016), for instance, is a prime example of research that often fails to consider the adaptive role of emotions that may be inconsistent with the somewhat impatient desire to resolve conflicts and shows zealous enthusiasm to regulate or eradicate these ostensibly destructive emotions.

Beyond Attachment: A Nuanced Understanding of Emotion Regulation

After a long drive with nothing to eat for hours, you spot a diner on the side of the road. It looks run down and deserted, but you are too hungry to care. You sit down and a very sweet old lady who runs the place takes your order. When the food arrives, it looks suspicious and smells bad. What should you do? You take a small bite and immediately feel nauseous. Should you regulate your feelings of disgust and wolf down your meal with plenty of water, or should you offend the owner who treated you so nicely, return the dish, and flee the premises? If you opted for the first solution, your good manners may carry the price of food poisoning and an unpleasant visit to the emergency room. Emotion regulation in this case may be maladaptive. Similarly, regulating your response to a truck mowing down tourists in the Ramblas or to a bear you encounter when hiking the back country may have deadly consequences.

Our emotions convey important information. They serve first and foremost as a warning system to alert us of threats much before our cognitive system is capable of fully recognizing the extent of the threat (Bechara, Damasio, Tranel, & Damasio, 1997). This is not to say that emotions cannot be falsely triggered due to biased perceptions (Gross, 2013), but, more often than not, emotions provide important information that increases the success of many cognitive processes such as negotiations, problem-solving, and decision making (Lerner, Yi, Valdesolo, & Kassam, 2015).

It appears that some of the research in the field confounds the attainment of a desired goal with the adaptive function of emotion such that when an emotion seems to stand as a barrier to goal attainment it is deemed maladaptive and unregulated. Relationship satisfaction and stability, mental health, and peaceful intergroup relations are not just important goals but the very reason many of us conduct research. Nevertheless, good science requires caution and a clear separation between personal desires and ideologies and an impartial observation of the social world. When emotions seem to stand in the way of attaining marital bliss, such as is often the case among insecurely attached individuals (Ben-Naim et al., 2013; Feeney, 2002; Hirschberger et al., 2009), or when emotions exacerbate rather than quell intergroup tensions (Halperin, 2016), these emotions may appear maladaptive. It is pertinent, however, that we consider the possibility that while these emotions are hindering the attainment of a desirable goal, they are conveying an important message. Sometimes an overzealous desire to resolve interpersonal and intergroup conflict may blind us to the possibility that seemingly undesirable emotions are reacting to signals that we cannot consciously detect or prefer to ignore. These emotions serve an adaptive function by turning our attention to threats that may slow down our progress toward a goal but for valid reasons (e.g., an abusive relationship, a duplicitous adversary). Social defense theory stands as a demonstration of how seemingly maladaptive emotions and emotion regulation strategies are in fact highly adaptive and paves the way for a more comprehensive and nuanced reconsideration of axiomatic notions of adaptivity and maladaptivity.

References

Aguirre, B. E., Wenger, D., & Vigo, G. (1998). *A test of the emergent norm theory of collective behavior*. Paper presented at the Sociological Forum.

Ainsworth, M. D., Blehar, M. C., Waters, E., & Wall, S. (1978). *Patterns of attachment: Assessed in the strange situation and at home*. Hillsdale, NJ: Erlbaum.

Bechara, A., Damasio, H., Tranel, D., & Damasio, A. R. (1997). Deciding advantageously before knowing the advantageous strategy. *Science, 275*, 1293–1295.

Ben-Naim, S., Hirschberger, G., Ein-Dor, T., & Mikulincer, M. (2013). An experimental study of emotion regulation during relationship conflict interactions: The moderating role of attachment orientations. *Emotion, 13*, 506–519.

Bowlby, J. (1973). *Attachment and loss: Vol. 2. Separation: Anxiety and anger*. New York, NY: Basic Books.

Bowlby, J. (1979). *The making & breaking of affectional bonds*. London, UK: Tavistock Publications Limited.

Bowlby, J. (1980). *Attachment and loss: Vol. 3. Sadness and depression.* New York, NY: Basic Books.

Bowlby, J. (1982). *Attachment and loss: Vol. 1. Attachment* (2nd ed.). New York, NY: Basic Books.

Buunk, B. P. (1997). Personality, birth order and attachment styles as related to various types of jealousy. *Personality and Individual Differences, 23*, 997–1006.

Calamari, E., & Pini, M. (2003). Dissociative experiences and anger proneness in late adolescent females with different attachment styles. *Adolescence, 38*, 287–303.

Cassidy, J., & Kobak, R. R. (1988). Avoidance and its relationship with other defensive processes. In J. Belsky & T. Nezworski (Eds.), *Clinical implications of attachment* (pp. 300–323). Hillsdale, NJ: Erlbaum.

Cassidy, J., & Shaver, P. R. (2008). *Handbook of attachment, second edition: Theory, research, and clinical applications.* New York, NY: The Guilford Press.

Catanzaro, A., & Wei, M. (2010). Adult attachment, dependence, self-criticism, and depressive symptoms: A test of a mediational model. *Journal of Personality, 78*, 1135–1162.

Čehajić-Clancy, S., Goldenberg, A., Gross, J. J., & Halperin, E. (2016). Social-psychological interventions for intergroup reconciliation: An emotion regulation perspective. *Psychological Inquiry, 27*, 73–88.

Chapman, C. A., & Chapman, L. J. (2000). Determinants of group size in primates: The importance of travel costs. In S. Boinski & P. A. Garber (Eds.), *On the move: How and why animals travel in groups* (pp. 24–42). Chicago, IL: The University of Chicago Press.

Coan, J. A. (2008). Toward a neuroscience of attachment. In J. Cassidy & P. R. Shaver (Eds.), *Handbook of attachment: Theory, research, and clinical applications* (2nd ed., pp. 241–265). New York, NY: Guilford Press.

Coifman, K. G., Flynn, J. J., & Pinto, L. A. (2016). When context matters: Negative emotions predict psychological health and adjustment. *Motivation and Emotion, 40*, 602–624.

Crawford, T. N., Livesley, W. J., Jang, K. L., Shaver, P. R., Cohen, P., & Ganiban, J. (2007). Insecure attachment and personality disorder: A twin study of adults. *European Journal of Personality, 21*, 191–208.

Davaji, R. B. O., Valizadeh, S., & Nikamal, M. (2010). The relationship between attachment styles and suicide ideation: The study of Turkmen students, Iran. *Procedia - Social and Behavioral Sciences, 5*, 1190–1194.

Davidovitz, R., Mikulincer, M., Shaver, P. R., Izsak, R., & Popper, M. (2007). Leaders as attachment figures: Leaders' attachment orientations predict leadership-related mental representations and followers' performance and mental health. *Journal of Personality and Social Psychology, 93*, 632–650.

Davis, D., Shaver, P. R., & Vernon, M. L. (2003). Physical, emotional, and behavioral reactions to breaking up: The roles of gender, age, emotional involvement, and attachment style. *Personality and Social Psychology Bulletin, 29*, 871–884.

Doron, G., Moulding, R., Kyrios, M., Nedeljkovic, M., & Mikulincer, M. (2009). Adult attachment insecurities are related to obsessive compulsive phenomena. *Journal of Social and Clinical Psychology, 28*, 1022–1049.

Dozier, M., & Kobak, R. (1992). Psychophysiology in attachment interviews: Converging evidence for deactivating strategies. *Child Development, 63*, 1473–1480.

Dutton, D. G., Saunders, K., Starzomski, A., & Bartholomew, K. (1994). Intimacy-anger and insecure attachment as precursors of abuse in intimate relationships. *Journal of Applied Social Psychology, 24*, 1367–1386.

Ein-Dor, T., & Doron, G. (2015). Attachment and psychopathology. In J. A. Simpson & S. Rholes (Eds.), *Attachment theory and research: New directions and emerging themes* (pp. 346–373). Washington, DC: American Psychological Association.

Ein-Dor, T., Doron, G., Solomon, Z., Mikulincer, M., & Shaver, P. R. (2010). Together in pain: Attachment-related dyadic processes and posttraumatic stress disorder. *Journal of Counseling Psychology, 57*, 317–327.

Ein-Dor, T., & Hirschberger, G. (2016). Rethinking attachment theory from a theory of relationships to a theory of individual and group survival. *Current Directions in Psychological Science, 25*, 223–227.

Ein-Dor, T., Mikulincer, M., Doron, G., & Shaver, P. R. (2010). The attachment paradox: How can so many of us (the insecure ones) have no adaptive advantages? *Perspectives on Psychological Science, 5*, 123–141.

Ein-Dor, T., Mikulincer, M., & Shaver, P. R. (2011a). Attachment insecurities and the processing of threat-related information: Studying the schemas involved in insecure people's coping strategies. *Journal of Personality and Social Psychology, 101*, 78–93.

Ein-Dor, T., Mikulincer, M., & Shaver, P. R. (2011b). Effective reaction to danger: Attachment insecurities predict behavioral reactions to an experimentally induced threat above and beyond general personality traits. *Social Psychological and Personality Science, 2*, 467–473.

Ein-Dor, T., & Orgad, T. (2012). Scared saviors: Evidence that people high in attachment anxiety are more effective in alerting others to threat. *European Journal of Social Psychology, 42*, 667–671.

Ein-Dor, T., & Perry, A. (2014). Full house of fears: Evidence that people high in attachment anxiety are more accurate in detecting deceit. *Journal of Personality, 82*, 83–92.

Ein-Dor, T., & Perry-Paldi, A. (2014). Human reaction to threats: Examining the interplay between personality dispositions and situational features. *Psychology Research, 4*, 599–622.

Ein-Dor, T., Perry-Paldi, A., & Hirschberger, G. (2017). Friend or foe? Evidence that groups of anxious people make accurate shooting decisions. *European Journal of Social Psychology, 47*, 783–788.

Ein-Dor, T., Perry-Paldi, A., Merrin, J., Efrati, Y., & Hirschberger, G. (2017). Effective disengagement: Insecure people are more likely to disengage from an ongoing task and take effective action when facing danger. *Journal of Personality*. Advance online publication. https://doi.org/10.1111/jopy.12308

Ein-Dor, T., Perry-Paldi, A., Merrin, J., & Hirschberger, G. (in press). Effective disengagement: Insecure people are more likely to disengage from an ongoing task and take effective action when facing danger. *Journal of Personality*. Advance online publication. https://doi.org/10.1111/jopy.12308

Ein-Dor, T., Perry-Paldi, A., Zohar-Cohen, K., Efrati, Y., & Hirschberger, G. (2017). It takes an insecure liar to catch a liar: The link between attachment insecurity, deception, and detection of deception. *Personality and Individual Differences, 113*, 81–87.

Ein-Dor, T., Viglin, D., & Doron, G. (2016). Extending the transdiagnostic model of attachment and psychopathology. *Frontiers in Psychology, 7*, 484.

Evans, C. S., Evans, L., & Marler, P. (1993). On the meaning of alarm calls: Functional reference in an avian vocal system. *Animal Behaviour, 46*, 23–38.

Feeney, B. C., & Collins, N. L. (2001). Predictors of caregiving in adult intimate relationships: An attachment theoretical perspective. *Journal of Personality and Social Psychology, 80*, 972–994.

Feeney, J. A. (2002). Attachment, marital interaction, and relationship satisfaction: A diary study. *Personal Relationships, 9*, 39–55.

Feeney, J. A., & Noller, P. (1990). Attachment style as a predictor of adult romantic relationships. *Journal of Personality and Social Psychology, 58*, 281–291.

Form, W. H., & Nosow, S. (1958). *Community in disaster*. New York, NY: Harper & Bros.

Fraley, R. C., & Shaver, P. R. (1997). Adult attachment and the suppression of unwanted thoughts. *Journal of Personality and Social Psychology, 73*, 1080–1091.

Goldenberg, A., Halperin, E., van Zomeren, M., & Gross, J. J. (2016). The process model of group-based emotion. *Personality and Social Psychology Review, 20*, 118–141.

Gross, J. J. (2013). Emotion regulation: Taking stock and moving forward. *Emotion, 13*, 359–365.

Gross, J. J. (2015). Emotion regulation: Current status and future prospects. *Psychological Inquiry, 26*, 1–26.

Halperin, E. (2016). *Emotions in conflict: Inhibitors and facilitators of peace making*. New York, NY: Routledge.

Hill, R., & Hansen, D. A. (1962). Families in disaster. In G. W. Baker & D. W. Chapman (Eds.), *Man and society in disaster* (pp. 185–221). New York, NY: Basic Books.

Hinojosa, A. S., Davis-McCauley, K., Randolph-Seng, B., & Gardner, W. L. (2014). Leader and follower attachment styles: Implications for authentic leader–follower relationships. *The Leadership Quarterly, 25*, 595–610.

Hirschberger, G., Srivastava, S., Marsh, P., Cowan, C. P., & Cowan, P. A. (2009). Attachment, marital satisfaction, and divorce during the first fifteen years of parenthood. *Personal Relationships, 16*, 401–420.

Horowitz, M. J. (1982). Psychological processes induced by illness, injury, and loss. In T. Millon, C. Green, & R. Meagher (Eds.), *Handbook of clinical health psychology* (pp. 53–68). New York, NY: Plenum Press.

Illing, V., Tasca, G. A., Balfour, L., & Bissada, H. (2010). Attachment insecurity predicts eating disorder symptoms and treatment outcomes in a clinical sample of women. *The Journal of Nervous and Mental Disease, 198*, 653–659.

Kobak, R., Cole, H., Ferenz-Gillies, R., & Fleming, W. (1993). Attachment and emotional regulation during mother-teen problem solving: A control theory analysis. *Child Development, 64*, 231–245.

Köster, G., Seitz, M., Treml, F., Hartmann, D., & Klein, W. (2011). On modelling the influence of group formations in a crowd. *Contemporary Social Science, 6*, 397–414.

Lavy, S., Bareli, Y., & Ein-Dor, T. (2015). The effects of attachment heterogeneity and team cohesion on team functioning. *Small Group Research, 46*, 27–49.

Lerner, J. S., Li, Y., Valdesolo, P., & Kassam, K. S. (2015). Emotion and decision making. *Annual Review of Psychology, 66*, 799–823.

Livesley, W. J. (1991). Classifying personality disorders: Ideal types, prototypes, or dimensions? *Journal of Personality Disorders, 5*, 52–59.

Marganska, A., Gallagher, M., & Miranda, R. (2013). Adult attachment, emotion dysregulation, and symptoms of depression and generalized anxiety disorder. *American Journal of Orthopsychiatry, 83*, 131–141.

Marshall, S. (1947). *Men against fire*. Norman, OK: University of Oklahoma Press.

Mawson, A. R. (2012). *Mass panic and social attachment: The dynamics of human behavior*. Burlington, VT: Ashgate.

Meyer, B., & Pilkonis, P. A. (2005). An attachment model of personality disorders. In M. F. Lenzenweger & J. F. Clarkin (Eds.), *Major theories of personality disorder* (pp. 231–281). New York, NY: Guilford.

Mikulincer, M. (1998). Adult attachment style and affect regulation: Strategic variations in self-appraisals. *Journal of Personality and Social Psychology, 75*, 420–435.

Mikulincer, M., & Florian, V. (2000). Exploring individual differences in reactions to mortality salience: Does attachment style regulate terror management mechanisms? *Journal of Personality and Social Psychology, 79*, 260–273.

Mikulincer, M., Florian, V., Birnbaum, G., & Malishkevich, S. (2002). The death-anxiety buffering function of close relationships: Exploring the effects of separation reminders on death-thought accessibility. *Personality and Social Psychology Bulletin, 28*, 287–299.

Mikulincer, M., Florian, V., & Tolmacz, R. (1990). Attachment styles and fear of personal death: A case study of affect regulation. *Journal of Personality and Social Psychology, 58*, 273–280.

Mikulincer, M., & Shaver, P. R. (2003). The attachment behavioral system in adulthood: Activation, psychodynamics, and interpersonal processes. In M. P. Zanna (Ed.), *Advances in experimental social psychology* (Vol. 35, pp. 52–153). New York, NY: Academic Press.

Mikulincer, M., & Shaver, P. R. (2007). *Attachment in adulthood: Structure, dynamics, and change*. New York, NY: Guilford Press.

Mikulincer, M., & Shaver, P. R. (2012). An attachment perspective on psychopathology. *World Psychiatry, 11*, 11–15.

Mikulincer, M., Shaver, P. R., & Pereg, D. (2003). Attachment theory and affect regulation: The dynamics, development, and cognitive consequences of attachment-related strategies. *Motivation and Emotion, 27*, 77–102.

Mikulincer, M., Shaver, P. R., Sapir-Lavid, Y., & Avihou-Kanza, N. (2009). What's inside the minds of securely and insecurely attached people? The secure-base script and its associations with attachment-style dimensions. *Journal of Personality and Social Psychology, 97*, 615–633.

Molero, F., Moriano, J. A., & Shaver, P. R. (2013). The influence of leadership style on subordinates' attachment to the leader. *The Spanish Journal of Psychology, 16*, E62.

Murray, H. A. (1943). *Thematic apperception test manual*. Cambridge, MA: Harvard University Press.

Pelled, L. H., Eisenhardt, K. M., & Xin, K. R. (1999). Exploring the black box: An analysis of work group diversity, conflict and performance. *Administrative Science Quarterly, 44*, 1–28.

Perry, R. W. (1994). A model of evacuation compliance behavior. In R. R. Dynes & K. J. Tierne (Eds.), *Disasters, collective behavior, and social organization* (pp. 85–98). Newark, DE: University of Delaware Press.

Quirin, M., Pruessner, J. C., & Kuhl, J. (2008). HPA system regulation and adult attachment anxiety: Individual differences in reactive and awakening cortisol. *Psychoneuroendocrinology, 33*, 581–590.

Refaeli, T. (2017). *Evidence that heterogeneity in attachment scores is linked with better performance of professional soccer teams*. Unpublished master's thesis. Interdisciplinary Center (IDC) Herzliya, Herzliya, Israel.

Rom, E., & Mikulincer, M. (2003). Attachment theory and group processes: The association between attachment style and group-related representations, goals, memories, and functioning. *Journal of Personality and Social Psychology, 84*, 1220–1235.

Schel, A. M., Townsend, S. W., Machanda, Z., Zuberbühler, K., & Slocombe, K. E. (2013). Chimpanzee alarm call production meets key criteria for intentionality. *PLoS One, 8*, e76674.

Shaver, P. R., & Hazan, C. (1993). Adult romantic attachment: Theory and evidence. *Advances in Personal Relationships, 4*, 29–70.

Shaver, P. R., & Mikulincer, M. (2002). Attachment-related psychodynamics. *Attachment and Human Development, 4*, 133–161.

Sime, J. D. (1983). Affiliative behaviour during escape to building exits. *Journal of Environmental Psychology, 3*, 21–41.

Sime, J. D. (1985). Movement toward the familiar person and place affiliation in a fire entrapment setting. *Environment and Behavior, 17*, 697–724.

Simpson, J. A., Ickes, W., & Grich, J. (1999). When accuracy hurts: Reactions of anxious-ambivalent dating partners to a relationship-threatening situation. *Journal of Personality and Social Psychology, 76*, 754–769.

Simpson, J. A., Kim, J. S., Fillo, J., Ickes, W., Rholes, W. S., Orina, M. M., & Winterheld, H. A. (2011). Attachment and the management of empathic accuracy in relationship-threatening situations. *Personality and Social Psychology Bulletin, 37*, 242–254.

Simpson, J. A., & Rholes, S. W. (2015). *Attachment theory and research: New directions and emerging themes*. New York, NY: The Guilford Press.

Smith, E. R., Murphy, J., & Coats, S. (1999). Attachment to groups: Theory and management. *Journal of Personality and Social Psychology, 77*, 94–110.

Solomon, R. C. (2000). The philosophy of emotions. In M. Lewis, J. M. Haviland-Jone, & L. F. Barrett (Eds.), *Handbook of emotions* (pp. 3–16). New York, NY: Guilford Press.

Soltis, J., King, L. E., Douglas-Hamilton, I., Vollrath, F., & Savage, A. (2014). African elephant alarm calls distinguish between threats from humans and bees. *PLoS One, 9*, e89403.

Sroufe, L. A., Duggal, S., Weinfield, N., & Carlson, E. A. (2000). Relationships, development, and psychopathology. In A. J. Sameroff, M. Lewis, & S. M. Miller (Eds.), *Handbook of developmental psychopathology* (2nd ed.). New York, NY: Kluwer Academic/Plenum Publishers.

Sroufe, L. A., Egeland, B., Carlson, E. A., & Collins, A. (2004). *The development of the person: The Minnesota study of risk and adaptation from birth to adulthood*. New York, NY: Guilford Press.

Vrtička, P., Bondolfi, G., Sander, D., & Vuilleumier, P. (2012). The neural substrates of social emotion perception and regulation are modulated by adult attachment style. *Social Neuroscience, 7*, 473–493.

Waters, H. S., & Waters, E. (2006). The attachment working models concept: Among other things, we build script-like representations of secure base experiences. *Attachment & Human Development, 8*, 185–197.

Chapter 4
Sadness, the Architect of Cognitive Change

Melissa M. Karnaze and Linda J. Levine

Abstract Emotions guide action in ways that are frequently adaptive. Fear, disgust, and anger motivate people to act to avoid danger, shun contamination, and overcome obstacles to their goals. But what good does feeling sad do? This seemingly passive state is often characterized by behavioral withdrawal and rumination. This chapter reviews theory and research concerning the types of situations that elicit sadness and the effects of sadness on expression, behavior, and cognition. Evidence suggests that, far from being passive, sadness is an architect of cognitive change, directing the challenging but essential work of reconstructing goals and beliefs when people face irrevocable loss.

In the Pixar film, *Inside Out*, 11-year-old Riley's emotions are depicted as cartoon characters living in her brain who help her respond to challenges. Riley's life is disrupted when her family moves to a new city, forcing her to leave behind everything familiar. The other emotions, Joy, Fear, Anger, and Disgust, all have clear functions. They urge Riley to celebrate the good things in her life, avoid danger, overcome obstacles, and shun contamination. But it is unclear to them, and to Sadness herself, what the function of Sadness might be. In the end, though, Sadness proves to be the hero of the tale. Only with Sadness' help does Riley come to terms with all she had to leave behind, allowing her to appreciate the inviting possibilities of her new life.

Researchers too have struggled to identify the functions of sadness. After all, sadness is often characterized by passivity and behavioral inhibition (e.g., Frijda, 1986). Sad people prefer activities framed as inactive to those framed as active (Rucker & Petty, 2004), and people report feeling fatigued when recalling experiences that made them sad (Keller & Nesse, 2005). Sadness is also a frequent companion to pessimism and rumination and a component of debilitating disorders such

M. M. Karnaze · L. J. Levine (✉)
Department of Psychology and Social Behavior, University of California, Irvine,
Irvine, CA, USA
e-mail: llevine@uci.edu

© Springer International Publishing AG, part of Springer Nature 2018   45
H. C. Lench (ed.), *The Function of Emotions*,
https://doi.org/10.1007/978-3-319-77619-4_4

as depression (Lyubomirsky & Nolen-Hoeksema, 1993; Mouchet-Mages & Baylé, 2008). This chapter reviews theories and evidence that sadness is nonetheless adaptive. Following Lench, Tibbett, and Bench (2016), an emotion is defined as adaptive if it promotes changes that result in better outcomes for individuals in the types of situations that typically evoke the emotion. This chapter first examines the types of situations that evoke sadness. It then reviews evidence that sadness is associated with specific changes in expressions, behavior, and cognition, some of which have been shown to promote successful resolution of the types of problems that evoke sadness. Research suggests that sadness is an architect of cognitive change, facilitating adaptation to irrevocable loss by soliciting aid and restructuring expectations and goals. Finally, the chapter discusses unresolved questions about the functions of sadness and directions for future research.

What Makes People Sad?

According to functionalist accounts of emotion, people are attuned to changes in the environment that are relevant to their goals and well-being. Emotions are evoked when people perceive that a goal has been attained or obstructed, making it necessary for them to revise their behavior or their goals and beliefs. Specific emotions are elicited by the perception of specific types of changes in the status of goals. For instance, people feel happy when they attain their goals. They feel afraid when they perceive a threat to their ability to attain a desired outcome or avoid an aversive one. They feel angry when they perceive an obstacle to goal attainment that might yet be overcome or removed. Once evoked, emotions facilitate behavioral and cognitive changes that help people respond adaptively to these changes (e.g., Frijda, 1986; Moors, Ellsworth, Scherer, & Frijda, 2013; Stein & Levine, 1987).

Sadness too is evoked by the perception of change in the status of a goal. People feel sad when they perceive that they are unable to maintain or attain a goal or valued state. In several studies, adults have been instructed to keep detailed diaries over days or weeks, recording events that evoked emotions and reporting how they appraised those events. Sadness was the most common emotional response to events perceived as the loss of a valued state (e.g., Nezlek, Vansteelandt, Van Mechelen, & Kuppens, 2008; Oatley & Duncan, 1994). Feelings of sadness often follow bereavement, separation from caregivers or significant others, dissolution of romantic relationships, job loss, social exclusion, and damage to valued possessions, as well as loss of anticipated valued states such as missed opportunities to engage in pleasurable activities (Carnelley, Wortman, Bolger, & Burke, 2006; Nesse, 1990; Sbarra, 2006).

The perception that goal failure is irrevocable is also an important component of sadness. Roseman (1984) argued that people feel sad when they are certain that they were unsuccessful at obtaining a reward and perceive themselves as having little power in the situation. When adults failed to attain social goals, the more they appraised themselves as having low control, the more intense sadness they experienced (Siemer, Mauss, & Gross, 2007). Young children also associate sadness with irrevocable loss. When presented with stories in which a protagonist failed to attain a goal, children were most likely to attribute sadness to the protagonist if they viewed failure as permanent (e.g., permanent damage to a prized possession). When children viewed the protagonist as able to reinstate his or her goal, they were more likely to attribute anger (Levine, 1995).

Evolutionary accounts posit that sadness results from significant changes in people's physical or social environment, such as the loss of an important resource, mate, or child, that negatively impact adaptive fitness or the prospect of passing genetic information to new generations. Loss of a child likely to pass on one's genes would be expected to elicit the most intense sadness (Tooby & Cosmides, 1990). Consistent with this view, one study assessed the intensity of grief that participants expected parents to experience following the death of a child. The child's age in these hypothetical scenarios ranged from 1 day to 50 years. Participants expected parents to feel more intense grief if a child was close to reproductive age at the time of death rather than younger or older (Crawford, Salter, & Jang, 1989). Among relatives who actually experienced a child's death, those with greater certainty of their genetic relatedness to the child (e.g., maternal rather than paternal grandmothers) reported more grief than those with less certainty (Littlefield & Rushton, 1986). Overall, then, people feel sad when they perceive loss or goal failure to be irrevocable, given their current resources. The intensity and duration of sadness increase with the importance of the loss (Carver, 2015; Lench et al., 2016; Verduyn, Delvaux, Van Coillie, Tuerlinckx, & Van Mechelen, 2009).

What Good Does It Do to Feel Sad?

Emotion theorists have proposed that sadness, like other emotions, was conserved throughout human evolution because it helped solve problems that ancestral humans often encountered (Gross & Barrett, 2011; Tooby, Cosmides, Sell, Lieberman, & Sznycer, 2008; Sznycer, Cosmides, & Tooby, 2017). When goal failure is irrevocable given a person's available resources, sadness is thought to serve two key functions. First, sad expressions and behaviors elicit aid by signaling to others that an individual needs assistance (Reed & DeScioli, 2017). Second, when assistance is unavailable or ineffective, sadness promotes cognitive changes that facilitate adaptation to irrevocable loss. If people are to pursue alternative goals, they must first understand the implications of loss, dismantle unrealistic beliefs and expectations, and withdraw investment from unattainable goals (Andrews & Thomson, 2009; Klinger, 1975; Nesse, 1991; Sznycer et al., 2017; Wrosch, Scheier, Carver, & Shulz, 2003).

Far from being passive, the cognitive restructuring instigated by sadness is effortful and challenging. Beliefs and goals are closely intertwined, and goals are hierarchically organized with lower-order goals serving as necessary conditions for achieving explicit and implicit higher-order goals (e.g., Cooper & Shallice, 2006;

Simon, 1967). For example, a student may believe she is capable of passing an academic course. Passing may also be necessary for attaining her explicit goals of getting a letter of recommendation and pursuing a particular career path and for maintaining her implicit goals of thinking well of her own abilities and pleasing her parents. Thus, sadness after failing the course prompts revision of an extensive network of beliefs and goals. Research indicates that sad people dwell, not just on their immediate loss but on its implications for their beliefs and goals (Lyubomirsky, Caldwell, & Nolen-Hoeksema, 1998; Reynolds & Brewin, 1999). Restructuring beliefs following irrevocable failure allows people to maintain representations that accurately reflect real-world constraints. Disengaging from unattainable goals sets the stage for adopting more realistic goals (Carver & Scheier, 1990; Levine & Edelstein, 2009; Heckhausen, Wrosch, & Schulz, 2010; Mendola, Tennen, Affleck, McCann, & Fitzgerald, 1990).

If sadness is adaptive, it should be accompanied by changes that generally serve to solicit aid or to facilitate adaptation to loss. Below, we review evidence that sadness is associated with distinctive changes in facial and vocal expressions, behavior, and cognition that may promote these outcomes.

Expressive and Behavioral Change

Across cultures, people express sadness in the face, often with raised inner corners of the eyebrows and depressed corners of the mouth (Keltner, Ekman, Gonzaga, & Beer, 2003). The sad expression shows low overlap with expressions of other emotions (Smith, Cottrell, Gosselin, & Schyns, 2005), and people recognize sad expressions in others at higher-than-chance levels (Elfenbein & Ambady, 2002). People show expressions of sadness in real-world settings when failing to obtain a desired goal, such as failing to win a gold medal at the Olympics (Matsumoto & Willingham, 2006). More pronounced expressions are correlated with reports of more intense sadness. For instance, when study participants watched a film clip depicting a child grieving over his father's death, the more intense sadness participants reported, the more they exhibited a sad facial expression (Mauss, Levenson, McCarter, Wilhelm, & Gross, 2005). Sadness is also frequently accompanied by crying, which includes vocal expression and tears (Vingerhoets & Bylsma, 2016).

Sadness also motivates behavior, some with clear benefits and some less so. When feeling sad, people tend to behave politely and generously. In one study, participants watched a video that induced sadness, happiness, or neutral affect and were then instructed to request a file from someone in a nearby office. Sad participants made more polite requests than those who felt happy or neutral affect (Forgas, 1999). When reading about an individual in need of material support, the more pronounced facial sadness and the more sympathy participants expressed, the more hours they anonymously committed to helping the individual in need (Eisenberg et al., 1989). After recalling a sad experience, rather than an anger-inducing or neutral experience, participants recommended providing more monetary assistance to an individual receiving welfare (Small & Lerner, 2008). This politeness and generosity may serve to elicit reciprocal support and generosity from others or alleviate sadness indirectly by contributing to the well-being of others (Cialdini et al., 1987).

Sadness also motivates behavior that, though potentially unhelpful in the long run, may make people feel better in the short run. People led to feel sad (versus disgust or neutral affect) were likely to accept an immediate monetary reward rather than choosing to wait 3 months to obtain a higher reward (Lerner, Li, & Weber, 2013). In another study, participants were induced to feel happy or sad and then asked to test snack food for an unrelated study (Tice, Bratslavsky, & Baumeister, 2001). Before the taste test, some participants were informed that research suggests eating would not make them feel better. This information did not affect the amount of snack food that happy participants ate. But among sad participants, those who had been informed that eating would not improve their mood ate less snack food than those who were not given this information. These findings suggest that sad people increased consumption of snack food with the aim of improving their mood. Thus, when people feel sad, they show susceptibility to immediate rewards that may improve their mood.

Cognitive Change

Sadness influences people's thoughts about the situation that evoked their negative feelings, referred to as integral cognition. People in a sad mood often ruminate about the causes and consequences of losses and defeats (e.g., Lyubomirsky et al., 1998; Reynolds & Brewin, 1999; Watkins & Teasdale, 2001). Rumination has been associated with mental health disorders such as depression (Nolen-Hoeksema & Schweizer, 2010). However, in individuals without a mental health disorder, rumination is not necessarily problematic. Researchers had two groups of US veterans complete daily diaries for 2 weeks. One group had been diagnosed with combat-related post-traumatic stress disorder (PTSD), and the other group did not have a diagnosis of PTSD. Overall, same-day rumination was positively associated with same-day negative affect. But for veterans without PTSD, the more they ruminated on a given day, the less intense negative affect they reported the following day (Kashdan, Young, & McKnight, 2012). In a laboratory study, participants who ruminated about how they could improve on a laboratory task performed better on a similar task in the future (Ciarocco, Vohs, & Baumeister, 2010). Thus, in nonclinical populations, thinking through the implications of loss when sad may be a precursor to mood repair and future goal attainment.

In another study, researchers elicited sadness or happiness by giving people negative or positive feedback on their leadership potential. When choosing a leadership mentor afterward, sad people were more likely than happy people to select the mentor who encouraged both imagining goal attainment and realistically assessing obstacles to goal attainment rather than a mentor who focused solely on goal attainment or solely on obstacles (Oettingen, Park, & Schnetter, 2001). A focus on goals, combined with realistic evaluation of obstacles to goals, was also found to characterize sadness across a series of studies using different mood induction techniques. This dual focus should promote future goal attainment when expectations of success are high and goal disengagement when expectations of success are low (Kappes, Oettingen, Mayer, & Maglio, 2011).

Sadness also influences cognitions about events that are incidental or unrelated to the source of sadness, serving to generally lower expectations. Chong and Park (2017) had undergraduates rate their feelings each week before taking a quiz. After each quiz students reviewed their scores and set a goal for the following week's quiz. The sadder students felt prior to the quizzes, the lower goals they set for subsequent quizzes, even accounting for grade point average and differences between students' goals and their actual quiz scores (Chong & Park, 2017, study 1). In summary, when feeling sad, people tend to dwell on the causes and consequences of goal failure and on obstacles to success. Bringing unrealistic beliefs and goals into line with external constraints may promote attainment of goals in the future.

Sadness Narrows Information Processing Research on incidental cognition has led to mixed findings concerning the information-processing strategies people use when sad. According to one view, negative affect triggers narrow, detail-oriented, and systematic information processing in the service of addressing problems (e.g., Schwarz, 2012; Andrews & Thomson, 2009). Consistent with this view, sad people have been shown to rely less on top-down processing strategies such as heuristics than people in a happy or neutral mood. Following emotion induction, sad people were less likely than happy people to make the fundamental attribution error, which involves exaggerating the role of personal attributes, and underestimating the role of situational factors, in causing people's behavior (Forgas, 1998). Inducing sadness also reduced people's tendency to make broad judgments about other people's traits or capabilities based on first impressions or small samples of behavior (Ambady & Gray, 2002). In a study of memory, participants viewed a series of images. Later, emotion was induced by having participants recall sad, happy, or neutral personal events. They were then tested for their memory for the images. The sadness induction improved memory by reducing the tendency to incorporate misleading information into memory reports (Forgas, Laham, & Vargas, 2005, study 1; for similar results, see Forgas et al., 2005, study 2). Thus, negative affect generally, and sadness specifically, can promote systematic, effortful, and detailed information processing. This processing style may help people figure out why things are going badly and how to change course.

Sadness Motivates People to Change Information-Processing Strategies
According to an alternative approach, rather than promoting the use of a particular information-processing strategy, positive affect and negative affect serve to reinforce or inhibit, respectively, whatever strategy a person is currently using (Huntsinger, Isbell, & Clore, 2014). Positive affect functions like a green light, signaling that goals are met and that the current information-processing strategy is

working. Negative affect serves as a red light, signaling the need to discontinue the current strategy and adopt a different strategy to address unresolved challenges. In support of this view, when participants were led to adopt a systematic information-processing strategy (characterized by narrowed attention to the details of presented stimuli), inducing sadness led them to shift to using more global processing, whereas inducing happiness led to continued use of local processing (Huntsinger et al., 2014; Huntsinger & Ray, 2016). In contrast, when participants were led to adopt a global information-processing strategy, inducing sadness led them to shift to using more local processing, whereas inducing happiness led to continued use of global processing. In summary, while previous research suggests that sadness promotes systematic, effortful, and detailed information processing, Huntsinger and colleagues found support for the alternative view that sadness triggers a shift from the current processing strategy to a new one that might be more successful for addressing current demands. Global processing tends to be the default strategy because it is less effortful than systematic processing. Thus, further research should assess whether previous findings linking sadness and systematic processing were due to sadness motivating a change from the default global strategy.

Sadness Broadens Information Processing   Other researchers have argued that the information-processing strategy conducive to well-being depends not on whether an emotion is positive or negative but on whether the emotion precedes or follows a change in the status of a goal. Pre-goal emotions, such as hope, fear, anger, and disgust, are experienced in the midst of goal pursuit (i.e., attempting to attain a desired state or avoid an aversive state). These emotions should narrow the scope of attention and memory to goal-relevant information. In contrast, post-goal emotions, such as happiness and sadness, signal that goal attainment or failure has already occurred. Post-goal emotions should broaden the scope of attention and memory, allowing people to think through the implications of change for related beliefs and goals (Harmon-Jones, Price, & Gable, 2012; Kaplan, Van Damme, Levine, & Loftus, 2016; Levine & Pizarro, 2004; Levine & Edelstein, 2009).

Gable and Harmon-Jones (2010) had participants view pictures that induced sadness, disgust, or neutral affect before each trial of an attentional task. In the task, participants viewed pictures that contained a large letter composed of several smaller letters and indicated as quickly as possible which letter was in the picture. Sadness broadened attention relative to neutral affect by reducing reaction times for identifying global targets. Disgust narrowed attention relative to neutral affect by reducing reaction times for identifying local targets. Harmon-Jones, Gable, and Price (2013) suggested that whether sadness broadens or narrows cognitive scope may depend on whether sadness occurs alone or co-occurs with pre-goal negative emotions, such as anger or fear. In other words, previous findings that sadness narrows attentional scope may have been due to researchers contrasting a blend of sadness and pre-goal negative emotions with post-goal positive emotion (e.g., happiness).

In another study, participants watched a slideshow of an interaction between a woman and her boyfriend and were encouraged to empathize with the woman's feelings (Van Damme, Kaplan, Levine, & Loftus, 2017). The woman was described as feeling either devastated or happy (post-goal emotions), fearful, or hopeful (pre-goal emotions) about her goal of maintaining a long-term relationship with her boyfriend. Later, participants were tested on their recognition of information from the slides that was true (present in the slide) or false (not present) and central or peripheral to the woman's goal. Participants who empathized with post-goal emotions were less susceptible to false memories about peripheral information than participants who empathized with pre-goal emotions, suggesting greater breadth in the scope of information attended to and remembered. Further research is clearly needed to address the mixed findings in the literature concerning the effects of sadness on information-processing strategies. It will be important to examine when and why sadness triggers detail-oriented and systematic information processing, promotes changing the current strategy, or broadens information processing to encompass the implications of failure for related beliefs and goals. Research on how sadness affects information processing has focused primarily on information, that is, incidental or unrelated to the cause of sadness. Further research is also needed on how sadness affects the processing of integral information, that is, the information that served to elicit sadness.

Evidence that Sadness Is Adaptive

The findings reviewed above indicate that sadness is associated with expressive, behavioral, and cognitive changes that, in principle, may be adaptive. But this evidence falls short of demonstrating that, when people encounter a loss that exceeds their capabilities, being sad leads to better outcomes than not being sad. A few studies provide more direct evidence of the benefits of sadness. Crying is a universal and potent expression of sadness, loss, and powerlessness throughout the life span (Vingerhoets & Bylsma, 2016). In infancy and early childhood, crying serves to maintain proximity to parents and solicit care and assistance (Bell & Ainsworth, 1972; Bowlby, 1980). Laboratory studies displaying pictures of adults with tears either digitally added or digitally removed show that tears serve as an important pre-attentive visual cue of sadness and evoke in others feelings of empathy, connectedness, and willingness to provide support (for a review see Vingerhoets & Bylsma, 2016). For example, researchers presented participants with photographs of sad and neutral faces for 50 ms. Recognition of sad faces was better when tears were digitally added to the photos than when no tears were added. Moreover, participants perceived greater need for social support in response to sad faces with tears (Balsters, Krahmer, Swerts, & Vingerhoets, 2013).

Expressing sadness without tears has also been shown to elicit help which benefits the sad individual. Participants in one study were asked to imagine a scenario in which their family needed medicine to survive but a neighboring family also needed the medicine (Dehghani, Carnevale, & Gratch, 2014). Participants gave more medicine to the neighboring family when a member of that family was depicted with a sad expression rather than a neutral or angry expression. In another study, participants engaged in a simulated fishing task with another person in order to earn money. The other person, who was actually a confederate, explained via video that she had lost all her fish. If there was uncertainty about the loss, participants donated more of their money when the confederate's account of losing fish was accompanied by a sad rather than neutral facial expression (Reed & DeScioli, 2017). Thus, sad expressions and tears elicit empathy and aid which can result in better outcomes for individuals who have suffered a loss.

When loss is irrevocable, sadness should promote revision of unrealistic expectations and disengagement from unattainable goals. These cognitive changes should result in both measurably better outcomes and enhanced well-being. One study assessed the effects of inducing a happy or sad mood on financial trading decisions (Au, Chan, Wang, & Vertinsky, 2003). Economics and finance students received information about financial markets to help them make trades. After a round of trading, they received randomized feedback that their decisions had led to high profit (happiness induction), substantial loss (sadness induction), or breaking even (control condition). In subsequent decision rounds, participants listened to music to maintain their assigned mood. Sad participants made more accurate judgments and more conservative trading decisions than did happy participants and, as a result, profited more than happy participants, though not more than control participants.

Carver (2015) has argued that emotions are self-regulating. Sadness, for example, motivates accommodation to loss by reducing the priority of unattainable goals. When goal disengagement is successful, feelings of sadness should abate, resulting in enhanced well-being. Several studies have demonstrated a link between disengaging from unattainable goals and greater well-being. Among female breast cancer survivors, the more participants reported the ability to disengage if they had to stop pursuing an important goal in their life, the lower their daily negative affect (Wrosch & Sabiston, 2013). In women past childbearing age, those who were able to disengage from the goal of bearing a child had greater subjective well-being (Heckhausen, Wrosch, & Fleeson, 2001). In a longitudinal study of older adults, functional disability and depressive symptoms increased over a 6-year period. But among those who reported greater ability to disengage when they had to stop pursing an important goal, functional impairment was less strongly related to depressive symptoms (Dunne, Wrosch & Miller, 2011).

Another study assessed adolescent girls' depressive symptoms (a measure broader than, but encompassing, sadness) and their self-reported ability to disengage from unattainable goals over the course of a year (Wrosch & Miller, 2009). At the start of the study, goal disengagement ability was not related to depressive symptoms. But the more depressive symptoms adolescents reported at baseline, the better they became at disengaging from unattainable goals over the course of the year. Indeed, baseline depressive symptoms explained approximately 21% of the variance in improvement in adolescents' ability to disengage from unattainable goals. In turn, controlling for levels of baseline depressive symptoms, the greater the increase over time in adolescents' ability to let go of futile goals, the more their depressive symptoms declined in the subsequent 6 months. Taken together, these findings suggest depressive symptoms facilitate disengaging from unattainable goals and that disengaging from unattainable goals enhances well-being.

Conclusions

In the film *Inside Out*, young Riley has difficulty adjusting to her new life when her family moves to a different city. The emotion Joy, who lives in Riley's brain, rounds up the other emotions – Sadness, Anger, Disgust, and Fear – to help Riley cope. Sadness slows the team down and appears to worsen Riley's situation but only when Riley expresses her grief to her parents and acknowledges the life she left behind is she able to adjust and pursue alternative goals, such as forging new friendships. The film illustrates that, when something valued is lost, sadness serves as a powerful signal to both the self and others that problems need to be addressed. External expressions of sadness recruit assistance from others. Internally, the sad individual is occupied with the challenging tasks of revising unrealistic beliefs and reprioritizing goals.

We have reviewed evidence concerning the several ways in which sadness is likely to be adaptive. However, finding that sadness motivates the difficult mental work of rethinking beliefs and reprioritizing goals does not mean that this work is always successful. If people are unable to revise their expectations and disengage from high priority goals, dwelling on the implications of loss can devolve into rumination, hopelessness, and depression (Nesse, 2000; Carver, 2015). Thus, further research is needed on when and why sadness is followed by adaptive versus maladaptive types of rumination (Ciarocco et al., 2010; Nolen-Hoeksema, Wisco, & Lyubomirsky, 2008). Further research is also needed to explicate the mixed findings concerning how sadness impacts information-processing strategies. Studies should directly compare the competing views that sadness prompts detail-oriented processing, that sadness leads people to change their current processing strategy whatever it may be, and that sadness broadens the scope of information processing in the service of understanding consequences of loss. Finally, disengaging from failed goals enhances well-being and makes it possible to prioritize new goals. Yet goal disengagement and reengagement are separable processes, and some evidence suggests that sadness promotes the former but not the latter (Wrosch et al., 2003). Thus, future work should assess whether sadness directly facilitates the pursuit of alternative goals.

In conclusion, research indicates that sadness is adaptive. When people face obstacles to their goals that outstrip their resources, their sad expressions, tears, and behaviors elicit empathy and aid from others. When goal failure is irrevocable, however, sadness serves as an architect of cognitive change, leading people to rebuild their beliefs and goals. The cognitive structures designed by sadness tend to be weather resistant, earthquake friendly, and low to the ground. Sadness prompts people to think through the implications of loss, disengage from unattainable goals, let go of unrealistic expectations, and forge more realistic ones. This restructuring is effortful and challenging but essential for maintaining representations that accurately reflect real-world constraints and for preventing people from squandering their time, effort, and resources pursuing unattainable goals (e.g., Ciarocco, Vohs, & Baumeister, 2010; Chong & Park, 2017; Kappes et al., 2011). Over time, disengaging from unattainable goals predicts enhanced well-being and makes it possible for people to successfully pursue new goals (Wrosch & Miller, 2009).

References

Ambady, N., & Gray, H. M. (2002). On being sad and mistaken: Mood effects on the accuracy of thin-slice judgments. *Journal of Personality and Social Psychology, 83*, 947–961.

Andrews, P. W., & Thomson, J. A., Jr. (2009). The bright side of being blue: Depression as an adaptation for analyzing complex problems. *Psychological Review, 116*, 620–654.

Au, K., Chan, F., Wang, D., & Vertinsky, I. (2003). Mood in foreign exchange trading: Cognitive processes and performance. *Organizational Behavior and Human Decision Processes, 91*, 322–338.

Balsters, M. J., Krahmer, E. J., Swerts, M. G., & Vingerhoets, A. J. (2013). Emotional tears facilitate the recognition of sadness and the perceived need for social support. *Evolutionary Psychology, 11*, 148–158.

Bell, S. M., & Ainsworth, M. D. S. (1972). Infant crying and maternal responsiveness. *Child Development, 43*, 1171–1190.

Bowlby, J. (1980). *Attachment and loss: Volume 3. Loss*. New York, NY: Basic Books.

Carnelley, K. B., Wortman, C. B., Bolger, N., & Burke, C. T. (2006). The time course of grief reactions to spousal loss: Evidence from a national probability sample. *Journal of Personality and Social Psychology, 91*, 476–492.

Carver, C. S. (2015). Control processes, priority management, and affective dynamics. *Emotion Review, 7*, 301–307.

Carver, C. S., & Scheier, M. F. (1990). Origins and functions of positive and negative affect: A control-process view. *Psychological Review, 97*, 19–35.

Chong, S., & Park, G. (2017). The differential effects of incidental anger and sadness on goal regulation. *Learning and Motivation, 58*, 1–15.

Cialdini, R. B., Schaller, M., Houlihan, D., Arps, K., Fultz, J., & Beaman, A. L. (1987). Empathy-based helping: Is it selflessly or selfishly motivated? *Journal of Personality and Social Psychology, 52*, 749–758.

Ciarocco, N. J., Vohs, K. D., & Baumeister, R. F. (2010). Some good news about rumination: Task-focused thinking after failure facilitates performance improvement. *Journal of Social and Clinical Psychology, 29*, 1057–1073.

Cooper, R. P., & Shallice, T. (2006). Hierarchical schemas and goals in the control of sequential behavior. *Psychological Review, 113*, 887–916.

Crawford, C. B., Salter, B. E., & Jang, K. L. (1989). Human grief: Is its intensity related to the reproductive value of the deceased? *Ethology and Sociobiology, 10*, 297–307.

Dehghani, M., Carnevale, P. J., & Gratch, J. (2014). Interpersonal effects of expressed anger and sorrow in morally charged negotiation. *Judgment and Decision making, 9*, 104–113.

Dunne, E., Wrosch, C., & Miller, G. E. (2011). Goal disengagement, functional disability, and depressive symptoms in old age. *Health Psychology, 30*, 763–770.

Eisenberg, N., Fabes, R. A., Miller, P. A., Fultz, J., Shell, R., Mathy, R. M., & Reno, R. R. (1989). Relation of sympathy and personal distress to prosocial behavior: A multimethod study. *Journal of Personality and Social Psychology, 57*, 55–66.

Elfenbein, H. A., & Ambady, N. (2002). On the universality and cultural specificity of emotion recognition: A meta-analysis. *Psychological Bulletin, 128*, 203–235.

Forgas, J. P. (1998). On being happy and mistaken: Mood effects on the fundamental attribution error. *Journal of Personality and Social Psychology, 75*, 318–331.

Forgas, J. P. (1999). On feeling good and being rude: Affective influences on language use and request formulations. *Journal of Personality and Social Psychology, 76*, 928–939.

Forgas, J. P., Laham, S. M., & Vargas, P. T. (2005). Mood effects on eyewitness memory: Affective influences on susceptibility to misinformation. *Journal of Experimental Social Psychology, 41*, 574–588.

Frijda, N. H. (1986). *The emotions: Studies in emotion and social interaction.* New York, NY: Cambridge University Press.

Gable, P., & Harmon-Jones, E. (2010). The blues broaden, but the nasty narrows: Attentional consequences of negative affects low and high in motivational intensity. *Psychological Science, 21*, 211–215.

Gross, J. J., & Barrett, L. (2011). Emotion generation and emotion regulation: One or two depends on your point of view. *Emotion Review, 3*, 8–16.

Harmon-Jones, E., Gable, P. A., & Price, T. F. (2013). Does negative affect always narrow and positive affect always broaden the mind? Considering the influence of motivational intensity on cognitive scope. *Current Directions in Psychological Science, 22*, 301–307.

Harmon-Jones, E., Price, T. F., & Gable, P. A. (2012). The influence of affective states on cognitive broadening/narrowing: Considering the importance of motivational intensity: Affect, motivation, and cognitive scope. *Social and Personality Psychology Compass, 6*, 314–327.

Heckhausen, J., Wrosch, C., & Fleeson, W. (2001). Developmental regulation before and after a developmental deadline: The sample case of "biological clock" for childbearing. *Psychology and Aging, 16*, 400–413.

Heckhausen, J., Wrosch, C., & Schulz, R. (2010). A motivational theory of life-span development. *Psychological Review, 117*, 32–60.

Huntsinger, J. R., Isbell, L. M., & Clore, J. L. (2014). The affective control of thought: Malleable, not fixed. *Psychological Review, 121*, 600–618.

Huntsinger, J. R., & Ray, C. (2016). A flexible influence of affective feelings on creative and analytic performance. *Emotion, 16*, 826–837.

Kaplan, R. L., Van Damme, I., Levine, L. J., & Loftus, E. F. (2016). Emotion and false memory. *Emotion Review, 8*, 8–13.

Kappes, H. B., Oettingen, G., Mayer, D., & Maglio, S. (2011). Sad mood promotes self-initiated mental contrasting of future and reality. *Emotion, 11*, 1206–1222.

Kashdan, T. B., Young, K. C., & McKnight, P. E. (2012). When is rumination an adaptive mood repair strategy? Day-to-day rhythms of life in combat veterans with and without posttraumatic stress disorder. *Journal of Anxiety Disorders, 26*, 762–768.

Keller, M. C., & Nesse, R. M. (2005). Is low mood an adaptation? Evidence for subtypes with symptoms that match precipitants. *Journal of Affective Disorders, 86*, 27–35.

Keltner, D., Ekman, P., Gonzaga, G. C., & Beer, J. (2003). Facial expression of emotion. In R. J. Davidson, K. R. Scherer, & H. H. Goldsmith (Eds.), *Series in affective science. Handbook of affective sciences* (pp. 415–432). New York, NY: Oxford University Press.

Klinger, E. (1975). Consequences of commitment to and disengagement from incentives. *Psychological Review, 82*, 1–25.

Lench, H. C., Tibbett, T. P., & Bench, S. W. (2016). Exploring the toolkit of emotion: What do sadness and anger do for us? *Social and Personality Psychology Compass, 10*, 11–25.

Lerner, J. S., Li, Y., & Weber, E. U. (2013). The financial costs of sadness. *Psychological Science, 24*, 72–79.

Levine, L. J. (1995). Young children's understanding of the causes of anger and sadness. *Child Development, 66*, 697–709.

Levine, L. J., & Edelstein, R. S. (2009). Emotion and memory narrowing: A review and goal-relevance approach. *Cognition and Emotion, 23*, 833–875.

Levine, L. J., & Pizarro, D. A. (2004). Emotion and memory research: A grumpy overview. *Social Cognition, 22*, 530–554.

Littlefield, C. H., & Rushton, J. P. (1986). When a child dies: The sociobiology of bereavement. *Journal of Personality and Social Psychology, 51*, 797–802.

Lyubomirsky, S., Caldwell, N. D., & Nolen-Hoeksema, S. (1998). Effects of ruminative and distracting responses to depressed mood on retrieval of autobiographical memories. *Journal of Personality and Social Psychology, 75*, 166–177.

Lyubomirsky, S., & Nolen-Hoeksema, S. (1993). Self-perpetuating properties of dysphoric rumination. *Journal of Personality and Social Psychology, 65*, 339–349.

Matsumoto, D., & Willingham, B. (2006). The thrill of victory and the agony of defeat: Spontaneous expressions of medal winners of the 2004 Athens Olympic games. *Journal of Personality and Social Psychology, 91*, 568–581.

Mauss, I. B., Levenson, R. W., McCarter, L., Wilhelm, F. H., & Gross, J. J. (2005). The tie that binds? Coherence among emotion experience, behavior, and physiology. *Emotion, 5*, 175–190.

Mendola, R., Tennen, H., Affleck, G., McCann, L., & Fitzgerald, T. (1990). Appraisal and adaptation among women with impaired fertility. *Cognitive Therapy and Research, 14*, 79–93.

Moors, A., Ellsworth, P. C., Scherer, K. R., & Frijda, N. H. (2013). Appraisal theories of emotion: State of the art and future development. *Emotion Review, 5*, 119–124.

Mouchet-Mages, S., & Baylé, F. J. (2008). Sadness as an integral part of depression. *Dialogues in Clinical Neuroscience, 10*, 321–327.

Nesse, R. M. (1990). Evolutionary explanations of emotions. *Human Nature, 1*, 261–289.

Nesse, R. M. (1991). What good is feeling bad? The evolutionary benefits of psychic pain. *The Sciences, 31*, 30–37.

Nesse, R. M. (2000). Is depression an adaptation? *Archives of General Psychiatry, 57*, 14–20.

Nezlek, J. B., Vansteelandt, K., Van Mechelen, I., & Kuppens, P. (2008). Appraisal-emotion relationships in daily life. *Emotion, 8*, 145–150.

Nolen-Hoeksema, S., & Schweizer, S. (2010). Emotion-regulation strategies across psychopathology: A meta-analytic review. *Clinical Psychology Review, 30*, 217–237.

Nolen-Hoeksema, S., Wisco, B. E., & Lyubomirsky, S. (2008). Rethinking rumination. *Perspectives on Psychological Science, 3*, 400–424.

Oatley, K., & Duncan, E. (1994). The experience of emotions in everyday life. *Cognition and Emotion, 8*, 369–381.

Oettingen, G., Pak, H. J., & Schnetter, K. (2001). Self-regulation of goal-setting: Turning free fantasies about the future into binding goals. *Journal of Personality and Social Psychology, 80*, 736–753.

Reed, L. I., & DeScioli, P. (2017). The communicative function of sad facial expressions. *Evolutionary Psychology, 15*, 1–9.

Reynolds, M., & Brewin, C. R. (1999). Intrusive memories in depression and posttraumatic stress disorder. *Behaviour Research and Therapy, 37*, 201–215.

Roseman, I. J. (1984). Cognitive determinants of emotion: A structural theory. *Review of Personality and Social Psychology, 5*, 11–36.

Rucker, D. D., & Petty, R. E. (2004). Emotion specificity and consumer behavior: Anger, sadness, and preference for activity. *Motivation and Emotion, 28*, 3–21.

Sbarra, D. A. (2006). Predicting the onset of emotional recovery following nonmarital relationship dissolution: Survival analyses of sadness and anger. *Personality and Social Psychology Bulletin, 32*, 298–312.

Schwarz, N. (2012). Feelings-as-information theory. In P. Van Lange, A. Kruglanski, & E. T. Higgins (Eds.), *Handbook of theories of social psychology* (pp. 289–308). London, UK: Sage.

Siemer, M., Mauss, I., & Gross, J. J. (2007). Same situation – different emotions: How appraisals shape our emotions. *Emotion, 7*, 592–600.

Simon, H. A. (1967). Motivational and emotional controls of cognition. *Psychological Review, 74*, 29–39.

Small, D. A., & Lerner, J. S. (2008). Emotional policy: Personal sadness and anger shape judgments about a welfare case. *Political Psychology, 29*, 149–168.

Smith, M. L., Cottrell, G. W., Gosselin, F., & Schyns, P. G. (2005). Transmitting and decoding facial expressions. *Psychological Science, 16*, 184–189.

Stein, N. L., & Levine, L. J. (1987). Thinking about feelings: The development and organization of emotional knowledge. *Aptitude, Learning, and Instruction, 3*, 165–197.

Sznycer, D., Cosmides, L., & Tooby, J. (2017). Adaptationism carves emotions at their functional joints. *Psychological Inquiry, 28*, 56–62.

Tice, D. M., Bratslavsky, E., & Baumeister, R. F. (2001). Emotional distress regulation takes precedence over impulse control: If you feel bad, do it! *Journal of Personality and Social Psychology, 80*, 53–67.

Tooby, J., & Cosmides, L. (1990). The past explains the present: Emotional adaptations and the structure of ancestral environments. *Ethology and Sociobiology, 11*, 375–424.

Tooby, J., Cosmides, L., Sell, A., Lieberman, D., & Sznycer, D. (2008). Internal regulatory variables and the design of human motivation: A computational and evolutionary approach. In A. J. Elliot (Ed.), *Handbook of approach and avoidance motivation* (pp. 251–271). New York, NY: Psychology Press.

Van Damme, I., Kaplan, R. L., Levine, L. J., & Loftus, E. F. (2017). Emotion and false memory: How goal-irrelevance can be relevant for what people remember. *Memory, 25*, 201–213.

Verduyn, P., Delvaux, E., Van Coillie, H., Tuerlinckx, F., & Van Mechelen, I. (2009). Predicting the duration of emotional experience: Two experience sampling studies. *Emotion, 9*, 83–91.

Vingerhoets, A. J., & Bylsma, L. M. (2016). The riddle of human emotional crying: A challenge for emotion researchers. *Emotion Review, 8*, 207–217.

Watkins, E., & Teasdale, J. D. (2001). Rumination and overgeneral memory in depression: Effects of self-focus and analytic thinking. *Journal of Abnormal Psychology, 110*, 353–357.

Wrosch, C., & Miller, G. E. (2009). Depressive symptoms can be useful: Self-regulatory and emotional benefits of dysphoric mood in adolescence. *Journal of Personality and Social Psychology, 96*, 1181–1190.

Wrosch, C., & Sabiston, C. M. (2013). Goal adjustment, physical and sedentary activity, and well-being and health among breast cancer survivors. *Psycho-Oncology, 22*, 581–589.

Wrosch, C., Scheier, M. F., Carver, C. S., & Shulz, R. (2003). The importance of goal disengagement in adaptive self-regulation: When giving up is beneficial. *Self and Identity, 2*, 1–20.

Chapter 5
On the Functions of Sadness and Grief

David Huron

Abstract An account of sadness and grief is offered that focuses on their evolutionary function. Sadness and grief are distinct yet complementary adaptive responses to stress. Sadness is characterized by low physiological arousal, whereas grief is characterized by higher physiological arousal and a propensity to weep. Three general responses to stress are proposed: (1) an immune response, principally an energy-conserving state that is coordinated with enhanced immune activity; (2) a cognitive response, principally a reflective disposition characterized by more realistic situational appraisals, ultimately encouraging adaptive actions; and (3) a social response, minimally an appeal to halt aggression and, more broadly, an appeal for altruistic assistance.

In *The Expression of the Emotions in Man and Animals*, Darwin (1872) observed how *sorrow* differs from *grief*: Darwin characterized grief as "frantic" and "energetic," whereas sorrow was "languid" and "resigned." In much modern emotion research, Darwin's distinction between grief and sorrow is ignored, and "sadness" is regarded as a single basic affect. The difference between these two states is readily observed among children: when unhappy, a child may engage in sustained crying or quiescent morose sadness.

Grief and *sadness* (the terms used here) are negative mood states precipitated by similar circumstances. However, this chapter will show that carefully delineating their physiological and psychological differences will lead to an evolutionary account that points to different, yet complementary, functions. It should be noted at the outset that the theory proposed here is not a theory of depression. Any biological system can assume pathological states. Freed (2009) has characterized depression as a "sadness disorder"—a claim that Horwitz and Wakefield (2007) note has been expressed by Western thinkers dating back to Hippocrates. Although the discussion will draw, from time to time, on research on depression, the focus here will be on

D. Huron (✉)
Center for Cognitive and Brain Sciences, Ohio State University, Columbus, OH, USA
e-mail: huron.1@osu.edu

© Springer International Publishing AG, part of Springer Nature 2018   59
H. C. Lench (ed.), *The Function of Emotions*,
https://doi.org/10.1007/978-3-319-77619-4_5

normal rather than pathological behaviors. The chapter reviews evidence that (normal) sadness and grief are evolved behaviors that usually enhance inclusive fitness.

An appropriate place to begin is with detailed descriptions of sadness and grief. An integrated description may include at least seven different perspectives. A biological description focuses on genetic, neurologic, endocrine, and general physiological correlates. Etiological description focuses on precipitating stressors (biological, physical, cognitive, or social) that might induce the state. Affective description identifies subjective feelings that are presumed to amplify motivation. Cognitive description identifies patterns of thought that correlate with the psychological state. A developmental perspective focuses on the emergence and possible changes in how the psychological state is manifested over a life span. Behavioral description stresses the characteristic actions, postures, or expressions associated with the state. Social-psychological description concentrates on how the state is communicated and interpreted by conspecifics within a social context. Finally, a cultural description identifies cultural manifestations of the state, including possible ritualization, as well as potential cultural origins of the state. As will be evident, the evolutionary account proposed here offers a plausible narrative at each of these descriptive levels.

Sadness

What causes sadness? Common etiology for sadness includes failures to achieve life goals, such as romantic, parental, or occupational goals. Sadness might be caused by the departure of a loved one, the breakup of a romantic relationship, parenting difficulties, loneliness, unemployment, financial problems, poor health, loss of social status, frustration in the pursuit of goals, or the inability to help others. Sadness can also arise from more basic vulnerabilities, such as from hunger, thirst, cold, injury, insecurity, or chronic fear. In general, sadness is associated with failure or powerlessness. In affluent societies, sadness is more likely to arise from social stressors—leading some researchers to conclude that sadness is exclusively social in origin (e.g., Allen & Badcock, 2003).

The main physiological symptom of sadness is *anergia* or low arousal. When sad, heart rate decreases and respiration is slower and shallower. Reduced levels of epinephrine, norepinephrine, acetylcholine, and serotonin are observed along with increased levels of the stress hormones cortisol and prolactin (although see Andrews & Thomson, 2009). In the peripheral nervous system, low acetylcholine is associated with poor muscle tone and slow muscle reactivity—making movement slow and lethargic (e.g., Siegel & Sapru, 2006). Low norepinephrine is associated with decreased attention and reduced engagement with the world (e.g., Viggiano, Ruocco, Arcieri, & Sadile, 2004). Low serotonin is linked to diminished self-esteem (e.g., Raleigh et al., 1991). Behaviorally, sadness commonly leads to reduced activity, slumped posture, slow movement, infrequent speech, weak voice, disrupted sleep, changes in appetite, diminished interest, and social withdrawal. Perhaps the most important behavioral change, however, is cognitive: sadness tends to lead to sustained reflection about one's life situation (Andrews & Thompson, 2009; Nesse, 1991).

Further behavioral characteristics are evident in the relaxation of all facial muscles. Relaxing the jaw causes the chin to drop downward. Relaxing the zygomatic muscles (involved in smiling) causes the cheeks to flatten—reducing the physical width of the face. The lowered chin and flattened cheeks contribute to the "long face" appearance—a description synonymous in several languages with being sad. Apart from the appearance of a longer face, the relaxation of the facial musculature is also associated with lowered head and drooping eyelids.

Sadness is also associated with characteristic changes in speech patterns. Sad or depressed speech is quieter and slower, with a lower overall pitch height. In addition, sad speech exhibits a more monotone prosody (narrow pitch movements), mumbled articulation, breathier voice, and a darker timbre or tone color (Banse & Scherer, 1996; Erickson et al., 2006; Kraepelin, 1899/1921; Murray & Arnott, 1993; Scherer, Johnstone, & Klasmeyer, 2003). However, the most important clinical observation regarding sad speech is the tendency for sad individuals to remain mute: sad people speak less (Kraepelin, 1899/1921).

The principal affective symptom of sadness is *anhedonia*. Many activities that are normally enjoyable lose their allure, including food, sex, play, and socializing. Apart from reduced pleasure in various activities, the phenomenal experience of sadness entails a distinctive gloomy qualia that is negatively valenced (Nesse, 1991).

Grief

The etiology of grief is similar to sadness. Like sadness, grief accompanies failures to achieve life goals, including romantic, social, or occupational goals. As with sadness, grief may be precipitated by extreme hunger, cold, poor health, insecurity, etc. In cultures around the globe, grief is most reliably induced by the death of a loved one (Rosenblatt, Walsh, & Jackson, 1976; p. 15). Whereas sadness can also be precipitated by failures to achieve life goals, grief more commonly accompanies the loss of already existing resources, including the reversal of current fortunes or the failure for highly anticipated outcomes to transpire. Interestingly, grief is more likely than sadness to occur in response to feelings of guilt or shame (Vingerhoets, 2013). Both grief and sadness are symptoms of adversity, failure, vulnerability, or powerlessness. Although grief and sadness are precipitated by similar circumstances, they differ principally in the magnitude of the loss or failure: grief is more likely to be associated with especially onerous failures or losses.

From a physiological perspective, grief (in contrast to sadness) is associated with an increase in epinephrine. The heart rate increases, blood pressure increases, and breathing becomes deeper and more erratic. The most characteristic symptom of grief is weeping. In its full-blown expression, weeping entails a flushed face, nasal congestion, constricted pharynx, punctuated exhaling, vocalized wailing, and the shedding of tears. Pharyngeal constriction is typically described as either "a lump in one's throat" or feeling "choked up."

Tears probably represent the most stereotypic visual feature of weeping. Physiologists distinguish three types of tears: basal, reflex, and psychic (Frey, 1985). *Basal tears* serve to lubricate the eyeballs and are constantly being secreted. *Reflex tears* are generated in response to irritation. *Psychic tears* are produced when we experience strong emotions (Lutz, 2001, pp. 67–68). Apart from grief, psychic tears can also be produced from laughing (Frey, 1985).

With regard to the development of grief, the most notable change is the reduced amount of weeping that occurs with increased age. Babies cry a lot, children less so, and adults cry rarely. The amount of weeping appears to be related to the dependency on others. As an individual becomes more autonomous—able to fend for herself/himself—the frequency of weeping is reduced. Crying tends to increase among the elderly, but here too, it may be related to feelings of dependency or vulnerability (Rosenblatt et al., 1976; Vingerhoets, 2013).

In terms of observable behavior, grief is easy to recognize. Ekman has described the main facial features as including an open mouth, with the corners of the lips turned down, cheeks raised as if squinting, downward turned eyes, with drooping upper eyelids, and the inner corners of the eyebrows pulled up (Ekman, 2003, pp. 95–96). Tears are a prototypical symptom of grief. When a person weeps for an extended period, the face tends to become red and puffy, with inflammation common surrounding the eyes, including redness of the eyes themselves—i.e., vasodilation of the blood vessels of the conjunctiva (Provine et al., 2011). Aside from the face, grief-related behaviors may include outstretched arms and occasional acts of self-injury such as slapping one's face, pulling one's hair, or beating one's chest (e.g., Gertsman, 2011; Maguire, 1977).

Apart from the visible behaviors, grief is also associated with characteristic sounds. Vocalized wailing, combined with punctuated breathing, produces the distinctive "ah-ah-ah-ah" weeping sound. Nasal congestion leads to nasalized vocal timbre, while the constriction of the pharynx leads to characteristic resonances described by linguists as "pharyngealized." Post-nasal drip encourages rapid inhalation—producing a characteristic sniffling sound. Frick (1985, p. 420) notes that crying appears to involve a general tendency to contract the muscles of the face and neck. Pharyngealization, for example, involves strong contraction of the muscles of the pharynx. Extended weeping often leads to a feeling of soreness at the back of the throat due to the intense muscle contraction. Creaky voice involves muscle contractions that draw the arytenoid cartilages together. Falsetto phonation involves tensing the edges of the vocal folds. The strong contractions in the region of the vocal folds also account for the instability between falsetto and modal phonation that is responsible for cracking or "breaking" voice (Švec & Pešák, 1994). Constriction of the pharynx also appears to be the source of ingressive phonation. That is, the narrowing of the throat would naturally lead to sounds we associate with gasping (while inhaling).

It is possible to experience degrees of grief with only some of the symptoms appearing. For example, a person might simply feel a tightening in the throat ("choked up") without any further symptoms. One might experience "incipient tears"—where tears simply well up along the lower eyelids without any tears actually dropping onto the cheeks, or where the eyes appear moist without any fluid evident. The corners of the mouth might turn downward without the mouth opening. In particular, the vocalizing can vary from no sound at all to quiet whimpering, moaning, crying, or loud wailing.

Phenomenologically, grief is characterized by a strongly negative affective state. Grief vies with physical pain for the most negatively valenced affect. Although grief is normally regarded as an agonizing or miserable feeling, the experience of grief has led to some of the most touching and profound of human expressions. We find compelling expressions or portrayals in poetry, literature, visual art, and music.

Grief can be private and individual; but grief can also be public and communal and therefore cultural. All over the world, cultures have shaped distinctive rituals for grieving, including funerary rites that provide both public and private contexts for grieving (e.g., Ebersole, 2000; Hockey, Katz, & Small, 2001; Marsella, Sartorius, Jablensky, & Fenton, 1985; Murphy, Wittkower, & Chance, 1964).

Many scholars have suggested that grief is an evolved behavior, and a few scholars have proposed phylogenetic precursors for human crying (e.g., Frey, Ahern, Gunderson, & Tuason, 1986; Hasson, 2009; Montagu, 1960; Murube, 2009; Roes, 1989; Trimble, 2012). Panksepp and Bernatzky (2002), for example, have suggested that human grief might have biological origins in the phenomenon of separation distress (see also Vingerhoets, 2013; Zeifman, 2001). When removed from their mothers, offspring will often make distinctive calls (Panksepp, 1998).

Although something similar to grief may be experienced by many animals, weeping appears to be uniquely human. From time to time, there are reports of other animals shedding tears (such as elephants); however, no consistent evidence has been assembled (Bard, 2000; Vingerhoets, 2013). Watery eyes in response to psychic loss have not been observed in our closest relatives—chimpanzees, bonobos, or gorillas (Bard, 2000).

Mourning Cycle

In *Mourning and Melancholia*, Freud proposed that sadness is a variant of grief (Freud, 1917). Following after Freud, Bowlby (1961, 1973) proposed that the active (grief) and passive (sadness) responses represent stages or phases in a grief event. However, subsequent studies suggest that the two responses do not represent stages (Hinde & Spencer-Booth, 1971; Spencer-Booth & Hinde, 1971, as cited in Archer, 1999, p. 56). Instead, the two states frequently alternate back and forth. When in a state of mourning, for example, it is common for a person to experience periods of active weeping alternating with periods of passive sadness (Hofer, 1984), which we refer to as the *mourning cycle*.

Signals and Cues

In comparing sadness and grief, it is helpful to review the signal/cue distinction in ethology (Lorenz, 1937; Maynard Smith & Harper, 2003). A *signal* is a functional communicative act. An example of a signal is a rattlesnake's rattle. The rattle is used as a warning when the snake encounters another animal that could cause harm. The aim is to avoid unnecessary conflict. By contrast, a *cue* is an unintended conveyance of information. An example of a cue is the sound of a buzzing mosquito prior to an attack. In both cases, the sounds convey information—alerting the observer to the possibility of being attacked. However, the source of the information differs. In the case of the snake's rattle, the communication is a functional behavior: the snake's interest is best served when the signal is perceived and recognized. In the case of the mosquito's buzzing, the communication (cue) is incidental—a by-product of the need for the mosquito to move its wings.

In the case of signals, ethologists interpret these displays as evolutionary adaptations and so ask "what is the adaptive value that a signal provides?" From an ethological perspective, if a smile is an innate behavior that serves an evolutionary purpose, then the smile must serve an adaptive purpose for the individual generating the smile. Accordingly, the purpose of a signal is to change the behavior of the observer to the benefit of the signaler (Bradbury & Vehrenkamp, 1998). Notice that if smiling led to reduced inclusive fitness, then smiling would be selected against and so disappear as a behavior.

If signals are intended to be overtly communicated, then signals should be obvious rather than subtle. The adaptive value of the signal depends on its successful communication. A signal is said to exhibit *redundancy* when the signal is repeated or sustained over time and over multiple channels (Johnstone, 1997; Wiley, 1983). Communication is more likely to occur if the signal involves more than one modality (Partan & Marler, 1999). In the case of the rattlesnake's rattle, the signal entails both a distinctive auditory feature (the rattling sound) as well as a distinctive visual feature (the raised shaking tail). On theoretical grounds then, ethological signals are more likely to exhibit features in more than one sensory modality.

Since cues are artifacts, they may exhibit either unimodal or multimodal features. Since cues are not intended to be communicative, unlike signals, there exists no selection pressure for an existing unimodal cue to accrue multimodal features that would enhance conspicuousness. Tinbergen (1952, 1964) cogently argued that all signals evolve from cues (see also Maynard Smith & Harper, 2003). That is, if a cue offers an adaptive advantage for the animal exhibiting the cue, then selection pressures would lead to enhancing or amplifying the communicative properties of the cue. One of the best ways to enhance the conspicuousness of a newly evolved signal is to add features in another modality. As we will see, this process provides helpful clues that illuminate the adaptive functions of sadness and grief.

Apart from their conspicuous design, signals also differ from cues in how they influence observers. Signals are functional acts that "push" information into the environment. Cues are incidental phenomena where an observant individual "pulls" unintended information out of the environment. Cues are deciphered purely for the benefit of the observer. However, signals initiate a transaction that is commonly beneficial to both the signaling and observing animals (Maynard Smith & Harper, 2003).

Consider, by way of example, the submission or capitulation display in dogs. When one dog is attacked by another, the attacked animal may produce a submission display by rolling on its back and (commonly) making a whimpering sound. This behavior typically has a dramatic impact on the aggressor animal—immediately terminating the attack. The benefit for the signaling dog is that the aggression is stopped, reducing the likelihood of life-threatening injury. However, this favorable outcome is purchased at the cost of a loss of social status. The gain for the attacking dog is that it has established a relative social dominance over the submissive animal. Both animals benefit from the interaction.

Unlike cues, in the case of signals, both the signaling behavior and the response of the observer are stereotypic: they coevolve. Under the appropriate circumstances, the signaling behavior is largely automatic despite its costliness (Zahavi & Zahavi, 1997). At the same time, the response of the observer is similarly largely automatic. That is, the responses are biologically prepared. Once again, we will see that these widely accepted concepts in ethology provide helpful clues regarding the adaptive functions of sadness and grief.

Sadness as Cue

From an ethological perspective, an appropriate question is whether sadness and grief represent signals or cues. This review begins with sadness. Recall the seven acoustic features of sad speech: What—we might ask—do quieter and slower speech, lower pitch, smaller pitch movement, more mumbled articulation, breathier voice, and darker timbre all share in common? The answer is that all seven features are associated with low physiological arousal. In the peripheral nervous system, low arousal is linked to reduced acetylcholine, which in turn reduces both tone and reactivity for skeletal muscles (Siegel & Sapru, 2006). Low arousal would therefore be associated with *relaxed* and *slow* muscles.

All of the peripheral muscles of the body are affected, including the muscles of the vocal folds, tongue, lips, chin, and pulmonary muscles. Reduced muscle tone will cause the vocal folds to be less tense, resulting in a lower overall pitch as well as breathier phonation (Hollien, 1960). A slower cricothyroid muscle will produce more sluggish pitch changes and therefore generate a more monotone prosody (Sundberg, 1987). Relaxed pulmonary muscles result in lower subglottal air pressure, causing a quieter voice. Slower reactivity of tongue, lips, and chin will result in a slower rate of speech and more slurred or mumbled articulation. When the zygomatic muscles of the face are relaxed, the lips tend to fall away from the teeth (in contrast to smiling); this results in a longer effective vocal tract length with a concomitant lower resonance—producing a darker timbre (Tartter, 1980). In short, *all* of the acoustic features of sad speech can be plausibly attributed to the effects of low physiological arousal—in particular, the effects of reduced acetylcholine.

Sadness is not the only state that will cause low arousal. Low arousal is most commonly experienced when people are relaxed, tired, or sleepy. In an unpublished experiment, we asked actors to distinguish sad voice from sleepy voice. Excluding the telltale sound of yawning, we found that listeners are unable to distinguish between feigned sadness and feigned sleepiness. Like sad speech, tired or sleepy speech exhibits quieter sound intensity, slower speaking rate, lower pitch, more monotone phonation, breathier voice, and more mumbled articulation.

Consider now the visual aspects associated with sadness. Recall that sadness is associated with slumped posture and relaxed facial muscles. Eyelids may droop slightly, and the eyes may gaze downward without focusing on particular objects. Relaxation of the zygomatic muscles tends to flatten the cheeks, and relaxation of the mouth tends to cause the chin to descend. As in the case of sad speech, all of these features are attributable to low physiological arousal.

By way of summary, the features associated with both sad speech and sad facial expressions appear to be indistinguishable from other low arousal states—notably sleepy, tired, or relaxed states. It may be that there exist reliable features that successfully distinguish sad from sleepy, tired, or relaxed states. However, the apparent ease of confusion is not consistent with the properties of conspicuousness and redundancy that ethologists consider important for signaling (Johnstone, 1997; Partan & Marler, 1999; Wiley, 1983). Moreover, recall that the most characteristic auditory feature of sad voice is the tendency for sad individuals to remain mute. The tendency to reduce or avoid vocalization is not consistent with signaling. In summary, sadness better conforms to the concept of an ethological cue than to that of an ethological signal.

Grief as Signal

Consider now the parallel ethological question regarding grief: is grief a cue or a signal? Visual features include a furrowed brow, squinting eyes, down-turned corners of the mouth, flushed red face, and of course tears (Ekman, 1982). Auditory features of grief include vocalized punctuated exhaling, long sustained tones (wails), ingressive vocalization, use of falsetto phonation, breaking voice, creaky voice, pharyngealization, and sniffling. When crying, sounds may range from quiet whimpering to loud sobbing or wailing. Tears can be shed without producing a sound, but prototypical crying involves notable spontaneous sound production.

The strongest evidence regarding the compulsion to vocalize is the phenomenon of *ingressive phonation*, where the vocal folds are activated while inhaling. When crying, puffs of air are forced through the vocal folds while exhaling. When inhaling, it is common to hear a gasping sound akin to a neutral vowel or schwa sound. Phoneticians are well aware of how unusual this behavior is: 99.99% of all human vocalizations occur while exhaling. In a small number of languages, linguists have shown that some phonemes involve ingressive phonation. However, across the majority of cultures, ingressive phonation is most commonly manifested in only two behaviors: crying and laughing.

The phenomenon of ingressive phonation is highly suggestive. When weeping, the motor system keeps the vocal folds continuously and closely engaged. Whether exhaling or inhaling, the air flows through the folds, ensuring that a sound is made. The physiological behavior is consistent with a resolute involuntary compulsion to vocalize. The contrast with sadness is striking: once again people tend not to vocalize when sad.

As noted earlier, the constriction of the pharynx changes the acoustic resonance of the vocal tract leading to a sort of "pinched" or pharyngealized sound. However, the pharyngeal constriction also leads to phonetic instability where the voice chaotically switches back and forth between modal and falsetto phonation. This results in a highly distinctive "cracking" or "breaking" voice, which—even more than whimpering or wailing—is the quintessential sound of weeping.

Perhaps the most compelling evidence that a particular behavior represents a true ethological signal is the presence of a dedicated anatomical feature or organ. In the case of the rattlesnake, the rattle represents a purpose-specific anatomical organ. This raises the question of whether weeping involves any purpose-specific anatomy. In general, the various elements of grief do not appear to be behaviorally unique. Tear ducts are used to shed irritant tears as well as psychic tears; the motor actions involved in punctuated exhaling are shared with laughter; falsetto phonation is found in infant-directed speech; a red face is shared with blushing; nasal congestion is an unwelcome companion of most colds; and frowning is shared with anger. Nevertheless, there is at least one component that appears to be unique.

As noted earlier, ophthalmologists distinguish basal (lubricant) tears, reflex (irritant) tears, and psychic (emotional) tears. Reflex and psychic tears originate in the same lacrimal sacs. However, reflex and psychic tears appear to be evoked by different neural pathways. An ophthalmologist can anesthetize the entire eye so that basal and reflex tears are inhibited. However, given a suitably emotional stimulus, an anesthetized patient can still cry psychic tears because of the existence of a separate neural pathway (Earley, personal communication; Kottler, 1996, p. 63). The existence of a distinct limbic path for producing psychic tears implies an evolved neuroanatomical feature, consistent with weeping as an evolved behavior, rather than being an artifact of some other process.

Recall that another characteristic feature of signals is that they tend to directly influence the behavior of others: signals are foremost intended to change the actions of the observer. Gelstein and her colleagues (2011) collected tears from women volunteers who were induced to weep by watching a sad scene from a movie. When asked to smell the collected tears, men were unable to distinguish actual tears from a control saline solution. Nevertheless, the real psychic tears produced a marked physiological effect: testosterone concentrations (as measured in the men's saliva) dropped significantly when the men were exposed to the real tears. In addition, other measures showed that smelling the tears significantly impeded sexual arousal. These behavioral changes suggest the presence of a pheromone in psychic tears.

The effect is unconscious and automatic. In short, the work of Gelstein et al. (2011) is consistent with crying as an ethological signal that induces a biologically prepared stereotypic response.

The main purpose of emotions is to act as motivational amplifiers (Tomkins, 1980). When we experience some affective state, we are more likely to behave in certain ways. When we encounter someone crying, feelings of compassion or sympathy encourage us to offer assistance (or terminate aggression). Consistent with an ethological signal, expressions of grief have a marked impact on the thoughts, feelings, and actions of those who witness them.

Finally, we need to ask whether grief expressions are subtle or obvious. A simple Internet search for photographs of people crying will confirm that weeping expressions are nearly always unmistakable. It is possible that confusion might arise for a person suffering from an allergy like hay fever. However, allergy sufferers typically do not show a furrowed brow, squinting eyes, or a down-turned mouth. Moreover, what photographs do not convey are the characteristic sounds of weeping: the punctuated vocalized exhaling, the sounds of whining or wailing, or the distinctive "cracking" voice. In contrast to sadness, grief appears to be obvious. Even when a grief-stricken person makes efforts to hide their face or otherwise mask their grief, observers seem to have little difficulty detecting weeping. It is not simply the case that grief is conspicuous; it also seems to be the case that people are especially sensitive and vigilant for the slightest indications that a person may be weeping.

By way of summary, human weeping appears to exhibit all of the hallmarks of an ethological signal. The features of weeping are multimodal, including distinctive visual, auditory, and olfactory elements. Together, the combination of elements makes weeping unmistakable. Weeping has a strong influence on the behavior of observers—an effect that appears limited to our own species. There appears to exist a separate limbic pathway for generating psychic tears, implying a unique evolved anatomical concomitant. In particular, the rare compulsion to vocalize while inhaling and the pheromonal effect of tears on the endocrine levels of observers provide especially strong evidence consistent with the notion that weeping is an ethological signal.

Weeping as Surrender/Solicit Signal

What is the biological function of weeping? The subject of human crying has attracted extensive theoretical speculation (e.g., Cornelius, 1997; Frey, 1985; Kottler, 1996; Lutz, 2001; Vingerhoets, 2013; Vingerhoets & Cornelius, 2001; Vingerhoets, Cornelius, Van Heck, & Becht, 2000). There exists a broad consensus that adult weeping is a form of help-seeking behavior (Becker, 1933; Bowlby, 1961; Engel, 1962; Farberow & Shneidman, 1961; Gorer, 1965; Henderson, 1974; Lewis, 1934; and many others). Moreover, this idea long predates modern research and can be found in ancient texts and commentaries in many cultures.

Kottler and Montgomery (2001, p. 10) offer an important supplement to this theory. Specifically, they characterize adult weeping as a *surrender display* analogous to raising a "white flag." The effect is illustrated in the following firsthand account relayed by Kottler (1996):

> A male physician had been verbally abusing a female hospital administrator. The more she apologized, the more he berated her. It was clear he was not accepting her [apology].
>
> All of a sudden, a tear welled up in her eye, just a single tear, and ran down her cheek. He stopped cold. This guy, big time surgeon and all, used to having his way and blustering onward, just stopped dead. This tiny spot of wetness communicated to him very clearly what he otherwise had not seen. He started backpedaling so fast, apologizing like crazy. That single tear had meaning for him a way that nothing else did. (Kottler, 1996, pp. 68–69)

The important observation here is the transformation in the affective state (and consequent behavior) of the surgeon—from aggression to compassion (and perhaps even embarrassment). This single anecdotal example is consistent with more representative empirical research. For example, Lane (2006) showed that in interpersonal conflict situations, weeping tends to bring the conflict to a resolution, whereas the absence of weeping is likely to lead to an escalation of the conflict.

In short, weeping appears to exhibit at least two functions: a specific appeal to terminate aggression and an appeal for assistance. With the surrender function, human weeping more closely resembles analogous displays that are ubiquitous among other social animals, such as the submission or capitulation display when a dog rolls over on its back in response to attack. As an ethological signal, weeping has a dramatic effect on observers, evoking feelings of compassion that commonly terminate aggression and encourage altruistic behaviors.

Depressive Realism

People commonly hold overly optimistic assessments of the likelihood of achieving certain goals (Alicke & Govorun, 2005; Brown & Marshall, 2000; Ross & Nisbett, 1991; Weinstein, 1987). One might suppose that people tend to become pessimistic when experiencing sadness; however, research suggests that we are at our most realistic when sad—a phenomenon called *depressive realism* (Alloy & Abramson, 1979; Moore & Fresco, 2012). Compared with happy or neutral affect, sadness promotes more detail-oriented thinking (Clore & Huntsinger, 2007), reduced stereotyping (Bless & Fiedler, 2006), less judgment bias (Clore & Huntsinger, 2007; Tan & Forgas, 2010), greater memory accuracy (Storbeck & Clore, 2005; Forgas, Goldenberg, & Unkelbach, 2009), reduced gullibility (Forgas & East, 2008), more task perseverance (Goldenberg & Forgas, 2012), more social attentiveness and politeness (Forgas, 1995, 2002), more accurate assessments of the emotional states of others (Weary & Edwards, 1994; Yost & Weary, 1996), and improved reasoning related to social risks (Badcock & Allen, 2003). Andrews and Thomson (2009) suggest that sad feelings are adaptive for analyzing complex problems. (See Karnaze &

Levine, Chap. 4, this volume, for a more detailed discussion of the cognitive benefits of sadness.)

Nesse (1991) has suggested that the optimism that characterizes normal mental
life encourages individuals to strive to achieve goals that might be attainable with
effort; conversely, depressive realism provides a mental "grounding" or "reality
check" when those same goals prove elusive. That is, low mood is likely to discour-
age futile efforts that may squander crucial resources. The benefits of depressive
realism have led a number of researchers over the past two decades to argue that
ordinary sadness is commonly beneficial and that depression is overly diagnosed in
Western cultures (e.g., Andrews & Thomson, 2009; Hagen, 2011; Horwitz &
Wakefield, 2007; Keedwell, 2008; Nesse, 2000; Sharot, 2011; Wilson, 2008).

The apparent cognitive benefits associated with sadness appear to contradict
classic adverse symptoms characteristic of major depressive disorders, namely,
rumination. Rumination is a cognitive state in which an individual repeatedly recalls
past situations or failures, dwelling on negative thoughts and self-assessments.
Rumination is broadly regarded as destructive and unhelpful. In a groundbreaking
study, Trapnell and Campbell (1999) carried out principal component analysis
involving a large sample of responses for items on the Self-Consciousness Scale
(Fenigstein, Scheier, & Buss, 1975; Scheier & Carver, 1985). They found a clear
disassociation between two independent components they designated *rumination*
and *reflection*. Rumination represents brooding thoughts dominated by negative
self-assessments. Reflection, by contrast, represents a pattern of thought related to
self-awareness and self-knowledge (see also Joireman, Parrott, & Hammersla,
2002).

The value of analytic processing is evident in several studies reviewed by
Andrews and Thomson (2009). For example, encouraging depressed patients to
reflect on their condition through expressive writing is more likely to alleviate
depressive symptoms than amplify them (e.g., Gortner, Rude, & Pennebaker, 2006;
Graf, Gaudiano, & Geller, 2008). Although reflective thoughts are typically more
negatively valenced than thoughts experienced when not sad, reflective thinking
exhibits greater verisimilitude. In short, the reflective thinking pattern described by
Trapnell and Campbell converges with research on depressive realism. Ruminative
thinking appears to be one of the main discriminators between (pathological) major
depressive disorders and (normal) sadness. Unlike rumination, reflective thinking
serves a useful role. On balance, normal sadness appears to be an adaptive behavior
likely to enhance inclusive fitness (Andrews & Thomson, 2009; see also Karnaze &
Levine, Chap. 4, this volume).

Purpose of Sadness and Grief

By way of summary, we have seen that sadness resembles an ethological cue,
whereas grief resembles an ethological signal. Recall that cues are not intended to
be communicative. Signals, by contrast, are overtly communicative and exist to

change the behavior of observers to the benefit of the signaler. In short, sadness is a self-directed state, whereas grief is an other-directed state (see also Hagen, 2011).

When a person faces difficulties in life, there are several possible resources that can be recruited to help deal with the situation. One resource is our own mental capacities. We have seen that normal sadness is associated with reflection (as opposed to rumination). This reflective state is characterized by improved memory, cognition, and assessment compared with normal (optimistic) mentation. Through careful analysis, less biased perception, consideration of options, and realistic appraisal, an individual can strategize—forming a plan of action that may help resolve, overcome, or ameliorate a difficult situation. A second resource is our social network. The support of others can be solicited. Companions, partners, acquaintances, and even complete strangers may be induced to intervene and provide crucial support in dealing with a stressful circumstance.

The theory proposed here is that sadness and grief are distinct yet complementary states that arise in response to difficult conditions (stress). Both sadness and grief normally contribute to inclusive fitness. When we fail or encounter a problem, sadness is intended to optimize our own behaviors; grief is intended to favorably change the behavior of those around us.

This view has repercussions for interpreting the commonly observed mourning cycle. According to the theory proposed here, the alternation between periods of quiescent sadness and periods of active grieving represents phases of inward-directed and socially directed behaviors. Notice that the proportion of time allotted to each behavior is likely to be shaped by the severity of the situation, the ability of the individual to cope with the situation alone, the capacity of others to be able to offer genuinely useful assistance, and the willingness of the individual to incur the social cost associated with appeals for help. Minor failures are apt to lead to sadness without grief. Major failures are apt to require the help of others and so result in grief. This chapter will consider the relative costs and benefits of various behaviors in more detail in a later section.

The suggestion that sadness is a self-oriented *cue* while grief is an other-oriented *signal* raises a number of questions. For example, if weeping is intended to change the behavior of observers, why would anyone cry alone? Similarly, if weeping is intended to be communicative, why would anyone attempt to suppress or hide their weeping? These and other questions will be addressed in due course.

Immune Response

Over the past decade, research on sadness and depression has drawn attention to the importance of the immune system (Felger & Lotrich, 2013; Miller, Haroon, Raison, & Felger, 2013; Raison, Capuron, & Miller, 2006). Along with cognitive and social stressors, basic forms of stress also include injury and illness. Coping with these latter kinds of stressors has long been the province of the immune system.

When highly active, the immune system places considerable demands on metabolic resources. Indeed, an active immune system is comparable to the brain as a high-demand energy consumer. The effectiveness of the immune response is reduced if the immune system must compete for metabolic resources. Of various energy-commanding systems, voluntary motor movements can be singled out as the most "optional." By refraining from movement, more metabolic resources are available for the immune system (Engel, 1962; Miller et al., 2013). In order to achieve this state, the individual must lose her/his motivation to move. Two feelings contribute to this desirable state: anergia (in the form of fatigue) and anhedonia. Anergia discourages movement itself. Anhedonia reduces the incentive to engage in what otherwise might be beneficial behaviors.

The classic symptom of virtually every kind of pathology is inflammation—a response arising from pro-inflammatory cytokines. Recent research implicates pro-inflammatory cytokines in feelings of both anergia and anhedonia. Capuron et al. (2002) found that administering pro-inflammatory cytokines decreases putamen and caudate activity, consistent with decreased dopamine synthesis or dopamine release. As might be expected, suppression of dopamine has repercussions for both motor movement and motivation. Specifically, the reduced activity is correlated with feelings of fatigue and anhedonia. Normally rewarding activities are experienced as significantly less appealing.

An example of a pro-inflammatory cytokine is interferon IFN-α, a powerful endogenous antiviral used to treat various infectious diseases, notably hepatitis C. Injecting interferon into a healthy individual precipitates a series of changes including a rise in body temperature, feelings of fatigue, muscle pain, and possible headache. In short, the person will feel sick. Between 30% and 50% of patients receiving IFN-α in a clinical application will also exhibit symptoms of depression (Capuron et al., 2002; Musselman et al., 2001; Raison et al., 2006). In summary, feelings of sadness or depression appear to enhance the effectiveness of the immune response by discouraging competition for metabolic resources, principally through feelings of anergia and anhedonia (Nesse & Williams, 1994). Activities that are normally enjoyable lose their appeal, and the person becomes less engaged with the world.

Further evidence of a close relationship between depression and the immune system is provided by the effects of sleep deprivation. Sleep deprivation has long been known to interfere with immune function (Rogers, Szuba, Staab, Evans, & Dinges, 2001). Ultimately, sleep deprivation leads to death through a catastrophic failure of immune responses (Everson, 1993). Interestingly, sleep deprivation has been used as an effective therapy for short-term treatment of major depressive disorders (Dallaspezia & Benedetti, 2011; Pflug & Tölle, 1971). That is, the relief of depressive symptoms is correlated with reduced immune function.

This simple story may make sense for injury and illness, but much sadness or depression in humans arises from other stressors, notably social stress. Although one might expect that inflammatory responses make no sense when dealing with cognitive forms of stress, the research suggests otherwise. The physiological mechanisms involved in cognitive or social stress appear to be elaborations of immune responses. Cytokines have been shown to target the dorsal anterior cingulate cortex (dACC)—a region associated with social pain. For example, Eisenberger and Lieberman (2004) showed that the dACC is activated when experiencing social rejection. Moreover, Slavich et al. (2010) found that the intensity of the inflammatory response is predictive of the magnitude of negative feelings arising from social rejection. In addition, antidepressants that are effective for cognitively induced depression have been shown to inhibit the production and release of pro-inflammatory cytokines and stimulate the production of anti-inflammatory cytokines (Kenis & Maes, 2002). Altogether, the research implies that ancient immune responses provide the foundation for addressing cognitive and social stressors as well as injury and microbial stressors.

Although ordinary sadness may commonly enhance fitness, a proportion of the population is disposed to suffer from major depressive disorders that are clearly pathological. The etiology of major depressive disorders remains a complex problem addressed by ongoing research. One part of the puzzle appears to involve a genetic concomitant. Meta-analyses of genome-wide association studies suggest that many of the genes implicated in depression are known to enhance immune effectiveness (Raison & Miller, 2013). Miller et al. (2013) argue that depression-related genes have been preserved in the human gene pool because of their adaptive value in protecting against pathogens.

Overall, recent research suggests a linkage between immune responsiveness and the negative feeling states associated with sadness and depression. In particular, the negative feeling states are closely linked with pro-inflammatory cytokines. There remains the question of why sadness would be associated with social withdrawal, rather than with social approach or appeal. Like voluntary movement, social engagement is likely to incur an energy cost; if the social cost of an appeal for help (via crying) is deemed too high, then avoidance of social interaction would be warranted as a means of conserving energy.

Ritualization

With this background, consider once again the symptoms of weeping: watery eyes, nasal congestion, constriction of the pharynx (lump in throat), and erratic breathing. When people cry for an extended period, they typically also experience red swollen eyes, and some individuals may experience urticaria (hives) in response to sustained weeping (Saul & Bernstein, 1941). As noted earlier, these are classic symptoms of a systemic allergic response. In short, weeping itself resembles yet another immune response, linked predominantly to yet another class of pro-inflammatory cytokines—histamines. Consequently, the characteristic features of weeping—from tears to cracking voice—amount to downstream manifestations of immune activity in response to stressors.

Ethologists have long proposed that signals evolve from cues through a process dubbed *ritualization* (Tinbergen, 1952, 1964). Through repetition and amplification, ritualization renders a cue more conspicuous and so more communicative (Maynard Smith & Harper, 2003). For example, the signaling of aggression by lowering the pitch of the voice originates from the association between large size and low frequency of oscillation. This association began as a cue, proved useful, and so was subsequently amplified to make it more conspicuous (Huron & Shanahan, 2013).

In light of the recent discoveries identifying the immunological concomitants of sadness, we propose an evolutionary-historical scenario of the process of ritualization by which crying or weeping arose as a signal among *Homo sapiens*. Long before the appearance of social animals, the principal response to physiological stress (either injury or illness) was immunological. Dealing with tissue damage and fighting pathogens was the main function of pro-inflammatory cytokines. As noted, the effectiveness of the immune response is enhanced if there are no other behaviors vying for metabolic resources. Notably, reduced motor movement is beneficial. Accordingly, the benefits from releasing cytokines are augmented when they influence motivation—mainly by evoking lethargic feelings that lead to reduced motor movement and by discouraging other normal goal-related behaviors by rendering hedonic rewards less appealing. In short, we might expect that at some point in evolutionary history, anergia and anhedonia were added to the effects of the release of pro-inflammatory cytokines. This would have arisen long before the appearance of humans.

At some point in hominini evolution, the release of pro-inflammatory cytokines was broadened to include the release of histamines, with predictable symptoms, including watery eyes, nasal congestion, and pharyngeal constriction. Notice that these allergic symptoms are among the most easily observed signs of immunological stress. Although profuse tears may not be common, watery eyes are symptomatic of infection or stress in many mammals and can be readily observed, for example, in sick dogs and cats. Accordingly, observant conspecifics learn to interpret these symptoms as suggesting that the observed individual is experiencing a stressed (or saddened) state. That is, allergic symptoms initially served as an ethological *cue* for dejected or depressed states—more generally indicating a reduced fitness in the observed individual.

Like many (artifactual) cues, this cue would have been easily misinterpreted. Notably, a dejected or saddened state would not have been distinguishable from a genuine allergic response. As discussed below, there are advantages for both observer and observed to transform the cue into a signal. Hence the symptoms involved in the cue (tears, congestion, constricted pharynx) undergo selection pressure that enhances their conspicuousness (i.e., ritualization). The small quantity of tears arising from the allergic response is amplified, so psychic tears become more profuse than is the case for an allergy. Most important in the transition from cue to signal is the introduction of an acoustical component that increases conspicuousness by adding another sensory modality. With the exception of occasional sniffling, sneezing, and nose-blowing, the allergy itself exhibits few sonic features. Added to the allergic response, then, is the compulsion to vocalize. This compulsion is evident, first, in sobbing, whining, or wailing. A second distinctive sound is ingressive phonation. As mentioned earlier, the rare behavior of vocalizing while inhaling testifies to a powerful motivation to keep the vocal folds engaged. Finally, two other characteristic sounds are directly attributable to the constricted pharynx. In the first instance, constricting the pharynx leads to the distinctive pharyngealized vocal resonance. In addition, the constricted pharynx produces phonetic instability, leading to abrupt transitions between modal and falsetto phonation producing the quintessential cracking or breaking voice. In effect, the constricted pharynx (originating from the allergic response) affords an exaptation for the ensuing acoustical components of a bona fide weeping signal (Gould & Vrba, 1982).

Vocalization is most communicative when it is loud. Loud vocalization, however, requires relatively high physiological arousal. As noted, sadness and depression are associated with low arousal. Engel (1962) argued that sadness-related anergia serves a resource-conserving function that is a useful response to stress. Miller et al. (2013) have argued more explicitly that anergia frees metabolic resources for healing wounds and fighting infection. Consequently, in the case of crying, there arises a conundrum regarding optimal arousal levels: the goal of tissue repair conflicts with the goal of communication. It is possible that these competing goals account for the wide energy range found in grief-related vocalizations—expressions that can range from quiet, subdued sobbing to loud, energetic wailing.

Coevolved Responsiveness

Apart from the changes in the signaling animal, ethological signals also entail the coevolution of a stereotypic response in conspecific observers. The selection pressures for the signaler are clear: weeping benefits the grief-stricken individual either by terminating an attack or by receiving support from an observer. However, what selection pressure exists for the observer to coevolve a helping behavior? In what way does the signal benefit the observer? Why would an observer experience a feeling such as compassion?

When an observer encounters an individual in need, opportunities arise for the observer to benefit through both kin-related altruism and reciprocal altruism (Trivers, 1971). Kin-related altruism contributes directly to inclusive fitness. However, altruistic acts directed toward non-kin can also contribute to inclusive fitness. Enhanced social status and implied reciprocal obligations for future resource sharing can often outweigh the proximal cost of helping someone in need.

In short, the act of weeping has the potential to benefit both signaling and observing individuals. It is this potential for mutually beneficial interaction that provides converging selection pressure that propels the ritualization—from cue to signal. What begins as an artifact of histamine release is reshaped into the ethological signal we call weeping.

By way of summary, crying or weeping behavior can be plausibly traced to an evolutionary history beginning with pro-inflammatory responses arising from injury, illness, or defeat. Expanded to include histamines, the readily perceived symptoms offer an ethological cue, informing observers of the sad, stressed, or depressed state of an individual. Altruistic acts by an observer benefit the signaler and can also benefit the observer. Consequently, allergy-related symptoms come under selection pressure that amplifies them and extends them to include multi-modal characteristics. An ethological cue is transformed into an ethological signal in accordance with the classic process of ritualization (Tinbergen, 1952, 1964).

The Differential Costs and Benefits of Weeping

The principal cost of weeping is the loss of social status. The principal benefit of weeping is the increased likelihood of terminating aggression and/or the increased likelihood of receiving altruistic assistance. These costs and benefits are not the same for all individuals. High social position is biologically important insofar as it impacts reproductive success (Ellis, 1995; Hopcroft, 2006). Moreover, among mammals, high social rank disproportionately benefits males. A high-ranked male can produce many more offspring than a high-ranked female. In summary, those who pay the greatest costs for weeping are reproductive individuals of highest social rank, with males incurring a greater cost than equivalently ranked females. Those individuals who have the least to lose by weeping are non-reproductive individuals and those at the bottom of the social hierarchy.

These theory-derived predictions accord remarkably well with empirical observations concerning the frequency of crying. The greatest amount of crying is evident in infancy. Crying decreases around 2–3 years of age, when toddlers become more socially engaged and so are more likely to suffer from the associated social penalty incurred by crying. Sex-linked differences in crying frequency are not evident in early life. Landreth (1941) carried out an extensive developmental study of crying among children between 2 and 5 years of age. She was the first researcher to observe that, in this age group, boys cry (slightly) more often than girls.

At puberty, a dramatic reduction in the frequency of crying is evident for both males and females. At the same time, marked sex-related differences appear at puberty, with males much less likely to cry than females (Delp & Sackeim, 1987). The difference in crying frequency between males and females is evident in nearly every culture observed; in addition, in many cultures, people of high social station (both male and female) exhibit less crying (Rosenblatt, Walsh, & Jackson, 1976).

With the onset of old age, sex-related differences are attenuated. Elderly men are slightly more likely to weep than younger men (Vingerhoets, 2013). This difference is consistent with changes in reproductive fitness among older people. Elderly men commonly retain some reproductive capacity, but typically exhibit reduced social status. A further reduction of social status due to weeping is less likely to impact reproductive success.

In conjunction with the costs incurred by weeping, one also needs to consider the benefits. Those who have the most to gain are those who are being attacked, those who have little access to resources, and those who lack the ability to acquire resources. Landreth (1941) found a significant negative correlation between crying frequency and IQ. To the extent that IQ correlates with a capacity for acquiring resources, this relationship is consistent with an increased value of crying for those individuals less able to provide for themselves.

Executive Control

In ethology, both the etiology of a signal (also known as a releaser) and the observer's responses are commonly stereotypic. The apparent automaticity of these behaviors led Lorenz (1937) to dub them "innate releasing mechanisms." However, subsequent research has played down the notion that the behaviors are fixed and automatic. For mammals in particular, some degree of executive control may override or modify behaviors that otherwise appear to be instinctive (Immelmann & Beer, 1989).

Compared with other animals, humans have a greater capacity for self-control. Large regions of the frontal cortex are known to serve inhibitory functions—suppressing, modifying, or masking otherwise compelling behaviors. Weak connections from the frontal lobes are implicated in impulsive behavior (Miller & Cummings, 2007).

Despite the fact that weeping appears to be largely involuntary, since weeping incurs a social cost, if the individual assesses the social cost as too burdensome, then the person may attempt to suppress, modify, or mask their weeping (Kraemer & Hastrup, 1988). Such executive control of weeping behavior is evident in several ways. The weeping signal can be physical masked by turning away, hiding one's face, or seeking privacy. If physical masking is impossible, various strategies exist for psychological masking. For example, a person moved to the edge of tears may consciously think of something else—typically something mundane—such as the need to fuel the car or what to prepare for dinner. That is, prefrontal "executive" control is used to mask or circumvent the propensity to weep.

Conversely, an individual might conclude that, under the circumstances, weeping would be advantageous. In this case, a reverse psychological strategy might be employed, such as thinking sad or tragic thoughts—as in recalling the death of a loved one.

In light of the costs and benefits associated with weeping, one might expect a complex calculus to exist concerning whether or not to weep in a given circumstance. Note, however, that the very fact that people hide their faces, pretend to have something in their eye, or think thoughts that either inhibit or facilitate weeping attests to the comparatively automatic etiology of the behavior—despite its malleability through executive control. That is, the modifications afforded by executive control notwithstanding, weeping exhibits the stereotypic tendencies seen in signaling among nonhuman animals.

The same arguments apply to how individuals respond when they observe weeping. Recall that the principal benefit to the observer is the long-term inclusive fitness conferred by engaging in kin-related or reciprocal altruistic assistance. Notice that potential benefits from reciprocal altruism depend on future interaction with the weeping individual. If the interaction is unique or "one-off," then the fitness advantage of altruistic assistance is negligible. Indeed, we find considerable anecdotal evidence of the failure for weeping to suspend an attack when the attacker and crier are strangers or when the potential for future interaction is limited. Both experimental research and game-theoretic models show that the likelihood for cooperation depends on the probability of repeated future interaction (Ahn, Janssen, & Ostrom, 2004; Andreoni & Miller, 1993; Axelrod & Hamilton, 1981). At the same time, the observer's response is apt to be shaped by such factors as the perceived honesty of the signal, reputation and history of past interactions, and the marginal cost to the observer of offering assistance.

In summary, there is a notable degree of automaticity both with regard to the circumstances leading to weeping and with regard to observer responses to weeping. However, humans exhibit a considerable capacity for executive control in which such biologically prepared behaviors can be inhibited or masked.

Crying Alone

The foregoing discussions provide answers to two questions posed earlier: If weeping is an ethological signal and if signals are intended to be communicative, why would anyone weep alone? Moreover, if signals are intended to be communicative, why do people often attempt to mask their weeping, by seeking privacy, hiding their face, or wiping away tears?

As was just noted, the very fact that people mask or hide their weeping suggests that the act of weeping is largely automatic and involuntary. Circumstances can dispose people to weep, whether they want to or not. This automaticity contributes to the honesty of the signal—reassuring the observer that the weeping is unlikely to arise from intentional manipulation. However, the largely involuntary character of weeping increases the likelihood that a person might weep, even when there is no audience to witness the signal.

Similarly, the second question has already been answered. Since weeping incurs a cost, cognitive appraisals (including cultural norms) might be expected to contribute to a complex calculus of whether the cost is prohibitively high. In these cases, efforts to mask or disguise weeping may be expected.

Infant Crying

As noted, the principal cost of weeping is the loss of social status. The loss of social status is more costly for high-status individuals of reproductive age. The least cost is incurred by non-reproducing individuals at the bottom of the social ladder, a group whose members include infants and children. Since these individuals incur the least cost associated with weeping, it follows that they have the most to gain from the altruistic responses evoked by weeping.

To the extent that adults are biologically prepared to respond to weeping with acts of compassion, and since children suffer little cost when they weep, children have much to gain from weeping behaviors. In short, there is a period in human development when the emergence of weeping allows children to tap into adult compassion at relatively little cost. This window of opportunity closes slightly when toddlers begin earnest social interaction and closes more fully with sexual maturity when social costs have greater consequences for reproductive success.

At birth, crying is most frequent in the *absence* of a caregiver, suggesting that the main purpose of infant crying is to maintain infant-caregiver contact (e.g., Panksepp & Bernatzky, 2002). However, by 2 years of age, crying is maximum in the *presence* of a caregiver, suggesting that the main purpose of toddler crying is to promote caregiver investment. Evidently, weeping provides an extraordinary tool through which an enterprising child can loosen the adult grip on resources through a biologically prepared disposition to acts of compassion.

The use of crying by infants to solicit resources is consistent with a further feature of infant crying—namely, the tendency for crying to be contagious. The crying of a single infant is apt to induce crying among nearby infants (Geangu, Benga, Stahl, & Striano, 2010; Hatfield, Cacioppo, & Rapson, 1994). This crying "contagion" might simply be a response to the unpleasantness of the sound of others crying. However, another possibility is that crying might represent a form of sibling competition. If caregiver attention is given disproportionately to the infant who cries, then a silent infant nearby is apt to receive less.

The costs incurred by infants and children from weeping can be so low that a real danger is the possibility of caregiver neglect, abuse, and even infanticide (Frodi, 1985; Frodi & Lamb, 1980). Such scenarios are consistent with classic parent-offspring conflict described by Trivers (1974).

As noted, reproducing adults pay a considerable cost for crying through the loss of social status. This chapter has suggested that the reason why infants and children incur so little cost for weeping is that the weeping behavior is crucial for adult social interaction; consequently, weeping simply must appear at some point in human development, and that moment of appearance necessarily occurs when social costs are low. Colic would be a nonadaptive artifact of this evolutionary scenario.

Cultural Coda

If weeping is an ethological signal, then it must be species-wide and therefore truly cross-cultural. The notion that weeping has a biologically prepared meaning might be expected to raise concerns among cultural anthropologists. Surprisingly, some anthropologists agree that weeping is an innate behavior. American anthropologist Jules Henry has commented on the "striking resemblance" of grief-related behaviors across cultures (Henry, 1941/1964, p. 66; quoted in Rosenblatt et al., 1976,

p. 18). Similarly, Greg Urban has remarked on the common humanity of grief expressions, referring to them as "natural" and "transparently understandable, not in need of detailed ethnographic description" (Urban, 1991, p. 151).

Nevertheless, weeping expressions exhibit a number of differences within and between cultures, and these differences raise challenges for any theory claiming that weeping has a biologically prepared social meaning. For example, in many cultures people experience tears of joy, such as those produced by beauty pageant winners. As noted earlier, in several cultures, weeping is sometimes accompanied by various forms of self-injury, including tissue damage that appears to contradict the claim the grief behaviors enhance inclusive fitness. There also exist ritualized forms of weeping, such as the "fake crying" used by the Tupinamba Indians to greet strangers— the so-called *welcome of tears*. These and other cultural behaviors raise challenges for any theory that purports any innate foundation for weeping behaviors.

In the space available here, we examine a single cultural expression—the crying of beauty pageant winners. If weeping is regarded as a response to loss or tragedy, then the tearful pageant winner appears to make no sense. Having triumphed over the competition, the winner is certainly not experiencing feelings of loss or disappointment. However, ethology tells us that the purpose of a signal is not to communicate the feeling state of the individual: the purpose of a signal is to change the behavior of observers to the benefit of the signaler. Once again, if weeping is a signal, we need to attend less to the feelings of the weeping person and more to the effect the signal has on observers.

If weeping is a signal of surrender, then the weeping beauty pageant winner is communicating submission. Unlike the winner of a sports competition who thrusts her arms into the air in joyful celebration (and possible gloating), the weeping pageant winner is exhibiting a remarkable display of humility. When a culture expects a winner to be magnanimous, gracious, and grateful, there is arguably no more powerful expression than to voluntarily mark oneself down in the social hierarchy.

By way of summary, the argument here is that the tears shed by a beauty pageant winner are not tears of joy. The feeling of joy is surely real, but the tears are not part of the joy. Tears may flow in response to intense stress, especially when executive control is relaxed or abandoned. However, the main effect would be how observers interpret the tears—as communicating humility and gratitude (as opposed to entitlement)—which, for many observers, would make the pageant winner more rather than less appealing.

This single example is offered merely as an illustration of how the analysis of cultural expressions related to weeping might be profitably approached from an ethological perspective.

Phenomenology

Evolutionary arguments such as those offered here have a long history of poor reception by the general public. It is not simply that Machiavellian motives to maximize inclusive fitness are offensive when viewed from common moral standards.

The accounts themselves simply do not accord with subjective experience when we observe weeping or when we ourselves weep.

Humans exist in a physical world of competing molecular patterns whose dynamics shape the deep motivations underlying behavior. However, our subjective experience has us living in a world of people and objects, social networks, and ineffable feelings. Love may simply be nature's way of encouraging pair-bonding and procreation, but the feeling of love is no less profound an experience despite its prosaic biochemical origin.

When we weep, our subjective experience is not one of manipulating others to help. Instead our experience is one of expressing true tragedy, accompanied by feelings of profound capitulation to an unhappy human condition. Similarly, when we observe others weeping, our phenomenological experience is not one of gleefully helping others, confident that they are incurring a great debt to us that may be repaid later. Instead our experience is one of expressing true compassion and empathy, often accompanied by a powerful feeling of social connection.

In our phenomenological world, sadness is about loss and regret; weeping is about vulnerability and compassion. In our shared world of phenomenological experience, sadness and grief are feelings of ultimate depth that touch and inspire us. Indeed, these feelings find expression in some of the most exquisite and affecting moments in poetry, drama, literature, and music (e.g., Kaufmann, 1992; Larson, 2010; Lewis, 1961; Young, 2010). When compared to the profundity of our subjective feelings, the presumed evolutionary origins will necessarily appear mundane and trivial.

Reprise

With this background, it is possible to offer a more systematic statement of the evolutionary theory proposed here for sadness and grief. Figure 5.1 provides a schematic summary of the proposed evolutionary history of stress-related responses. The following numbered summary is intended to clarify the logic of the theory, with the potential to better expose weakness. The summary may also provide a guide for identifying components of the theory amenable to empirical testing.

1. **Three responses to stress**. Animals experience many kinds of stress. These include physical injury, pathogens, hunger, cognitive challenges, and social threats such as social exclusion. When faced with difficulty, an individual can draw on at least three broad types of resources: *physiological resources* that fight infection, repair injury, and conserve energy, *cognitive resources* that encourage realistic reflection and strategizing, and *social resources* where conspecifics are induced to terminate aggression and/or offer assistance.
2. **Immune responsiveness**. Physical injury and illness provoke ancient immune responses. These responses are metabolically expensive, accounting for nearly 20% of metabolic energy consumption when fully activated.

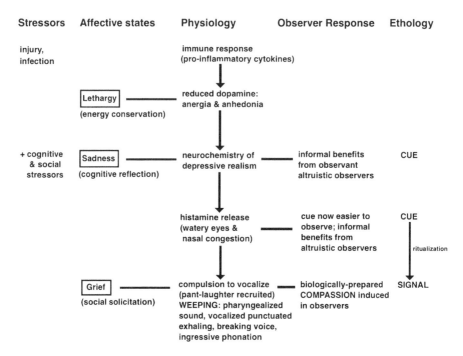

Fig. 5.1 Schematic summary of a proposed evolutionary history of stress-related responses. Three affective states are distinguished: *lethargy*, whose purpose is to minimize metabolic competition that impedes immune responsiveness; *sadness*, whose purpose is to promote cognitive assessment and planning to deal with stresses; and *grief*, whose purpose is to terminate conspecific aggression and/or solicit assistance. Five historical stages are represented: (1) an immune response that is limited to fighting infection and repairing tissue damage, (2) supplemented by motivational changes that enhance immune effectiveness through feelings of anergia and anhedonia, (3) neuro-chemical changes that promote improved cognitive processing ("depressive realism") and expand the range of stressors addressed to include cognitive and social stresses, (4) histamine-related changes that enhance visible symptoms of stress and may result in assistance, and (5) a full-fledged ethological signal in which a distinctive display (weeping) induces biologically prepared *compassion* in conspecifics

3. **Anergia**. In the presence of injury or illness, energetic motor behaviors reduce fitness by competing with the immune system for metabolic resources. Fitness is enhanced if voluntary energetic activities are suppressed. Energy conservation can be achieved through the proximal feelings of fatigue.

4. **Anhedonia**. Many behaviors are motivated by hedonic rewards. A second effective strategy for reducing energy-depleting motor movement is to render normally enjoyable activities less enjoyable or appealing. This is achieved through the proximal feelings of anhedonia or apathy.

5. **Dopamine and lethargy**. The principal neurochemical concomitant of decreased motivation and motor activity (collectively "lethargy") is reduced dopamine.

6. **Pro-inflammatory cytokines**. In order to facilitate tissue repair and defense against pathogens, the immune system releases pro-inflammatory cytokines. These cytokines are implicated in anergia, anhedonia, dopamine suppression, and depressive feelings. In addition, pro-inflammatory cytokines are implicated in social pain, such as that arising from social exclusion.
7. **Reflection**. When under stress, appropriate mental activities may include cognitive reflection, where alternative adaptive strategies are formed and assessed.
8. **Depressive realism**. In difficult conditions, normally "optimistic" thinking has less utility than "realistic" thinking. Accurate memory recall, unbiased judgment, and realistic assessment are favored.
9. **Sadness versus grief**. Sadness and grief are different yet complementary states. Sadness is a quiescent state whose purpose is to promote cognitive reflection and strategizing. Grief is a socially directed signal intended to terminate aggression and/or solicit the assistance of others.
10. **Mourning cycle**. For minor stresses, the cost of weeping is likely to outweigh the benefits, and so minor stresses are apt to lead to sadness without grief. For major stresses, the benefits of weeping are more likely to outweigh the costs, and so sadness is apt to be supplemented by bouts of grief, where inward-directed sadness alternates with outward-directed grief, producing a "mourning cycle."
11. **From inflammation to lethargy to sadness to grief**. Since injury and illness are ubiquitous threats, immune responses ("inflammation") must have appeared very early in animal evolution. The beneficial consequences of anergia and anhedonia ("lethargy") are likely to have arisen next. The compulsion for cognitive reflection ("sadness") would have appeared subsequently. Finally, a grief signal ("weeping") appears to be a ritualization of histamine release, unique to the hominini line.
12. **Histamines**. One class of pro-inflammatory cytokines includes histamines. Histamine release leads to allergic symptoms, including watery eyes, nasal congestion, and pharyngeal constriction. Note that histamines also disrupt sleep, reduce libido, and interfere with attention and vigilance—classic symptoms of depression (Cará et al., 1995; Falus, Grosman, & Darvas, 2004).
13. **Manifest allergies**. Of the various immunological responses, allergic symptoms are among the most easily perceived by observers. Nasal congestion and moist eyes are symptoms of immunological stress.
14. **Allergy as cue**. In the ancient past, watery eyes and nasal congestion acted as ethological cues—indexing a robust immune response to allergen stress. However, as these immune responses broadened to deal with other stressors (notably social stress), these symptoms also became observable cues indicating cognitive or social stress. Observant conspecifics learned to associate these symptoms with an individual experiencing stress. However, this cue was easily confused with a true allergic response. That is, an observer could not confidently distinguish those symptoms arising from allergen stress from those symptoms arising from cognitive or social stress.

15. **Ritualization**. Signals evolve from cues through the process of ritualization. Allergy-like cues would occasionally provoke altruistic assistance from observers. In light of the benefits for the stressed individual, the allergic symptoms arising from histamine release underwent selection pressure, transforming a *stress-induced allergy cue* into a *stress-induced weeping signal*.

16. **Conspicuousness**. Since signals are intended to be communicative, signals evolve toward conspicuousness and redundancy.

17. **Psychic tears**. The most conspicuous visual feature of weeping is the proliferation of tears. Although the neuroanatomy remains obscure, independent limbic activation of lacrimal sacs implies an anatomical connection, which in turn suggests a genetic (therefore innate) basis for psychic tears.

18. **Compulsion to vocalize**. An important aspect of conspicuousness is making a signal multimodal. Apart from sniffling, sneezing, and nose-blowing, the allergy exhibits no distinctive sonic element. The *compulsion to vocalize* (which is not part of a histamine-engendered allergic response) enhances the communicative effect of tears, contributing to the transformation from an ethological cue into an ethological signal.

19. **Ingressive phonation**. Especially compelling evidence in support of the compulsion to vocalize is found in ingressive phonation, where the vocal folds remain activated even while inhaling. This leads to distinctive gasping sounds.

20. **Breaking voice and pharyngealization**. As part of the allergic response, the constriction of the pharynx originally functioned to impede the entry of allergens. With the development of weeping, pharyngeal constriction affords two characteristic acoustic features: breaking or cracking voice (due to instability between modal and falsetto phonation) and a pharyngealized acoustic resonance or formant. In the evolution from a *stress-induced allergy cue* to a *stress-induced weeping signal*, pharyngeal constriction qualifies as an exaptation.

21. **Pant-laughter**. The punctuated vocalized exhaling responsible for the distinctive "ah-ah-ah-ah" sound of weeping appears to be phylogenetically related to primate pant-laughter.

22. **Mutualism**. Signals evolve only if they serve both the signaling animal and the observing animal. The advantage of weeping for the signaling individual is the termination of attack and the effective soliciting of social assistance. The advantage for the observing individual is an enhanced social status, improved reputation, possible kin selection, and/or future opportunities to benefit from reciprocal altruism.

23. **Compassion**. For the observing individual, the proximal motivation to terminate aggression and to engage in resource sharing is a feeling of compassion, commonly followed by feelings of pride or virtue.

24. **Pheromonal tears**. Psychic tears appear to contain a pheromone that encourages compassionate behaviors. This discovery holds three important implications. First, the research indicates that weeping activates at least three sensory modalities—visual, auditory, and olfactory—consistent with the multimodal conspicuousness of ethological signals. Second, since exposure to tears changes the behavior of the observer to the benefit of the signaler, this effect is

consistent with the claim that weeping is an ethological signal. Third, the apparent presence of a pheromone provides further indirect evidence of genetic factors underlying weeping behaviors, with the additional implication that weeping is an evolved behavior.

25. **Biologically prepared tendencies**. Taken altogether, the anatomical, physiological, phenomenological, behavioral, and social evidence is consistent with weeping exhibiting the stereotypic tendencies commonly observed in signaling among nonhuman animals. That is, there are biologically prepared tendencies to weep under certain circumstances and biologically prepared tendencies for observers to respond in certain ways toward weeping individuals. There is a notable degree of automaticity to these behaviors.

26. **Executive control**. Compared with other animals, humans exhibit greater executive control. Among humans, otherwise compelling behaviors (such as weeping) are susceptible to suppression, modification, or masking.

27. **Frequency of crying**. The likelihood of crying is proportional to the magnitude of the stressor and inversely proportional to a person's social status and reproductive fitness. Crying is less common during reproductive years, least common among reproductive males, and more common among those with lower social status.

28. **Responsiveness to weeping**. The tendency to respond to weeping by terminating attack and/or offering assistance is mediated by several factors, including the degree of relatedness between observer and crier, the likelihood of future sustained interaction, the perceived honesty of the signal, the reputation and history of past interactions, the presence of an audience, and the marginal cost to the observer of offering assistance.

29. **Infant crying**. Crying incurs much lower costs for infants and children than for adults. As a result, there are few limits to the amount of infant crying.

30. **An autoimmune disorder**. Depression appears to be another type of autoimmune disorder.

References

Ahn, T. K., Janssen, M. A., & Ostrom, E. (2004). Signals, symbols, and human cooperation. In R. W. Sussman & A. R. Chapman (Eds.), *The origins and nature of sociality* (pp. 122–140). Hawthorne, NY: Aldine de Gruyter.

Alicke, M. D., & Govorun, O. (2005). The better-than-average effect. In M. D. Alicke & J. I. Krueger (Eds.), *Studies in self and identity. The self in social judgment* (pp. 85–108). New York, NY: Psychology Press.

Allen, N. B., & Badcock, P. B. T. (2003). The social risk hypothesis of depressed mood: Evolutionary, psychosocial, and neurobiological perspectives. *Psychological Bulletin, 129*, 887–913.

Alloy, L. B., & Abramson, L. Y. (1979). Judgment of contingency in depressed and nondepressed students: Sadder but wiser? *Journal of Experimental Psychology: General, 108*, 441–485.

Andreoni, J., & Miller, J. H. (1993). Rational cooperation in the finitely repeated prisoner's dilemma: Experimental evidence. *Economic Journal, 103*, 57–85.

Andrews, P. W., & Thomson, J. A., Jr. (2009). The bright side of being blue: Depression as an adaption for analyzing complex problems. *Psychological Review, 116*, 620–654.

Archer, J. (1999). *The nature of grief: The evolution and psychology of reaction to loss*. London, UK: Routledge.

Axelrod, R., & Hamilton, W. D. (1981). The evolution of cooperation. *Science, 211*, 1390–1396.

Badcock, P. B. T., & Allen, N. B. (2003). Adaptive social reasoning in depressed mood and depressive vulnerability. *Cognition and Emotion, 17*, 647–670.

Banse, R., & Scherer, K. R. (1996). Acoustic profiles in vocal emotion expression. *Journal of Personality and Social Psychology, 70*, 614–636.

Bard, K. A. (2000). Crying in infant primates: Insights into the development of crying in chimpanzees. In R. G. Barr, B. Hopkins, & J. A. Green (Eds.), *Crying as a sign, a symptom, and a signal: Clinical, emotional and developmental aspects of infant and toddler crying, Clinics in Developmental Medicine No. 152* (pp. 157–175). New York, NY: Cambridge University Press.

Becker, H. (1933). The sorrow of bereavement. *Journal of Abnormal and Social Psychology, 27*, 391–410.

Bless, H., & Fiedler, K. (2006). Mood and the regulation of information processing and behavior. In J. P. Forgas (Ed.), *Affect in social thinking and behavior* (pp. 65–84). New York, NY: Psychology Press.

Bowlby, J. (1961). Process of mourning. *International Journal of Psycho-Analysis, 42*, 317–340.

Bowlby, J. (1973). *Attachment and loss; Vol. 2: Separation*. London, UK: Hogarth.

Bradbury, J. W., & Vehrenkamp, S. L. (1998). *Principles of animal communication*. Sunderland, MA: Sinauer.

Brown, J. D., & Marshall, M. A. (2000). Great expectations: Optimism and pessimism in achievement settings. In D. C. Change (Ed.), *Optimism and pessimism: Implications for theory, research, and practice* (pp. 239–256). Washington, DC: American Psychological Association.

Capuron, L., Gumnick, J. F., Musselman, D. L., Lawson, D. H., Reemsnyder, A., Nemeroff, C. B., & Miller, A. H. (2002). Neurobehavioral effects of interferon-alpha in cancer patients: Phenomenology and paroxetine responsiveness of symptom dimensions. *Neuropsychopharmacology, 26*, 643–652.

Cará, A. M., Lopes-Martins, R. A., Antunes, E., Nahoum, C. R., & De Nucci, G. (1995). The role of histamine in human penile erection. *British Journal of Urology, 75*, 220–224.

Clore, G. L., & Huntsinger, J. R. (2007). How emotions inform judgment and regulate thought. *Trends in Cognitive Science, 11*, 393–399.

Cornelius, R. R. (1997). Toward a new understanding of weeping and catharsis? In A. J. J. M. Vingerhoets, F. J. Van Bussel, & A. J. W. Boelhouwer (Eds.), *The (non)expression of emotions in health and disease* (pp. 303–321). Tilburg, Netherlands: Tilburg University Press.

Dallaspezia, S., & Benedetti, F. (2011). Chronobiological therapy for mood disorders. *Expert Review of Neurotherapeutics, 11*, 961–970.

Darwin, C. R. (1872). *The expression of emotions in man and animals*. London, UK: John Murray.

Delp, M. J., & Sackeim, H. A. (1987). Effects of mood on lacrimal flow: Sex differences and asymmetry. *Psychophysiology, 24*, 550–556.

Ebersole, G. L. (2000). The function of ritual weeping revisited: Affective expression and moral discourse. *History of Religions, 39*, 211–246.

Eisenberger, N. I., & Lieberman, M. D. (2004). Why rejection hurts: A common neural alarm system for physical and social pain. *Trends in Cognitive Science, 8*, 294–300.

Ekman, P. (1982). *Emotion in the human face*. New York, NY: Cambridge University Press.

Ekman, P. (2003). *Emotions revealed: Understanding faces and feelings*. New York, NY: Times Books.

Ellis, L. (1995). Dominance and reproductive success among nonhuman animals: A cross-species comparison. *Ethology and Sociobiology, 16*, 257–333.

Engel, G. L. (1962). Anxiety and depression-withdrawal. The primary affects of unpleasure. *International Journal of Psychoanalysis, 43*, 89–97.

Erickson, D., Yoshida, K., Menezes, C., Fujino, A., Mochida, T., & Shibuya, Y. (2006). Exploratory study of some acoustic and articulatory characteristics of sad speech. *Phonetica, 61*, 1–25.

Everson, C. A. (1993). Sustained sleep deprivation impairs host defense. *American Journal of Physiology, 265*, R1148–R1154.

Falus, A., Grosman, N., & Darvas, Z. (2004). *Histamine: Biology and medical aspects*. Budapest, Hungary: SpringMed.

Farberow, N. L., & Shneidman, E. S. (1961). *The cry for help*. New York, NY: Blakiston Division, McGraw-Hill.

Felger, J. C., & Lotrich, F. E. (2013). Inflammatory cytokines in depression: Neurobiological mechanisms and therapeutic implications. *Neuroscience, 246*, 199–229.

Fenigstein, A., Scheier, M. F., & Buss, A. H. (1975). Public and private self-consciousness: Assessment and theory. *Journal of Consulting and Clinical Psychology, 43*, 522–527.

Forgas, J. P. (1995). Mood and judgment: The Affect Infusion Model (AIM). *Psychological Bulletin, 116*, 39–66.

Forgas, J. P. (2002). Feeling and doing: Affective influences on interpersonal behavior. *Psychological Inquiry, 13*, 1–28.

Forgas, J. P., & East, R. (2008). How real is that smile? Mood effects on accepting or rejecting the veracity of emotional facial expressions. *Journal of Nonverbal Behavior, 32*, 157–170.

Forgas, J. P., Goldenberg, L., & Unkelbach, C. (2009). Can bad weather improve your memory? A field study of mood effects on memory in a real-life setting. *Journal of Experimental Social Psychology, 54*, 254–257.

Freed, P. (2009). Is sadness an evolutionarily conserved brain mechanism to dampen reward seeking? Depression may be a "sadness disorder". *Neuropsychoanalysis, 11*, 61–66.

Freud, S. (1917). Trauer und Melancholie. *Internationale Zeitschrift für Psychoanalyse, 4*, 288–301.

Frey, W. H. (1985). *Crying: The mystery of tears*. Minneapolis, MN: Winston Press.

Frey, W. H., Ahern, C., Gunderson, B. D., & Tuason, V. B. (1986). Biochemical behavioral and genetic aspects of psychogenic lacrimation: The unknown function of emotional tears. In E. J. Holly (Ed.), *The preocular tear film*. Lubbock, TX: Dry Eye Institute.

Frick, R. W. (1985). Communicating emotion: The role of prosodic features. *Psychological Bulletin, 97*, 412–429.

Frodi, A. (1985). When empathy fails: Aversive infant crying and child abuse. In B. Lester & C. F. Boukydis (Eds.), *Infant crying* (pp. 263–277). New York, NY: Plenum Press.

Frodi, A., & Lamb, M. E. (1980). Child abusers' responses to infant smiles and cries. *Child Development, 51*, 238–241.

Geangu, E., Benga, O., Stahl, D., & Striano, T. (2010). Contagious crying beyond the first days of life. *Infant Behavior and Development, 33*, 279–288.

Gelstein, S., Yeshurun, Y., Rozenkrantz, L., Shushan, S., Frumin, I., Roth, Y., & Sobel, N. (2011). Human tears contain a chemosignal. *Science, 331*, 226–230.

Gertsman, E. (2011). *Crying in the Middle Ages: Tears of history*. London, UK: Routledge.

Goldenberg, L., & Forgas, J. P. (2012). *Can happiness make us lazy? Hedonic discounting can make us reduce perseverance and the motivation to perform*. Sydney, NSW: University of New South Wales.

Gorer, G. (1965). *Death, grief, and mourning*. New York, NY: Doubleday.

Gortner, E. M., Rude, S. S., & Pennebaker, J. W. (2006). Benefits of expressive writing in lowering rumination and depressive symptoms. *Behavior Therapy, 37*, 292–303.

Gould, S. J., & Vrba, E. S. (1982). Exaptation – a missing term in the science of form. *Paleobiology, 8*, 4–15.

Graf, M. C., Gaudiano, B. A., & Geller, P. A. (2008). Written emotional disclosure: A controlled study of the benefits of expressive writing homework in outpatient psychotherapy. *Psychotherapy Research, 18*, 389–399.

Hagen, E. H. (2011). Evolutionary theories of depression: A critical review. *Canadian Journal of Psychiatry, 56*, 716–726.

Hasson, O. (2009). Emotional tears as biological signals. *Evolutionary Psychology, 7*, 363–370.

Hatfield, E., Cacioppo, J. T., & Rapson, R. L. (1994). *Emotional contagion.* New York, NY: Cambridge University Press.

Henderson, S. (1974). Care-eliciting behavior in man. *Journal of Nervous and Mental Disease, 159*, 172–181.

Henry, J. (1964). *Jungle people: A Kaingáng tribe of the highlands of Brazil.* New York, NY: Vintage Books. (Original work published 1941).

Hinde, R. A., & Spencer-Booth, Y. (1971). Effects of brief separation from mother on rhesus monkeys. *Science, 173*, 111–118.

Hockey, J. L., Katz, J., & Small, N. (2001). *Grief, mourning, and death ritual.* Buckingham, UK: Open University Press.

Hofer, M. A. (1984). Relationships as regulators: A psychobiologic perspective on bereavement. *Psychosomatic Medicine, 46*, 183–197.

Hollien, H. (1960). Some laryngeal correlates of vocal pitch. *Journal of Speech and Hearing Research, 3*, 52–58.

Hopcroft, R. L. (2006). Sex, status, and reproductive success in the contemporary United States. *Evolution and Human Behavior, 27*, 104–120.

Horwitz, A., & Wakefield, J. (2007). *The loss of sadness: How psychiatry transformed normal sadness into depressive disorder.* Oxford, UK: Oxford University Press.

Huron, D., & Shanahan, D. (2013). Eyebrow movements and vocal pitch height: Evidence consistent with an ethological signal. *Journal of the Acoustical Society of America, 133*, 2947–2952.

Immelmann, K., & Beer, C. (1989). *A dictionary of ethology.* Cambridge, MA: Harvard University Press.

Johnstone, R. A. (1997). The evolution of animal signals. In J. R. Krebs & N. B. Davies (Eds.), *Behavioural ecology* (pp. 155–178). Oxford, UK: Oxford University Press.

Joireman, J., Parrott, L., & Hammersla, J. (2002). Empathy and the self-absorption paradox: Support for the distinction between self-rumination and self-reflection. *Self and Identity, 1*, 53–65.

Kaufmann, W. (1992). *Tragedy and philosophy.* Princeton, NJ: Princeton University Press.

Keedwell, P. (2008). *How sadness survived: The evolutionary basis of depression.* Oxford, UK: Radcliffe.

Kenis, G., & Maes, M. (2002). Effects of antidepressants on the production of cytokines. *International Journal of Neuropsychopharmacology, 5*, 401–412.

Kottler, J. A. (1996). *The language of tears.* San Francisco, CA: Jossey-Bass.

Kottler, J. A., & Montgomery, M. J. (2001). Theories of crying. In A. J. J. M. Vingerhoets & R. R. Cornelius (Eds.), *Adult crying: A biopsychosocial approach* (pp. 1–-7). East Sussex, UK: Brunner-Routledge.

Kraemer, D. L., & Hastrup, J. L. (1988). Crying in adults: Self-control and autonomic correlates. *Journal of Social and Clinical Psychology, 6*, 53–68.

Kraepelin, E. (1921). Psychiatrie. Ein Lehrbuch für Studierende und Ärzte [Manic-depressive insanity and paranoia]. In G. M. Robertson (Ed.), R. M. Barclay (Trans.), *Text-book of psychiatry vols. iii and iv* (8th ed.). Edinburgh, Scotland: Livingstone. (Original work published 1899)

Landreth, C. (1941). Factors associated with crying in young children in the nursery school and the home. *Child Development, 12*, 81–97.

Lane, C. J. (2006). *Evolution of gender differences in adult crying* (Doctoral dissertation). University of Texas at Arlington, Arlington, TX.

Larson, T. (2010). *The saddest music ever written: The story of Samuel Barber's Adagio for Strings.* New York, NY: Pegasus Books.

Lewis, A. J. (1934). Melancholia: A clinical survey of depressive states. *British Journal of Psychiatry, 80*, 277–378.

Lewis, C. S. (1961). *A grief observed.* New York, NY: Seabury Press.

Lorenz, K. (1937). Über die Bildung des Instinktbegriffes. *Naturwissenschaften, 25*, 289–300. 307–318, 324–331.

Lutz, T. (2001). *Crying: A natural and cultural history of tears*. New York, NY: Norton.

Maguire, H. (1977). The depiction of sorrow in Middle Byzantine art. *Dumbarton Oaks Papers, 31*, 123–174.

Marsella, A. J., Sartorius, N., Jablensky, A., & Fenton, F. R. (1985). Cross-cultural studies of depressive disorders: An overview. In A. Kleinman & B. Good (Eds.), *Culture and depression: Studies in the anthropology and cross-cultural psychiatry of affect and disorder* (pp. 299–324). Berkeley, CA: University of California Press.

Maynard Smith, J. M., & Harper, D. (2003). *Animal signals*. Oxford, UK: Oxford University Press.

Miller, A. H., Haroon, E., Raison, C. L., & Felger, J. C. (2013). Cytokine targets in the brain: Impact on neurotransmitters and neurocircuits. *Depression and Anxiety, 30*, 297–306.

Miller, B. L., & Cummings, J. L. (2007). *The human frontal lobes: Functions and disorders*. New York, NY: Guilford Press.

Montagu, A. (1960). Natural selection and the origin and evolution of weeping in man. *Journal of the American Medical Association, 174*, 392–397.

Moore, M. T., & Fresco, D. (2012). Depressive realism: A meta-analytic review. *Clinical Psychology Review, 32*, 496–509.

Murphy, H. B. M., Wittkower, E., & Chance, N. (1964). Cross-cultural inquiry into the symptomatology of depression. *Transcultural Psychiatric Research Review, 1*, 5–21.

Murray, I. R., & Arnott, J. L. (1993). Toward the simulation of emotion in synthetic speech: A review of the literature on human vocal emotion. *Journal of the Acoustical Society of America, 93*, 1097–1108.

Murube, J. (2009). Hypotheses on the development of psychoemotional tearing. *The Ocular Surface, 7*, 171–175.

Musselman, D. L., Lawson, D. H., Gumnick, J. F., Manatunga, A. K., Penna, S., Goodkin, R. S., … Miller, A. H. (2001). Paroxetine for the prevention of depression induced by high-dose interferon alfa. *New England Journal of Medicine, 344*, 961–966.

Nesse, R. M. (1991). What good is feeling bad? The evolutionary benefits of psychic pain. *The Sciences, 31*, 30–37.

Nesse, R. M. (2000). Is depression an adaptation? *Archives of General Psychiatry, 57*, 14–20.

Nesse, R. M., & Williams, G. C. (1994). *Why we get sick: The new science of Darwinian medicine*. New York, NY: Times Books.

Panksepp, J. (1998). *Affective neuroscience: The foundations of human and animal emotions*. Oxford, UK: Oxford University Press.

Panksepp, J., & Bernatzky, G. (2002). Emotional sounds and the brain: The neuro-affective foundations of musical appreciation. *Behavioural Processes, 60*, 133–155.

Partan, S., & Marler, P. (1999). Communication goes multimodal. *Science, 283*, 1272–1273.

Pflug, B., & Tölle, R. (1971). Disturbance of the 24-hour rhythm in endogenous depression and the treatment of endogenous depression by sleep deprivation. *International Pharmacopsychiatry, 6*, 187–196.

Provine, R. R., Cabrera, M. O., Brocato, N. W., & Krosnowski, K. A. (2011). When the whites of the eyes are red: A uniquely human cue. *Ethology, 117*, 1–5.

Raison, C. L., Capuron, L., & Miller, A. (2006). Cytokines sing the blues: Inflammation and the pathogenesis of depression. *Trends in Immunology, 27*, 24–31.

Raison, C. L., & Miller, A. H. (2013). The evolutionary significance of depression in Pathogen Host Defense (PATHOS-D). *Molecular Psychiatry, 18*, 15–37.

Raleigh, M. J., McGuire, M. T., Brammer, G. L., Pollack, D. B., & Yuwiler, A. (1991). Serotonergic mechanisms promote dominance acquisition in adult male vervet monkeys. *Brain Research, 559*, 181–190.

Roes, F. L. (1989). On the origin of crying and tears. *Human Ethology Newsletter, 5*, 5–6.

Rogers, N. L., Szuba, M. P., Staab, J. P., Evans, D. L., & Dinges, D. F. (2001). Neuroimmunologic aspects of sleep and sleep loss. *Seminars in Clinical Neuropsychiatry, 6*, 295–307.

Rosenblatt, P. C., Walsh, R. P., & Jackson, D. A. (1976). *Grief and mourning in cross-cultural perspective*. New Haven, CT: Human Relations Area Files.

Ross, L., & Nisbett, R. E. (1991). *The person and the situation: Perspectives of social psychology.* New York, NY: McGraw-Hill.

Saul, L. J., & Bernstein, C. (1941). The emotional settings of some attacks of urticaria. *Psychosomatic Medicine, 3*, 349–369.

Scheier, M. F., & Carver, C. S. (1985). The self-consciousness scale: A revised version for use with general populations. *Journal of Applied Social Psychology, 15*, 687–699.

Scherer, K. R., Johnstone, T., & Klasmeyer, G. (2003). Vocal expression of emotion. In R. J. Davidson, K. R. Scherer, & H. Goldsmith (Eds.), *Handbook of the affective sciences* (pp. 433–456). Oxford, UK: Oxford University Press.

Sharot, T. (2011). *The optimism bias: A tour of the irrationally positive brain.* New York, NY: Pantheon Books.

Siegel, A., & Sapru, H. N. (2006). *Essential neuroscience.* London, UK: Lippincott Williams & Wilkins.

Slavich, G. M., Way, B. M., Eisenberger, N. I., & Taylor, S. E. (2010). Neural sensitivity to social rejection is associated with inflammatory responses to social stress. *Proceedings of the National Academy of Sciences, 107*, 14817–14822.

Spencer-Booth, Y., & Hinde, R. A. (1971). Effects of brief separations from mothers during infancy on behavior of rhesus monkeys 6-24 months later. *Journal of Child Psychology and Psychiatry, 12*, 157–172.

Storbeck, J., & Clore, G. L. (2005). With sadness comes accuracy; with happiness, false memory: Mood and the false memory effect. *Psychological Science, 16*, 785–791.

Sundberg, J. (1987). *The science of the singing voice.* DeKalb, IL: Northern Illinois University Press.

Švec, J. G., & Pešák, J. (1994). Vocal breaks from the modal to the falsetto register. *Folia Phoniatrica et Logopaedica, 46*, 97–103.

Tan, H. B., & Forgas, J. P. (2010). When happiness makes us selfish, but sadness makes us fair: Affective influences on interpersonal strategies in the dictator game. *Journal of Experimental Social Psychology, 46*, 571–576.

Tartter, V. C. (1980). Happy talk: Perceptual and acoustic effects of smiling on speech. *Perception & Psychophysics, 27*, 24–27.

Tinbergen, N. (1952). "Derived" activities; their causation, biological significance, origin, and emancipation during evolution. *Quarterly Review of Biology, 27*, 1–32.

Tinbergen, N. (1964). The evolution of signaling devices. In W. Etkin (Ed.), *Social behavior and organization among vertebrates* (pp. 206–230). Chicago, IL: University of Chicago Press.

Tomkins, S. S. (1980). Affect as amplification: Some modifications in theory. In R. Plutchik & H. Kellerman (Eds.), *Emotion: Theory, research and experience* (pp. 141–164). New York, NY: Academic Press.

Trapnell, P. D., & Campbell, J. D. (1999). Private self-consciousness and the five-factor model of personality: Distinguishing rumination from reflection. *Journal of Personality and Social Psychology, 76*, 284–304.

Trimble, M. (2012). *Why humans like to cry: Tragedy, evolution, and the brain.* Oxford, UK: Oxford University Press.

Trivers, R. L. (1971). The evolution of reciprocal altruism. *Quarterly Review of Biology, 46*, 35–57.

Trivers, R. L. (1974). Parent-offspring conflict. *American Zoologist, 14*, 249–264.

Urban, G. (1991). *A discourse-centered approach to culture: Native South American myths and rituals.* Austin, TX: University of Texas Press.

Viggiano, D., Ruocco, L. A., Arcieri, S., & Sadile, A. G. (2004). Involvement of norepinephrine in the control of activity and attentive processes in animal models of attention deficit hyperactivity disorder. *Neural Plasticity, 11*, 133–149.

Vingerhoets, A. J. J. M. (2013). *Why only humans weep: Unravelling the mysteries of tears.* Oxford, UK: Oxford University Press.

Vingerhoets, A. J. J. M., & Cornelius, R. R. (2001). *Adult crying: A biopsychosocial approach.* East Sussex, UK: Brunner-Routledge.

Vingerhoets, A. J. J. M., Cornelius, R. R., Van Heck, G. L., & Becht, M. C. (2000). Adult crying: A model and review of the literature. *Review of General Psychology, 4*, 354–377.

Weary, G., & Edwards, J. A. (1994). Social cognition and clinical psychology: Anxiety, depression, and the processing of social information. In R. S. Wyer Jr. & T. K. Srull (Eds.), *Handbook of social cognition* (pp. 289–338). Hillsdale, NJ: Erlbaum.

Weinstein, N. D. (1987). Unrealistic optimism about susceptibility to health problems: Conclusions from a community-wide sample. *Journal of Behavioral Medicine, 10*, 481–500.

Wiley, R. H. (1983). The evolution of communication: Information and manipulation. In T. R. Halliday & P. J. B. Slater (Eds.), *Communication* (pp. 82–113). Oxford, UK: Blackwell.

Wilson, E. (2008). *Against happiness: In praise of melancholy.* New York, NY: Farrar, Straus and Giroux.

Yost, J. H., & Weary, G. (1996). Depression and the correspondent inference bias: Evidence for more effortful cognitive processing. *Personality and Social Psychology Bulletin, 22*, 192–200.

Young, K. (Ed.). (2010). *The art of losing: Poems of grief and healing.* New York, NY: Bloomsbury.

Zahavi, A., & Zahavi, A. (1997). *The handicap principle: A missing piece of Darwin's puzzle.* Oxford, UK: Oxford University Press.

Zeifman, D. M. (2001). An ethological analysis of human infant crying: Answering Tinbergen's four questions. *Developmental Psychobiology, 39*, 265–285.

Chapter 6
Boredom: What Is It Good For?

James Danckert, Jhotisha Mugon, Andriy Struk, and John Eastwood

Abstract Boredom is an ubiquitous and consequential human emotion. This chapter argues that it functions as a self-regulatory signal indicating that our cognitive resources are not engaged. It provides a definition of state boredom before developing the broad notion that trait boredom represents a chronic disposition toward maladaptively responding to the boredom signal (i.e., state boredom). The chapter reviews the nascent research employing functional neuroimaging to understand boredom and casts it as being mired in the "here and now" with no clear avenues for escape. Next, it outlines a specific hypothesis that trait boredom arises in circumstances of regulatory non-fit – when our preferred mode of goal pursuit does not match our current behavior. Finally, the chapter explores the notion that state boredom is not intrinsically good or bad. The signal itself does not evaluate what we are doing in any obvious way but merely indicates that change is needed.

> The boredom of God on the seventh day of creation would be a subject for a great poet.
>
> – Friedrich Nietzsche (1996)

Why would God be bored after having created the universe and everything in it? Tired, sure, but bored? What Nietzsche's quote suggests is that inherent in the act of completing one task is the need to figure out the answer to the obvious question your success provokes – what next? And if what you've just completed is as monumental as having created the universe, perhaps you would be faced with the daunting possibility that there are no goals left worth pursuing. Hence, God gets bored! Although obviously just a touch facetious, the conundrum highlights some key aspects of the emotional, cognitive, and motivational components of boredom (Eastwood, Frischen, Fenske, & Smilek, 2012). As an emotion, boredom signals that we are

J. Danckert (✉) · J. Mugon · A. Struk
Department of Psychology, University of Waterloo, Waterloo, ON, Canada
e-mail: jdancker@uwaterloo.ca

J. Eastwood
Department of Psychology, York University, Toronto, ON, Canada

© Springer International Publishing AG, part of Springer Nature 2018   93
H. C. Lench (ed.), *The Function of Emotions*,
https://doi.org/10.1007/978-3-319-77619-4_6

dissatisfied with whatever it is we are currently doing or whatever lies in front of us as options for engagement. We are not simply disengaged – we are dissatisfied and feel that dissatisfaction as negative affect. As a drive state, boredom is crucial for what could be thought of as the "push" to engage in something different (Bench & Lench, 2013; Elpidorou, 2014). While it is born of dissatisfaction, is clearly uncomfortable, and as such, undesirable, the function of boredom is nevertheless adaptive. Successfully responding to the boredom signal is important for effective control of goal-directed behaviors.

What Is Boredom?

The authors have argued elsewhere that boredom is the aversive feeling associated with being cognitively unengaged (Eastwood et al., 2012; Fahlman, Mercer-Lynn, Flora, & Eastwood, 2013). Selectively attending to and processing internal or external stimuli are adaptive. Our survival would be short-lived if we were unable to engage our cognitive abilities in the service of achieving our goals or responding adroitly to environmental demands. Thus, it is reasonable to assume that we have been shaped by evolutionary forces to experience the aversive state of boredom when our cognitive resources are not being optimally utilized. To be clear, being cognitively engaged is not the same as exerting mental effort. In fact, we can "relax" and let our mind drift without any intention to engage with particular stimuli or events, with no concomitant exertion of mental effort and still be cognitively engaged (e.g., perhaps in unintentional mind-wandering or even fantasizing – "What would I do if I won the lottery?", e.g., Seli, Risko, Smilek, & Schacter, 2016). Flow is another example of effortless cognitive engagement (Csikszentmihalyi, 1990). Where mental effort indicates what was required to *become* engaged, boredom indicates that our cognitive abilities *are not engaged*. Nevertheless, this cognitive account of boredom is not complete. Boredom also represents a specific motivational bind. Namely, boredom is the aversive feeling associated with wanting to be cognitively engaged (because it is aversive when we are not) but not being able to find anything in that moment with which to become engaged. When bored, we are restless, agitated, not merely resigned to our fate, but aggressively dissatisfied by it (Danckert, 2013). Disengagement from one's surroundings without that concomitant feeling of dissatisfaction is simply not boredom but is more akin to apathy (Goldberg, Eastwood, LaGuardia, & Danckert, 2011). While boredom and apathy share some things in common, they are clearly distinct cognitive-affective experiences (Goldberg et al., 2011; van Tilburg & Igou, 2011). Unlike apathy, a clear functional account for boredom presents itself – boredom acts as the impetus to find something to do that is more engaging (Bench & Lench, 2013; Elpidorou, 2014). Boredom has also been consistently associated with depression, with each construct sharing a strong negative valence (Farmer & Sundberg, 1986; Goldberg et al., 2011). However, unlike boredom, depression is characterized by unremitting sadness and a difficulty experiencing pleasure (American Psychiatric Association, 2013). The depressed person's interest in doing things is dulled, whereas a distinguishing feature of boredom is the *drive* to find something engaging. In short, then, boredom can best be thought of as a failure to satisfy a desire to be engaged with the world – "a desire for desires" (Tolstoy, 1899). That is, when bored we cannot find anything that we want to do in our current surroundings, but we desperately want to want to do something. In other words, we may not know *what* it is we want to do (or may not feel that the available options are likely to satisfy), but we most definitely know that we want *something* to do.

This description of boredom has it tightly coupled with the pursuit of goals. In the first instance, boredom would not arise without the desire to have one's mental faculties engaged in the pursuit of some goal. And in the second instance, as hinted at by Nietzsche (and more directly argued by Schopenhauer, 1995), boredom may be most prevalent in the *transition between* goals. The argument below posits that boredom represents a kind of self-regulatory failure in which the bored individual knows they want something to engage with but fails to see a viable avenue for goal pursuit that would satisfy that desire. Boredom becomes problematic only when an individual adopts maladaptive behaviors in their attempt to find something satisfying. That is, boredom merely goads us into seeking out satisfying activity; how we respond to that prompt determines whether it is a positive or negative force in our lives. Many people remark to the authors, upon hearing about research on boredom, that they are "never bored." This is unlikely, and what they are really expressing is the fact that, in general, they respond adaptively to the boredom signal.

An analogy to pain should clarify the point: the function of pain is not to *cause* us to feel hurt. The sensation of hitting one's thumb with a hammer certainly hurts and is something we would rather avoid, but that subjective experience of pain does little to describe its *function*. Pain, like boredom, is a signal to the organism that a behavioral response is required. Whether that is an automatic reaction (e.g., drop the hammer and suck your thumb) or a more deliberate response (e.g., get an ice pack), pain signifies the need to act (Inzlicht & Legault, 2014). This functional account of pain is not new. Pain has long been seen as an experience that interrupts our current focus of attention and motivates action, on the one hand to escape the painful experience and on the other to restore the goals we had been pursuing before the pain began (Eccleston & Crombez, 1999). By analogy, this chapter suggests that boredom operates as a self-regulatory signal for the control of behavior. Like pain this is a twofold process: first to escape the sensation of boredom and second to articulate and pursue a goal that would successfully engage our mental faculties. Those who claim never to be bored likely act in ways that address the needs signaled by the onset of boredom. For those who claim to suffer from boredom, the experience is negative precisely because of the failure to *adaptively* heed the signal.

Casting boredom as a self-regulatory signal suggests it is a singular construct, which may appear in different guises depending on our responses to it. This is far from uncontroversial, with many authors suggesting that there are in fact many types of boredom (Goetz et al., 2014; Nett, Goetz, & Hall, 2011). One of the earliest descriptions of boredom comes from a psychoanalytic case study in the 1950s (Greenson, 1953), in which the author proposed a distinction between agitated and apathetic boredom – states his patient claimed to experience at different times. Greenson's account represents the first attempt to carve boredom at some imagined joints. Indeed, the scale most commonly used to measure trait boredom – the boredom proneness scale (BPS; Farmer & Sundberg, 1986) – led researchers (including ourselves) to propose at least two distinct factors underlying boredom proneness: the need for either internal or external stimulation (Malkovsky, Merrifield, Goldberg, & Danckert, 2012; Merrifield & Danckert, 2014; Struk, Scholer, & Danckert, 2016; Vodanovich, 2003a). Although the authors and many others have published work implying the existence of distinct types of boredom proneness in the past (as many as five subtypes in academic settings; Goetz et al., 2014), the authors no longer see a meaningful way to carve boredom into separate subtypes for a number of reasons. With respect to the distinction Greenson made, boredom is an agitated state and what he called apathetic boredom is simply apathy (Goldberg et al., 2011). One key component in the present definition of boredom is that the individual is motivated to engage, a factor that is precluded by the term apathy. With respect to the dichotomy of the need for either external or internal stimulation in trait boredom, evidence has shown that this is likely an artifact of the scale used (Struk, Carriere, Cheyne, & Danckert, 2017). Not only has that two-factor structure been difficult to replicate (Melton & Schulenberg, 2009), it disappears entirely when reverse-worded items are reworded and items with poor discriminatory value are omitted (Struk et al., 2017). This shorter version of the scale is now clearly a one-factor measure, suggesting that trait boredom is a unitary construct characterized by the motivation to engage in something satisfying.

The Physiology of Boredom

Greenson's initial distinction between agitated and apathetic boredom raises another controversy in the literature – should boredom be considered a high or low arousal state? At first blush, the present definition of boredom as an aggressively dissatisfying experience leans toward the high arousal camp. But is it that simple? Using self-report measures, Van Tilburg and colleagues (2011, 2013) consistently find that boredom is reported to be a low arousal experience. This may reflect a hindsight bias, such that when evaluated in retrospect, we associate boredom with doing nothing and so remember it as being under-stimulating and under-arousing. In constrast, "in-the-moment" boredom, characterized as the desire to engage in something meaningful, would be highly arousing. This highlights a key challenge for boredom research (and perhaps for emotion researchers more broadly). Boredom is a dynamic experience that changes over time. High arousal states associated with the desire to engage may eventually give way to a kind of discouragement about the prospect of becoming engaged – something that would likely be appraised as a low arousal state (Eastwood et al., 2012; Fahlman et al., 2013).

Beyond self-report measures, several authors have examined the physiological signature of state boredom using metrics such as heart rate and skin conductance levels (Merrifield & Danckert, 2014; Pattyn, Neyt, Henderickx, & Soetens, 2008). Here too, results are mixed. Some have suggested that boredom is consistently associated with a state of low arousal attributed to situations that offer inadequate stimulation (Barmack, 1939; Geiwitz, 1966; Mikulas & Vodanovich, 1993; Pattyn et al., 2008; Russell, 1980; Vogel-Walcutt, Fiorella, Carper, & Schatz, 2012). Barmack (1939) even suggests that inadequate stimulation associated with boredom results in a physiological state that approaches that of sleep. In contrast, others suggest that boredom is best characterized as an agitated or restless state associated with higher physiological arousal (Berlyne, 1960; Jang, Park, Park, Kim, & Sohn, 2015; London, Schubert, & Washburn, 1972; Lundberg, Melin, Evans, & Holmberg, 1993; Merrifield & Danckert, 2014; Ohsuga, Shimono, & Genno, 2001). A recent study induced boredom via a video mood induction (the video showed two men hanging laundry) and measured skin conductance levels (SCL), heart rate (HR), and cortisol levels (Merrifield & Danckert, 2014). Compared to an induction of sadness, boredom was associated with a pattern known as *directional fractionation* (Lacey, 1959; Lacey & Lacey, 1970). Directional fractionation refers to changes in SCL and HR related to internal and external demands for attention. When attention is focused externally, both HR and SCL decrease (Lacey, 1959; Lacey & Lacey, 1970). Indeed, a study from the late 1970s showed, somewhat counterintuitively, that HR *decelerated* when people read sexually explicit material (Fehr & Schulman, 1978). In contrast, HR increases and SCL decreases when attention wanes. The recent study showed precisely this pattern when people were induced into a state of boredom – HR increased and SCL decreased indicative of a failure to engage attention on the video mood induction (Merrifield & Danckert, 2014). In addition, cortisol levels rose suggesting the experience of boredom was stressful. Jang et al. (2015) partially replicated these results showing decreased SCL when people were bored. In their study boredom was compared to pain and surprise inductions, so it is perhaps not surprising that HR was lowest in the boredom condition.

It is plausible that the resolution to this debate would be to suggest that the experience of boredom includes *both* high and low arousal states (Eastwood et al., 2012; Fahlman et al., 2013). In a recent study, people read different passages of text intended to be either boring (an excerpt from a text on the properties of soil) or interesting (an excerpt from a Harry Potter novel) while their blink rates were measured along with periodic subjective reports of boredom, restlessness, mind-wandering, and sleepiness (Danckert et al., under consideration). Highly boredom-prone people had higher blink rates indicative of poor sustained attention (Smilek, Carriere, & Cheyne, 2010). Furthermore, boredom and mind-wandering were highest, as expected, when reading about the joys of soil. Intriguingly for the arousal debate, self-reports of *both* restlessness *and* sleepiness rose sharply when reading the boring story – particularly when this was the second story read by participants (Danckert et al., under consideration). Asking people how sleepy they felt was intended as an indirect measure of arousal. As Barmack (1939) suggested, the low arousal bored state may approximate sleep in a physiological sense. But at the same time, people were reporting being under-aroused; they were also reporting increasing levels of restlessness. Clearly, more work is needed to explore the dynamics of state boredom. It may be the case that the physiological changes associated with boredom lead to distinct subjective evaluations as captured by this definition of boredom from Vogel-Walcutt et al. (2012):

> State boredom occurs when an individual experiences *both* the (objective) neurological state of low arousal *and* the (subjective) psychological state of dissatisfaction, frustration, or disinterest …. (p. 104; emphasis added).

Clearly, a sense of dissatisfaction and frustration represent *high* arousal negative affective evaluations (Russell, 1980). In addition, differences in the subjective experience of boredom-related arousal might follow distinct stages of goal pursuit: that is, the subjective experience of arousal likely depends on the specific stage of goal pursuit/engagement we are currently experiencing. For example, consider trying to complete a task we do not want to do – like finishing our taxes. This task may fail to hold our attention and engage our cognitive abilities – thus, we experience boredom. Initially, when unengaged we may be experiencing low arousal as the task of doing taxes is not very stimulating. If we decide to redouble our efforts and push through to completion, this clearly requires an increase in arousal. It is difficult to maintain attention when under-aroused. We may strategically try to upregulate our arousal by fidgeting, tapping our pencil, or drinking a third coffee for the night. If we still fail to become cognitively engaged by our taxes, we will now likely be experiencing a higher level of arousal, a restless, irritable agitation. The point here is that we may be equally unable to focus our attention and engage our cognitive abilities with the task during both phases (i.e., equally bored), but our arousal levels would differ during the early and late phases.

One possible key to this arousal conundrum relates to one's sense of autonomy or control – more specifically, arousal levels may track the *prospect* of attaining successful engagement of our cognitive faculties (Struk, Scholer, & Danckert, 2015). That is, as our taxes example above highlights, when we first realize that what we are doing has not engaged our cognitive abilities sufficiently, we are likely experiencing lowered levels of arousal. That realization, the initial phase of the boredom signal, may rapidly lead to increasing levels of arousal as we attempt to engage our cognitive resources with the boring situation (or, if possible, engage in a novel situation). In other words, as we seek out new activities or find our continued attempts to engage with the current activity failing, arousal levels will increase. Should a failure to engage persist, frustration and high arousal boredom will give way to discouragement with an eventual return to lower levels of arousal as we find ourselves mired in boredom, unable to successfully respond to the need for engagement. A recent study explored this possibility by having people play the children's game of "rock, paper, scissors" against a computer opponent (Struk et al., 2015). The subjective sense of control was manipulated in the task by having one group win 100% of the time regardless of their plays and another group lose 100% of the time. Those who won all the time reported the highest levels of boredom – the task was facile, monotonous, and hence, boring. For those who lost all the time, initial subjective reports were indicative of increased arousal as they tried in vain to "figure out" their opponent's strategy. This high arousal soon dissipated as failure continued. In a follow-up study, two groups played against an opponent that adopted a uniform play strategy (i.e., choosing each option equally often; Struk et al., 2015). One group were told of this circumstance and therefore understood that there was no way for them to win more than one third of the time. A second group was erroneously told that their opponent was playing an exploitable strategy that they had to "figure out" in order to win more often. This latter group reported lower levels of boredom suggesting that the mere prospect of gaining control over a circumstance was enough to ward off boredom. What this work highlights is that subjective feelings of boredom and the associated judgements of arousal likely depend to some extent on our belief in the possibility of attaining successful engagement.

This Is Your Brain on Boredom

Functional neuroimaging work has only recently examined the neural circuits active when we are bored (Dal Mas & Wittmann, 2017; Danckert & Isacescu, 2017; Danckert & Merrifield, in press; Ulrich, Keller, & Grön, 2016; Ulrich, Keller, Hoenig, Waller, & Grön, 2014). Two networks are critical to the understanding of boredom: the default mode network (DMN; Andrews-Hanna, 2012; Greicius, Krasnow, Reiss, & Menon, 2003; Mason et al., 2007; Weissman, Roberts, Visscher, & Woldorff, 2006) and the salience network (SN; Menon & Uddin, 2010). Originally reported in the early 2000s, the DMN is a collection of brain regions including the posterior cingulate, precuneus, and medial prefrontal cortex that has been associated with "off-task" thinking – anything from internally focused thoughts (i.e., thinking of the past, imagining the future) to mind-wandering (Christoff, Gordon, Smallwood, Smith, & Schooler, 2009; Fox, Spreng, Ellamil, Andrews-Hanna, & Christoff, 2015; Mason et al., 2007; Weissman et al., 2006). The DMN is typically active when there are few external demands on attention and is commonly associated with concomitant decreases in activation of frontal cortical regions comprising the central executive network (CEN; Andrews-Hanna, 2012; Buckner, Andrews-Hanna, & Schacter, 2008). The second network critical to understanding boredom is the so-called *salience network* (SN) that consists primarily of the insular cortex and its connections with the CEN. The SN is important for detecting behaviorally relevant events in the environment ultimately to engage the CEN when needed. In a sense then, the SN switches between the DMN and the CEN in response to goal-relevant information (Menon & Uddin, 2010; Sidlauskaite et al., 2014; Uddin, 2015).

Ulrich et al. (2014) contrasted the experience of boredom with that of flow – a state of optimal engagement in which attention is so focused on the task at hand that everything else fades to the background (Csikszentmihalyi, 1990; Csikszentmihalyi & Csikszentmihalyi, 1992). They had participants complete a series of mathematical sums that varied in difficulty level from too easy (which they presumed led to boredom, much like the 100% win rate in rock, paper, scissors), too hard (which they referred to as a cognitive overload condition), or "just right" (i.e., problems titrated to an individual's ability, presumably leading to flow). They observed increased CEN activity and decreased DMN activity when people were in a state of flow – doing math problems experienced to be at a "Goldilocks" level of difficulty. This condition also led to increased activity in the insula indicative of engagement with the task at hand. When doing the easy math sums, participants were bored and demonstrated increased activity in the DMN with concomitant decreases in CEN activity.

Rather than exploring boredom as a consequence of a primary task as Ulrich et al. (2014, 2016) have done, a recent study used the mood induction film of two men hanging laundry to directly induce boredom (Danckert & Isacescu, 2017; Danckert & Merrifield, in press). Activity while watching this mind-numbingly dull film was contrasted with a more traditional resting state scan in which people are instructed to simply relax for 8 min with nothing but a fixation cross to look at (Buckner et al., 2008). Importantly, differences in these two scans will reflect differences between being bored and simply having nothing to do. As with the Ulrich study, boredom was associated with upregulation of the DMN. Much the same network was also observed when people were simply at rest. Where the two conditions differed was with respect to insula activity. When bored, the insular cortex was anticorrelated with the DMN. That is, as the DMN was upregulated, the insula was downregulated. No such relationship was evident in the rest condition, a result recently replicated (Danckert & Isacescu, 2017; Danckert & Merrifield, in press). The key distinction between the rest and boredom mood induction conditions is the presence or absence of something to at least try to engage with. During rest there was little to nothing in the external environment to engage with. In this case, DMN upregulation may reflect mind-wandering (e.g., Christoff et al., 2009; Mason et al., 2007). The biggest task in this scanning session is to avoid falling asleep! The boredom video is a different beast altogether – something is constantly happening on screen (although one might be loathe to call it action, things are happening). Anticorrelated activity in the insula may reflect continued failed attempts to engage with what is a monotonous, uninteresting series of events. There is really only so much one can do to engage with a video of two men hanging laundry! Successful engagement would presumably involve the SN signaling the CEN that something relevant and of interest is present in the world. At the same time, attending to the movie would be expected to lead to downregulation of the DMN, which was clearly not the case. One prominent theory regarding the anterior insular suggests that it represents our conscious, embodied experience of the here and now (Craig, 2009). We have claimed that state boredom is adaptive, functioning as a signal telling us that we are currently underutilizing our cognitive abilities. But some situational factors make it impossible to act on that adaptive signal, and thus the feeling of boredom becomes protracted and we feel stuck. The inescapable environs of an fMRI experiment in which participants were made to watch two men hang laundry are one such circumstance that both prompt the boredom signal and prevent any action to respond adaptively to it. They cannot, for example, fully give themselves over to mind-wandering because they are supposed to be watching the film. Boredom signaled the need to engage in something else, but the circumstance prevents it.

Finally, Dal Mas and Wittmann (2017) recently had people perform three different tasks – first, deciding whether a picture frame was blurry or not (the boredom condition); second, performing a somewhat challenging visual search task; and third, simply reporting their preference for visual images (i.e., "How much do you like this image?"). After doing these tasks, participants were asked how much they would be willing to pay for a music download. The logic was that, when bored, people ought to be more willing to pay higher amounts for music – a metric of how desperate they were to avoid boredom. Indeed, when people were bored, they were willing to pay more for music. Interestingly, activity in the insula was associated with just *how willing* people were to pay to avoid boredom – higher willingness to pay for music (which presumably eliminated boredom) was associated with increased activity in the insula (Dal Mas & Wittmann, 2017). On the one hand, then, *failures* to engage are reflected in downregulation of the insula (Danckert & Isacescu, 2017; Danckert & Merrifield, in press), while an increased *desire to be engaged* (by paying more to *avoid* boredom) is associated with upregulation of the insula (Dal Mas & Wittmann, 2017).

If the insular cortex is important for switching between the large-scale neural networks involved in off-task thinking on the one hand (i.e., the DMN) and goal-directed behavior on the other (i.e., the CEN), then boredom may represent a kind of interminable present. That is, activity in the insula may be a metric of the desire to engage, with inactivation reflecting the inability to extricate oneself from the current circumstance. Certainly, when bored, we often complain about being *stuck* in the moment. In this sense, boredom is a desire to engage that is at its most intense when that desire goes unfulfilled.

Self-Regulation and Boredom

Up to this point, the focus has been mostly on state boredom. Far more work has been conducted looking at boredom through the lens of an individual trait (see Eastwood et al., 2012 for review). This chapter has cast the function of *state* boredom as an adaptive self-regulatory signal pushing the individual to seek satisfaction and optimal utilization of cognitive resources. Despite voluminous research, the concept, definition, and measurement of *trait* boredom are underdeveloped (Struk et al., 2017; Vodanovich & Watt, 2016). The functional account of state boredom offers a precise and testable way of thinking about trait boredom. Namely, trait boredom arises from a chronic failure to respond successfully to the self-regulatory signal of state boredom. This approach links state and trait boredom in a coherent way and provides a parsimonious account for the myriad relations between state boredom and other negative affective states and outcomes (e.g., depression, anxiety, increased aggression, impulsivity, increased sensation seeking, and a susceptibility to addictive behaviors from problem gambling to drugs of abuse; Blaszczynski, McConaghy, & Frankova, 1990; Isacescu, Struk, & Danckert, 2016; Iso-Ahola & Crowley, 1991; Johnston & O'Malley, 1986; Mercer & Eastwood, 2010; Rupp &

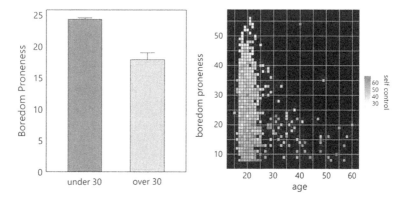

Fig. 6.1 The left panel shows boredom proneness scores for those under (orange) and over (yellow) 30 years of age. The right panel shows boredom as a function of both age and individual trait levels of self-control (Data adapted from Isacescu et al. (2016)

Vodanovich, 1997; Sommers & Vodanovich, 2000; Vodanovich, Verner, & Gilbride, 1991; Watt & Vodanovich, 1992; but see Mercer-Lynn, Flora, Fahlman, & Eastwood, 2011, for discussion of the influence of which boredom measures are used in determining the nature and direction of these associations). These well-replicated associations appear to reveal that trait boredom is a failure of self-regulation. Put another way, a failure to appropriately regulate one's own thoughts, feelings, and actions may be at the heart of each of these distinct relationships. If the state of boredom represents a signal to act (do something more engaging than your current activity), then the trait, more than simply reflective of increased frequency and intensity, reflects maladaptive responses – borne of poor self-regulatory control – to the boredom signal.

The authors have shown that those who have a higher propensity to experience boredom also report lower levels of self-control (Isacescu et al., 2016; Struk et al., 2016), which fits well with the findings touched on above. This casts lower levels of self-control as the cause of maladaptive responses to the boredom signal (not necessarily the cause of boredom itself). Depending on the age range tested, age has been shown to be a *negative* predictor of boredom proneness (Essed et al., 2006; Hill, 1975; Isacescu et al., 2016; Vodanovich & Kass, 1990; although see Spaeth, Weichold, & Silbereisen, 2015, showing *increases* in boredom with age during early adolescence). As we approach our late teens and early 20s, we also attain higher levels of self-control which may in turn reduce the susceptibility to experiencing protracted boredom (Fig. 6.1; Isacescu et al., 2016). This narrow age range encompasses a period of neurodevelopment in which the frontal cortices, that part of the brain critically important for effective self-control and self-regulation, reach full maturity (Anderson, Anderson, Northam, Jacobs, & Catroppa, 2001; Gogtay et al., 2004; Keating, 2012; Poletti, 2009).

Further evidence supporting a link between self-control, frontal maturation, and trait boredom comes from work with patients who have suffered traumatic brain injuries (TBI; e.g., Seel & Kreutzer, 2003). That is, TBI, commonly arising from acceleration-deceleration injuries (e.g., concussions, car crashes), prominently involves the orbitofrontal cortex – part of the brain involved in reward processing (Elliott, Newman, Longe, & Deakin, 2003; Gottfried, O'Doherty, & Dolan, 2003; O'Doherty, Kringelbach, Rolls, Hornak, & Andrews, 2001). The sine qua non of TBI is the dysexecutive syndrome in which patients exhibit increased impulsivity, sensation seeking, and poor inhibitory control – many of the same issues prevalent in those high in boredom proneness (Dockree et al., 2004, 2006; Joireman, Anderson, & Strathman, 2003; Kass & Vodanovich, 1990; Mercer & Eastwood, 2010; O'Keeffe, Dockree, Moloney, Carton, & Robertson, 2007). Studies showed recently that boredom proneness was indeed elevated in patients who had suffered moderate to severe TBI (Isacescu & Danckert, 2017; see Kenah et al., in press for a recent review).

Self-control is a rather vague term encompassing the regulation of thoughts, behaviors, and emotions (Baumeister & Vohs, 2003; Struk et al., 2016; Tangney, Baumeister, & Boone, 2004). Self-regulation in the pursuit of goals has been explored in more nuanced ways that examine an individual's preferred mode of goal pursuit (Kruglanski et al., 2000). In that context, boredom proneness may be related to two distinct regulatory modes – locomotion and assessment (Kruglanski et al., 2000; Mugon, Struk, & Danckert, under consideration; Struk et al., 2015). Locomotion refers to individuals who prefer to get on with things moving rapidly from one action state to another – in other words, preferring to "just do it." In contrast, the assessment regulatory mode represents a preference for carefully considering options before moving from one goal to another – in other words, preferring to "do the right thing" (Kruglanski et al., 2000). One could consider these distinctions in terms of calculations of risk. A person who adopts the assessment mode (i.e., an assessor) values minimizing the "risk" of making the wrong behavioral choice, whereas a person adopting the locomotion mode (i.e., a locomotor) has a higher risk tolerance for making the wrong choice and instead values efficiently achieving the goal at hand. Consider the following anecdote: You're on a long road trip with your family and need to stop over in a small town for lunch before continuing to drive to your destination. While the town is small, there are a number of dining options. You see a sign for "Mom and Pop's Diner" – the first restaurant on the right as you come into town – and pull over. Your spouse meanwhile is still busy with a smartphone evaluating the myriad options for dining in the small hamlet of *where-the-hell-are-we* and is decidedly unimpressed by Mom and Pop's. You, in this scenario, are a locomotor, preferring to just get things done and move on toward the ultimate goal of finishing the road trip (and the next goal and the next). Your spouse is an assessor and is not willing to risk a less than average meal; instead, your spouse carefully evaluates the available options to ensure that does not happen. While this description of our locomotor may sound like "satisficing" (e.g., Schwartz et al., 2002), the emphasis here is less on the locomotor's decision to choose the first restaurant he sees and more on the fact that she/he wants to get quickly to the end goal – the final trip destination. As Kruglanski and colleagues put it, getting on with things in a "straightforward and direct manner, without undue distractions or delays"

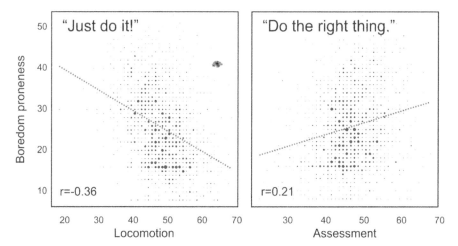

Fig. 6.2 Correlations between boredom proneness (as measured by the shortened version of the BPS; Struk et al., 2015) and locomotion (left) and assessment (right) regulatory modes (n = 1,727, collected in the winter term of 2016; see also Struk et al., 2015 for regression analyses of similar data and Mugon et al., under consideration for a full discussion of multiple data sets). Larger data points reflect the fact that multiple individuals fall at those data points

(Kruglanski et al., 2000, p. 794). Thus, the locomotor is characterized by a preference for action. Assessors should not be construed as merely maximizers – the assessor is not characterized by attempts to maximize value or utility. Rather, the assessor is characterized by a preference for deliberation so as to do the right thing and avoid doing the wrong thing – eating at a substandard restaurant in the example (Kruglanski et al., 2000). Clearly, avoiding the wrong choice (a motivating consideration for the assessor) is different than maximizing value or reward.

In large samples of undergraduate students (ranging from 927 to 2,660) over multiple terms (n = 7), there are consistent relationships between trait boredom, as measured by the boredom proneness scale, and these regulatory modes (Mugon et al., in press). For locomotion the correlation is consistently negative (ranging from −0.27 to −0.39) suggesting that engaging in an action of some kind acts as a prophylactic against boredom (Fig. 6.2). In contrast, there is a modest but highly consistent positive correlation between boredom proneness and the assessment regulatory focus (ranging from 0.21 to 0.28; Fig. 6.2).

This raises an intriguing possibility: those most prone to experiencing boredom may be stuck in a decision phase, trying (but failing) to decide on the best possible outlet for their desire to engage. This chapter has cast boredom as a failure to be effectively engaged by the world. Although speculative at this stage, one potential antecedent of this failure is a fruitless rumination on the potential options for engagement. That is, those who adopt a locomotion mode of goal pursuit have little trouble deciding what to do next and simply get on with it. Those with an assessment mode of goal pursuit may be more prone to boredom for many reasons: first, interminable evaluation of potential options for engagement leads to a kind of "failure to launch" into an activity. Second, all options for engagement may be tarred with the same gray brush – that is, they fail to see *any one action* as more valuable than another. Third, highly boredom-prone individuals may have an elevated fear of failure impeding their ability to get started on a task. Finally, willingness to commit to a goal may be lower in the highly boredom prone. This last hypothesis is striking for its counterintuitive nature – surely an agitated individual desperate for engagement would do anything to achieve that? The reduced willingness to commit makes some sense if one considers the common parental anecdote of the bored child imploring them for a remedy. As any parent knows, despite the child demanding that the parent solve their ennui for them, all suggestions to redress their boredom are immediately discounted as though none are appealing enough or the effort to achieve them is deemed not worth it. While research is clearly needed to more directly address these hypotheses, the subjective sense that each consequence of fruitless rumination outlined above represents an impediment to effective engagement, and hence elevated boredom proneness, is appealing.

The notion that boredom proneness may be underpinned by a ruminative cognitive style may also shed light on the link between boredom and depression (Farmer & Sundberg, 1986; Goldberg et al., 2011; Vodanovich, 2003a). Excessive rumination is also a key component of the syndrome of depression (Aldao, Nolen-Hoeksema, & Schweizer, 2010; Mor & Winquist, 2002; Nolen-Hoeksema, Wisco, & Lyubomirsky, 2008). Whereas for depression those ruminations tend to be self-focused and negative in an evaluative sense, for boredom proneness, the ruminations are outwardly focused – the world is not enough. Although this chapter has reviewed evidence that boredom is distinct from depression, the two still share a large amount of variance (Goldberg et al., 2011). The focus of ruminations may represent one factor that helps to differentiate the two affective experiences. Interestingly, a study exploring the effect of citalopram on depression in cancer patients found that patients who reported high levels of both boredom and depression showed early improvements in symptoms of depression, but no improvements in boredom until much later (Theobold, Kirsh, Holtsclaw, Donaghy, & Passik, 2003). It may be the case that repeated failures to engage with the world, a key determinant of boredom, precede the sense of helplessness that is characteristic of depression and turns ruminations inward. This casts boredom as a risk factor for depression. Clearly, there is a complex relationship at play that warrants further exploration.

Boredom proneness may not only be related to an assessment regulatory mode orientation, it may also be related to what is referred to as regulatory fit (Avnet & Higgins, 2003; Higgins, 2005). Regulatory fit refers to the match, or non-match, between the strategic means used to achieve a goal and a person's regulatory mode orientation. That is, although an individual could be said to have a *preferred* regulatory mode (i.e., beliefs and values that represent a locomotion or assessment orientation), it is possible to use each regulatory mode in the moment to achieve particular goals. Indeed, different situations may be more optimally suited toward one regulatory mode or another. Returning to the travelling family, consider the driver who wants to stop at the first greasy spoon he/she sees to keep acting and moving efficiently to the final goal. If her/his regulatory mode orientation is indeed locomotion, there is no conflict if the family stops at "Mom and Pop's Diner" to eat – she/he wants to get on with things and acts accordingly. The assessor on their smartphone, however, who would normally carefully deliberate before acting, would experience some level of conflict between the assessment regulatory mode orientation and the choice imposed by the locomotor to eat at the first available restaurant. Highly boredom-prone individuals may subjectively report that they prefer to adopt an assessment mode of goal pursuit (Fig. 6.2) but may chronically behave at odds with this stated preference. That is, regulatory non-fit conflicts may arise more commonly in the highly boredom prone.

The authors have preliminary evidence to support this notion of regulatory non-fit as a potential component driving increased boredom proneness. For a larger study, examining the genetic correlates of regulatory mode and boredom proneness, people performed a virtual foraging task (Struk, Mugon, Scholer, Sokolowski, & Danckert, in preparation; Fig. 6.3). Using a touch screen, people navigated through a virtual environment of berries (red circles of varying sizes distributed evenly on a green "grasslike" background). They were instructed to pick, simply by tapping the screen, as many "berries" as they could within a 5-min time window (a counter indicating how many berries they had collected and a clock counting down the time were present in the upper right corner). The study examined associations between preferred regulatory mode and distinct behaviors in our foraging environment. To do so, a composite variable was created to capture preferences for exploring the environment vs. exploiting the "resources" of the berry patch: the former was captured by the number of moves an individual made and the latter by the number of berries picked (a score of zero suggests no bias for either exploration or exploitation). One might assume that a locomotor would maximize berry picking by moving around the environment quickly gathering the immediately and easily accessible berries, but moving on from a patch of berries before all were picked (i.e., exploring the environment). In contrast, an assessor might be expected to maximize berry picking by making sure to collect *all* the berries in a patch before moving on to a new patch (i.e., exploiting the environment). Regulatory non-fit would be evident in an individual espousing a preference for the assessment regulatory mode while exhibiting an action preference for movement over berry picking (and vice versa). Indeed, assessors tended to pick more berries, and locomotors tended to move on before all berries were picked. Interestingly, individuals reporting a preference for the assessment regulatory mode who nevertheless engaged in exploration (i.e., moving on from a patch of berries before all were picked) were most prone to boredom (Fig. 6.3).

The assessor typically behaves in a manner that minimizes the "risk" of leaving berries behind. The locomotor has higher risk tolerance and typically wants to simply move on to a new patch of berries that might have greater riches (i.e., more berries). However, individuals who report preferring an assessment regulatory mode but actually engage in behaviors normally adopted by locomotors are essentially at odds with themselves. This disconnect between stated values and actual behavior may reflect dysfunctional or disorganized self-regulation and thus be especially related to the tendency to experience boredom (Fig. 6.3).

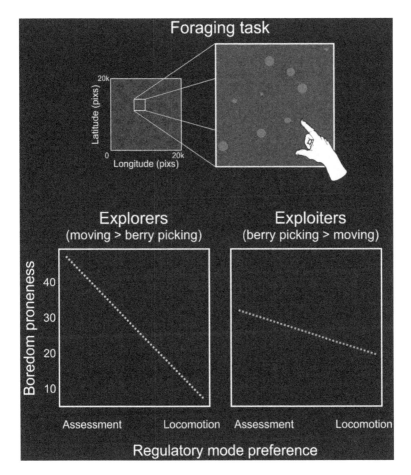

Fig. 6.3 Upper panel is a schematic of the foraging task. Participants began in the center of a touch screen. The environment spanned 20,000 × 20,000 pixels, and to move around it, they simply swiped their finger across the touch screen. Berries, which differed in size, were "picked" by tapping the screen and in this case were uniformly distributed throughout the environment. Lower panel shows boredom proneness as a function of regulatory mode preference and behavior on a composite measure of foraging which indicates preference for either moving (explorers – left panel) or berry picking (exploiters – right panel). Regulatory non-fit occurs when assessors exhibit a bias for exploring (and vice versa). Those with a preference for an assessment regulatory mode were generally higher in boredom proneness but were highest if they exhibited nonregulatory fit, that is, adopting an explorer strategy (left panel; Struk et al., in preparation)

What Causes Boredom?

Many situational causes for boredom spring easily to mind: from the drudgery of particular topics of conversation (e.g., "Politics bores me!") to the absurdity of minimally changing activities/events (e.g., "It was like watching paint dry/grass grow."). While the list of potential environmental causes for boredom may seem endless, two factors have been prominently touted as critical to the experience – monotony (i.e., nothing to do) and constraint (i.e., having to do something we do not want to do; although see Daschmann, Goetz, & Stupnisky, 2011, for an eight-factor account of the causes of boredom within an educational setting; Thackray, 1981; Tze, Klassen, & Daniels, 2014; van Tilburg & Igou, 2011). That is, circumstances that are monotonous or are in some sense inescapable cause us to feel bored. But are these factors sufficient and direct causes of boredom? Is it possible to establish objective situational factors that reliably cause boredom? This chapter argues that the answer is no.

Boredom is the disagreeable feeling that arises when our mental capacities are not being optimally utilized – when our mind is unengaged. Like an idling car, our engine is revved up and we are itching to go, but we can't. We do not have anything we want to do, but we want to have *something we want* to do. You might be thinking at this point, "Hold on a minute, that doesn't make sense. I know exactly what I want to do when I am stuck in a monotonous situation – and therefore bored out of my skull. I want to be at home reading a novel (or anything else that you *know* will engage you). Reading would engage and use my cognitive resources and, presto, I won't be bored anymore." Indeed, situational factors are important *indirect* determinants of boredom. Some situations force us to do something we do not want to do, and others offer up very few desirable options for things to do. The point, however, is that *given the reality of the situation in which we find ourselves*, there is nothing that we want to do. However, we would not be bored if we could just find some reason to commit ourselves to the task at hand. Moreover, we would not be bored if we were forced to do something that we already wanted to do anyway. Thus, situational factors like constraint and monotony powerfully increase the chances of boredom, but they are not, in and of themselves, sufficient. Our inability to *formulate an object of our desire for engagement* is itself the sufficient and direct cause of boredom. Hence, as Tolstoy said, boredom is the desire for desires.

Monotony is perhaps the most common situational factor thought to cause boredom. First discussed by human factors researchers in the early part of the twentieth century (e.g., Vernon, 1926; see also Smith, 1981; Thackray, Bailey, & Touchstone, 1977), monotony however is far from a straightforward causal factor of boredom. It is possible to avoid boredom during a monotonous task if some reason for doing the task (or some other parallel engagement in the midst of the task) can be found that engenders something of value to do in the situation. The dedicated philatelist who spends hours arranging stamps by country of origin, decade of issue, and quality could be said to be engaged in a fairly monotonous task. But most passionate devotees of this hobby would not describe the experience as even remotely boring. Csikszentmihalyi (1990) describes a factory worker with an incredibly monotonous task on an assembly line, coping by trying to beat his own "personal best" times in each hour of work. The task for the worker has not changed and on its own has little to no meaning. But imbued with a challenge the individual sees as worthwhile, it is no longer boring. The worker cannot change the task but can control the way in which he/she frames it.

Similarly, constraint or lack of autonomy is often thought to cause boredom (e.g., Fisher, 1993; Troutwine & O'Neal, 1981). However, it is easy to imagine being forced to do something that you want to do at the outset. In such circumstances, the fact of being forced to do the task would not be sufficient to cause boredom. Moreover, even if you do not initially want to do a task, if the task is imbued with some semblance of meaning, then boredom can be averted. For example, Sansone, Weir, Harpster, and Morgan (1992) found that a task was perceived as more engaging and hence less boring, if people believed that it had some inherent health benefits. This capacity to reframe a forced situation to have more meaning or to be more engaging is also prominent in the educational literature (see Mugon, Danckert, & Eastwood, in press). Those who can reappraise a circumstance or task to be meaningful in some way experience less boredom and attain higher levels of achievement (Daniels, Tze, & Goetz, 2015; Nett, Goetz, & Daniels, 2010; Nett et al., 2011). Such reappraisals are within the control of the individual – in other words, they are independent of the external constraint itself. Finally, sitting down to do your taxes is something we all have to do – the government dictates this activity relieving us of autonomous control. While most of us may not like the task for other reasons and may even say we are bored by it, the mere fact that we are compelled to do it by some external agent (i.e., the government) does not itself *make the task boring.*

The relation between meaningless situations and boredom is somewhat nuanced; but again it does not appear that meaningless activities necessarily *cause* boredom. There appears to be an asymmetrical relationship between meaninglessness and boredom. In sum, if a person is bored, then the activity will be seen as meaningless; but if the activity is meaningless, a person will not necessarily feel bored. Let us unpack that claim. If a person is bored, then they will undoubtedly say the situation they find themselves in is meaningless. This kind of lack of situational meaning is perhaps best cast as a *key part* of the experience of boredom rather than a cause. (This does not obviate the possibility that a more general sense that life itself is meaningless – something akin to nihilism – may operate as a cause of boredom.) The in-the-moment experience of boredom is in part constituted by the absence of subjective value and meaning. However, the converse does not follow. A person can find an activity meaningless but not feel bored while they engage in it. Consider, for example, coming home from a hard day's work and binge-watching the Kardashians on television. This could hardly be considered a meaningful activity to engage in, but it might hold our attention and occupy our mental faculties; and if so, we would not experience boredom.

To conclude, situational factors powerfully increase our chances of experiencing boredom. But they are not sufficient or direct causes of boredom. When situational factors do cause boredom, they do so indirectly by preventing us from being able to articulate and sustain an actionable desire. What is common to monotony, lack of meaning, and a loss of autonomy is the notion that each may reflect the calculation of opportunity costs (Kurzban, Duckworth, Kable, & Myers, 2013). That is, at any given moment we could choose to engage in numerous goals or activities. The need to choose one activity over all others necessarily involves some calculation of reward or value. Opportunity costs refer to the potential loss of reward/value from failing to pursue something different than our current task (Kurzban et al., 2013; see also Gomez-Ramirez & Costa, 2017, for a computational model of boredom that takes into account opportunity costs). The notion of opportunity costs is best highlighted by foraging behavior in animals. When foraging for food, the animal must balance the need to *exploit* current resources (e.g., berries in a bush) with the costs of failing to *explore* the environment for potentially better resources (e.g., a more full bush of berries around the corner; Charnov, 1976). The decision to move on to a new patch of berries reflects some calculation of diminishing rewards obtained from the current patch (Gallistel, 1990). By analogy, when a task becomes monotonous, this could be cast in the context of other potentially more varied avenues for engagement. An activity we deem meaningless, by definition, hints at other things we could be doing that would be more meaningful. Finally, when we feel we have diminished control over the outcome, the reward value of that task diminishes as we consider other things we could be doing that would afford higher levels of autonomy. In each instance, monotony, meaninglessness, and lack of control represent not causes of boredom but sources of opportunity costs signaled by the experience of boredom. In other words, opportunity costs are essentially the boredom signal, telling us to move on (Bench & Lench, 2013; Elpidorou, 2014). This is not to suggest that boredom directly *calculates what it is about our current activity* that is boring or, for that matter, evaluates the likelihood of other activities to satisfy our needs. Instead, boredom signals the fact that opportunity costs have risen above some threshold for engagement, pushing the organism to act. In other words, rather than asking specifically what situations or personal factors cause boredom, we should be asking what does boredom signal? One plausible answer is that boredom signals rising opportunity costs (Gomez-Ramirez & Costa, 2017; Kurzban et al., 2013).

Can Boredom Help?

The not so subtle reference to the Edwin Starr song with the chorus "War, huh, what is it good for? Absolutely nothing." in the title to this chapter might suggest that boredom is not good for much. On the contrary, this chapter argues that boredom is absolutely good for something. Boredom signals that our mental faculties are not engaged. Arguments about the desirability of "being engaged" hinge on the fact that conscious awareness is finite. We are only conscious of a small subset of possible stimuli at any given moment. Mentions of being "cognitively engaged" are referring to the processes needed to selectively engage with some stimuli or task and would further claim that such selective processing is essential to our survival. Persisting in a state of cognitive disengagement is, at best, a waste of time. Our time is better spent being cognitively engaged, and boredom will not let us rest comfortably in a state of being unengaged. Unfortunately, however, this does not mean that boredom is a reliable indicator that *what we are doing* in the moment is a waste of time or has no value. Nor does it necessarily mean that it is best to drop what we are doing and move on to something else. It might mean that we should "double down" and find a way to *become* engaged with what we are doing. The point here is that boredom is the feeling associated with the sense that we are not optimally utilizing our cognitive resources or realizing our goals. Like feelings of pain associated with tissue damage, boredom pushes us out of a state that is potentially harmful for our well-being. However, as mentioned above with respect to opportunity costs, the boredom signal does not arise from any kind of evaluation of the specific activity itself. Instead, it simply reflects the fact that we are not engaged with whatever that activity is. The current activity is not boring because it pales in comparison to some other potential activity. Boredom, simply, but very powerfully and helpfully, tells us that what we are currently doing is not engaging our cognitive resources *sufficiently*. We might want boredom to do more for us, but as a self-regulatory signal, it achieves the important goal of pushing the organism toward mental engagement without doing the hard work of specifying what that action might, or even ought to, be. In other words, boredom's job ends with the signaling of a problem.

The things boredom gets blamed for are obvious and do not need reiterating here. But the narrative will pause for a moment to examine one area where boredom gets too much credit – namely, as a creativity boosting force (Vodanovich, 2003b). There is certainly anecdotal evidence that some of the most creative people are spurred on by boredom. When Mike Bloomfield of The Paul Butterfield Blues Band, an eventual inductee into the Rock and Roll Hall of Fame, first heard Jimi Hendrix play he asked him after the show where he had been hiding. Hendrix replied "I been playin' the chitlin circuit and I got bored shitless. I didn't hear any guitar players doing anything new and I was bored out of my mind" (Tolinski & Di Perna, 2016, p. 218). Hendrix's assertion aside, actual demonstrations that state boredom leads to increased creativity are thin on the ground. There are only three studies that have directly examined whether being bored gets the creative juices flowing. Larson (1990) asked students to report their levels of boredom while working on an essay at four key points in time. After each boredom report, they handed in a draft of their work. Independent judges evaluated the originality, organization, and overall quality of the essays. The findings showed that higher levels of boredom were associated with lower quality essays. However, a big limitation of this study is that Larson (1990) did not experimentally make students feel more or less bored; thus, among other things, leaving open the possibility that the absence of creative ideas resulted in more boredom and not the other way around. Gasper and Middlewood (2014) actually made research participants feel bored, elated, distressed, or relaxed by asking them to watch different video clips. Boredom and elation were grouped together as examples of promotion-focused emotions, that is, motivated by the attempt to *obtain* something desirable, whereas, distress and relaxation were grouped together as examples of prevention-focused emotions, that is, motivated by the attempt to *avoid* something undesirable. The results showed that promotion-focused emotions were associated with more creativity than prevention-focused emotions. However, the study did not examine the creativity boosting ability of boredom specifically. Elation was always paired with boredom in the statistical analyses. Previous research has established that elation has a large and robust positive impact on creativity (e.g., Adaman & Blaney, 1995), and this particular emotion likely drove the positive effect for the class of promotion-focused emotions. Finally, Mann and Cadman (2014) made half of their participants bored by asking them to write out or read out numbers from a telephone book for 15 min before having them perform a task in which people are asked to think of as many alternate uses as they can for an every-day object (e.g., a paper cup, a brick; there are many variants of this kind of test – see Guilford, 1971; Mednick & Mednick, 1968; Wallach & Kogan, 1965). The other half of the participants completed the alternate uses task, an indirect measure of creativity, right away without undergoing a boredom manipulation. Mann and Cadman then zeroed in on the participants in the boredom condition who also reported daydreaming during the boredom induction. They did so because they proposed that daydreaming is a way of eliminating boredom and that daydreaming might, in turn, facilitate creativity. Indeed, they found that participants who were bored *and* who reported daydreaming demonstrated greater creativity compared to those who did not undergo an emotion manipulation. Unfortunately, however, the creativity level of the participants who remained bored after the manipulation is unknown (i.e., those that did not escape boredom by daydreaming). Nor is it clear if daydreaming while in a potentially boring situation is an indicator of a creative personality per se.

Although an enticing idea, there is simply not yet any compelling evidence to suggest that actually being bored enhances creativity. However, perhaps it is not being bored in the moment that is the key driver of creativity. Rather, it may be that the drive to avoid potential boredom – coupled with successful evasion of boredom – is associated with higher levels of creativity. In retrospect, it is a bit odd to think that someone who is currently caught up in the throes of boredom would be more creative. Rather, the notion that creativity reflects the successful sidestepping of boredom seems to have more face validity to us. Thus, Hendrix might have been correct in his assertion that boredom played a role in his creativity. However, it is unlikely that he was bored at the moment of creating his masterpieces. Indeed, his innovation may have been borne out of previous episodes of boredom and a disdain for what others were doing at the time. There is a sense then in which our capacity for boredom is good for creativity.

Trait boredom, on the other hand, does indeed appear to be good for "absolutely nothing." This chapter defined trait boredom as essentially a chronic pattern of responding to the signal of boredom in an ineffectual manner. To return to the analogy of pain, it is like the boredom-prone person feels the pain of boredom but then cannot rectify the problem. Clearly, this conceptualization of trait boredom as a problem of self-control and action regulation needs considerable development and elaboration. However, even if this way of understanding trait boredom in terms of self-regulation proves unhelpful, it seems clear that trait boredom itself is utterly unhelpful. Trait boredom, as mentioned earlier, is correlated with a large range of psychosocial problems ranging from problem gambling (Blaszczynski et al., 1990) to impoverished life meaning (Fahlman, Mercer, Gaskovski, Eastwood, & Eastwood, 2009) to anxiety (Sommers & Vodanovich, 2000). Moreover, trait boredom has incremental validity (Mercer-Lynn, Hunter, & Eastwood, 2013). For example, trait boredom uniquely predicts depression and anger over and above several other trait variables including neuroticism, impulsivity, emotional awareness, inattention, behavioral inhibition, and activation. Thus, while the state of boredom may be an important signal that leads to adaptive behavior, to date there is no reason to celebrate trait boredom.

What Is Next for Boredom Research?

Thankfully, we are not at the seventh day of boredom research – there is still a great deal to learn. The dynamics of the state and its relation to our sense of autonomy and self-efficacy represent an important avenue to pursue further. It may be that those who report never experiencing the state simply have high levels of self-esteem and a strong sense of self-efficacy in the pursuit of goals. Although we know that boredom diminishes as the frontal cortex reaches full maturation levels in the early 20s, we know far less about boredom in the preschool and pre-teen years or, for that matter, at the other end of the age spectrum. How boredom manifests in the seventh and eighth decades of life and beyond is likely to be different than its expression in the first few decades of life. The relation between boredom and depression is a ground-zero research finding – but little else is known about it, beyond its existence. Do increased levels of boredom lead to depression? If symptoms of depression resolve more rapidly than does the experience of boredom, can treatments be augmented by focusing on better boredom coping strategies? Recent work using psychophysiological measures and neuro-imaging hints at the possibility of developing a biological signature of state boredom. This could address the arousal conundrum directly and, when coupled with self-reports, may move the field forward in understanding the dynamics of both state and trait boredom proneness. This leads to an important goal of boredom research – to discover the most adaptive means of responding to the boredom signal. Although this chapter has characterized boredom as a unitary self-regulatory signal, this does not necessarily mean there will be a singular solution to coping with it. Any successful strategy will likely need to be tailored to the group or circumstance under consideration. For example, asking TBI patients who exhibit diminished attentional functioning to engage in mindfulness training to overcome boredom may be setting them up to fail. Counterintuitive solutions may help address the lack of fit between a preferred regulatory mode (e.g., assessment) and actual behavior (e.g., restlessness). For example, encouraging a highly boredom-prone individual to fidget more or doodle on scrap paper as a secondary task may in fact alleviate their boredom by simply providing an outlet for their pent-up energy and the sense that their capacities and skill set are currently underutilized. Finally, a deeper understanding of boredom has the potential to inform theories of motivated, goal-directed behavior more broadly (Gomez-Ramirez & Costa, 2017). In short, the boredom signal and how we respond to it has far-reaching consequences for the human condition that represent a fecund and fascinating path forward for researchers interested in goal-pursuit writ large.

References

Adaman, J. E., & Blaney, P. H. (1995). The effects of musical mood induction on creativity. *The Journal of Creative Behaviour, 29*, 95–108.

Aldao, A., Nolen-Hoeksema, S., & Schweizer, S. (2010). Emotion-regulation strategies across psychopathology: A meta-analytic review. *Clinical Psychology Review, 30*, 217–237.

American Psychiatric Association. (2013). *Diagnostic and statistical manual of mental disorders* (5th ed.). Arlington, VA: American Psychiatric Publishing.

Anderson, V. V., Anderson, P., Northam, E., Jacobs, R., & Catroppa, C. (2001). Development of executive functions through late childhood and adolescence in an Australian sample. *Developmental Neuropsychology, 20*, 385–406.

Andrews-Hanna, J. R. (2012). The brain's default network and its adaptive role in internal mentation. *The Neuroscientist, 18*, 251–270.

Avnet, T., & Higgins, E. T. (2003). Locomotion, assessment, and regulatory fit: Value transfer from "how" to "what.". *Journal of Experimental Social Psychology, 39*, 525–530.

Barmack, J. E. (1939). Studies on the psychophysiology of boredom: Part I. The effect of 15 mgs. Of benzedrine sulfate and 60 mgs. Of ephedrine hydrochloride on blood pressure, report of boredom and other factors. *Journal of Experimental Psychology, 25*, 494–505.

Baumeister, R. F., & Vohs, K. D. (2003). Self-regulation and the executive function of the self. In *Handbook of self and identity* (Vol. 1, pp. 197–217). New York: Guilford Press.

Bench, S. W., & Lench, H. C. (2013). On the function of boredom. *Behavioral Sciences, 3*, 459–472.

Berlyne, D. E. (1960). *Conflict, arousal, and curiosity*. New York, NY: McGraw-Hill.

Blaszczynski, A., McConaghy, N., & Frankova, A. (1990). Boredom proneness in pathological gambling. *Psychological Reports, 67*, 35–42.

Buckner, R. L., Andrews-Hanna, J. R., & Schacter, D. L. (2008). The brain's default network. *Annals of the New York Academy of Sciences, 1124*, 1–38.

Charnov, E. L. (1976). Optimal foraging, the marginal value theorem. *Theoretical Population Biology, 9*, 129–136.

Christoff, K., Gordon, A. M., Smallwood, J., Smith, R., & Schooler, J. W. (2009). Experience sampling during fMRI reveals default network and executive system contributions to mind wandering. *Proceedings of the National Academy of Sciences, 106*, 8719–8724.

Craig, A. D. (2009). How do you feel-now? The anterior insula and human awareness. *Nature Reviews Neuroscience, 10*, 59–70.

Csikszentmihalyi, M. (1990). *Flow: The psychology of optimal experience*. New York, NY: Harper & Row.

Csikszentmihalyi, M., & Csikszentmihalyi, I. S. (1992). *Optimal experience: Psychological studies of flow in consciousness*. Cambridge, England: Cambridge University Press.

Dal Mas, D. E., & Wittmann, B. C. (2017). Avoiding boredom: Caudate and insula activity reflects boredom-elicited purchase bias. *Cortex, 92*, 57–69.

Danckert, J. (2013). Descent of the doldrums. *Scientific American Mind, 24*, 54–59.

Danckert, J., Hammerschmidt, T., Marty-Duga, J., & Smilek, D. (2017). Boredom: Under-aroused and restless. Submitted to *Consciousness & Cognition*.

Danckert, J., & Isacescu, J. (2017). The bored brain: Insular cortex and the default mode network. *PsyArXiv Preprints*. Advance online publication. https://doi.org/10.17605/OSF.IO/AQBCD.

Danckert, J., & Merrifield, C. (in press). Boredom, sustained attention and the default mode network. *Experimental Brain Research*.

Daniels, L. M., Tze, V. M., & Goetz, T. (2015). Examining boredom: Different causes for different coping profiles. *Learning and Individual Differences, 37*, 255–261.

Daschmann, E. C., Goetz, T., & Stupnisky, R. H. (2011). Testing the predictors of boredom at school: Development and validation of the precursors to boredom scales. *British Journal of Educational Psychology, 81*, 421–440.

Dockree, P. M., Bellgrove, M. A., O'Keeffe, F. M., Moloney, P., Aimola, L., Carton, S., & Robertson, I. H. (2006). Sustained attention in traumatic brain injury (TBI) and healthy controls: Enhanced sensitivity with dual-task load. *Experimental Brain Research, 168*, 218–229.

Dockree, P. M., Kelly, S. P., Roche, R. A., Hogan, M. J., Reilly, R. B., & Robertson, I. H. (2004). Behavioural and physiological impairments of sustained attention after traumatic brain injury. *Brain Research Cognitive Brain Research, 20*, 403–414.

Eastwood, J. D., Frischen, A., Fenske, M. J., & Smilek, D. (2012). The unengaged mind defining boredom in terms of attention. *Perspectives on Psychological Science, 7*, 482–495.

Eccleston, C., & Crombez, G. (1999). Pain demands attention: A cognitive-affective model of the interruptive function of pain. *Psychological Bulletin, 125*, 356–366.

Elliott, R., Newman, J. L., Longe, O. A., & Deakin, J. W. (2003). Differential response patterns in the striatum and orbitofrontal cortex to financial reward in humans: A parametric functional magnetic resonance imaging study. *Journal of Neuroscience, 23*, 303–307.

Elpidorou, A. (2014). The bright side of boredom. *Frontiers in Psychology, 5*, 1–4.

Essed, N. H., van Staveren, W. A., Kok, F. J., Ormel, W., Zeinstra, G., & de Graaf, C. (2006). The effect of repeated exposure to fruit drinks on intake, pleasantness and boredom in young and elderly adults. *Physiology & Behaviour, 89*, 335–341.

Fahlman, S. A., Mercer, K. B., Gaskovski, P., Eastwood, A. E., & Eastwood, J. D. (2009). Does a lack of life meaning cause boredom? Results from psychometric, longitudinal, and experimental analyses. *Journal of Social and Clinical Psychology, 28*, 307–340.

Fahlman, S. A., Mercer-Lynn, K. B., Flora, D. B., & Eastwood, J. D. (2013). Development and validation of the multidimensional state boredom scale. *Assessment, 20*, 68–85.

Farmer, R., & Sundberg, N. D. (1986). Boredom proneness-the development and correlates of a new scale. *Journal of Personality Assessment, 50*, 4–17.

Fehr, F. S., & Schulman, M. (1978). Female self-report and autonomic responses to sexually pleasurable and sexually aversive readings. *Archives of Sexual Behavior, 7*, 443–453.

Fisher, C. D. (1993). Boredom at work: A neglected concept. *Human Relations, 46*, 395–417.

Fox, K. C., Spreng, R. N., Ellamil, M., Andrews-Hanna, J. R., & Christoff, K. (2015). The wandering brain: Meta-analysis of functional neuroimaging studies of mind-wandering and related spontaneous thought processes. *NeuroImage, 111*, 611–621.

Gallistel, C. R. (1990). *The organization of learning: Learning, development, and conceptual change*. Cambridge, MA: MIT Press.

Gasper, K., & Middlewood, B. L. (2014). Approaching novel thoughts: Understanding why elation and boredom promote associative thought more than distress and relaxation. *Journal of Experimental Social Psychology, 52*, 50–57.

Geiwitz, P. J. (1966). Structure of boredom. *Journal of Personality and Social Psychology, 3*, 592–600.

Goetz, T., Frenzel, A. C., Hall, N. C., Nett, U. E., Pekrun, R., & Lipnevich, A. A. (2014). Types of boredom: An experience sampling approach. *Motivation and Emotion, 38*, 401–419.

Gogtay, N., Giedd, J. N., Lusk, L., Hayashi, K. M., Greenstein, D., Vaituzis, A. C., … Thompson, P. M. (2004). Dynamic mapping of human cortical development during childhood through early adulthood. *Proceedings of the National Academy of Science of the United States of America, 101*, 8174–8179.

Goldberg, Y. K., Eastwood, J. D., LaGuardia, J., & Danckert, J. (2011). Boredom: An emotional experience distinct from apathy, anhedonia, or depression. *Journal of Social and Clinical Psychology, 30*, 647–666.

Gomez-Ramirez, J., & Costa, T. (2017). Boredom begets creativity: A solution to the exploitation-exploration trade-off in predictive coding. *Bio-Systems, 162*, 168–176.

Gottfried, J. A., O'Doherty, J., & Dolan, R. J. (2003). Encoding predictive reward value in human amygdala and orbitofrontal cortex. *Science, 301*, 1104–1107.

Greenson, R. R. (1953). On boredom. *Journal of the American Psychoanalytic Association, 1*, 7–21.

Greicius, M. D., Krasnow, B., Reiss, A. L., & Menon, V. (2003). Functional connectivity in the resting brain: A network analysis of the default mode hypothesis. *Proceedings of the National Academy of Sciences, 100*, 253–258.

Guilford, J. P. (1971). *Creativity tests for children: A manual of interpretations.* Orange, CA: Sheridan Psychological Services.

Higgins, E. T. (2005). Value from regulatory fit. *Current Directions in Psychological Science, 14*, 209–213.

Hill, A. B. (1975). Work variety and individual differences in occupational boredom. *Journal of Applied Psychology, 60*, 128–131.

Inzlicht, M., & Legault, L. (2014). No pain, no gain: How distress underlies effective control (and unites diverse psychological phenomena). In J. Forgas & E. Harmon-Jones (Eds.), *The control within: Motivation and its regulation* (pp. 115–132). New York, NY: Psychology Press.

Isacescu, J., & Danckert, J. (in press). Exploring the relationship between boredom proneness and self-control in traumatic brain injury (TBI). *Experimental Brain Research.*

Isacescu, J., Struk, A. A., & Danckert, J. (2016). Cognitive and affective predictors of boredom proneness. *Cognition and Emotion, 31*, 1741–1748.

Iso-Ahola, S. E., & Crowley, E. D. (1991). Adolescent substance abuse and leisure boredom. *Journal of Leisure Research, 23*, 260–271.

Jang, E. H., Park, B. J., Park, M. S., Kim, S. H., & Sohn, J. H. (2015). Analysis of physiological signals for recognition of boredom, pain, and surprise emotions. *Journal of Physiological Anthropology, 34*, 1–12.

Johnston, L. D., & O'Malley, P. M. (1986). Why do the nation's students use drugs and alcohol? Self-reported reasons from nine national surveys. *Journal of Drug Issues, 16*, 29–66.

Joireman, J., Anderson, J., & Strathman, A. (2003). The aggression paradox: Understanding links among aggression, sensation seeking, and the consideration of future consequences. *Journal of Personality and Social Psychology, 84*, 1287–1302.

Kass, S. J., & Vodanovich, S. J. (1990). Boredom proneness: Its relationship to type a behaviours and sensation seeking. *Psychology: A Journal of Human Behaviour, 27*, 7–16.

Keating, D. P. (2012). Cognitive and brain development in adolescence. *Enfance, 64*, 267–279.

Kenah, K., Bernhardt, J., Cumming, T., Spratt, N., Luker, J. & Janssen, H. (in press). Boredom in patients with acquired brain injuries during rehabilitation: A scoping review. *Disability and Rehabilitation.*

Kruglanski, A. W., Thompson, E. P., Higgins, E. T., Atash, M., Pierro, A., Shah, J. Y., & Spiegel, S. (2000). To "do the right thing" or to "just do it": Locomotion and assessment as distinct self-regulatory imperatives. *Journal of Personality and Social Psychology, 79*, 793–815.

Kurzban, R., Duckworth, A., Kable, J. W., & Myers, J. (2013). An opportunity cost model of subjective effort and task performance. *Behavioral and Brain Sciences, 36*, 661–679.

Lacey, J. I. (1959). Psychophysiological approaches to the evaluation of psychotherapeutic process and outcome. In E. A. Rubinstein & M. B. Parloff (Eds.), *Research in psychotherapy.* Washington, DC: American Psychological Association.

Lacey, J. I., & Lacey, B. C. (1970). Some autonomic-central nervous system interrelationships. In P. Black (Ed.), *Physiological correlates of emotion* (pp. 205–228). New York, NY: Academic.

Larson, R. W. (1990). Emotions and the creative process: Anxiety, boredom, and enjoyment as predictors of creative writing. *Imagination, Cognition and Personality, 9*, 275–292.

London, H., Schubert, D. S., & Washburn, D. (1972). Increase of autonomic arousal by boredom. *Journal of Abnormal Psychology, 80*, 29–36.

Lundberg, U., Melin, B., Evans, G. W., & Holmberg, L. (1993). Physiological deactivation after two contrasting tasks at a video display terminal: Learning vs repetitive data entry. *Ergonomics, 36*, 601–611.

Malkovsky, E., Merrifield, C., Goldberg, Y., & Danckert, J. (2012). Exploring the relationship between boredom and sustained attention. *Experimental Brain Research, 221*, 59–67.

Mann, S., & Cadman, R. (2014). Does being bored make us more creative? *Creativity Research Journal, 26*, 165–173.

Mason, M. F., Norton, M. I., Van Horn, J. D., Wegner, D. M., Grafton, S. T., & Macrae, C. N. (2007). Wandering minds: The default network and stimulus-independent thought. *Science, 315*, 393–395.

Mednick, M. T., & Mednick, S. A. (1968). The remote associations test. *The Journal of Creative Behaviour, 2*, 213–214.

Melton, A. M., & Schulenberg, S. E. (2009). A confirmatory factor analysis of the boredom proneness scale. *The Journal of Psychology, 143*, 493–508.

Menon, V., & Uddin, L. Q. (2010). Saliency, switching, attention and control: A network model of insula function. *Brain Structure and Function, 214*, 655–667.

Mercer, K. B., & Eastwood, J. D. (2010). Is boredom associated with problem gambling behaviour? It depends on what you mean by 'boredom'. *International Gambling Studies, 10*, 91–104.

Mercer-Lynn, K. B., Flora, D. B., Fahlman, S. A., & Eastwood, J. D. (2011). The measurement of boredom: Differences between existing self-report scales. *Assessment, 20*, 585–596.

Mercer-Lynn, K. B., Hunter, J. A., & Eastwood, J. D. (2013). Is trait boredom redundant? *Journal of Social and Clinical Psychology, 32*, 897–916.

Merrifield, C., & Danckert, J. (2014). Characterizing the psychophysiological signature of boredom. *Experimental Brain Research, 232*, 481–491.

Mikulas, W. L., & Vodanovich, S. J. (1993). The essence of boredom. *The Psychological Record, 43*, 3–12.

Mor, N., & Winquist, J. (2002). Self-focused attention and negative affect: A meta-analysis. *Psychological Bulletin, 128*, 638–662.

Mugon, J., Danckert, J., & Eastwood, J. (in press). The costs and benefits of boredom in the classroom. In *The Cambridge handbook on motivation and learning*. Cambridge, England: Cambridge University Press.

Mugon, J., Struk, A., & Danckert, J. (in press). A failure to launch: Exploring the self-regulatory profile of boredom. *Frontiers in Psychology*.

Nett, U. E., Goetz, T., & Daniels, L. M. (2010). What to do when feeling bored?: Students' strategies for coping with boredom. *Learning and Individual Differences, 20*, 626–638.

Nett, U. E., Goetz, T., & Hall, N. C. (2011). Coping with boredom in school: An experience sampling perspective. *Contemporary Educational Psychology, 36*, 49–59.

Nietzsche, F. (1996). *Human, all too human: A book for free spirits.* (R.J. Hollingdale, Trans.). Cambridge texts in the history of philosophy. Cambridge, England: Cambridge University Press.

Nolen-Hoeksema, S., Wisco, B. E., & Lyubomirsky, S. (2008). Rethinking rumination. *Perspectives on Psychological Science, 3*, 400–424.

O'Doherty, J., Kringelbach, M. L., Rolls, E. T., Hornak, J., & Andrews, C. (2001). Abstract reward and punishment representations in the human orbitofrontal cortex. *Nature Neuroscience, 4*, 95–102.

O'Keeffe, F. M., Dockree, P. M., Moloney, P., Carton, S., & Robertson, I. H. (2007). Characterising error-awareness of attentional lapses and inhibitory control failures in patients with traumatic brain injury. *Experimental Brain Research, 180*, 59–67.

Ohsuga, M., Shimono, F., & Genno, H. (2001). Assessment of phasic work stress using autonomic indices. *International Journal of Psychophysiology, 40*, 211–220.

Pattyn, N., Neyt, X., Henderickx, D., & Soetens, E. (2008). Psychophysiological investigation of vigilance decrement: Boredom or cognitive fatigue? *Physiology & Behavior, 93*, 369–378.

Poletti, M. (2009). Adolescent brain development and executive functions: A prefrontal framework for developmental psycho-pathologies. *Clinical Neuropsychiatry: Journal of Treatment Evaluation, 6*, 155–165.

Rupp, D. E., & Vodanovich, S. J. (1997). The role of boredom proneness in self-reported anger and aggression. *Journal of Social Behavior and Personality, 12*, 925–936.

Russell, J. A. (1980). A circumplex model of affect. *Journal of Personality and Social Psychology, 39*, 1161–1178.

Sansone, C., Weir, C., Harpster, L., & Morgan, C. (1992). Once a boring task always a boring task? Interest as a self-regulatory mechanism. *Journal of Personality and Social Psychology, 63*, 379–390.

Schopenhauer, A. (1995). *The world as will and idea.* (J. Berman, Trans.). (Book Two Section 29, page 85). London, England: Everyman.

Schwartz, B., Ward, A., Monterosso, J., Lyubomirsky, S., White, K., & Lehman, D. R. (2002). Maximizing versus satisficing: Happiness is a matter of choice. *Journal of Personality and Social Psychology, 83*, 1178–1197.

Seel, R. T., & Kreutzer, J. S. (2003). Depression assessment after traumatic brain injury: An empirically based classification method. *Archives of Physical Medicine and Rehabilitation, 84*, 1621–1628.

Seli, P., Risko, E. F., Smilek, D., & Schacter, D. L. (2016). Mind-wandering with and without intention. *Trends in Cognitive Science, 20*, 605–617.

Sidlauskaite, J., Wiersema, J. R., Roeyers, H., Krebs, R. M., Vassena, E., Fias, W., … Sonuga-Barke, E. (2014). Anticipatory processes in brain state switching—Evidence from a novel cued-switching task implicating default mode and salience networks. *NeuroImage, 98*, 359–365.

Smilek, D., Carriere, J. S., & Cheyne, J. A. (2010). Out of mind, out of sight: Eye blinking as indicator and embodiment of mind wandering. *Psychological Science, 21*, 786–789.

Smith, R. P. (1981). Boredom: A review. *Human Factors, 23*, 329–340.

Sommers, J., & Vodanovich, S. J. (2000). Boredom proneness: Its relationship to psychological- and physical-health symptoms. *Journal of Clinical Psychology, 56*, 149–155.

Spaeth, M., Weichold, K., & Silbereisen, R. K. (2015). The development of leisure boredom in early adolescence: Predictors and longitudinal associations with delinquency and depression. *Developmental Psychology, 51*, 1380–1394.

Struk, A., Scholer, A., & Danckert, J. (2015). *Perceived control predicts engagement and diminished boredom. Poster presented at the Canadian Society for Brain.* Ottawa, Canada: Behaviour and Cognitive Science.

Struk, A. A., Carriere, J. S., Cheyne, J. A., & Danckert, J. (2017). A short boredom proneness scale: Development and psychometric properties. *Assessment, 24*, 346–359.

Struk, A. A., Mugon, J., Scholer, A. A., Sokolowski, M. B., & Danckert, J. (in preparation). Of fruit flies and men: Self-regulation and the foraging gene (PRKG1) in humans.

Struk, A. A., Scholer, A. A., & Danckert, J. (2016). A self-regulatory approach to understanding boredom proneness. *Cognition and Emotion, 30*, 1388–1401.

Tangney, J. P., Baumeister, R. F., & Boone, A. L. (2004). High self-control predicts good adjustment, less pathology, better grades, and interpersonal success. *Journal of Personality, 72*, 271–324.

Thackray, R. I. (1981). The stress of boredom and monotony: A consideration of the evidence. *Psychosomatic Medicine, 43*, 165–176.

Thackray, R. I., Bailey, J. P., & Touchstone, R. M. (1977). Physiological, subjective, and performance correlates of reported boredom and monotony while performing a simulated radar control task. In R. R. Mackie (Ed.), *Vigilance* (pp. 203–215). Boston, MA: Springer.

Theobold, D. E., Kirsh, K. L., Holtsclaw, E., Donaghy, K., & Passik, S. D. (2003). An open label pilot study of citalopram for depression and boredom in ambulatory cancer patients. *Palliative & Supportive Care, 1*, 71–77.

Tolinski, B., & Di Perna, A. (2016). *Play it loud: An epic history of the style, sound, & revolution of the electric guitar.* New York, NY: Doubleday.

Tolstoy, L. N. (1899). *Anna Karénina.* New York, NY: Thomas Y. Crowell Co.

Troutwine, R., & O'Neal, E. D. (1981). Volition, performance of a boring task, and time estimation. *Perceptual and Motor Skills, 52*, 865–866.

Tze, V. M., Klassen, R. M., & Daniels, L. M. (2014). Patterns of boredom and its relationship with perceived autonomy support and engagement. *Contemporary Educational Psychology, 39*, 175–187.

Uddin, L. Q. (2015). Salience processing and insular cortical function and dysfunction. *Nature Reviews Neuroscience, 16,* 55–61.

Ulrich, M., Keller, J., & Grön, G. (2016). Neural signatures of experimentally induced flow experiences identified in a typical fMRI block design with BOLD imaging. *Social Cognitive and Affective Neuroscience, 11,* 496–507.

Ulrich, M., Keller, J., Hoenig, K., Waller, C., & Grön, G. (2014). Neural correlates of experimentally induced flow experiences. *NeuroImage, 86,* 194–202.

van Tilburg, W. A., & Igou, E. R. (2011). On boredom: Lack of challenge and meaning as distinct boredom experiences. *Motivation and Emotion, 36,* 181–194.

van Tilburg, W. A., Igou, E. R., & Sedikides, C. (2013). In search of meaningfulness: Nostalgia as an antidote to boredom. *Emotion, 13,* 450–461.

Vernon, H. M. (1926). The human factor and industrial accidents. *International Labour Review, 13,* 673–683.

Vodanovich, S. J. (2003a). Psychometric measures of boredom: A review of the literature. *The Journal of Psychology, 137,* 569–595.

Vodanovich, S. J. (2003b). On the possible benefits of boredom: A neglected area in personality research. *Psychology and Education: An Interdisciplinary Journal, 40,* 28–33.

Vodanovich, S. J., & Kass, S. J. (1990). A factor analytic study of the boredom proneness scale. *Journal of Personality Assessment, 55,* 115–123.

Vodanovich, S. J., Verner, K. M., & Gilbride, T. V. (1991). Boredom proneness: Its relationship to positive and negative affect. *Psychological Reports, 69,* 1139–1146.

Vodanovich, S. J., & Watt, J. D. (2016). Self-report measures of boredom: An updated review of the literature. *Journal of Psychology, 150,* 196–228.

Vogel-Walcutt, J. J., Fiorella, L., Carper, T., & Schatz, S. (2012). The definition, assessment, and mitigation of state boredom within educational settings: A comprehensive review. *Educational Psychology Review, 24,* 89–111.

Wallach, M. A., & Kogan, N. (1965). *Modes of thinking in young children.* New York, NY: Holt, Rinehart & Winston.

Watt, J. D., & Vodanovich, S. J. (1992). Relationship between boredom proneness and impulsivity. *Psychological Reports, 70,* 688–690.

Weissman, D. H., Roberts, K. C., Visscher, K. M., & Woldorff, M. G. (2006). The neural bases of momentary lapses in attention. *Nature Neuroscience, 9,* 971–978.

Chapter 7
The Adaptive Functions of Jealousy

Jose C. Yong and Norman P. Li

Abstract Jealousy is a troublesome emotional experience for those afflicted by its onset. The grip of the "green-eyed monster" has been known to cause misery and produce some drastic coping behaviors ranging from paranoid stalking to violent aggression. But rather than a product of civilized culture gone wrong or a mental disorder as some thinkers have claimed jealousy to be, the current chapter proposes from an evolutionary perspective that jealousy plays an important role in our lives by serving a critical adaptive function for humans—the vigilance over and protection of relationships that are valuable to us.

> I saw the light on the night that I passed by her window
> I saw the flickering shadows of love on her blind
> She was my woman!
> As she deceived me, I watched and went out of my mind
> My my my Delilah
> Why why why Delilah?
> I could see, that girl was no good for me
> But I was lost like a slave that no man could free
> At break of day when that man drove away I was waiting
> I crossed the street to her house and she opened the door
> She stood there laughing!
> I felt the knife in my hand and she laughed no more.
>
> —*Delilah*, Tom Jones

Popularly personified as the "green-eyed monster"—a term attributed to William Shakespeare—jealousy has had a longstanding reputation as one of the most toxic of human emotions. Across various assessments by theologians, philosophers, artists, and writers, jealousy is known for triggering bitter feelings that may erupt into reactions as violent as that of Tom Jones's popular song, "Delilah." There is a socially shared obsession with the drama of jealousy which makes shows like *The*

J. C. Yong (✉) · N. P. Li
School of Social Sciences, Singapore Management University, Singapore, Singapore
e-mail: jc.yong.2012@phdps.smu.edu.sg

© Springer International Publishing AG, part of Springer Nature 2018
H. C. Lench (ed.), *The Function of Emotions*,
https://doi.org/10.1007/978-3-319-77619-4_7

Good Wife and *Survivor* so engaging to watch, but jealousy far predates modern television. The famed sibling rivals from biblical times, Cain and Abel, are but one of the many ancient examples of the poisonous effects of jealousy. At a cocktail party, it is not uncommon for everyone's eager attention to be turned to a juicy, scandalous story where jealousy takes center stage.

This chapter reviews research on jealousy and, in particular, its function via an evolutionary lens. In contrast to other theoretical accounts of jealousy, evolutionary psychology, with its focus on the functional, adaptive origins of psychological traits, views jealousy not so much as "toxic" or "poisonous" but instead as playing an important, purposive role in our lives, thus justifying its presence within our psychological repertoire. Further, the utility of the evolutionary perspective will be explicated by discussing additional insights and predictions that prior, non-evolutionary theories of jealousy fail to elucidate. Through an analysis of its adaptive function, we may also better understand the factors that trigger jealousy, which include the various ways that the modern world we live in may be mismatched to our evolved psychological mechanisms and thus be especially conducive for maladaptive jealousy to breed.

Jealousy

"Jealousy" is a concept in many cultures that—in its broadest meaning—describes affective and behavioral responses to real or imagined situations where a highly valued possession, often a social relationship, is threatened to be diverted elsewhere and lost (Buss, 2000; Pfeiffer & Wong, 1989; Daly, Wilson, & Weghorst, 1982; Mathes, Adams, & Davies, 1985). Jealousy can be experienced for a wide range of interpersonal situations. For instance, one may fear losing a best friend to the new friends that he or she meets. When the valued relationship is a privileged or preferential working relationship with a boss, threats may come from impressive rival co-workers. When the valued relationship is a romantic mateship, threats may come from attractive or desirable "mate poachers" (Buss, 2000). Jealousy has been observed in children as young as toddlers who are sensitive to the loss of parental attention to another and try to disrupt the undesired, ongoing attention (Dunn, 1988; Hart, Field, Del Valle, & Letourneau, 1998). In many of these situations, rivals do not necessarily have to be clearly impressive, attractive, desirable, or even human. When we expect to have an exclusive relationship with a person but he or she displays interest in someone or something else, such as when a spouse is more attentive to the pet cat or devotes more time to golf, jealous feelings can also arise.

Inherent in the experience of jealousy is the experience of competitive threat—specifically the competition for valued relationships, the potential loss of these valued relationships to rivals, and the urge to act in ways that prevent such loss from occurring (Mathes et al., 1985). Jealousy is therefore subtly but significantly different from another closely related emotion: envy. Envy occurs in two-person situations in which we lack but covet a desired attribute enjoyed by another, whereas jealousy is a "triangle of relations" where a special relationship we (believe ourselves to) possess is perceived to be at risk of being taken away by a third rival individual or interest (Parrott, 1991; p. 16).

Consequences of Jealousy

People engage in a wide array of possible coping responses when they have appraised the threat of a rival relationship. Although studies suggest that some of these jealous reactions may lead to positive outcomes, such as when it serves as a reminder to stop taking one's romantic partner for granted (Elphinston, Feeney, & Noller, 2011; Pines, 1992), the preponderance of findings points to its destructive effects, especially in romantic relationships (e.g., Marazziti et al., 2003).

The experience of jealousy is associated with many distinct negative feelings: outrage, fear, sadness, depression, embarrassment, and humiliation (Buss, 2000). When one might lose a beloved to someone else when in a relationship that is expected to be exclusive, feelings of outrage and betrayal can arise because expectations of the beloved's faithfulness or fidelity are violated. When faced with the looming threat of potential loss, paranoia and fear may grip individuals suffering from jealousy. Finally, the actual loss of a beloved to a rival can elicit sadness as well as humiliation if one feels less worthy or inferior to the rival after the loss.

These negative feelings may prompt a range of destructive behaviors that can ironically undermine the very relationship that the jealous individual is trying to preserve (Buss & Duntley, 2011). Jealousy can lead to self-harm through substance abuse as a means of distraction or seeking alternative sources of pleasure (Michael, Mirza, Mirza, Babu, & Vithayathil, 1995; Nesse & Berridge, 1997). Jealousy can inconvenience or harm others through acts of suspicion, accusation, stalking, and violence (Buss & Shackelford, 1997). Jealousy can cause the cutting off of a partner's relationships with family and acquaintances, which in turn causes the partner to experience isolation, reduced self-esteem, and fear for personal safety (Buss, 2000; Daly et al., 1982). Jealousy is a major cause of spousal battering (Daly et al., 1982) and intimate partner violence ranging from minor slaps to brutal beatings, some of which have led to miscarriages if a man suspects that his pregnant mate is carrying a child that is not his (Buss & Duntley, 2011).

The experience of jealousy is significantly responsible for a large number of murders committed by people, in particular men, on their current and previous relationship partners (Daly & Wilson, 1988). According to Buss (2013), men's murderous tendencies are triggered by two main factors: (1) when the man suspects or knows that his partner has been sexually unfaithful and when she leaves the relationship and (2) when the man believes that the departure is irrevocable or permanent. Jealousy can also cause just as much danger to those who befriend, consort with, or show interest in a mate or ex-mate. For example, Ron Goldman—suspected as having an affair with Nicole Brown Simpson—was killed when he happened to be with Ms. Simpson at the time of her murder. Suspected or known mate poachers are frequent targets of homicidal ideation and same-sex rival murders (Duntley, 2005). Women are less likely to murder their mates out of jealousy, but women have been documented to resort to murder as self-defense against men who abuse them during episodes of jealous rage (Daly & Wilson, 1988).

Finally, because of the acute emotional effects that jealousy has on those who experience it, jealousy can also be used instrumentally by those seeking to manipulate others. "Romantic jealousy induction" is a strategic behavioral process designed to elicit a jealous reaction from a partner—for instance, openly flirting with the opposite sex in front of one's partner—to achieve a goal (de Miguel & Buss, 2011; Shackelford, Goetz, & Buss, 2005), such as to escalate attention and commitment from the partner (Jonason, Li, & Buss, 2010) or to test or control the relationship (White, 1980). Summarily, although some studies suggest that jealousy may produce positive outcomes, the vast majority of research points to the detrimental effects of jealousy on psychological well-being and social relationships.

Early Theories of Jealousy

Research on jealousy only began reaching scientifically acceptable standards in the 1980s and 1990s (Hart & Legerstee, 2010). These studies provided empirical data describing the "hows" and "whats" of jealousy, thus shedding light on the precursors and outcomes associated with jealous episodes. However, noticeably absent are theories elucidating the "whys" of jealousy. Although research has consistently indicated that perceived threats to valued relationships play a leading role in triggering the experience of jealousy (e.g., Pfeiffer & Wong, 1989), thereby hinting at an important function of jealousy in terms of relationship maintenance, this insight did not influence mainstream social science theories of jealousy over the last century. As jealousy is often viewed in a negative light due to the unpleasant outcomes it leads to, various theories have adopted as their starting point jealousy as an undesirable aberration of human nature to explain its origins and existence.

One such view of jealousy states that it originates from various cultural forces and socialization. According to Hupka (1991), the socialization of gender roles gives rise to jealousy: "The desire to control the sexual behavior of mates is the consequence of the social construction of the gender system. Social construction refers in this context to the arbitrary assignment of activities and qualities to each gender" (p. 260). From this perspective, men and women are culturally assigned roles and expected behaviors, and men are presumed to be assigned the role of controlling the sexuality of their partners. If the social construction of gender roles is arbitrary, it then follows that some (but not all) cultures should exist where only the men are jealous but the women are not, as well as vice versa.

Similarly, Bhugra (1993) argued that people are socialized to be jealous; but rather than being a product of gender roles, jealousy is instead a product of "capitalist societies," which place a premium on personal possessions and property, which then also extends to persons and "taking the partner to be the individual's personal possession or property" (p. 272). The corollary of this view is that people living in noncapitalist (e.g., socialist or dictatorship) societies should be free of jealousy. When socialization theories of jealousy are taken together, because "motives for jealousy are a product of the culture" (Bhugra, 1993; p. 273) and social constructions are arbitrary, we should expect to find a wide variability in jealous motives across cultures.

A second set of theories invokes psychological defects or poor mental health as the cause of jealousy. These range from mild or subclinical factors such as low self-esteem, immaturity, or deviance (cf., Bhugra, 1993) to severe psychopathology (cf., Buss, 2000, 2013). According to this train of thought, normal, psychologically healthy, and well-adjusted people should experience little to no jealousy. If psychological defects create malfunctions of the human mind and give rise to jealousy, then the absence of or the curing of those defects should minimize the incidences of jealousy.

Another important perspective is the first psychological theory that was ever formulated to explain jealousy by Freud (1910). Although Freud might have also viewed jealousy as a troublesome psychological experience, his theory differs from accounts based on socialization and psychological defects in that he believed jealousy to be an integral and not so unusual feature of human nature. In his view, jealousy originated in the "Oedipus complex" where a young boy realizes that his father is a mating competitor for the affection of his mother. Later, Jung (1913) proposed and coined the term "Electra complex" to represent the female version of this intrasexual competition—between that of a young girl and her mother for the father.

Some of these explanations reflect reality to some extent. For instance, jealousy can potentially result from the mental trauma of boxing or warfare (Johnson, 1969), and the severity of expressions of jealousy can vary according to culture (e.g., among the Kipsigis in Kenya, the offended husband might simply demand a refund on the bride price he paid for his wife, whereas jealous rivals in the Ache of Paraguay settle disputes through violent ritual fights; Borgerhoff Mulder, 1988; Hill & Hurtado, 1996). However, these explanations are often inconsistent with much of the empirical data on jealousy. In particular, jealousy is a largely commonplace occurrence for many people who are socially well-adjusted and do not have psychological defects. Individuals labeled as suffering from "pathological jealousy" often *do* have partners who are indeed romancing other people (Buss, 2013). Moreover, the experience of jealousy appears to be culturally universal. That children below the age of one can experience jealousy (Hart, 2015) also suggests that jealous feelings do not have to be learned.

Anthropologists with a romanticized view of human nature have tried to unearth cultures from tropical paradises that are untainted by modernization and are thus supposedly free of jealousy. For instance, Mead (1928) made assertions based on her anthropological research that Samoans are devoid of destructive passions such as anger between a cuckold and a seducer and have no thirst for revenge. However, later anthropological studies have refuted these claims, finding instead that jealousy is a prominent cause of violence against rivals and mates, and the Samoans even have a word for it: *fua* (Freeman, 1983). Among the Ammassalik Eskimos in Greenland, another culture that is sometimes exemplified as lacking jealousy, it is not unusual for a husband to kill an interloper who had sexual intercourse with his wife (Mirsky, 1937). Indeed, killing a wife and affair partner caught in the act of infidelity was legal in Texas until 1974 (Buss, 2000), and the killing of wives due to adultery was often treated as a "legitimate defense of honor" in Brazil up until 1991 (Brooke, 1991; although in some areas of Brazil, this is still a practice).

The Freudian view that jealousy originates from a young person's perception of his or her same-sex parent as a competitor for his or her opposite sex parent's sexual resources has not found empirical support (Buss, 2013). However, the theory may still be half right. Daly and Wilson (1990) argue that Freud conflated two different types of rivalries, one of which holds weight according to theories of parent-child conflict where a child expresses annoyance at the loss of attention or affection from one parent to another parent or even vice versa whereby a stepfather is jealous of a mother's attention to her own biological children, both of which are well-documented (e.g., Burlingham, 1973; Cavanagh, Dobash, & Dobash, 2007). According to Daly and Wilson (1990), a boy and his father may compete for the mother's attention, time, and resources, but they certainly do not compete for sexual access to the mother, and similarly this is unlikely to be the case for girls competing with mothers for sexual access to the father. Although Freudian accounts of jealousy are errone-ous in terms of the types of relationship or resources that are at stake, a major insight can be gleaned whereby jealousy might be viewed as a normal feature of the human condition, rather than an abnormality unique to modern society or a malfunctioning psychology.

Jealousy from an Evolutionary Perspective

The evolutionary biologist and Eastern Orthodox Christian Theodosius Dobzhansky (1973) once wrote that "nothing in biology makes sense except in the light of evolu-tion." It is difficult, for instance, to understand and predict the complicated work-ings of a stomach (e.g., the functional relationship between digestive tracts, stomach acid, and gastric pains) without awareness of the adaptive functions of nutrition and hunger. Similarly, the intricacies of our mind cannot be fully understood without knowing what it was designed to do. The evolutionary perspective thus begins its analysis of psychology with a simple question: If a psychological trait appears to be commonplace, for what specific purpose might it have been designed to serve?

All living organisms today, including humans, are well-preserved "fossils" hous-ing a raft of traits that provide windows into the ancestral past. For instance, our callus-producing mechanisms indicate that our evolutionary ancestors repeatedly dealt with friction to the skin, and our strong desires for sugar, fat, and protein sug-gest that ripe fruits and succulent meat were scarce and valuable food sources in ancestral environments. Likewise, the powerful emotion of jealousy suggests that infidelity or relationship defection posed serious adaptive problems. Many of the physical and psychological traits we carry with us today are therefore mechanisms shaped by evolution to help us do things that facilitated survival and reproduction (Tooby & Cosmides, 1992; Williams, 1966).

This focus on functional aspects means that a comprehensive understanding of jealousy resides in knowing what posed as adaptive problems to humans in the ancestral past and, correspondingly, what was therefore also valued. Throughout evolutionary history, both men and women faced the adaptive problem of producing and caring for offspring. As a result, humans have evolved to prize reproductively viable partners and commitment to share the long-term responsibility of raising children (Buss, 1989). Likewise, people face various other adaptive problems such as gaining social acceptance or social status (Baumeister & Leary, 1995). As a result, the possession of relationships with valuable individuals who were able to help us overcome those problems, such as a popular friend or a respected mentor, is also prized and guarded. The loss of such relationships to rivals becomes an important secondary adaptive challenge because losing the benefits provided by these valuable individuals can be detrimental to one's own survival and reproductive interests. Hence, sensitivity toward the health and vigilance against the loss of such relations likely was selected for over evolutionary time. People who were more careful at guarding their prized, valuable relationships were more likely to survive and reproduce than those who were less careful, and thus the genes that coded for such a psychology get passed down the generations and are present in people today (Tooby & Cosmides, 1992). Where crucial benefits and resources are at stake, from an evolutionary perspective, some of the extreme lengths to which jealous individuals will go to guard them may especially make sense. Neither is social learning necessary to experience jealousy; young children who have never had a prior episode of relationship threat can also get triggered by appropriate stimuli denoting such threats (Hart, 2015), thus suggesting that this mechanism is innate.

Specificity is an important consideration within an evolutionary analysis of psychological mechanisms. Just as the visual system evolved specifically to process light rays to see and not to process food for nutrition, our psychological mechanisms also evolved to attend to specific, distinctive stimuli and elicit correspondingly specific responses. However, as with many adaptations, distinct emotion adaptations may also share common subcomponents. The visual system, for instance, is utilized in both the mechanism for food selection (e.g., to select berries with cues to ripeness) and the mechanism for mate selection (e.g., to select mates with cues to health and fertility). Despite sharing the visual system as a common component, the mechanism for food consumption is a functionally distinct adaptation from the mechanism for sexual consummation. Likewise, envy and jealousy may appear similar as they share some affective components such as anger, but they also respond to distinct inputs, produce distinct psychological behavioral outputs, and are thus regarded as functionally distinct adaptations (Buss, Haselton, Shackelford, Bleske, & Wakefield, 1998).

To illustrate this point, "a woman might become *enraged* at a peer getting a promotion she felt she deserved instead and [similarly] become *enraged* at a husband caught *in flagrante delicto* with their neighbor's wife. However, as envy and jealousy have distinct social inputs, the input of a man having an affair provokes rage if the man is her husband, but not if the man is her co-worker. The input of a man getting an undeserved promotion provokes rage if the man is her rival co-worker, but not if the man is her husband" (Buss, 2013; p. 156). The specific behaviors that result from experiencing either of the two emotions also differ depending on the worth of the promotion or relationship and available response options. For example, the woman envious of her co-worker might increase her work efforts or try to undermine her co-worker's projects, while the woman experiencing jealousy from her husband's infidelity might engage in a retaliatory affair or seek a divorce.

The evolutionary perspective therefore provides greater specification on the conditions that will trigger jealousy. In principle, one could go through life entirely without experiencing jealousy if one's beloved, best friend, or any other valued persons never threatened defection or attended to anything else and if rivals showed no interest in these valued persons. One could also be less prone to jealousy if the context of the relationship is not intended to be long-term or exclusive. Symons (1979) proposed some mating contexts in which romantic jealousy can be suppressed, such as in the context of polyamory, open relationships, "swinging," and partner-swapping. Because such mateships do not entail expectations of exclusivity and faithfulness, violations of these expectations and feelings of betrayal are less likely to occur. Symons also suggests that men who opt for such relationships are also motivated by sexual variety and are thus willing to trade-off the monopolization of a mate and allow other men to have sex with their wives. Nonetheless, studies of swingers and polyamorous communities do note that jealousy still occurs (Buss, 2000), suggesting that it can be difficult to suppress the trigger of witnessing or knowing that a partner is having sex with others.

From this perspective, rather than being a product of socialized cultural or gender roles, jealousy is instead a product of evolutionary pressure—a mechanism designed to be attuned to specific stimuli denoting the potential loss of valued persons to rivals; signaling the potential loss through negative emotions such as fear, anxiety, or paranoia; and preventing that loss by taking action either against the rival or the valued person. And rather than being an inconvenient offshoot of psychopathology, jealousy instead played a significant role in the survival and reproductive success of our ancestral forebears and will continue to do so in modern as well as future generations of humans.

Implications from Considering Jealousy's Ultimate Functions

An evolutionary perspective addresses research gaps left behind by previous theories of jealousy, such as why jealousy is ubiquitous across cultures, expressed in psychologically healthy men as well as women, and capable of being elicited without being learned. Further, the evolutionary perspective also has utility in improving our understanding of the nature of jealousy, with various implications that follow from these improved insights.

Jealousy as a Basic Emotion One such reconsideration of jealousy is whether it should be viewed as a "complex" or "basic" emotion. Basic, primary, or fundamental emotions regulate us in response to environmental challenges and opportunities in a typically instinctive and automatic manner. Conversely, complex emotions are regarded as less automatic and composed of a blend of basic emotions. Basic emotions are often described as evolutionarily adaptive emotions, whereas most theories do not consider complex emotions to be adaptations. Much of the current research regards jealousy not as a basic emotion but instead as a complex emotion derived from a mix of different basic emotions such as anger, fear, and sadness (Buss, 2013). For an emotion to be considered basic, among various other criteria, Ekman (1994) proposed that it must be present in other primates, while Plutchik (1980) argued that it must function to help humans solve adaptive problems of survival.

Jealousy does not meet most of these traditional criteria as it is not always clearly observed in nonhumans, and romantic jealousy can also be detrimental to survival, such as when a romantically jealous man attempts to physically assault a mate poacher (Buss, 2013). Yet, there are good reasons to reevaluate the validity of these frameworks and reconsider jealousy as a basic emotion. An examination of whether an emotion or any other psychological mechanism is basic, according to modern evolutionary principles (e.g., Dawkins, 1982; Tooby & Cosmides, 2005; Williams, 1966), requires a consideration of whether it contributes not just to *survival* but also to *reproductive success*. Sexually reproducing organisms that survive well but do not mate will not pass on their genes, thus constituting evolutionary dead ends. Survival without reproduction in evolutionary terms is therefore ultimately pointless, and thus differential reproductive success, not differential survival success, is more accurately the fundamental "engine" of the evolutionary selection process (Miller, 2000). Moreover, some adaptations are detrimental to survival, but they still evolved anyway because they promote greater success in mating. Some examples include the cumbersome plumage of peacocks and elevated appetites for risk and aggression in human males (Wilson & Daly, 1985). Such traits often lead to shorter life spans for the males encumbered by them but nonetheless still exist because of their contributions to reproductive success.

This shift in the level of analysis from survival success to reproductive success is important because romantic jealousy is not designed for solving problems of survival. Rather, romantic jealousy exists because it contributed to solving the specific adaptive problem of mating and reproduction. The primary functions of male romantic jealousy include deterring sexual infidelity, deterring mate poachers, and deterring defection from the mateship—outcomes which, when successfully enacted, improve a man's reproductive success by increasing the certainty that he is the actual father of the children he is raising and monopolizing his mate's reproductive resources (Buss, 2013). The irrelevance of romantic jealousy to survival therefore does not disqualify jealousy from being basic or fundamental.

The modern evolutionary psychological framework also does not require existence in any other living organisms for an emotion or any other adaptive trait to be considered basic. To wit, "no one would deem the adaptation of echolocation not 'basic' in bats, even if it exists rarely outside of bat species" (Buss, 2013; p. 158). Likewise, just because the existence of language can hardly be found outside of humans (Pinker & Bloom, 1990) does not disqualify the capacity for language from being an adaptation that is "basic" to humans. According to this modern framework, although many emotions may indeed exist in other species or exist in precursor forms in earlier lineages, such presence in other species is neither necessary nor sufficient for deeming an emotion as basic. Taken together, a strong case can be made that jealousy is indeed a basic or fundamental emotion, thus cementing its role as an important contributor to human survival and, more importantly, reproductive success.

Sex differences in the Cues that Trigger Jealousy The evolutionary perspective also makes another key contribution to our understanding of jealousy through sex-differentiated predictions of cues that trigger jealousy. The first evolutionary-based proposition of sex differences in jealousy was posited by Symons (1979) as he suggested that "a wife's experience of sexual jealousy varies with the degree of threat to herself that she perceives in her husband's adultery, whereas a husband's experience of sexual jealousy is relatively invariant, his wife's adultery is almost always being perceived as threatening" (p. 232). Symons clarifies that this is because male sexual jealousy functions to prevent one's wife from conceiving another man's child, and yet when wives experience jealousy, their experiences can be just as strong as their husbands' jealousy. Indeed, studies that assess jealousy using "global" measures such as "how often do you experience jealousy" or "when jealous, how intense are your feelings" mostly show no sex differences (Buss, 2000).

To understand the basis of this proposed psychological sex difference, it is important to consider some fundamental biological differences between men and women. For humans to reproduce, women must invest heavily in offspring because fertilization, gestation, and placentation occur internally, and women also carry the additional parental burden associated with lactation after offspring are born (Symons, 1979; Trivers, 1972). These costs of pregnancy and childbirth impose a great deal of vulnerability on women, particularly during ancestral periods in the absence of modern food production, healthcare, and social welfare (Daly & Wilson, 1983). Women therefore value the ability of a partner to provide sustained protection and resources to her and her children (Buss & Schmitt, 1993). Men, on the other hand, face a different adaptive issue. Because human reproductive biology entails internal female fertilization, men face the problem of investing resources in children that are actually sired by rival men—an adaptive problem not faced by women.

From this insight, sex differences in romantic jealousy become apparent. Both men and women equally face the problem of losing the mating partner to an intra-sexual rival if the mating partner leaves the relationship entirely (Wilson & Daly, 1996). However, a female partner's sexual infidelity may lead a man to invest in other men's offspring but not the other way around (sexual infidelity per se from a male partner is not likely to induce a woman to unknowingly invest in another woman's child). Thus, men may have evolved to value sexual loyalty more than women have. Accordingly, men's jealousy, relative to women's, is more likely to be focused on guarding against sexual infidelity.

Although women's probability of maternity is not affected by her husband's sexual infidelity, a man's infidelity could divert his valuable investments, attention, and resources from a woman and her children to the female sexual interloper instead. Therefore, women's jealousy, relative to men's, is more likely to be heavily focused on guarding against the loss of a mate's attention, protection, and resources. Because the reproductive consequences of infidelity and partner loss are parallel for men and women in some respects and asymmetric in others, the sexes are predicted to be similarly jealous in some respects and also different where their adaptive problems diverge. That is, men more than women may focus on cues to a partner's potential sexual contact with others—termed *sexual* jealousy—while women more than men should focus on cues to the long-term diversion of a partner's commitment of time, attention, energy, and effort—termed *emotional* jealousy (Buss, Larsen, Westen, & Semmelroth, 1992).

As researchers began differentiating between sexual infidelity and emotional infidelity in their assessments of jealousy, sex differences emerged where they weren't previously observed. Buss et al. (1992) asked American college students to compare two distressing events: (a) their partner having sexual intercourse with someone else, or (b) their partner becoming emotionally involved with someone else. For emotional infidelity, 83% of women found this upsetting, whereas only 40% of the men did. In contrast, 60% of the men experienced their partner's sexual infidelity as more distressing, whereas only 17% of the women did. This sex differ- ence was even more pronounced in people who are dispositionally more jealous (Miller & Maner, 2009), and despite criticisms from some researchers (e.g., Harris, 2000), these findings have been replicated across various cultures (e.g., Brase, Caprar, & Voracek, 2004; Buunk, Angleitner, Oubaid, & Buss, 1996; de Souza, Verderane, Taira, & Otta, 2006; Whitty & Quigley, 2008; Wiederman & Kendall, 1999).

These sex differences are also reflected in physiological responses. Buss et al. (1992) assessed men and women's responses based on corrugator muscle strain (a measure of frowning), electrodermal response (a measure of sweating), and heart rate when imagining these two jealousy scenarios (e.g., "your partner having sex with someone else" and "your partner falling in love with someone else") and found that, across all measures, men were more physiologically distressed by sexual infi- delity whereas women were more physiologically distressed by emotional infidel- ity. Some of these physiological effects were as severe as drinking three cups of strong coffee at one time. These findings were replicated by Pietrzak, Laird, Stevens, and Thompson (2002) who also included a fourth physiological measure—skin temperature. A subsequent study by Takahashi et al. (2006) using fMRI techniques that measure neurophysiological activation also found support for the predicted sex differences. All in all, the evidence has been quite robust for sex-differentiated psy- chologies for sexual jealousy.

While a partner's infidelities constitute key threats to a valued romantic relation- ship, another key threat comes from intrasexual rivals, and the evolutionary perspective also predicts differences in how men and women consider rivals threatening—specifically whether a rival exceeds an individual on key components of mate value. As men especially value sexual resources in a mate, key components of women's mate value include cues to fertility, such as physical attractiveness, health, and youth (since female fertility sharply declines as a function of age). Conversely, women especially value the ability to acquire and provide resources in a partner; thus, key components of men's mate value include cues to social status and dominance (Buss, 1989; Buss & Schmitt, 1993). Indeed, women's self-assessments of their value as a marriage partner were undermined by exposure to highly physically attractive women but not by exposure to socially dominant women, whereas men's self-assessments were undermined by the social dominance than by the physical attractiveness of the men to whom they were exposed (Gutierres, Kenrick, & Partch, 1999).

Across various cultures, men more than women report greater distress when a rival surpasses them on physical strength and financial or job prospects, whereas women report greater distress than do men when rivals surpass them on physical attractiveness (Buss, Shackelford, Choe, Buunk, & Dijkstra, 2000). This distress is also not simply an artifact of unfounded insecurity. Kenrick, Neuberg, Zierk, and Krones (1994) found that when male participants were exposed to physically attractive as compared with average or socially dominant female targets, they rated their current relationships less favorably. In contrast, female participants' evaluations of their current relationships were unaffected by exposure to physically attractive males but were lower after exposure to targets high in dominance. Distress about intrasexual rivals who excel in the traits sought after by one's partner therefore reflects actual concerns about the partner's interest in those rivals with high mate value.

In summary, a considerable body of empirical evidence ranging from cross-cultural studies to physiological experiments has been amassed documenting the presence of sex differences in romantic jealousy. Specifically, men and women differ in their relative upset about sexual and emotional infidelity, which correspond to the sex-differentiated adaptive problems they historically faced in the context of forming long-term mateships.

Behavioral outputs of Jealousy From an evolutionary perspective, emotions are functional mechanisms that motivate behaviors in ways that are aimed at promoting survival and reproductive success (Nesse, 1990). Research on the behavioral outputs of romantic jealousy has focused on a broad class of behaviors called mate retention tactics (Buss & Shackelford, 1997). These tactics can be classified in terms of vigilance (e.g., checking up on a partner, dropping by unexpectedly, snooping through messages) or violence (e.g., physical threats, hitting, murder).

As predicted by evolutionary theory, mate retention intensity varies as a function of how desirable one's partner is to potential rivals. As men value youth and physical attractiveness which are associated with fertility in a mate, men's intensity of mate retention, but not women's, is predicted by their partner's age and physical attractiveness. Men who were married to younger women, relative to men who were married to older women, were more likely to conceal their wives from other men; monopolize their time; punish flirting and other behavioral signals of unfaithfulness; engage in emotional manipulation; ratchet up their signals of relationship commitment; increase the flow of resources; demonstrate possession of the wife with words, physical proximity, and jewelry adornments; threaten rivals with violence; and actually direct violence toward potential mating rivals (Buss & Shackelford, 1997; Daly & Wilson, 1988). Similarly, men whose partners are physically very attractive were more likely than men whose partners are less physically attractive to exhibit higher levels of vigilance, commitment, resource display, verbal and physical signals of possession, and threats against other men (Buss, 2013; Haselton & Gangestad, 2006).

On the flipside, women's mate retention efforts, but not men's, are predicted by their partner's financial income and ambitiousness (Buss & Shackelford, 1997). Men who are ambitious and strive for status often find themselves rubbing shoulders with other driven, successful individuals and drawing the respect and admiration of peers and subordinates, particularly that of women (Buss & Barnes, 1986; Nettle, 2005). Consequently, women married to men who exhibit high levels of ambition and status-striving tended to punish their mates for flirting and demonstrating other cues to infidelity, engaged in emotional manipulation such as guilt induction, provided sexual inducements, enhanced their appearance, and engaged in more verbal signals of possession in public contexts. Women married to men with higher earnings also engaged in more vigilance, appearance enhancement, and possessive ornamentation than women married to men who earned less. Consistent with the expectations derived from an evolutionary perspective of jealousy, men more than women reported using resource displays and intrasexual threats to retain their mates, whereas women more than men reported using appearance enhancements and verbal signals of possession in public contexts to retain their mates (Buss & Shackelford, 1997).

People are faced with a major decision when they discover that a romantic partner has been unfaithful: Should they forgive the partner and remain in the relationship or should they break up and terminate the relationship? Although the cross-cultural finding that infidelity is a major cause of divorce suggests that many choose to break up (Betzig, 1989), a sizable minority chooses to forgive. The aftermath of infidelity certainly depends on a variety of factors, such as family pressure, the presence of dependent children, and whether the betrayed partner is economically dependent on the unfaithful partner. Another key influence resides in the nature of the infidelity or more specifically whether it involved sexual, emotional, or economic components. Men, more so than women, felt that forgiving a sexual infidelity would be harder than an emotional infidelity (Shackelford, Buss, & Bennett, 2002). This is reflected in actual behavior as men, more so than women, are more likely to end a current romantic relationship following a partner's sexual infidelity compared with an emotional infidelity. Women showed the opposite pattern of responses, being more likely, relative to men, not to forgive and to end a relationship following an emotional infidelity than a sexual infidelity. These findings have been replicated (Confer & Cloud, 2011).

Taken together, the behavioral outputs of sexual jealousy correspond with those predicted by evolutionary theory. Sex differences in the components of mate value—in particular men's resources and social status versus women's youth and physical attractiveness—predict the intensity of sex-differentiated effort allocated toward retaining mates. Men devote more effort to mate retention when their partners are young and attractive, whereas women devote more effort to mate retention when their partners are well paid and display an appetite for status-striving. Men and women also differ predictably in the types of mate retention tactics employed, with appearance enhancements being used more often by women and resource displays being used more often by men. Finally, whether men and women forgive their partners following an infidelity depends to a significant degree on whether the infidelity involved a sexual liaison or a deep emotional involvement.

Future Directions: Maladaptive Jealousy in Modern Contexts

As this chapter suggests, a fair amount of knowledge has accumulated over the years on jealousy; nevertheless, there may be various avenues for future research to pursue. For instance, there seems to be a paucity of longitudinal studies in this area—does jealousy tend to increase or decrease the stability of a relationship over time? Additionally, it may be fruitful for researchers to investigate how modern contexts may interact with—and likely increase, rather than decrease—people's jealousy psychology. That is, especially in recent years, technology has allowed humans to live in environments that differ vastly from (and are mismatched to) the ancestral conditions to which evolved psychological mechanisms (including jealousy) are adapted. As such, many cues that psychological mechanisms process as inputs have changed in intensity or number, and their relation to adaptive consequences may also have significantly changed (Li, van Vugt, & Colarelli, 2018; Tooby & Cosmides, 1990). For example, tastes for sweet things, which evolved to adaptively impel humans to eat fruits and other natural foods high in calories and nutrients, are now inducing people to ingest modern foods manufactured with high levels of sugars (e.g., candy bars, soda). For jealousy, mismatched modern environments may lead to an excessive triggering of its onset and thus, to greater subjective distress and relationship stress.

The presentation and consumption of social information, including those that can potentially cause jealousy, can be excessively skewed by social network sites (SNSs) such as Facebook, Twitter, and Instagram in today's world of profuse, ubiquitous technological usage (Yong, Li, Valentine, & Smith, 2017). SNSs give us far more access to the activities and interactions of many other people than our ancestors ever had. Through the ease of communicating with or "following" a myriad of other individuals on SNSs, we can closely keep up with the lives of others, observe what others are talking about in public comment threads as well as in private group chats, and also partake in those conversations. A mismatch that arises from this is the often high level of importance we place on social events and information that has little relation or consequence to our own lives. In an ancestral village of approximately 100–230 people (Dunbar, 1992), events that occurred to a person would be maximally only three degrees of separation away from anybody else in that village (Christakis & Fowler, 2009). Thus, any social information was likely to be self-relevant and important because of the small size of a village community, and therefore we likely evolved to be sensitive to social information, such as gossip, and take much of it seriously.

Although the use of SNSs has its benefits, such as providing an efficient platform for maintaining social interactions, a range of psychologically detrimental effects can also arise due to mismatched interactions between our evolved psychological mechanisms and modern media technologies (cf., Yong et al., 2017). People often compare themselves and their own lives to the skewed impressions of reality presented on SNSs. As people tend to carefully select and curate the things they upload on SNSs, SNSs tend to portray only the most perfect aspects of people's lives, such as flattering photographs, nice holidays, and work success (Siibak, 2009). Our evolved psychological mechanism for digesting social information takes the information we see on SNSs seriously. As SNSs continually present information about how good-looking others are or how well others are doing, avid SNS users are apt to experience envy and dissatisfaction with various aspects of their own lives (Tandoc Jr., Ferrucci, & Duffy, 2015).

Likewise, SNSs trigger excessive jealousy by being a source of more information than people are evolved to need. Increased Facebook use is associated with increased jealousy because of a feedback loop whereby using Facebook exposes people to ambiguous information about their partner that they may not otherwise have access to, which then motivates further use to seek more information that may unwittingly be biased or self-confirming to resolve the ambiguity (Muise, Christofides, & Desmarais, 2009). Before the advent of SNSs, flirty gestures of interest or signs of subtle disregard remained relatively private and within a person's own control, and partners in intimate relationships were not subjected to the scrutiny afforded by SNSs today of their exchanges with other contacts (Utz & Beukeboom, 2011). Seeing on an SNS that one's partner had placed an arm around a member of the opposite sex or that one's partner had "liked" a post by a member of the opposite sex can also be appraised as a relationship threat. Texts on SNSs are also often ambiguous because they are devoid of emotional cues. A neutral message left by a woman on a man's public post on Facebook, such as "hey how r u," can be reinterpreted to be more flirtatious than it really is by the man's jealous partner.

SNSs also offer more avenues for partner monitoring (Utz & Beukeboom, 2011). Jealous individuals generally feel the urge to monitor their partners, such as searching their partner's bags or room when their partner isn't looking. However, jealous individuals are usually aware that such behavior is not socially accepted and forms a trust violation in itself. Visiting the SNS profiles of one's partner and related contacts, however, is a normal aspect of many users' SNS routine. This may be done with the purpose of maintaining contact and keeping up to date with others, and yet in the process, one has the opportunity to monitor the partner and check his or her activities, a practice popularly known as "stalking" (Lyndon, Bonds-Raacke, & Cratty, 2011).

Our evolved propensity for jealousy was designed for a world where the persons we were exposed to did not exceed 100–230 in a village, and social information we had access to was relatively more important, less ambiguous, and less excessive than that of the SNS-laden world we live in today. Future research may therefore examine the ways in which our sensitivity to cues denoting relationship threats can be hijacked by information on SNSs, thus overfeeding the green-eyed monster in modern contexts.

Conclusion

As reviewed in this chapter, jealousy is an emotion that, although commonly associated with negative feelings and relationship conflict, serves as an important function of preventing sexual and other resources from leaving relationships. The application of modern evolutionary theory on the analysis of jealousy not only puts many of the experiences and behaviors associated with jealousy in perspective but also raises important discussions about the nature of jealousy (e.g., jealousy as a basic emotion) and yields many specific predictions that are obscured from prior scientific research (e.g., sex differences in jealousy). Far from being some arbitrary product of culture or psychological defects, our psychology for jealousy is a typical feature of a healthy mind, an adaptive mechanism which has been carefully refined through long periods of evolutionary pressure. Yet, our minds are also vulnerable to various contexts that may excessively trigger jealousy. Armed with a better awareness of the specific cues that our evolved mechanisms for jealousy are sensitive toward, further research examining the features of our modern environment that trigger jealousy can also help us understand how best to manage this often painful and destructive emotion. An evolutionary analysis of jealousy ultimately reveals that despite it being a powerful and potentially destructive emotion, jealousy has likely contributed, over human history, to the prolonged survival of many relationships.

References

Baumeister, R. F., & Leary, M. R. (1995). The need to belong: Desire for interpersonal attachments as a fundamental human motivation. *Psychological Bulletin, 117*, 497–529.

Betzig, L. L. (1989). Causes of conjugal dissolution. *Current Anthropology, 30*, 654–676.

Bhugra, D. (1993). Cross-cultural aspects of jealousy. *International Review of Psychiatry, 5*, 271–280.

Borgerhoff Mulder, M. (1988). Kipsigis bridewealth payments. In L. L. Betzig, M. Borgerhoff Mulder, & P. Turke (Eds.), *Human reproductive behavior* (pp. 65–82). New York, NY: Cambridge University Press.

Brase, G. L., Caprar, D. V., & Voracek, M. (2004). Sex differences in responses to relationship threats in England and Romania. *Journal of Social and Personal Relationships, 21*, 763–778.

Brooke, J. (1991). 'Honor' killing of wives is outlawed in Brazil. *The New York Times*. Retrieved 17 Sept 2017 from: http://www.nytimes.com/1991/03/29/us/honor-killing-of-wives-is-outlawed-in-brazil.html.

Burlingham, D. (1973). The preoedipal infant-father relationship. *Psychoanalytic Study of Child, 28,* 23–47.

Buss, D. M. (1989). Sex differences in human mate preferences: Evolutionary hypotheses tested in 37 cultures. *Behavioral and Brain Sciences, 12,* 1–14.

Buss, D. M. (2000). *The dangerous passion: Why jealousy is as necessary as love and sex.* New York, NY: Simon & Schuster.

Buss, D. M. (2013). Sexual jealousy. *Psychological Topics, 22,* 155–182.

Buss, D. M., & Barnes, M. F. (1986). Preferences in human mate selection. *Journal of Personality and Social Psychology, 50,* 559–570.

Buss, D. M., & Duntley, J. D. (2011). The evolution of intimate partner violence. *Aggression and Violent Behavior, 16,* 411–419.

Buss, D. M., Haselton, M. G., Shackelford, T. K., Bleske, A. L., & Wakefield, J. C. (1998). Adaptations, exaptations, and spandrels. *American Psychologist, 53,* 533–548.

Buss, D. M., Larsen, R., Westen, D., & Semmelroth, J. (1992). Sex differences in jealousy: Evolution, physiology, and psychology. *Psychological Science, 3,* 251–255.

Buss, D. M., & Schmitt, D. P. (1993). Sexual strategies theory: An evolutionary perspective on human mating. *Psychological Review, 100,* 204–232.

Buss, D. M., & Shackelford, T. K. (1997). From vigilance to violence: Mate retention tactics in married couples. *Journal of Personality and Social Psychology, 72,* 346–361.

Buss, D. M., Shackelford, T. K., Choe, J., Buunk, B. P., & Dijkstra, P. (2000). Distress about mating rivals. *Personal Relationships, 7,* 235–243.

Buunk, A. P., Angleitner, A., Oubaid, V., & Buss, D. M. (1996). Sex differences in jealousy in evolutionary and cultural perspective: Tests from the Netherlands, Germany, and the United States. *Psychological Science, 7,* 359–363.

Cavanagh, K., Dobash, R. E., & Dobash, R. P. (2007). The murder of children by fathers in the context of child abuse. *Child Abuse and Neglect, 31,* 731–746.

Christakis, N. A., & Fowler, J. H. (2009). *Connected: The surprising power of our social networks and how they shape our lives.* New York, NY: Little Brown.

Confer, J. C., & Cloud, M. D. (2011). Sex differences in response to imagining a partner's heterosexual or homosexual affair. *Personality and Individual Differences, 50,* 129–134.

Daly, M., & Wilson, M. (1983). *Sex, evolution, and behavior.* Boston, MA: Willard Grant Press.

Daly, M., & Wilson, M. (1988). *Homicide.* Hawthorne, NY: Aldine.

Daly, M., & Wilson, M. (1990). Is parent-offspring conflict sex linked? Freudian and Darwinian models. *Journal of Personality, 58,* 163–189.

Daly, M., Wilson, M., & Weghorst, S. J. (1982). Male sexual jealousy. *Ethology and Sociobiology, 3,* 11–27.

Dawkins, R. (1982). *The extended phenotype.* Oxford, UK: Oxford University Press.

de Miguel, A., & Buss, D. M. (2011). Mate retention tactics in Spain: Personality, sex differences, and relationship status. *Journal of Personality, 79,* 563–586.

de Souza, A. A., Verderane, M. P., Taira, J. T., & Otta, E. (2006). Emotional and sexual jealousy as a function of sex and sexual orientation in a Brazilian sample. *Psychological Reports, 98,* 529–535.

Dobzhansky, T. (1973). Nothing in biology makes sense except in the light of evolution. *American Biology Teacher, 35,* 125–129.

Dunbar, R. I. M. (1992). Neocortex size as a constraint on group size in primates. *Journal of Human Evolution, 22,* 469–493.

Dunn, J. (1988). Sibling influences on childhood development. *Journal of Child Psychology and Psychiatry, 29,* 119–127.

Duntley, J. D. (2005). Adaptations to dangers from humans. In D. M. Buss (Ed.), *The handbook of evolutionary psychology* (pp. 224–249). New York, NY: Wiley.

Ekman, P. (1994). All emotions are basic. In P. Ekman & R. J. Davidson (Eds.), *The nature of emotion: Fundamental questions* (pp. 56–58). New York, NY: Oxford University Press.

Elphinston, R. A., Feeney, J. A., & Noller, P. (2011). Measuring romantic jealousy: Validation of the multidimensional jealousy scale in Australian samples. *Australian Journal of Psychology, 63*, 243–251.

Freeman, D. (1983). *Margaret mead and Samoa: The making and unmaking of an anthropological myth*. New York, NY: Viking Penguin.

Freud, S. (1910). Contributions to the psychology of love. *Papers XI, XII, XIII in Collected Papers, 4*, 192–235.

Gutierres, S. E., Kenrick, D. T., & Partch, J. (1999). Beauty, dominance, and the mating game: Contrast effects in self-assessment reflect gender differences in mate selection criteria. *Personality and Social Psychology Bulletin, 25*, 1126–1134.

Harris, C. R. (2000). Psychophysiological responses to imagined infidelity: The specific innate modular view of jealousy reconsidered. *Journal of Personality and Social Psychology, 78*, 1082–1091.

Hart, S. L. (2015). *Jealousy in infants: Laboratory research on differential treatment*. New York, NY: Springer.

Hart, S. L., Field, T., Del Valle, C., & Letourneau, M. (1998). Infants protest their mothers' attending to an infant-size baby doll. *Social Development, 7*, 54–61.

Hart, S. L., & Legerstee, M. (2010). *Handbook of jealousy: Theories, principles and multidisciplinary approaches*. West-Sussex, UK: Blackwell.

Haselton, M. G., & Gangestad, S. W. (2006). Conditional expression of women's desires and men's mate guarding across the ovulatory cycle. *Hormones and Behavior, 49*, 509–518.

Hill, K., & Hurtado, A. M. (1996). *Ache life history*. New York, NY: Aldine De Gruyter.

Hupka, R. B. (1991). The motive for arousal of romantic jealousy: Its cultural origin. In P. Salovey (Ed.), *The psychology of jealousy and envy* (pp. 252–270). New York, NY: Guilford Press.

Johnson, J. (1969). Organic psychosyndromes due to boxing. *British Journal of Psychiatry, 115*, 45–53.

Jonason, P. K., Li, N. P., & Buss, D. M. (2010). The costs and benefits of the dark triad: Implications for mate poaching and mate retention tactics. *Personality and Individual Differences, 48*, 373–378.

Jung, C. G. (1913). The theory of psychoanalysis. *Psychoanalytic Review, 1913-15*, 1–2.

Kenrick, D. T., Neuberg, S. L., Zierk, K. L., & Krones, J. M. (1994). Evolution and social cognition: Contrast effects as a function of sex, dominance, and physical attractiveness. *Personality and Social Psychology Bulletin, 20*, 210–217.

Li, N. P., van Vugt, M., & Colarelli, S. M. (2018). The evolutionary mismatch hypothesis: Implications for psychological science. *Current Directions in Psychological Science, 27*, 38–44.

Lyndon, A., Bonds-Raacke, J., & Cratty, A. D. (2011). College students' Facebook stalking of ex-partners. *Cyberpsychology, Behavior, and Social Networking, 14*, 711–716.

Marazziti, D., Di Nasso, E., Masala, I., Baroni, S., Abelli, M., Mengali, F., … Rucci, P. (2003). Normal and obsessional jealousy: A study of a population of young adults. *European Psychiatry, 18*, 106–111.

Mathes, E. W., Adams, H. E., & Davies, R. M. (1985). Jealousy: Loss of relationship rewards, loss of self-esteem, depression, anxiety, and anger. *Journal of Personality and Social Psychology, 48*, 1552–1561.

Mead, M. (1928). *Coming of age in Samoa: A psychological study of primitive youth for western civilisation*. New York, NY: Morrow.

Michael, A., Mirza, S., Mirza, K. A., Babu, V. S., & Vithayathil, E. (1995). Morbid jealousy in alcoholism. *British Journal of Psychiatry, 167*, 668–672.

Miller, G. F. (2000). *The mating mind: How sexual choice shaped the evolution of human nature*. New York, NY: Doubleday.

Miller, S. L., & Maner, J. K. (2009). Sex differences in response to sexual versus emotional infidelity: The moderating role of individual differences. *Personality and Individual Differences, 46*, 287–291.

Mirsky, J. (1937). The Eskimo of Greenland. In M. Mead (Ed.), *Cooperation and competition among primitive peoples* (pp. 51–86). New York, NY: McGraw-Hill.

Muise, A., Christofides, E., & Desmarais, S. (2009). More information than you ever wanted: Does facebook bring out the green-eyed monster of jealousy? *CyberPsychology and Behavior, 12*, 441–444.

Nesse, R. M. (1990). Evolutionary explanations of emotions. *Human Nature, 1*, 261–289.

Nesse, R. M., & Berridge, K. C. (1997). Psychoactive drug use in evolutionary perspective. *Science, 278*, 63–66.

Nettle, D. (2005). An evolutionary approach to the extraversion continuum. *Evolution and Human Behavior, 26*, 363–373.

Parrott, W. G. (1991). The emotional experiences of envy and jealousy. In P. Salovey (Ed.), *The psychology of jealousy and envy* (pp. 3–30). New York, NY: Guilford Press.

Pfeiffer, S. M., & Wong, P. T. P. (1989). Multidimensional jealousy. *Journal of Social and Personal Relationships, 6*, 181–196.

Pietrzak, R. H., Laird, J. D., Stevens, D. A., & Thompson, N. S. (2002). Sex differences in human jealousy: A coordinated study of forced-choice, continuous rating-scale, and physiological responses on the same subjects. *Evolution and Human Behavior, 23*, 83–94.

Pines, A. M. (1992). Romantic jealousy: Five perspectives and an integrative approach. *Psychotherapy: Theory, Research, Practice, Training, 29*, 675–683.

Pinker, S., & Bloom, P. (1990). Natural language and natural selection. *Behavioral and Brain Sciences, 13*, 707–727.

Plutchik, R. (1980). *Emotion: A psychoevolutionary synthesis.* New York, NY: Harper & Row.

Shackelford, T. K., Buss, D. M., & Bennett, K. (2002). Forgiveness or breakup: Sex differences in responses to a partner's infidelity. *Cognition and Emotion, 16*, 299–307.

Shackelford, T. K., Goetz, A. T., & Buss, D. M. (2005). Mate retention in marriage: Further evidence of the reliability of the mate retention inventory. *Personality and Individual Differences, 39*, 415–425.

Siibak, A. (2009). Constructing the self through the photo selection: Visual impression management on social networking websites. *Cyberpsychology: Journal of Psychosocial Research on Cyberspace, 3*(1). https://cyberpsychology.eu/article/view/4218/3260 (Retrieved 27 Sept 2017).

Symons, D. (1979). *The evolution of human sexuality.* New York, NY: Oxford University Press.

Takahashi, H., Matsuura, M., Yahata, N., Koeda, M., Suhara, T., & Okubo, Y. (2006). Men and women show distinct brain activations during imagery of sexual and emotional infidelity. *NeuroImage, 32*, 1299–1307.

Tandoc, E. C., Jr., Ferrucci, P., & Duffy, M. (2015). Facebook use, envy, and depression among college students: Is facebooking depressing? *Computers in Human Behavior, 43*, 139–146.

Tooby, J., & Cosmides, L. (1990). The past explains the present: Emotional adaptations and the structure of ancestral environments. *Ethology and Sociobiology, 11*, 375–424.

Tooby, J., & Cosmides, L. (1992). The psychological foundations of culture. In J. Barkow, L. Cosmides, & J. Tooby (Eds.), *The adapted mind* (pp. 19–136). New York, NY: Oxford University Press.

Tooby, J., & Cosmides, L. (2005). Conceptual foundations of evolutionary psychology. In D. M. Buss (Ed.), *The handbook of evolutionary psychology* (pp. 5–67). New York, NY: Wiley.

Trivers, R. L. (1972). Parental investment and sexual selection. In B. Campbell (Ed.), *Sexual selection and the descent of man, 1871–1971* (pp. 136–179). Chicago, IL: Aldine.

Utz, S., & Beukeboom, C. J. (2011). The role of social network sites in romantic relationships: Effects on jealousy and relationship happiness. *Journal of Computer-Mediated Communication, 16*, 511–527.

White, G. L. (1980). Inducing jealousy: A power perspective. *Personality and Social Psychology Bulletin, 6*, 222–227.

Whitty, M. T., & Quigley, L. L. (2008). Emotional and sexual infidelity offline and in cyberspace. *Journal of Marital and Family Therapy, 34*, 461–468.

Wiederman, M. W., & Kendall, E. (1999). Evolution, sex, and jealousy: Investigation with a sample from Sweden. *Evolution and Human Behavior, 20*, 121–128.

Williams, G. C. (1966). *Adaptation and natural selection*. Princeton, NJ: Princeton University Press.

Wilson, M. I., & Daly, M. (1985). Competitiveness, risk taking, and violence: The young male syndrome. *Ethology and Sociobiology, 6*, 59–73.

Wilson, M. I., & Daly, M. (1996). Male sexual proprietariness and violence against wives. *Current Directions in Psychological Science, 5*, 2–7.

Yong, J. C., Li, N. P., Valentine, K. A., & Smith, A. R. (2017). Female virtual intrasexual competition and its consequences: An evolutionary mismatch perspective. In M. L. Fisher (Ed.), *The Oxford handbook of women and competition* (pp. 657–680). New York, NY: Oxford University Press.

Chapter 8
Functions of Anger in the Emotion System

Ira J. Roseman

Abstract This chapter considers the functions of anger as an emotion within an often functional emotion system. It is proposed that emotions are general-purpose coping strategies, usually comprising phenomenological, physiological, expressive, behavioral, and emotivational goal components, each of which fulfills specific functions within an emotion's strategy. For example, typical instances of anger involve thoughts about undeserved harm, feeling hot and ready to explode, activity in circuits running through the medial amygdala and hypothalamus, lowered brows and squarish mouth, readiness to attack, and a goal of hurting its target or compelling change in the target's behavior. Together they implement a strategy of interpersonal coercion. Emotions are typically elicited by combinations of appraisals about significant changes in motive-attainment (e.g., goal blockage caused by other persons, when there may be something that can be done about it, eliciting anger) and function to provide alternative ways to attain one's motives (alternative to each other and to action governed by what have traditionally been considered motives, such as hunger and the need for achievement) in particular types of situations. The Emotion System theory offers an account of why people and other organisms have emotions and why they have the particular emotions that they do. Explanations for emotion dysfunctions, such as anger disorders, are also discussed. Finally, the theory is applied to examine anger in the political domain.

> *I have spent years overcoming the issues that have surrounded my abandonment by [identity withheld]...I'm angry because he will not simply acknowledge that what he did was wrong and take his responsibility for it. I'm angry because of everything I had to go through because of his choices. [He] will not claim responsibility for his choices. He acts like he has no blame in the situation and that it was entirely my fault, even though I was a child. He refuses to acknowledge that him kicking me out with nowhere to go was neglect and abandonment...It is an almost uncontrollable feeling. I feel like I have no control. I feel like breaking things, hurting things, yelling, and screaming. I want desperately to make [him] feel what I felt because I feel that is the only way he will understand what he put me through*

I. J. Roseman (✉)
Department of Psychology, Rutgers University, Camden, NJ, USA
e-mail: ira.roseman@rutgers.edu

© Springer International Publishing AG, part of Springer Nature 2018   141
H. C. Lench (ed.), *The Function of Emotions*,
https://doi.org/10.1007/978-3-319-77619-4_8

and maybe that would make him take responsibility. I want him to hurt. At the same time, I don't want him in my life. I want him gone.

[What thoughts is anger making you think?]

That he needs to suffer. That I didn't deserve this. That it's unfair. That he needs to be punished.

[What physical sensations is anger making you feel?]

I feel hot, perspiring a little. My body is shaking, my hands trembling.

[What is anger making you feel like doing?]

Hurting something; breaking something; yelling; screaming; calling him to yell and scream.

[What is anger making you want?]

It makes me want some kind of justice, some kind of amends, some kind of closure. It also makes me want to hurt those who hurt me so that they know what it was like.

-Research participant describing something that is causing anger right now more than any other emotion (Roseman, Steele, & Goodvin, 2017)

What Is an Emotion: A Functional Approach

Like a number of other concepts in the social sciences, such as culture (e.g., Jahoda, 2012), leadership (Northouse, 2016), and religion (Hill et al., 2000), and in the natural sciences, such as the limbic system (Kotter & Stephan, 1997), autism (Rutter, 2005), and arousal (Jing, Gilette, & Weiss, 2009), there are varying definitions of emotion. Building on prior theory and research (e.g., Averill, 1980; Kleinginna & Kleinginna, 1981; Lazarus, 1991; Roseman, 2011; Scherer, 2009), emotions are conceptualized here as alternative, general-purpose response syndromes that have evolved as strategies to cope adaptively in reaction to specific perceptions about the fate of motives. The following sections elucidate this conceptualization, with special attention to anger.

Elicitors of Anger and Other Emotions in the Emotion System

To understand the functions of emotions, it is necessary to specify when they typically occur. Many contemporary theories maintain that emotions are usually evoked by appraisals, rather than by events themselves (e.g., Arnold, 1960; Roseman & Smith, 2001), and most appraisal theories hold that particular emotions are elicited by *combinations* of appraisals (e.g., Lazarus, 1991; Roseman, 2001; Scherer, 2009; Smith & Kirby, 2011). The Emotion System theory (Roseman, 2013) proposes that 7 appraisals combine to elicit 17 distinct emotions (16 positive or negative emotions, plus the neutral-valenced emotion of surprise).

These appraisals are:

1. *Unexpectedness: not unexpected/unexpected*—whether the event violates the expectations of the person feeling the emotions (cf. Reisenzein, 2000)

2. *Situational State*: *motive-consistency/inconsistency*—whether the event is wanted vs. unwanted by the person (cf. Frijda, 1986, concern match vs. mismatch; Scherer, 2009, goal conducive vs. obstructive; Smith & Kirby, 2011, goal congruent vs. incongruent)
3. *Motivational State*: *appetitive/aversive*—whether the event is related to a motive that seeks more of something pleasant vs. less of something unpleasant (cf. Carver & Scheier, 2012, goals vs. anti-goals)
4. *Probability*: *uncertain/certain*—whether the occurrence of motive-relevant aspects of the event is possible vs. definite (cf. Scherer, 2009, outcome probability)
5. *Agency*: *unspecified or impersonal/other person/self*—what or who, if anyone, is seen as causing the motive-relevant event (cf. Scherer, 2009, agent, intention; Smith & Kirby, 2011, accountability)
6. *Control Potential*: *low/high*—whether there is nothing one can do vs. something one can do about the motive-relevant aspects of negative events (cf. Scherer, 2009, control, power; Smith & Kirby, 2011, problem-focused coping potential)
7. *Problem Type*: *instrumental/intrinsic*—whether a motive-inconsistent event is unwanted because it has negative effects (e.g., blocks attainment of a goal) vs. unwanted because of some inherent attribute (cf. Janoff-Bulman, 1979, behavioral vs. characterological blame)

Hypothesized relationships between appraisals and emotional responses, and the place of anger in the system, are shown in Fig. 8.1.

The Emotion System theory proposes that anger is elicited by appraising an event as having motive-inconsistent effects (e.g., a goal blockage), caused by another person, when one's control potential is seen as relatively high. Research has found support for motive-inconsistency (e.g., Frijda, Kuipers, & ter Schure, 1989; Roseman, Antoniou, & Jose, 1996; Scherer & Fontaine, 2013), goal blockage (e.g., Ceulemans, Van Mechelen, & Kuppens, 2012), and other-person-agency (e.g., Frijda et al., 1989; Roseman et al., 1996; Tong, 2010) as involved in eliciting anger. Regarding the latter, Averill's (1982) survey of community residents and students found that anger was felt toward other persons in the vast majority of instances; a small number of exceptions involved treating a nonhuman target "as if it were a person" (p. 166; cf. Fernandez & Wasan, 2010). Ellsworth and Tong (2006) studied cases of anger at the self. I suggest that these are instances in which the self is chastised as if it were another person ("Dammit, why did you leave your briefcase in the middle of the floor!") co-occurring with other emotions—guilt, shame, and regret were also elevated in this study, along with appraisals of self-responsibility.

There have been mixed results regarding appraisals of power or control potential contributing to anger elicitation (e.g., Frijda et al., 1989; Kuppens, Van Mechelen, Smits, & De Boeck, 2003; Roseman et al., 1996). This may reflect a dual relationship of control or control potential to anger (Roseman & Fischer, 2017): the angry individual lacked sufficient control to prevent the angering event, but may have enough potential control to do something about it. Consistent with this view, Litvak, Lerner, Tiedens, and Shonk (2010) suggest that anger is unpleasant looking back on

	Positive Emotions		Negative Emotions	
	Motive-Consistent		Motive-Inconsistent	
	Appetitive Motive (+)	Aversive Motive (-)	Appetitive Motive (+)	Aversive Motive (-)

(Circumstance-caused) Unexpected

Surprise
PHE: unexpectedness; stunned
EXP: brows raised, arched; eyes wide; mouth open, oval; gasp
BEH: interrupt, inquire
EMV: understand
<suspend movement>

Not Unexpected / Uncertain

Hope
PHE: potential; focused
EXP: brows slightly raised, eyes widened, upward gaze
BEH: anticipate, approach
EMV: make happen
<prepare to move toward or to stop moving away from it>

Fear
PHE: danger; cold; heart pounding
EXP: brows raised, straight; eyes wide; lips drawn back
BEH: vigilance, inhibition or flight
EMV: get to safety, prevent
<prepare to move away from or to stop moving toward it>

(Low Control Potential)

Certain

Joy (+)
PHE: attainment; excited, light
EXP: smile
BEH: jump up, celebrate
EMV: sustain
<move toward it>

Relief (-)
PHE: amelioration; calming
EXP: exhalation, sigh
BEH: rest, relax
EMV: return to normal
<stop moving away from it>

Sadness (+)
PHE: missing, lethargy, throat lump
EXP: weep, inner brows raised
BEH: inaction
EMV: recover
<stop moving toward it>

Distress (-)
PHE: harm; agitated
EXP: cry out
BEH: move around, leave
EMV: terminate, get away
<move away from it>

Uncertain

Hope
PHE: potential; focused
EXP: brows slightly raised, eyes widened, upward gaze
BEH: anticipate, approach
EMV: make happen
<prepare to move toward or to stop moving away from it>

Frustration
PHE: obstacle; tense
EXP: brows lowered
BEH: exert effort
EMV: overcome
<move against it>

Disgust
PHE: repulsiveness; nausea
EXP: wrinkled nose
BEH: expel, purge, reject
EMV: remove
<move it away from you>

(High Control Potential)

Certain

Joy (+)
PHE: attainment; excited, light
EXP: smile
BEH: jump up, celebrate
EMV: sustain
<move toward it>

Relief (-)
PHE: amelioration; calming
EXP: exhalation, sigh
BEH: rest, relax
EMV: return to normal
<stop moving away from it>

Other-caused / Uncertain / Certain

Love
PHE: appreciation; drawn to someone
EXP: sustained relaxed eye contact, lean toward
BEH: touch, hold
EMV: connect
<move toward other>

Dislike
PHE: other unappealing; cold
EXP: refuse eye contact
BEH: decrease attention to
EMV: dissociate, avoid interaction
<move away from other>

(Low Control Potential)

Uncertain / Certain

Anger
PHE: injustice; explosive
EXP: brows lowered, square mouth
BEH: yell, hit, criticize
EMV: hurt, get revenge, compel
<move against other>

Contempt
PHE: other unworthy; revulsion
EXP: sneer, "tse," head raised
BEH: look down on, disparage
EMV: exclude
<move other away>

(High Control Potential)

Self-caused / Uncertain / Certain

Pride
PHE: self-worth; big, powerful
EXP: head back, expanded posture
BEH: exhibit, assert
EMV: recognition, dominance
<move toward self>

Regret
PHE: mistake; sick, sinking
EXP: eyes closed; lips stretched, pressed together
BEH: do over, do differently
EMV: correct, improve
<move away from self>

(Low Control Potential)

Uncertain / Certain

Guilt
PHE: transgression; heavy
EXP: shift gaze
BEH: reproach, punish self
EMV: oblige, redress
<move against self>

Shame
PHE: self unworthy; small
EXP: head and gaze down
BEH: withdraw, hide, submit
EMV: conceal
<move self away>

(High Control Potential)

Instrumental Problem | Intrinsic Problem

Note. Emotion components: PHE=phenomenological; EXP=expressive; BEH=behavioral; EMV=emotivational goal. Strategies integrating the response components for each emotion are given in angle brackets. Appraisal combinations eliciting each emotion are found by proceeding outward from an emotion box to its borders around the chart.

• Contacting family appraisal, emotions.   • Distancing family appraisal, emotions.   • Attack family appraisal, emotions.   • Rejection family appraisal, emotions.

Fig. 8.1 Hypothesized structure of the Emotion System, showing appraisals and some resulting emotional responses. (Adapted and revised from Roseman, 2013) (Note: Emotion components: *PHE* phenomenological, *EXP* expressive, *BEH* behavioral, *EMV* emotivational goal. Strategies integrating the response components for each emotion are given in angle brackets. Appraisal combinations eliciting each emotion are found by proceeding outward from an emotion box to its borders around the chart)

eliciting events, but pleasant when one looks forward, anticipating overcoming obstacles and opponents, or taking revenge. Such envisioned outcomes indicate appraised control potential. Keltner, Young, Heerey, Oemig, and Monarch (1998) found that fraternity members in positions of greater power showed more angry facial expressions in teasing interactions than members in lower power positions.

In two studies of recalled anger experiences, Lemay, Overall, and Clark (2012) found that anger intensity was significantly correlated with appraisals of control.

In addition, appraisals of injustice or unfairness correlate with anger (Averill, 1982; Kuppens et al., 2003; Shaver, Schwartz, Kirson, & O'Connor, 1987; Tong, 2010) and can provide a measure of control potential (French & Raven, 1959, "legitimate power"). Lerner (2015) has described how people become committed to the belief that one will "most of the time, and in most part," get what one deserves (p. 211) and has detailed much research supporting the existence of (an often pre-conscious) belief in a just world across many contexts. This provides strong evidence that perceived injustice will often confer control potential—a sense that ultimately wrongs will be righted. Having justice on one's side may also enable one to influence a harm-doer's behavior or recruit assistance from third parties (Roseman, 1984). Perceived unfairness may not be a *necessary* determinant of anger, given anger-related responses in animals (e.g., Blanchard & Blanchard, 2003) and 4- to 8-month-old infants (Lewis, Alessandri, & Sullivan, 1990). Instead, infants show such reactions when they learn that they can exercise control over events (Lewis et al., 1990).

Even when control potential is objectively lacking, perceiving that a person should not have done something, or an event should not have happened, may create at least a primitive or temporary sense of control potential (a sense that one *should* be able to do something about the situation; cf. "arrogant entitlement," Kuppens et al., 2003). Appraisals of control potential may help explain why children's "protest" reactions to separation (Bowlby, 1969), including temper tantrums, precede "despair" reactions, which are characterized by despondency (Simpson & Belsky, 2008) as a caregiver's continued absence eventually erodes the child's sense that something can be done to bring him/her back at that time. Among adults, data fitting the J-curve theory of revolutions (Davies, 1962) indicate that protests, riots, and rebellions (which, as discussed below, often involve anger) are likely to occur not when oppression is most intense but rather when a downturn follows a period of improvement. In such instances, the history of rising expectations may suggest that change is possible.

There is controversy about whether any or all of these appraisals are necessary or sufficient to elicit emotions, including anger (Kuppens et al., 2003). As Izard (1993) observed, claims of appraisal necessity are challenged by instances of non-cognitive emotion generation, such as from physiological manipulations (e.g., psychoactive drugs; brain stimulation), enacted expressions (e.g., Ekman, Levenson, & Friesen, 1983), or emotion contagion (Hatfield, Cacioppo, & Rapson, 1994). However, insofar as there can be more than one cause of an effect, such findings are not incompatible with appraisal being the typical elicitor of anger and other emotions.

More problematic is evidence that the specified appraisal combinations can occur without the consequent emotions. For example, in a careful investigation of "pure" experiences of anger, sadness, fear, and guilt, Tong (2010) found that each of the appraisals that he studied was associated with greater likelihood of experiencing the theoretically linked emotions, but the appraisal-emotion relationships were probabilistic. Nevertheless, this study found that anger became more likely as the number of its measured determinants increased. The conditional probability of experiencing anger given an appraisal of unfairness was 0.21; given the combination of unfairness and unpleasantness, 0.33; and given unfairness, unpleasantness, and responsibility of others, 0.39 (the addition of an appraisal of obstacles did not increase the conditional probability above 0.39). This raises the possibility that adding other key appraisals could further increase the likelihood of experiencing the hypothesized emotions, and Tong (2010, p. 699) notes that "this study might have overlooked critical appraisals." The Emotion System theory suggests that control potential may be such a key appraisal determinant, e.g., in cases where unfairness yields insufficient expectation of countering a negative outcome. Wortman and Brehm (1975) concluded that expectations of control differentiated depression-like learned helplessness vs. more anger-like reactance in response to non-contingent outcomes.

Anger and Other Emotions as Response Syndromes

How are the responses of anger similar to and distinct from those of other emotions in the emotion system? Different theorists and researchers have focused on different responses as characteristic of emotions, including subjective feelings (e.g., Davitz, 1969; Barrett, Mesquita, Ochsner, & Gross, 2007), thoughts (e.g., Lerner & Tiedens, 2006; Ortony, Clore, & Collins, 1988), physiological responses (e.g., Kreibig, 2010; Panksepp, 2017), facial expressions (e.g., Ekman, 2003; Keltner, Tracy, Sauter, Cordaro, & McNeil, 2016), behaviors (e.g., Frijda, 1986; Plutchik, 1980), and motivations (e.g., Izard, 1991; Tomkins, 1970).

Many see emotions as encompassing multiple response sytems. The conceptualization proposed here, like that of Scherer (2009), includes all five of the above response types as components of emotion syndromes. Note that appraisals (perceptions of the fate of motives, such as in anger, undeserved harm caused by another person) can be antecedent causes of emotions and also part of the phenomenology of an emotion once it occurs. But the phenomenological component also includes thoughts other than appraisals, that arise when an emotion is triggered (e.g., in anger, thoughts about hurting the target). Conceptualizing emotions as syndromes (Averill, 1980) indicates that specified properties of an emotion tend to co-occur, but no particular property is essential for the emotion to be present (cf. Fehr & Russell, 1984; Shaver et al., 1987). It is also possible that a modified syndrome conceptualization (e.g., with some common neural circuitry variably expressed in other components; see Potegal & Stemmler, 2010) will better characterize emotions, though a number of researchers maintain that meta-analytic evidence for unique brain-emotion patterning is lacking (e.g., Clark-Polner, Wager, Satpute, & Barrett, 2016).

The *phenomenological* component includes thoughts and feelings that are typical of an emotion, such as in anger, thoughts about injustice (Averill, 1982), appraisals of certainty (Lerner & Keltner, 2001), and ruminations about revenge

(Sukhodolsky, Golub, & Cromwell, 2001); and feeling aroused, hot, and as if one would explode (Kövecses, 2010; Roseman, Wiest, & Swartz, 1994; Scherer & Wallbott, 1994). For example, in the deidentified sample narrative that began this chapter, the research participant says that his suffering was underserved and unfair, is sure of what the target of his anger will not "acknowledge," "can't seem to let go of that anger," and thinks that the target "needs to be punished." He also reports that his anger is making him feel hot, perspiring a little.

The *physiological* component encompasses central and peripheral patterns of neural, chemical, and muscular responses. For example, it has been proposed that the physiology of anger or rage includes activity in neural circuits running from the medial amygdala (Potegal & Stemmler, 2010) through the hypothalamus and midbrain periaqueductal gray (Blair, 2016; Panksepp, 2017), increases in both adrenaline and noradrenaline levels (Stemmler, 2010), increased general peripheral resistance (due to vascular constriction) but vasodilation in active muscles (Goldstein, Edelberg, Meier, & Davis, 1989) and facial skin (Stemmler, 2010), and increased muscle tension (Ax, 1953).

The *expressive* component consists of facial, vocal, and postural responses, as well as movements, that signal one's emotion to others. According to Matsumoto, Keltner, Shiota, O'Sullivan, and Frank (2008), research indicates anger is associated with the following action units from the Facial Action Coding System (Ekman, Friesen, & Hager, 2002): 4 (eyebrows lowered and drawn together, forming a furrowed brow); 5 (upper eyelid raised, widening the eyes, and creating the appearance of a fixed stare) or 7 (upper and lower eyelids tightened, narrowing the eyes); 23 (tightened lips, making their red parts seem narrower); and 22 (funneled lips which can expose teeth, as in Fig. 8.2a, similar to the squarish mouth associated with anger in Izard's, 1983 MAX coding) or 24 (lips pressed together). Vocalizations that research participants identify as anger tend to be loud, fast, and rising in pitch (Green, Whitney, & Gustafson, 2010). A stance with the head bent back, shoulders straight, and arms raised forward and upward (resembling a fighting pose) was differentially identified as anger in a study by Coulson (2004; Fig. 8.2b). Across

Fig. 8.2 (**a**) Facial expression of anger (from Matsumoto & Hwang, 2011). (**b**) Posture most reliably identified as anger (from Coulson, 2004)

American, British, and Kreung cultures, Parkinson, Walker, Memmi, and Wheatley (2017) found that fast movement with arms thrust forcefully downward distinguished anger from disgust, fear, sadness, and happiness.

The *behavioral* component comprises tendencies and readiness to take particular actions when feeling an emotion. Anger has been associated with readiness to engage in aggressive behaviors (e.g., Berkowitz, 2012; Frijda et al., 1989). Averill's (1982) landmark study found that 93% of community residents and students reported feeling like acting aggressively in anger incidents in the week prior to filling out his survey and that 83% actually did so. More than twice as many (82%) felt like aggressing verbally as compared with those who felt like engaging in physical aggression (40%; see also Kassinove, Sukhodolsky, Tsytsarev, & Solovyova, 1997). Non-aggressive responses, such as talking about the angering incident with the instigator or a neutral third party, were reported by 75% of respondents (though at least some of these could be attempts to reduce the anger). Shaver et al. (1987) found a majority of anger incidents characterized by verbal attack and shouting. Similarly, Roseman et al. (1994) found recalled anger experiences differentiated from other negative emotions by the items "say something nasty" and "feel like yelling." The research participant in the anger narrative quoted at the start of this chapter felt like breaking something, yelling, and screaming.

The *emotivational* component consists of goals that people want to pursue when experiencing an emotion (Roseman, 1984; cf. De Rivera, 1977; Frijda, 1986), as distinct from goals (e.g., maintaining self-esteem; completing a task) whose blockage may have elicited the emotion (though blockage of emotivational goals can elicit additional emotions). Goals proposed as characteristic of anger include removal of an obstruction (e.g., Frijda, 1986; cf. Lench & Levine, 2008), correcting some injustice (e.g., Averill, 1982), or getting revenge (e.g., Aristotle, 1966; Roseman, 2011). If aggression involves intent to harm (e.g., Anderson & Bushman, 2002) and readiness for aggression is associated with anger, then hurting in some way (even if it only involves making the target feel bad) seems at least one short-term goal of anger (Roseman, 2011). For example, Roseman et al. (1994) found that participants recalling anger experiences agreed they wanted to hurt someone and get back at someone. In the anger narrative above, among other goals, the participant says he wants the target of his anger "to hurt."

However, while hurting the target in some way can be a salient immediate goal in anger, it is unclear whether it is a primary or ultimate emotivational goal of anger. Our research participant said "I want to hurt those who hurt me so that they know what it was like." He wants that "because I feel that is the only way [the harm doer] will understand what he put me through and maybe that would make him take responsibility." He also reports wanting "some kind of justice, some kind of amends, some kind of closure." The goal of revenge suggests not merely harm, but a connection or calibration of harm inflicted to harm returned (see Frijda, 1994). Perhaps harm-seeking should be understood as an intermediate goal of anger—a means to making the target change behavior and deterring similar instances of harm (Fessler, 2010).

Gollwitzer, Meder, and Schmitt (2011) found that research participants who take revenge against a partner's unfair actions feel more satisfied, or feel that everyone got what they deserved, if offenders acknowledge having done harm and admit fault (rather than merely suffering, which would have been consistent with a harm-seeking goal). Though felt satisfaction in their studies was not empirically related to anger, such findings raise the possibility that revenge-seeking in anger also aims at (a) restoring status lost through victimization, and/or (b) obtaining reason to believe the offensive conduct will not be repeated (Gollwitzer et al., 2011).

The goal of *compelling others' behavior* may also better encompass instances of anger felt toward friends and loved ones (in Averill's, 1982 survey, a loved one or friend was the target in 54% of anger instances). Coding narratives of emotions in marital relationships, Fitness and Fletcher (1993) found an urge to physically hurt the partner in only 7% of anger incidents, and an impulse to revenge in only 2%. Parent-child anger may be similar, with instances of actually wanting to hurt the target being relatively rare. Similarly, although revenge may sometimes be desired in parent-child anger, there are many cases in which it seems to play no part. If a parent is angry at a child for not cleaning his room, or a child at a parent for refusing to allow her to go to a party, the goal seems often to be influencing the target's behavior (and if the behavior changes, anger is likely to diminish). Consistent with this view, Fischer and Roseman (2007) found that anger was more associated than contempt with a goal they called "coercion." Three of the four items measuring this goal ("I wanted the other not to do this again," "I wanted the other to realize that he/she has gone too far," "I wanted the other to apologize") specify or imply seeking behavior change (the fourth item, "I wanted to get even with this person," seems to tap revenge). Smetana, Daddis, and Chuang (2003) found that parent-adolescent conflicts in middle-class African-American families were typically resolved by adolescents giving in and occasionally by compromise (and in resolved conflicts parental use of punishment was lower).

In Fig. 8.1 "compel" is proposed as a characteristic goal in anger, rather than "coerce," as the angry person may not want to utilize threats to induce behavior change. Again, it is considering anger at friends or loved ones which suggests that threatening may not be integral to the goals of angry persons—making the target act (or not act) in a certain way seems more characteristic across instances. It is also possible that "impel" is a better description than "compel" of the typical goal pursued in anger. According to grammarist.com (n.d.), "A person who is *impelled* has been persuaded to do something (perhaps based on moral grounds) and does so at least partially of his or her own volition. *Compel* implies that the person being compelled has no choice in the matter and is being coerced. For the person being compelled, the coercion is so strong that choice and morality don't enter into it." However, insofar as—at least in some instances—the angry person wants to influence the target's action whether or not the target is willing, "compel" may be the more generally applicable formulation. Three studies by Lemay et al. (2012) found that in recalled experiences relevant to anger, anger intensity was correlated with the goal of changing the target's behavior.

An alternative hypothesis is that a goal when experiencing anger is to make the target feel bad (more or rather than to inflict physical harm). Pursuing that goal would fit with the proposed strategy and function of anger (discussed below). As already noted, the literature on hostile aggression shows there are instances in which people do intend to harm the targets of their rage. Research is needed to elucidate the conditions under which anger results in intent to harm or, if harm is generally intended in anger, to identify the determinants of the degree of harm sought (from making the target feel bad to inflicting physical injury). In recognition of this gap in knowledge, Fig. 8.1 retains revenge and hurting (with degree unspecified) as emotivational goals, along with the goal of compelling the target's behavior.

Fischer and Roseman (2007) also found that, compared with contempt, anger was more associated with reconciliation ("making up," "talking it over," "solving the problem"). This finding could be interpreted as indicating that one of the emotivational goals of anger is to maintain a relationship with the target of the emotion (e.g., de Vos, van Zomeren, Gordijn, & Postmes, 2016). However, the score for anger on Fischer and Roseman's (2007) reconciliation index was below the scale midpoint, suggesting that anger is associated with reconciliation only in comparison to contempt. Moreover, the targets of the recalled anger incidents were relatively intimate with the angry person, and the desire for reconciliation was reported as a reaction after some days, whereas the immediate response involved attack (confrontation, tough language, unfriendly remarks, and criticism). These considerations all call into question whether reconciliation and relationship maintenance are part of anger or rather separate goals operative especially when the target of anger is someone with whom one already has a close relationship—goals that can follow or coexist with anger more easily than with contempt. Fischer and Roseman (2007) proposed that reconciliation may occur especially if undesired outcomes are altered.

De Vos, van Zomeren, Gordijn, and Postmes (2013, Study 1) found that Dutch students perceived German students as wanting a relationship with the Dutch more if the Germans communicated anger about discrimination than if they did not mention anger. However, in that experiment, the ascribed goal of having a relationship may be attributable to the context (a fictitious newspaper story described the German students as having come to the Netherlands to study, and reacting to Dutch students who were arguing they should stay in Germany instead) rather than to anger itself. Anger in that case may be compatible with the desire for a relationship, and even arise from perceiving the Dutch students as blocking this goal. Analogously, anger in attachment relationships (Bowlby, 1973, p. 278, cited in de Vos et al., 2016) may arise when proximity-seeking or other relationship goals are thwarted. But the relationship goals are separable from the anger (they exist prior to and subsequent to the anger response) and indeed may be diminished when one is feeling anger, as when some infants temporarily refuse to interact with an attachment figure after separation (as with the "insecure resistant" group in Waters, 2002), or adults feel a lessening of closeness and desire for intimacy when angry at a romantic partner (see Bozman & Beck, 1991).

Emotions as Coping Strategies: The Functions of Emotions

As discussed in Roseman (2011), examining the constituents of emotion syndromes suggests that the various responses characteristic of each particular emotion appear to be related to each other, forming distinctive strategies for coping with particular types of situations (see also Lazarus, 1991). These emotional coping strategies, like reproductive strategies (Kenrick & Keefe, 1992), have been shaped through natural selection and need not be consciously pursued by the person feeling an emotion. Each emotion's strategy fulfills the functions of that emotion.

Tolman (1923) observed that emotions are not just reactions to events, but responses that "act back" on those events, in order to influence them. Response syndromes in positive emotions function to "get more" of something, such as by moving toward something (an emotion-eliciting stimulus), by forming a relationship with someone (when motive fulfillment may be provided by another person), or by exhibiting characteristics and actions of the self (when outcomes are self-caused). Response syndromes of negative emotions function to "get less of something" by moving away from something, by moving something away the self, or by moving against something (see Fig. 8.1). According to the Emotion System theory, the strategy of anger is to *move against another person*.

Functions of the Emotion Components within an Emotion Strategy

Within emotion syndromes, each response component has a functional role to play in implementing the strategy of the emotion (here, moving against the target of one's anger). The emotivational component comprises goals that motivate and guide instrumental behavior. For example, in anger, the goal of hurting the target in some way (Roseman et al., 1994), or compelling the target's actions, motivates behaviors aiming to create some negative consequence (e.g., guilt, shame, regret, physical pain, loss of some benefit, or fear of any of these) for the target's unwanted actions. The behavioral component suggests behaviors that evolutionary history or experience has indicated may succeed in furthering the emotion's strategy. For example, in anger, protesting, yelling, and hitting (e.g., Potegal & Qiu, 2010) are behaviors that move against the target and could pressure the target to act or to refrain from acting in a particular way. The expressive component transmits communications that can lead perceivers to act in ways consistent with the expresser's strategy. Facial, vocal, and postural responses of anger communicate strength (Sell, Cosmides, & Tooby, 2014) and threaten aggressive behavior (e.g., Eibl-Eibesfeldt, 1989).

The phenomenological component primes potentially relevant thoughts, makes salient important features of situations, and cues retrieval of other experiences of the emotion and associated information. Prototypical thoughts in anger focus attention on injustices and harms perceived as caused by the target, and ways of preventing, halting, or avenging them (Sukhodolsky et al., 2001). Labeling one's state as anger, and feeling hot and ready to explode, connect current instances to previous experiences of anger, also potentially priming relevant behaviors and enhancing access to information about responses that have or have not achieved emotivational goals in similar situations–thereby helping to guide goal-directed emotional behavior.

The physiological component prepares for, organizes, facilitates, and provides the physical substrate for the various responses within an emotion's strategy. In anger, particular patterns of neural activity in the amygdala-hypothalamus-PAG circuits mentioned previously–perhaps modulated by the ventromedial prefrontal cortex calculating potential rewards of aggression and the orbitofrontal cortex processing potential punishments (Potegal & Stemmler, 2010)–may motivate, organize, and shape aggressive action; increases in respiration and blood pressure increase energy available for attack; facial muscle movements and flushing signal and communicate anger; and afferent feedback from such processes to the cerebral cortex contributes to the emotion's phenomenology. White, Brislin, Sinclair, and Blair (2014) found that in response to unfair offers in the Social Fairness Game, there was increased activity in the PAG and decreased activity in the vmPFC, both associated with increased punishment of the partner making the unfair offer.

From Emotion Strategies to Emotion Functions

Emotion strategies exist within a functional context, connecting situation types to coping responses, within a set of available coping alternatives. Thus the function of an emotion may correspond to the likely effect of an emotion strategy in the type of situation which elicits that emotion.

Various functions have been proposed for anger. Some identify relatively specific functional effects, such as:

- *Safeguarding physical survival* by removing threats to the self (Keltner & Haidt, 2001)
- *Terminating and deterring transgressions* by the target and other people (Fessler, 2010)
- *Redressing injustice* (Solomon, 1990)
- Motivating the angry person to avoid negative outcomes by *averting subordination* and *gaining superiority* (Stemmler, 2010)
- *Decreasing willingness to cooperate with* and *increasing willingness to impose costs upon the target*, thus increasing the target's willingness to cooperate and decreasing the target's willingness to impose costs upon the angry person (Tooby & Cosmides, 2008)

Others are more general:

- *Confrontationally increasing short-term social distance* between the self and the target (Fischer & Manstead, 2016)

- *Overcoming obstacles to goals* (Lench, Bench, Darbor, & Moore, 2015)
- *Mobilizing resources* (both physical and psychological) to cope with adversity, *energizing aggressive action* to correct a problem, and *conveying displeasure* (thus *promoting conflict resolution*; Novaco, 2010)

Each of these theories makes a contribution to understanding anger's functions. Transgressions and injustices are prototypical causes of anger (Kuppens et al., 2003), subordination predicts vulnerability to future harm, and threats to survival are of ultimate importance. Yet, anger can be elicited by and cope with challenges to *any* motive (as will be discussed below). Obstacles to goals can elicit anger (Ceulemans et al., 2012), and the overcoming function encompasses instances of anger at inanimate objects and the self. But typical responses of anger (e.g., threatening expressions, readiness for and actual verbal or physical aggression, seeking to make the target feel bad) are especially suited to dealing with other people, who can understand communications of displeasure, protest, and threat, and experience the psychological and physical pain of criticism, animus, and aggression.

Anger does function to change targets' behavior but so do other negative emotions, such as sadness (soliciting assistance) or shame (avoiding censure), and even positive emotions, such as joy (encouraging continued provision of reward). Indeed it is plausible that *all* human emotions have evolved in part to influence others' actions within the species' social context, which is why emotions have expressions. Thus a more specific account is required for anger. Given anger's distinctive responses (moving against another person by confrontational or aggressive action) and the situations in which they occur (goal blockage or harm, caused by other persons, when there may be something one can do about it), the most precise description of the specific function of anger may be to *coerce another person's action* (forcefully changing it from what it would otherwise have been).

According to the American Heritage Dictionary (n.d.), coerce means "to pressure, intimidate, or force (someone) into doing something." It is an intended effect of the strategy of moving against another person, and it makes functional sense in situations that are accurately appraised as involving relatively high control potential. As will be discussed in more detail in the section on appraisal-emotion relationships, the hypothesized coercion function fits both the response profile of anger and the situations in which it typically occurs.

Variability in Emotional Response

It is important to acknowledge that manifestations of an emotion syndrome may differ across individuals, time, and situations (Barrett, 2009; Roseman, 2011). For example, an angry facial expression may include pressed together lips as well as bared teeth (Matsumoto, Keltner, Shiota, O'Sullivan, & Frank, 2008), and anger may occur without facial expression (Ekman, 1972; Kerr & Schneider, 2008). Angry behavior can involve verbal aggression (e.g., hostile comments), physical aggression (e.g., hitting, kicking), indirect aggression (e.g., spreading malicious rumors), passive aggression (e.g., giving the silent treatment), and even non-aggressive attempts to resolve a conflict (Averill, 1982).

There are at least seven explanations for such variability (cf. Roseman, 2011). First, variation in emotion intensity can affect whether a facial expression (e.g., an angry glare) or action tendency (e.g., yelling) will be manifest (these are more likely as intensity increases; Frijda, Ortony, Sonnemans, & Clore, 1992), and perhaps which action it will be (e.g., stamping at lower intensity and screaming at higher intensity; Potegal & Qiu, 2010).

Second, emotional responses are often modulated by emotion regulation processes, which differ among individuals and over time (John & Gross, 2004). For example, people may intensify, dampen, or mask their expressions of anger (Ekman, 1972). Attempts to talk over an angry incident with the instigator (Averill, 1982), or reconcile after a confrontation (Fischer & Roseman, 2007), may reduce or control (rather than manifest) the emotion.

Third, multiple patterns of action readiness may be potentiated by a given emotion (Frijda, 1986), such as yelling at versus hitting someone in anger. While each of these may be more likely to occur than if the emotion were not being felt, the specific action prompted may also depend on situational variables, such as the angry person's power relative to the target, and the relationship, if any, that exists between them (e.g., strangers; friends; parent and child). Moreover, the multiple patterns of action readiness that are characteristics of emotions are not fixed action patterns, but rather are complex suites of interrelated responses (Frijda, 1986; Lazarus, 1991) that vary depending on changing external stimulus conditions (e.g., the physical distance between the angry person and the target), feedback from prior actions (e.g., the target's response), and internal determinants (e.g., SNS arousal; testosterone and serotonin levels). In an angry confrontation, whether or how to yell or hit can be continually recalculated as conditions change.

Fourth, apart from (relatively impulsive) action tendencies, the particular *instrumental* action that is taken in pursuit of emotivational goals likely depends on situational conditions. For example, whether yelling versus giving the silent treatment is more likely to make a target of anger feel bad may depend on the number and identity of other people present, as well as the goals and sensitivities of the target.

Fifth, multiple emotions (e.g., fear, anger, and guilt, each with differing effects on action) may be elicited by the same event (e.g., disobedience that puts one's child in danger) and occur simultaneously or in rapid succession.

Sixth, emotions can co-occur with motives, cognitions, and other nonemotional determinants of behavior, which may modify emotional and nonemotional responses taking place at the same time. For example, high need for approval (Taylor, 1970), normative beliefs about anger expression (Gibson & Callister, 2010), and ongoing action sequences such as eating or driving can each alter the facial expressions and actions of anger, as well as other simultaneously occurring behavior.

Finally, insofar as all behaviors, expressions, and other manifest responses are organized and carried out by the brain and body, each of these variations will correspond to variations in physiology occurring in an emotion episode. If, for example, refusing to speak to someone, yelling at, and hitting the person are all anger responses, and such responses may be regulated or combined with other emotions and nonemotional responses, it should come as no surprise that there are few if any single neural, chemical, or muscular signatures found in all instances of anger.

Yet despite such variability, different instantiations of anger are recognizable as alternative means to attaining the emotivational goals of making the target feel bad, or compelling the target's action. All may be understood as in some way manifesting anger's function of coercing the target to change behavior from what it would otherwise have been.

Emotions as General-Purpose Coping Strategies

Which behaviors of a target person does anger coerce? Any action of another person, or the failure of a person to take any particular action, could become the focus of someone's anger. For example, various research participants describing angry incidents (in Scherer, 1988) "tried to make [the target] compare me with others of my age," "make [the target] stick to his word," or get the target to stop "excessive drinking" (Appendix E, participants 26, 28, and 30). That is, each emotion is a general-purpose coping strategy, applicable to an infinite variety of specific situations of a particular type (in the case of anger, as indicated above, some motive-inconsistency appraised as caused by other persons, when one has potential to do something about it).

Emotions as Alternatives to Motives

The anger incidents just described involved the blockage of diverse goals: going out to a party with friends, co-authoring a seminar report, reducing drinking by a relationship partner (Scherer, 1988). Indeed, there is no limit to the varieties of motive-inconsistency that can elicit anger. Each of these could be pursued in motive-specific ways (e.g., asking a parent's permission, meeting to divide up report responsibilities, pointing out harmful effects of excessive alcohol consumption). In contrast, reacting with anger may coerce a target's behavior in (and thus be useful in coping with) any of these or other situations. Emotions are thus *general-purpose* responses that function to provide alternative ways to attain whatever one's motives may be.

Why should humans and other organisms have two systems—motives and emotions—to energize and direct behavior? According to Tomkins (1970), motives ("drives" such as hunger) direct behavior toward relatively specific ends (e.g., edible objects), whereas emotions ("affects") are more general with respect to their object (e.g., the limitless variety of behaviors people may attempt to compel in anger, and outcomes one may try to avoid in fear or celebrate in joy). Tomkins also proposed that affects have primacy over drives in influencing behavior.

It is proposed in this chapter that the generality and primacy of emotions are related—the emotion system has evolved to preempt the relatively specific-purpose pursuit of motives with the general-purpose coping strategies of emotions when fast action may be needed (Roseman, 2008; cf. the "control precedence" of emotional action tendencies in Frijda's 1986 theory). Motivated behavior is often more deliberative (though much "deliberation" may occur unconsciously), as executive functions process whether particular responses will result in rewarding or aversive consequences and may compare the relative efficacy of different instrumental actions (e.g., taking food from the refrigerator, preparing a meal, or going to a restaurant to satisfy one's hunger). In contrast, emotional behavior is often more impulsive, involving greater reliance on relatively pre-specified patterns of action readiness (e.g., yelling or hitting in anger, freezing or running in fear). Though some motive-linked behavior is habitual or automatic, people seem more able to deliberatively consider how to get food when hungry than how to attack when angry (see Lerner & Tiedens, 2006).

However, emotional behavior is not always so impulsive (as in cyberstalking triggered by anger over a breakup; Strawhun, Adams, & Huss, 2013). In addition to readiness for specific actions, the emotivational goals of emotion syndromes (e.g., getting revenge, or making the target feel bad, in anger) can prompt an infinite variety of instrumental actions (e.g., insulting, threatening, revealing private information) whose likely effects can be evaluated in light of situational conditions. As will be discussed below, behavior governed by emotivational goals may typically have more control precedence than other motivated behavior (because emotivational goals have higher priority or urgency than other goals), but less than behavior governed by emotional action tendencies.

Emotions as Alternatives to Each Other

In addition to being alternatives to motives, particular emotions are alternatives to each other, forming coherent sets of coping options that shed light on why the human species has particular emotions (discussed in more detail in Roseman, 2011). Fig. 8.1 includes four *emotion families*, each of which contains related emotions that have evolved to cope either with motive-relevant events in general (surprise, hope, joy, relief, fear, sadness, distress, frustration, and disgust), events caused by other people (love, interpersonal dislike, anger, and contempt), or events caused by the self (pride, regret, guilt, and shame). The five positive emotions (shown in green in Fig. 8.1) comprise a family of *contacting emotions*, whose strategies increase proximity to or interaction with impersonal, interpersonal, or intrapersonal stimuli. Fear, sadness, distress, interpersonal dislike, and regret constitute a family of *distancing emotions*, which move the self away from emotion elicitors. Disgust, contempt, and shame are *rejection emotions*, which move eliciting stimuli away from the self. Frustration, anger, and guilt are *attack emotions*, which move against impersonal elicitors, other persons, and the self, respectively. Surprise, which is not inherently positive or negative, and whose status as an emotion is thus controversial (e.g., Ortony, Clore, & Collins, 1988), suspends action and seeks information.

Among the attack emotions, anger's threatening facial expressions, behaviors such as criticizing or hitting, and goals of revenge or harm-seeking are specialized ways of moving against animate agents who can understand hostile communications, feel pain, and anticipate negative consequences. The self-reproach, self-punishment, and reparative responses (e.g., apology) of guilt (Roseman et al., 1994) are specialized for moving against the self, compelling changes in one's own behavior. Responses in frustration, which involve increased effort and forcefully overcoming obstacles (e.g., Amsel, 1992; Roseman et al., 1994), are suitable for moving against all types of interference with one's motives, including those impersonally caused.

Anger can also be contrasted with interpersonal dislike and contempt, two alternative negative emotions felt toward other people. Responses of interpersonal dislike move away from (rather than against) people in physical and social space, e.g., by avoidance, decreasing interaction, and dissociation (Feldman, 1969; Roseman et al., 1994), which function to get away from negative consequences others might cause. Responses in contempt (e.g., condescension, gossiping about, social exclusion, and social rejection; Fischer & Roseman, 2007) move target persons both physically and socially away from the self, which can reduce their impact.

Functional Relationships between Eliciting Appraisals and Emotions

According to the Emotion System theory, appraisals encode key properties of situations and events that predict–typically without the necessity for complex deliberative calculation–whether non-affective, motivational, or emotional responses are likely to be adaptive; and if the latter, which particular emotion strategy is most likely to succeed in coping adaptively.

Appraisals Influencing Non-affective Vs. Motivated Vs. Emotional Behavior The prevailing system of behavior governance at a given time appears to be determined at least in part by appraisals of a situation's *degree of consistency and inconsistency* with various motives (which can be conceptualized as biological and psychological reference states that function as goals or anti-goals; Carver & Scheier, 2012). For example, an individual may have a characteristic set point, range, or responsiveness to the peptide hormone ghrelin (Buss et al., 2014) or a particular level of success (or failure) that he or she seeks to approach (or avoid; Elliot & Church, 1997). Greater distance from goals or greater closeness to anti-goals may shift control away from non-affective (e.g., cognitive) processes and produce more intense motivation and more motivated action (e.g., food-seeing, achievement attempts).

Change in motive-consistency generates emotions (Frijda, 1986, cf. Scherer, 2009), with increases producing positive emotions and decreases (i.e., change in the direction of motive-*in*consistency) producing negative emotions (Roseman,

Antoniou, & Jose, 1996). Inconsistency with expectations (i.e., the occurrence of unexpected events) elicits surprise (Reisenzein, 2000).

The more important the motive and the greater the change in motive-consistency (e.g., from an average grade to a failing grade, rather than from an average to a just-below average grade; or from outstanding success to total failure, rather than from outstanding success to an intermediate outcome), the more intense the emotional reaction is likely to be (Roseman, 2008, 2017).

The importance and extent of change in consistency with motives and expectations influence which system of behavior governance is dominant because they predict the potential urgency of rapid response. The larger and more important the change, the more quickly one may need to cope with the situation. Large changes in the degree to which important motives are or may be fulfilled are therefore appraised as crises or potentially time-limited opportunities, which may make more deliberative processes of action production too costly.

Each system of behavior governance is comparatively likely to be functional under the conditions of its characteristic elicitation by these appraisals. If there is little inconsistency with goals and little consistency with anti-goals, *non-affective* processes can allow relatively unconstrained behavior generation, by situational cues, response tendencies or hierarchies, or automatic or deliberative cognition. Larger degrees of goal inconsistency or anti-goal consistency engender *motivations* (e.g., hunger; competence; achievement motivation), which produce action that is still quite flexible, though influenced by the perceived or associated likelihood of moving in the direction of greater motive-consistency. (Note that instrumental behavior, such as food-seeking, can be variable, even if consumption behaviors, such as eating, are stereotypic).

As actual or potential *change* in motive-consistency is perceived (and increases), *emotions* such as those in Fig. 8.1 are elicited (and intensify), and their emotivational goals become increasingly salient and influential. Emotional intensity is also greater the more important the motive, the greater the rate of change in motive-consistency, and the more imminent the change (Roseman, 2008). Increasing emotion intensity reduces action flexibility by increasingly constraining goal selection to correspond to the general-purpose emotivational goals of the emotion (e.g., making target others feel bad or compelling their behavior in anger) in place of more time-consuming processing of multiple specific-purpose goals, although the latter may remain operative subordinately. For example, other conditions being equal, the longer participant 26 in Scherer (1988, Appendix E) waited for his seminar partner to show up for their appointment, the angrier he was likely to become, with the goal of making the target "stick to his word" becoming increasingly prominent in consciousness. When the partner ultimately did not come to the seminar, forcing the participant to present alone, he is likely to have gotten even angrier.

As perceived change in motive-consistency and consequent emotion intensity increase still further, behavior may become increasingly constrained toward emotional action readinesses, such as yelling in anger, perhaps via interference with deliberative processing of alternative instrumental actions (Easterbrook, 1959; Gable, Poole, & Harmon-Jones, 2015). Here, consideration of fewer actions permits faster response. At the time of writing about his experience, participant 26 said of the target of his anger "If I saw him now, I guess I wouldn't be able to keep control over myself" (Scherer, 1988, p. 232).

Appraisals Influencing which Emotion Occurs in Emotion-Eliciting Situations Given sufficient perceived change in motive-consistency (heightened or diminished by greater or lesser motive importance, rate of change, and imminence of change), the seven appraisals specified earlier combine to influence which particular emotion (e.g., from Fig. 8.1) will be elicited. The function of these particular appraisals is to sort situations into categories for which particular emotions are most likely to be adaptive, due to their different response strategies (Roseman, 1984).

As shown in Fig. 8.1, the Emotion System model proposes that anger is elicited by appraising an event as a motive-inconsistent effect or goal blockage, caused by another person, when one's control potential is seen as relatively high. Given this combination of appraisals, the response strategy of anger—attacking to coerce the behavior of another person—is relatively likely to succeed (compared with the strategies of other emotions in the emotion system). Let us compare the theoretically specified appraisal-emotion relationships to those that would pertain if any one of the appraisals in the anger-eliciting combination were altered (while holding the others constant), in order to better understand the functional dynamics (see also Roseman, 2013, for additional discussion of these seven appraisals and their functional connections to each of the 17 emotions encompassed within the Emotion System theory).

If an event caused by another person is *not* motive-inconsistent, the effort required to coerce someone's behavior would be unnecessary. Indeed, if another person is causing motive-*consistent* events, the emotion predicted in Fig. 8.1 (some form of liking or love, whose strategy involves moving toward that person, e.g., by forming or strengthening an interpersonal relationship) is much likelier to be adaptive than angry attack.

If motive-inconsistency is due to an *intrinsic* quality of another person (e.g., the person's character or a personality trait or genetic attribute), rather than a goal blockage or negative effect produced by the person, changing this is likely to be more difficult, if not impossible. Holding the other typically anger-eliciting appraisals constant, the emotion predicted to result from another person's motive-inconsistent intrinsic quality is the rejection emotion of contempt. Its strategy of moving the contemptible person away from the self (implemented through derogation and disparagement, and other behaviors pursuant to the goal of social exclusion; Fischer & Roseman, 2007; Roseman, in press) would be more likely to successfully minimize that person's impact on attainment of one's motives.

If appraisal indicates that one *lacks* potential to control the motive-relevant aspects of the emotion-eliciting event, attacking would be unlikely to succeed in coercing the target to alter the behavior. Moreover, if the angry person is weaker than the target, and has no legitimate claim that could prospectively influence the target, enlist the aid of others, or suggest ultimate redress, then moving against the target in anger could result in injurious retaliation. Given such low potential to control motive-inconsistency caused by another person, the distancing emotion of inter-personal dislike would more likely be adaptive. As shown in Fig. 8.1, the strategy of dislike involves moving away from the disliked person. Moving away from some-one (e.g., by avoiding interaction) limits one's freedom of action and is likely to be more disruptive than moving the person away from the self (e.g., via social exclu-sion). However, this method of creating distance may be more likely to succeed in reducing the other's negative impact when one is relatively weak.

Finally, if the motive-inconsistency is not caused by, and could not be remedied by, another person taking action or refraining from some action, then attacking to coerce that person's behavior would be ineffective in promoting one's motive-attainment. For example, if harm was caused by inanimate objects or impersonal forces and could not be remedied by other persons, then the emotion of "frustration" (which is similar to what Smith & Kirby, 2009, refer to as "challenge") seems like-lier to be adaptive. Its strategy, as shown in Fig. 8.1, involves increasing effort to overcome obstacles. If the self is causing motive-inconsistent effects (e.g., by harm-ing others or thwarting one's own goals or values), the self-directed attack emotion of guilt would be more likely to result in motive-attainment. As shown in Fig. 8.1, guilt moves against the self (e.g., by self-reproach) to compel one's own behavior.

Anger Dysfunction

The discussion to this point has focused on ways that emotions are often functional in the situations within which they occur. Yet the extensive literature on emotional disorders (e.g., American Psychiatric Association, 2013; Rottenberg & Johnson, 2007) provides abundant evidence of emotional dysfunction.

Types of Emotion Dysfunction Prototypical examples of emotional disorders involve too much emotion, as in phobias (excessive fear) or bipolar disorder (which involves successive episodes of excess positive and negative emotion). However, there are also disorders that involve too little emotion (e.g., psychopathy) or emo-tion that is inappropriate to the situations in which it occurs, even if its frequency or intensity is within the normal range (e.g., reactive attachment disorder).

Historically, and still today, individuals with dysfunctional anger often wind up interacting with the police and justice system (e.g., after assault or murder) rather than psychologists. But psychologists and psychiatrists have increasingly concluded that some cases should be viewed as instances of anger disorders (e.g., DiGiuseppe & Tafrate, 2007; Kassinove, 1995; Novaco, 2010). According to a review by Fernandez and Johnson (2016), DSM-5 recognizes anger as a key criterion in five disorders: intermittent explosive disorder (IED), oppositional defiant disorder (ODD), disruptive mood dysregulation disorder (DMDD), borderline personality disorder (BPD), and bipolar disorder (BD).

According to the DSM-5 definitions of these disorders, they vary in the way anger is manifested and in additional diagnostic criteria. For example, DSM-5 identifies IED with repeated angry or aggressive episodes that are sudden and impulsive; ODD with irritability, defiance, and vindictiveness; DMDD with severe temper outbursts and persistent irritability or anger; BPD with affective lability, fears of abandonment, and suicidality; and BD with irritable mood, especially in the context of a manic episode.

Fernandez and Johnson (2016) also discuss hypotheses about distinctive etiologies for different anger-related disorders. For example, IED has been associated with low central serotonin activity and childhood maltreatment, particularly physical (but not sexual or emotional) abuse; ODD with the long form of the serotonin transporter gene and caretaker hostility; BPD with an invalidating childhood environment, disturbed attachment, and prefrontal cortex deficits; and BD with heightened approach motivation, frustration, and diminished executive functioning.

However, Fernandez and Johnson (2016) suggest that there may be significant transdiagnostic similarities across the disorders. These include excessive attention to and rumination about negative events; tendencies to perceive wrongdoing, blame others, and interpret their behavior as antagonistic; and deficits in executive function that may underlie impulsivity and poor emotion regulation.

In light of the existing literature, it seems that anger is likely to become dysfunctional if it results from inaccurate or distorted appraisals (such as hostile attribution bias, Dodge, 2006–a dysfunction in the emotion generation process); or if its expression, action tendencies, or emotivational goals are insufficiently constrained by situational contingencies (e.g., likely negative consequences), norms, or other goals and priorities of the angry individual, indicating dysfunction in the emotion regulation process. And although anger can be adaptive in all the ways discussed above (defending against threats, deterring transgressions, redressing injustice, etc.), frequent anger also puts one at risk for cardiovascular disease (e.g., Williams, 2010), generalized anxiety and depressive disorders (Stringaris, Cohen, Pine, & Leibenluft, 2009), and interpersonal difficulties (such as decreased marital satisfaction; Renshaw, Blais, & Smith, 2010).

Is Anger Relevant to Politics?

This section examines the literature on anger in the political domain, to see whether or not it corresponds to the functional account of anger presented here and whether it provides additional insights into the functions of anger. Anger has been front and center in descriptions of recent political events and developments in the United States and elsewhere (e.g., Banks, 2014; Cloninger & Leibo, 2017; Hochschild, 2016; Zernike, 2010).

In a Pew Research Center (2016) survey conducted during the US presidential primaries, nearly half of all Republican and Democrat respondents (and nearly 60% of those high in political engagement) reported that the opposition party makes them feel angry. Shortly before the election, data from a Cooperative Congressional Election Study module showed anger to be the negative emotion experienced at least some of the time by the largest number of Democrats, Independents, and Republicans toward both Hillary Clinton and Donald Trump (Roseman, Redlawsk, Mattes, & Katz, 2017). The American National Election Studies (2016) yielded similar data on Clinton and Trump in its whole sample, though a larger number of respondents reported feeling "disgusted" (a term whose lay meaning reflects anger as much as repulsion; Nabi, 2002) toward Trump, and nearly as many reported feeling afraid ("because of the kind of person he is or something he has done"). Indeed, the importance of anger as a political emotion has long been recognized (in his *Rhetoric*, Aristotle discussed it as an emotion that orators could employ).

Appraisals As in other domains, anger is felt toward political actors seen as causing or responsible for harm to oneself or one's group. For example, in the 2005–2010 British Election Survey, respondents who blamed someone for the financial crisis reported more anger than respondents who blamed no one or did not know whom to blame (Wagner, 2014).

Consistent with the Emotion System theory's analysis of anger's appraisal determinants, there is also some evidence that being in a position of strength increases the likelihood of political anger. For example, seeing newspaper headlines supportive of one's group's opinion increases anger felt toward members of an opposing group (Mackie, Devos, & Smith, 2000). Americans' self-rated group efficacy was correlated with anger in response to viewing photographs of the September 11 terrorist attacks (Cheung-Blunden & Blunden, 2008). Having confidence in the government's ability to respond to the threat of terrorism was correlated with anger felt toward terrorists (Musgrove & McGarty, 2008). An item measuring "internal efficacy" (believing one is able to understand what is going on in politics and government) predicted anger toward the two candidates in the 1992 US presidential election (Valentino, Gregorowicz, & Groenendyk, 2009). Perceived efficacy in preventing tuition fees contributed to students' anger regarding rejection of an argument against the fees (Tausch & Becker, 2013).

However, as in non-political domains, there are also conflicting findings. In an earlier paper, Tausch et al. (2011) found that anger was positively correlated with group efficacy in one study, was not correlated with it in another, and inversely correlated with political efficacy in a third. Group efficacy and expectation to win the wars in Afghanistan and Iraq were not significantly related to anger when other variables were taken into account in path analyses conducted by Cheung-Blunden and Blunden (2008).

It is noteworthy, however, that anger was predicted by perceived injustice in all three studies by Tausch et al. (2011) and by negative attitudes toward terrorism (including items indicating that terrorism is unjustified) in the studies by Cheung-Blunden and Blunden (2008). For example, Tausch et al. (2011) found that perceiving British government foreign policy in the Middle East, Iraq, and Afghanistan as immoral and illegitimate was associated with greater anger among Muslims living in the United Kingdom. Indeed, much evidence indicates that perceptions of unjust treatment contribute to feeling anger about political events. Garrett and Bankert (2018) have also found that basing issue opinions on moral values is associated with greater anger at opposing partisans.

As discussed above, legitimacy (e.g., perceiving one has justice on one's side) may confer power (French & Raven, 1959) or control potential (Roseman, 1984) and thereby contribute to eliciting anger. A similar view has been articulated in the political domain by Huddy (2013, p. 756) who contends that "Group strength does not just lie with military might or an electoral victory, it also includes a sense of moral strength" and leads to anger. Klandermans, van der Toorn, and van Stekelenberg (2008) found that immigrants who thought they were discriminated against felt angry if they also perceived themselves as efficacious (and felt fear in the absence of perceived efficacy). This supports the hypothesis that while perceived injustice can contribute to an appraisal of control potential, the latter is the more proximal determinant leading to attack emotions such as anger (rather than distancing emotions, such as fear; Roseman, 1984).

Finally, the likelihood of reacting to politically relevant events (such as the September 11 attacks or the prospective loss of an election) with anger is increased by stronger group identification (Brown, Wohl, & Exline, 2008, study 2; Rydell et al., 2008) and greater partisanship (Groenendyk & Banks, 2014; Huddy, Mason, & Aarøe, 2015). Insofar as identification with a group is correlated with endorsement of group goals, and greater partisanship with stronger endorsement of those goals, these findings fit Emotion System theory predictions of greater motive intensity fueling higher emotion intensity (see also Griner & Smith, 2000).

Angry Responses in Politics   Are the phenomenology, expressions, behaviors, and emotivational goals of anger manifest in the political domain? Political anger is certainly characterized by unfavorable thoughts and feelings about its targets and opposition to policies associated with them. For example, anger toward presidential candidates predicts unfavorable feelings toward them in multiple elections (Johnston, Roseman, & Katz, 2014; Roseman et al., 2012). Banks (2014, 2016) manipulated emotions by asking research participants to recall and write about things that make them feel anger and fear as depicted in facial expression photographs. He found that anger (more than fear) increased opposition to "Barack Obama and the Democrats' healthcare reform bill" among whites who scored high on a measure of symbolic racism (Banks, 2014) and increased opposition to immigration and affirmative action among whites who were relatively unfavorable to blacks (Banks, 2016). Webster (in press) also manipulated incidental anger and found that this (more than in a control group that was not asked to recall a time they felt very angry about politics) led to perceptions that the government is unresponsive to public interests and concerns.

Many theorists and researchers have linked anger to political *action*. For example, based on a review of sociological research on social movements, Jasper (2014) maintains that perceived injustice ("moral shocks") can elicit anger and thus motivate action. Sparks (2015) argues that anger is a critical resource for mobilizing activists and political movements, and can promote solidarity among people who are united in anger against some target. In elections from 1984 to 2008, Groenendyk and Banks (2014) found that anger has been consistently related to four measures of political participation (talking to people about how they should vote, wearing a campaign button or displaying a campaign sticker, attending a meeting or rally, and donating to a candidate or party). Anger (but not fear) also mediated the effect of party affiliation strength on these activities.

Consistent with an Emotion System theory analysis, anger is especially linked to negative attitudes and actions that *attack* political targets. Empirically, felt anger toward particular candidates *lowered* the likelihood of voting for 2014 Democratic Party U.S. senate candidates Cory Booker and Bruce Braley (Redlawsk, Roseman, Mattes, & Katz, 2018), and Republican Party U.S. presidential candidates Donald Trump, Ted Cruz, and Marco Rubio in the 2016 Iowa Caucuses (Redlawsk, Roseman, Mattes, & Katz, in press). Tausch et al. (2011) found that feelings of anger predicted British Muslims' willingness to engage in non-violent actions to change British foreign policy toward Muslim countries (e.g., signing petitions, lobbying, or joining a peaceful rally, protest, or demonstration), as well as support for violent actions *against* Western military targets. Contempt rather than anger was associated with support for violence against civilians. Matsumoto, Hwang, and Frank (2014) report that increases in anger, contempt, and disgust in the speeches of leaders in multiple countries preceded acts of *aggression* (e.g., war, invasion, revolution) but not acts of resistance (non-violent protest). In experimental research, Lerner, Gonzalez, Small, and Fischhoff (2003) manipulated whether Americans thought about anger reactions versus fear reactions to the September 11 attacks, and found that anger predicted advocating relatively *punitive* policies.

Smith (1993) proposed that anger is central to prejudice and discrimination, and may be manifested in behaviors that harm an outgroup by taking away benefits perceived as undeserved. This fits with Banks' (2016) finding that anger increased whites' opposition to affirmative action. Though not explicitly measuring anger, a measure of "modern racism" correlated 0.46 with support for Donald Trump (Pettigrew, 2017), and measures of "hostile sexism" and "denial of racism" predicted intention to vote for Trump in the 2016 presidential election (Schaffner, MacWilliams, & Nteta, 2017). In an August 2016 poll (Rasmussen Reports, 2016), 96% of likely voters who supported Trump reported feeling angry at current federal government policies (compared with 36% of Clinton supporters).

Evidence also relates the posited emotivational goals of vengeance or hurting the target to political anger. For example, according to Lickel's (2012) review of the literature on revenge, emotions "lie at the heart of retribution" (p. 90), and anger, "clearly a dominant emotion in response to intergroup provocations" (p. 92), predicts intergroup aggression (and aggression, as noted earlier, is typically defined in terms of intent to harm). In Cheung-Blunden and Blunden's (2008) study, described above, Americans' anger about the September 11 attacks predicted support for the U.S. wars in Afghanistan and Iraq and for killing people in those two countries (Osama bin Laden, Saddam Hussein, their officers and fighters, and perhaps even civilians). Sadler, Lineberger, Correll, and Park (2005) found that self-reported anger in response to video clips of the September 11 attacks predicted Americans' rated acceptability of defacing a mosque, verbally confronting a Muslim person, and leaving a threatening message on a Muslim family's answering machine. In the former Yugoslavia, Spanovic, Lickel, Denson, and Petrovic (2010) found that anger predicted Serbian undergraduates' self-reported motivation to vote for military action, economic restrictions, and restrictions on the rights of Albanian Muslims.

Garrett and Bankert (2018) measured "affective polarization in everyday life" with a five-item scale that included one question asking how often thinking about the opposition party makes the respondent angry, and another question asking how often the respondent has worn political apparel or merchandise "hoping it would upset" opposition party members. The two items were significantly correlated ($r = 0.5$, $p < 0.05$; K. N. Garrett, personal communication, Nov. 9, 2017), linking anger to the goal of making its targets feel bad. Lambert et al. (2010) manipulated anger (by having participants think of a time they were treated extremely unfairly) and found increased support for politicians who advocated "powerful military action...crushing the known enemies of America" (p. 897).

Are vengeance and inflicting harm the end goals sought in political anger, or are they intermediate objectives aimed at compelling behavior change? According to van Stekelenburg and Klandermans (2013, p. 175), social psychological analyses of emotions view anger as "*the* prototypical protest emotion." Republicans and Republican leaners who agree with the Tea Party in the United States have been angrier than other Americans (Pew Research Center, 2013)—*opposing* high taxes (Arceneaux & Nicholson, 2012) and government spending (e.g., on mortgage "bailouts" and Obama's healthcare proposals; Sparks, 2015; Zernike, 2010). Van Zomeren, Spears, and Leach (2008) found that group-based anger predicts collective action to *stop* increases of college fees in the Netherlands; Tausch and Becker (2013) found it motivated action against the introduction of such fees in Germany. Anger in Study 3 by Tausch et al. (2011) predicted measured willingness to engage in actions "to change British foreign policy toward Muslim countries" and support for violence "to stop Western interference in Muslim countries" (p. 139). The "punitive" policies supported by Americans focusing on anger over the September 11 attacks involved deporting foreigners who lacked valid visas, which could be seen as a means to prevent another terrorist attack. Americans' support for wars in Afghanistan and Iraq and for killing Saddam Hussein, Osama bin Laden, and their supporters (Cheung-Blunden & Blunden, 2008) could be similarly understood. It could even be argued that the acceptability of killing of civilians in that study and confronting and threatening Muslims (Sadler et al., 2005), as well as other acts of revenge, are interpretable as aiming to deter future injurious conduct.

Whether vengeance, inflicting harm, or making targets feel bad are viewed as end goals in these instances of anger or as intermediate objectives aimed at the goal of compelling change, political anger, like anger in other domains, appears to aim at coercing the behavior of other people. As such, it makes functional sense for anger to be elicited by appraising others as causing harm when there is potential to do something about it, in light of one's power in the situation or deservingness predicting that one's cause will ultimately prevail. In fact, the observed manifestations of anger in politics highlight the importance of power and legitimacy appraisals in generating this attack emotion, as well as the coercive function of anger's strategy of moving against its targets to force change in their behavior.

References

American Heritage Dictionary (n.d.). Coerce. Retrieved from https://ahdictionary.com/word/search.html?q=coerce.

American National Election Studies. (2016). *ANES 2016 time series study*. Ann Arbor, MI: Interuniversity Consortium for Political and Social Research.

American Psychiatric Association. (2013). *Diagnostic and statistical manual of mental disorders* (5th ed.). Arlington, VA: American Psychiatric Publishing.

Amsel, A. (1992). *Frustration theory: An analysis of dispositional learning and memory*. Cambridge, UK: Cambridge University Press.

Anderson, C. A., & Bushman, B. J. (2002). Human aggression. *Annual Review of Psychology, 53*, 27–51.

Arceneaux, K., & Nicholson, S. P. (2012). Who wants to have a tea party? The who, what, and why of the tea party movement. *Political Science & Politics, 45*, 700–710.

Aristotle (1966). Rhetoric. In *Aristotle's Rhetoric and Poetics* (W. R. Roberts, Trans.). New York, NY: Modern Library. (Original work published 350 B.C.)

Arnold, M. B. (1960). *Emotion and personality*. New York, NY: Columbia University Press.

Averill, J. R. (1980). A constructivist view of emotion. In R. Plutchik & H. Kellerman (Eds.), *Emotion: Theory, research and experience* (Vol. 1, pp. 305–339). New York, NY: Academic Press.

Averill, J. R. (1982). *Anger and aggression: An essay on emotion*. New York, NY: Springer-Verlag.

Ax, A. F. (1953). The physiological differentiation between fear and anger in humans. *Psychosomatic Medicine, 15*, 433–442.

Banks, A. J. (2014). The public's anger: White racial attitudes and opinions toward health care reform. *Political Behavior, 36*, 493–514.

Banks, A. J. (2016). Are group cues necessary? How anger makes ethnocentrism among whites a stronger predictor of racial and immigration policy opinions. *Political Behavior, 38*, 635–657.

Barrett, L. F. (2009). Variety is the spice of life: A psychological construction approach to understanding variability in emotion. *Cognition and Emotion, 23*, 1284–1306.

Barrett, L. F., Mesquita, B., Ochsner, K. N., & Gross, J. J. (2007). The experience of emotion. *Annual Review of Psychology, 58*, 373–403.

Berkowitz, L. (2012). A different view of anger: The cognitive-neoassociation conception of the relation of anger to aggression. *Aggressive Behavior, 38*, 322–333.

Blair, R. J. (2016). The neurobiology of impulsive aggression. *Journal of Child and Adolescent Psychopharmacology, 26*, 4–9.

Blanchard, D. C., & Blanchard, R. J. (2003). What can animal aggression research tell us about human aggression? *Hormones and Behavior, 44*, 171–177.

Bowlby, J. (1969). *Attachment and loss (Vol. 1: Attachment)*. New York, NY: Basic Books.

Bowlby, J. (1973). *Attachment and loss (Vol. 2: Separation)*. New York, NY: Basic Books.

Bozman, A. W., & Beck, J. G. (1991). Covariation of sexual desire and sexual arousal: The effects of anger and anxiety. *Archives of Sexual Behavior, 20*, 47–60.

Brown, R. P., Wohl, M. J., & Exline, J. J. (2008). Taking up offenses: Secondhand forgiveness and group identification. *Personality and Social Psychology Bulletin, 34*, 1406–1419.

Buss, J., Havel, P. J., Epel, E., Lin, J., Blackburn, E., & Daubenmier, J. (2014). Associations of ghrelin with eating behaviors, stress, metabolic factors, and telomere length among overweight and obese women: Preliminary evidence of attenuated ghrelin effects in obesity? *Appetite, 76*, 84–94.

Carver, C. S., & Scheier, M. F. (2012). Cybernetic control processes and the self-regulation of behavior. In R. M. Ryan (Ed.), *The Oxford handbook of human motivation* (pp. 28–42). New York, NY: Oxford University Press.

Ceulemans, E., Kuppens, P., & Mechelen, I. V. (2012). Capturing the structure of distinct types of individual differences in the situation-specific experience of emotions: The case of anger. *European Journal of Personality, 26*, 484–495.

Cheung-Blunden, V., & Blunden, B. (2008). The emotional construal of war: Anger, fear, and other negative emotions. *Peace and Conflict: Journal of Peace Psychology, 14*, 123–150.

Clark-Polner, E., Wager, T. D., Satpute, A. B., & Barrett, L. F. (2016). Neural fingerprinting: Meta-analysis, variation and the search for brain-based essences in the science of emotion. In L. F. Barrett, M. Lewis, & J. M. Haviland-Jones (Eds.), *Handbook of emotions* (4th ed., pp. 146–165). New York, NY: Guilford Press.

Cloninger, S. C., & Leibo, S. A. (2017). *Understanding angry groups*. Santa Barbara, CA: Praeger.

Coulson, M. (2004). Attributing emotion to static body postures: Recognition accuracy, confusions, and viewpoint dependence. *Journal of Nonverbal Behavior, 28*, 117–139.

Davies, J. C. (1962). Toward a theory of revolution. *American Sociological Review, 27*, 5–19.

Davitz, J. R. (1969). *The language of emotion*. New York, NY: Academic Press.

de Rivera, J. H. (1977). A structural theory of the emotions. Psychological issues monograph 40. New York, NY: International Universities Press.

de Vos, B., van Zomeren, M., Gordijn, E. H., & Postmes, T. (2013). The communication of "pure" group-based anger reduces tendencies toward intergroup conflict because it increases outgroup empathy. *Personality and Social Psychology Bulletin, 39*, 1043–1052.

de Vos, B., van Zomeren, M., Gordijn, E. H., & Postmes, T. (2016). When does the communication of group-based anger increase outgroup empathy in intergroup conflict? The role of perceived procedural unfairness and outgroup consensus. *Group Processes & Intergroup Relations*. Retrieved from https://doi.org/10.1177/1368430216674340.

DiGiuseppe, R., & Tafrate, R. C. (2007). *Understanding anger disorders*. New York, NY: Oxford University Press.

Dodge, K. A. (2006). Translational science in action: Hostile attributional style and the development of aggressive behavior problems. *Development and Psychopathology, 18*, 791–814.

Easterbrook, J. A. (1959). The effects of emotion on cue utilization and the organization of behavior. *Psychological Review, 66*, 183–201.

Eibl-Eibesfeldt, I. (1989). *Human ethology*. New York, NY: Aldine De Gruyter.

Ekman, P. (1972). Universals and cultural differences in facial expressions of emotion. In J. K. Cole (Ed.), *Nebraska symposium on motivation, 1971* (Vol. 19, pp. 207–283). Lincoln, NE: University of Nebraska Press.

Ekman, P. (2003). *Emotions revealed*. New York, NY: Holt.

Ekman, P., Friesen, W. V., & Hager, J. C. (2002). *Facial action coding system: The manual*. Salt Lake City, UT: A Human Face.

Ekman, P., Levenson, R. W., & Friesen, W. V. (1983). Autonomic nervous system activity distinguishes among emotions. *Science, 221*, 1208–1210.

Elliot, A. J., & Church, M. A. (1997). A hierarchical model of approach and avoidance achievement motivation. *Journal of Personality and Social Psychology, 72*, 218–232.

Ellsworth, P. C., & Tong, E. M. W. (2006). What does it mean to be angry at yourself? Categories, appraisals, and the problem of language. *Emotion, 6*, 572–586.

Fehr, B., & Russell, J. A. (1984). Concept of emotion viewed from a prototype perspective. *Journal of Experimental Psychology: General, 113*, 464–486.

Feldman, R. A. (1969). Group integration and intense interpersonal disliking. *Human Relations, 22*, 405–413.

Fernandez, E., & Johnson, S. L. (2016). Anger in psychological disorders: Prevalence, presentation, etiology and prognostic implications. *Clinical Psychology Review, 46*, 124–135.

Fernandez, E., & Wasan, A. (2010). The anger of pain sufferers: Attributions to agents and appraisals of wrongdoings. In M. Potegal, G. Stemmler, & C. Spielberger (Eds.), *International handbook of anger* (pp. 449–464). New York, NY: Springer.

Fessler, D. M. (2010). Madmen: An evolutionary perspective on anger and men's violent responses to transgression. In M. Potegal, G. Stemmler, & C. Spielberger (Eds.), *International handbook of anger* (pp. 361–381). New York, NY: Springer.

Fischer, A. H., & Manstead, A. S. R. (2016). Social functions of emotion and emotion regulation. In L. F. Barrett, M. Lewis, & J. M. Haviland-Jones (Eds.), *Handbook of emotions* (4th ed., pp. 424–439). New York, NY: Guilford Press.

Fischer, A. H., & Roseman, I. J. (2007). Beat them or ban them: The characteristics and social functions of anger and contempt. *Journal of Personality and Social Psychology, 93,* 103–115.

Fitness, J., & Fletcher, G. J. O. (1993). Love, hate, anger and jealousy in close relationships: A prototype and cognitive appraisal analysis. *Journal of Personality and Social Psychology, 65,* 942–958.

French, J. R. P., & Raven, B. (1959). The bases of social power. In D. Cartwright & A. Zander (Eds.), *Group dynamics* (pp. 150–167). New York, NY: Harper & Row.

Frijda, N. H. (1986). *The emotions.* New York, NY: Cambridge University Press.

Frijda, N. H. (1994). The Lex Talionis: On vengeance. In S. H. Van Goozen, N. E. Van de Poll, & J. A. Sergeant (Eds.), *Emotions: Essays on emotion theory* (pp. 263–289). Hillsdale, NJ: Erlbaum.

Frijda, N. H., Kuipers, P., & ter Schure, E. (1989). Relations among emotion, appraisal, and emotional action readiness. *Journal of Personality and Social Psychology, 57,* 212–228.

Frijda, N. H., Ortony, A., Sonnemans, J., & Clore, G. L. (1992). The complexity of intensity: Issues concerning the structure of emotion intensity. In M. S. Clark (Ed.), *Review of personality and social psychology* (Vol. 13, pp. 60–89). Thousand Oaks, CA: Sage.

Gable, P. A., Poole, B. D., & Harmon-Jones, E. (2015). Anger perceptually and conceptually narrows cognitive scope. *Journal of Personality and Social Psychology, 109*(1), 163–174.

Garrett, K. N., & Bankert, A. (2018). The moral roots of partisan division: How moral conviction heightens affective polarization. *British Journal of Political Science,*1-20. https://doi.org/10.1017/S000712341700059X.

Gibson, D. E., & Callister, R. R. (2010). Anger in organizations: Review and integration. *Journal of Management, 36,* 66–93.

Goldstein, H. S., Edelberg, R., Meier, C. F., & Davis, L. (1989). Relationship of expressed anger to forearm muscle vascular resistance. *Journal of Psychosomatic Research, 33*(4), 497–504.

Gollwitzer, M., Meder, M., & Schmitt, M. (2011). What gives victims satisfaction when they seek revenge? *European Journal of Social Psychology, 41,* 364–374.

Gramarist.com (n.d.) Compel vs. impel. retrieved from http://grammarist.com/usage/compel-impel/

Green, J. A., Whitney, P. G., & Gustafson, G. E. (2010). Vocal expressions of anger. In M. Potegal, G. Stemmler, & C. Spielberger (Eds.), *International handbook of anger* (pp. 139–156). New York, NY: Springer.

Griner, L. A., & Smith, C. A. (2000). Contributions of motivational orientation to appraisal and emotion. *Personality and Social Psychology Bulletin, 26,* 727–740.

Groenendyk, E. W., & Banks, A. J. (2014). Emotional rescue: How affect helps partisans overcome collective action problems. *Political Psychology, 35,* 359–378.

Hatfield, E., Cacioppo, J. T., & Rapson, R. L. (1994). *Emotional contagion.* Cambridge, UK: Cambridge University Press.

Hill, P. C., Pargament, K. I., Hood, R. W., McCullough, M. E., Jr., Sawyers, J. P., Larson, D. B., & Zinnbauer, B. J. (2000). Conceptualizing religion and spirituality: Points of commonality, points of departure. *Journal for the Theory of Social Behaviour, 30,* 51–77.

Hochschild, A. R. (2016). *Strangers in their own land: Anger and mourning on the American right.* New York, NY: The New Press.

Huddy, L. (2013). From group identity to political cohesion and commitment. In L. Huddy, D. O. Sears, & J. S. Levy (Eds.), *The Oxford handbook of political psychology* (pp. 737–773). New York, NY: Oxford University Press.

Huddy, L., Mason, L., & Aarøe, L. (2015). Expressive partisanship: Campaign involvement, political emotion, and partisan identity. *American Political Science Review, 109,* 1–17.

Izard, C. E. (1983). *The maximally discriminative facial movement coding system (MAX)* (Rev. ed.). Newark, DE: Information Technologies and University Media Services, University of Delaware.

Izard, C. E. (1991). *The psychology of emotions.* New York, NY: Plenum.

Izard, C. E. (1993). Four systems for emotion activation: Cognitive and noncognitive processes. *Psychological Review, 100,* 68–90.

Jahoda, G. (2012). Critical reflections on some recent definitions of "culture". *Culture & Psychology, 18*, 289–303.

Janoff-Bulman, R. (1979). Characterological versus behavioral self-blame: Inquiries into depression and rape. *Journal of Personality and Social Psychology, 37*, 1798–1809.

Jasper, J. M. (2014). Constructing indignation: Anger dynamics in protest movements. *Emotion Review, 6*, 208–213.

Jing, J., Gillette, R., & Weiss, K. R. (2009). Evolving concepts of arousal: Insights from simple model systems. *Reviews in the Neurosciences, 20*, 405–428.

John, O. P., & Gross, J. J. (2004). Healthy and unhealthy emotion regulation: Personality processes, individual differences, and life span development. *Journal of Personality, 72*, 1301–1334.

Johnston, G., Roseman, I., & Katz, S. (2014). *Discrete emotions mediate perceptions of presidential candidates: A study using a nationally representative sample*. Poster session presented at the 26th annual meeting of the Eastern Psychological Association, Boston, MA.

Kassinove, H. (1995). *Anger disorders: Definition, diagnosis, and treatment*. Washington, DC: Taylor & Francis.

Kassinove, H., Sukhodolsky, D. G., Tsytsarev, S. V., & Solovyova, S. (1997). Self-reported anger episodes in Russia and America. *Journal of Social Behavior and Personality, 12*(2), 301–324.

Keltner, D., & Haidt, J. (2001). Social functions of emotions. In T. Mayne & G. Bonanno (Eds.), *Emotions: Current issues and future directions* (pp. 192–213). New York, NY: Guilford Press.

Keltner, D., Tracy, J., Sauter, D. A., Cordaro, D. C., & McNeil, G. (2016). Expression of emotion. In L. F. Barrett, M. Lewis, & J. M. Haviland-Jones (Eds.), *Handbook of emotions* (4th ed., pp. 467–482). New York, NY: Guilford Press.

Keltner, D., Young, R. C., Heerey, E. A., Oemig, C., & Monarch, N. D. (1998). Teasing in hierarchical and intimate relations. *Journal of Personality and Social Psychology, 75*, 1231–1247.

Kenrick, D. T., & Keefe, R. C. (1992). Age preferences in mates reflect sex differences in human reproductive strategies. *Behavioral and Brain Sciences, 15*(1), 75–91.

Kerr, M. A., & Schneider, B. H. (2008). Anger expression in children and adolescents: A review of the empirical literature. *Clinical Psychology Review, 28*, 559–577.

Klandermans, B., Van der Toorn, J., & Van Stekelenburg, J. (2008). Embeddedness and identity: How immigrants turn grievances into action. *American Sociological Review, 73*, 992–1012.

Kleinginna, P., Jr., & Kleinginna, A. (1981). A categorized list of emotion definitions, with suggestions for a consensual definition. *Motivation and Emotion, 5*, 345–379.

Kötter, R., & Stephan, K. E. (1997). Useless or helpful? The" limbic system" concept. *Reviews in the Neurosciences, 8*, 139–145.

Kövecses, Z. (2010). Cross-cultural experience of anger: A psycholinguistic analysis. In M. Potegal, G. Stemmler, & C. Spielberger (Eds.), *International handbook of anger* (pp. 157–174). New York, NY: Springer.

Kreibig, S. D. (2010). Autonomic nervous system activity in emotion: A review. *Biological Psychology, 84*, 394–421.

Kuppens, P., Van Mechelen, I., Smits, D. J., & De Boeck, P. (2003). The appraisal basis of anger: Specificity, necessity and sufficiency of components. *Emotion, 3*, 254–269.

Lambert, A. J., Scherer, L. D., Schott, J. P., Olson, K. R., Andrews, R. K., O'Brien, T. C., & Zisser, A. R. (2010). Rally effects, threat, and attitude change: An integrative approach to understanding the role of emotion. *Journal of Personality and Social Psychology, 98*, 886–903.

Lazarus, R. S. (1991). *Emotion and adaptation*. New York, NY: Oxford University Press.

Lemay, E. P., Jr., Overall, N. C., & Clark, M. S. (2012). Experiences and interpersonal consequences of hurt feelings and anger. *Journal of Personality and Social Psychology, 103*, 982–1006.

Lench, H. C., & Levine, L. J. (2008). Goals and responses to failure: Knowing when to hold them and when to fold them. *Motivation and Emotion, 32*, 127–140.

Lench, H. C., Bench, S. W., Darbor, K. E., & Moore, M. (2015). A functionalist manifesto: Goal-related emotions from an evolutionary perspective. *Emotion Review, 7*, 90–98.

Lerner, J. S., Gonzalez, R. M., Small, D. A., & Fischhoff, B. (2003). Effects of fear and anger on perceived risks of terrorism: A national field experiment. *Psychological Science, 14*, 144–150.

Lerner, J. S., & Keltner, D. (2001). Fear, anger, and risk. *Journal of Personality and Social Psychology, 81*, 146–159.

Lerner, J. S., & Tiedens, L. Z. (2006). Portrait of the angry decision maker: How appraisal tendencies shape anger's influence on cognition. *Journal of Behavioral Decision Making, 19*, 115–137.

Lerner, M. J. (2015). Understanding how the justice motive shapes our lives and treatment of one another: Exciting contributions and misleading claims. In R. S. Cropanzano & M. L. Ambrose (Eds.), *The Oxford handbook of justice in the workplace* (pp. 205-234). New York, NY: Oxford University Press.

Lewis, M., Alessandri, S. M., & Sullivan, M. W. (1990). Violation of expectancy, loss of control, and anger expressions in young infants. *Developmental Psychology, 26*, 745–751.

Lickel, B. (2012). Retribution and revenge. In L. R. Tropp (Ed.), *The Oxford handbook of intergroup conflict* (pp. 89–105). New York, NY: Oxford University Press.

Litvak, P. M., Lerner, J. S., Tiedens, L. Z., & Shonk, K. (2010). Fuel in the fire: How anger impacts judgment and decision-making. In M. Potegal, G. Stemmler, & C. Spielberger (Eds.), *International handbook of anger* (pp. 287–310). New York, NY: Springer.

Mackie, D. M., Devos, T., & Smith, E. R. (2000). Intergroup emotions: Explaining offensive action tendencies in an intergroup context. *Journal of Personality and Social Psychology, 79*, 602–616.

Matsumoto, D., & Hwang, H. S. (2011). Reading facial expressions of emotion. *Psychological Science Agenda.* Retrieved from http://www.apa.org/science/about/psa/2011/05/facial-expressions.aspx

Matsumoto, D., Hwang, H. C., & Frank, M. G. (2014). Emotions expressed in speeches by leaders of ideologically motivated groups predict aggression. *Behavioral Sciences of Terrorism and Political Aggression, 6*(1), 1–18.

Matsumoto, D., Keltner, D., Shiota, M. N., O'Sullivan, M., & Frank, M. (2008). Facial expressions of emotion. In M. Lewis, J. M. Haviland-Jones, & L. F. Barrett (Eds.), *Handbook of emotions* (3rd ed., pp. 211–234). New York, NY: Guilford Press.

Musgrove, L., & McGarty, C. (2008). Opinion-based group membership as a predictor of collective emotional responses and support for pro-and anti-war action. *Social Psychology, 39*, 37–47.

Nabi, R. (2002). The theoretical versus the lay meaning of disgust: Implications for emotion research. *Cognition and Emotion, 16*, 695–703.

Northouse, P. G. (2016). *Leadership: Theory and practice* (7th ed.). Thousand Oaks, CA: Sage.

Novaco, R. W. (2010). Anger and psychopathology. In M. Potegal, G. Stemmler, & C. Spielberger (Eds.), *International handbook of anger* (pp. 465–497). New York, NY: Springer.

Ortony, A., Clore, G. L., & Collins, A. (1988). *The cognitive structure of emotions.* New York, NY: Cambridge University Press.

Panksepp, J. (2017). Instinctual foundations of animal minds: Comparative perspectives on the evolved affective neural substrate of emotions and learned behaviors. In J. Call, Gordon M. Burghardt, I. M. Pepperberg, C. T. Snowdon, & T. Zentall (Eds.). *APA handbook of comparative psychology.* Washington, DC: American Psychological Association. *1*, 475–500.

Parkinson, C., Walker, T. T., Memmi, S., & Wheatley, T. (2017). Emotions are understood from biological motion across remote cultures. *Emotion, 17*, 459–477.

Pettigrew, T. F. (2017). Social psychological perspectives on Trump supporters. *Journal of Social and Political Psychology, 5*, 107–116.

Pew Research Center (2013). *Anger at government most pronounced among conservative Republicans.* Retrieved from http://www.people-press.org/2013/09/30/anger-at-government-most-pronounced-among-conservative-republicans/.

Pew Research Center (2016). *Partisanship and Political Animosity in 2016.* retrieved from http://www.people-press.org/2016/06/22/partisanship-and-political-animosity-in-2016/

Plutchik, R. (1980). A general psychoevolutionary theory of emotion. In R. Plutchik & H. Kellerman (Eds.), *Emotion: Theory, research, and experience: Vol. 1. Theories of emotion* (pp. 3–33). New York, NY: Academic Press.

Potegal, M., & Qiu, P. (2010). Anger in children's tantrums: A new, quantitative, behaviorally based model. In M. Potegal, G. Stemmler, & C. Spielberger (Eds.), *International handbook of anger* (pp. 193–217). New York, NY: Springer.

Potegal, M., & Stemmler, G. (2010). Cross-disciplinary views of anger: Consensus and controversy. In M. Potegal, G. Stemmler, & C. Spielberger (Eds.), *International handbook of anger* (pp. 3–7). New York, NY: Springer.

Rasmussen Reports (2016). *Trump Voters Don't Like the Feds, Clinton Voters Do*. Retrieved from http://www.rasmussenreports.com/public_content/politics/elections/election_2016/trump_voters_don_t_like_the_feds_clinton_voters_do.

Redlawsk, D. P., Roseman, I. J., Mattes, K., & Katz, S. (2018). *They're laughable, they lie: The role of contempt in negative campaigning*. Manuscript submitted for publication.

Redlawsk, D. P., Roseman, I. J., Mattes, K., & Katz, S. (in press). Donald Trump, contempt, and the 2016 GOP Iowa caucuses. *Journal of Elections, Public Opinion & Parties*.

Reisenzein, R. (2000). The subjective experience of surprise. In H. Bless & J. P. Forgas (Eds.), *The message within: The role of subjective experience in social cognition and behavior* (pp. 262–279). Philadelphia, PA: Psychology Press.

Renshaw, K. D., Blais, R. K., & Smith, T. W. (2010). Components of negative affectivity and marital satisfaction: The importance of actor and partner anger. *Journal of Research in Personality, 44*, 328–334.

Roseman, I. J. (1984). Cognitive determinants of emotions: A structural theory. In P. Shaver (Ed.), *Review of personality and social psychology* (Vol. 5, pp. 11–36). Beverly Hills, CA: Sage Publications.

Roseman, I. J. (2001). A model of appraisal in the emotion system: Integrating theory, research, and applications. In K. R. Scherer, A. Schorr, & T. Johnstone (Eds.), *Appraisal processes in emotion: Theory, methods, research* (pp. 68–91). New York, NY: Oxford University Press.

Roseman, I. J. (2008). Motivations and emotivations: Approach, avoidance, and other tendencies in motivated and emotional behavior. In A. J. Elliot (Ed.), *Handbook of approach and avoidance motivation* (pp. 343–366). New York, NY: Psychology Press.

Roseman, I. J. (2011). Emotional behaviors, emotivational goals, emotion strategies: Multiple levels of organization integrate variable and consistent responses. *Emotion Review, 3*, 434–443.

Roseman, I. J. (2013). Appraisal in the emotion system: Coherence in strategies for coping. *Emotion Review, 5*, 141–149.

Roseman, I. J. (2017). Transformative events: Appraisal bases of passion and mixed emotions. *Emotion Review, 9*, 133–139.

Roseman, I. J. (in press). Rejecting the unworthy: The causes, components, and consequences of contempt. In M. Mason (Ed.), *The moral psychology of contempt*. London: Rowman & Littlefield.

Roseman, I. J., Antoniou, A. A., & Jose, P. E. (1996). Appraisal determinants of emotions: Constructing a more accurate and comprehensive theory. *Cognition and Emotion, 10*, 241–277.

Roseman, I. J., & Fischer, A. H. (2017). *Anger, dislike, contempt, and hatred*. Manuscript submitted for publication.

Roseman, I. J, Johnston, B. M., Garguilo, S., Floman, J. L., Bryant, A. D., Frazier, I. R., & Nugent, M. K. (2012, May). *Are some emotions more politically potent than others?* Poster session presented at the 24th Annual Convention, Association for Psychological Science, Chicago, IL.

Roseman, I. J., Redlawsk, D. P., Mattes, K., & Katz, S. (2017, July). *"Little Marco," "Lyin' Ted," and "Crooked Hillary": The power of contempt in American electoral politics and beyond*. In I. J. Roseman (Chair) "The power and perils of contempt: advances in understanding." Symposium presented at the International Society for Research on Emotions biannual conference, St. Louis, MO.

Roseman, I. J., & Smith, C. A. (2001). Appraisal theory: Overview, assumptions, varieties, controversies. In K. R. Scherer, A. Schorr, & T. Johnstone (Eds.), *Appraisal processes in emotion: Theory, methods, research* (pp. 3–19). New York, NY: Oxford University Press.

Roseman, I. J., Steele, A., & Goodvin, A. (2017). *Anger, contempt, hatred, and dislike*. Rutgers University: Unpublished raw data.

Roseman, I. J., Wiest, C., & Swartz, T. S. (1994). Phenomenology, behaviors, and goals differentiate discrete emotions. *Journal of Personality and Social Psychology, 67*, 206–221.

Rottenberg, J. E., & Johnson, S. L. (2007). *Emotion and psychopathology: Bridging affective and clinical science.* Washington, DC: American Psychological Association.

Rutter, M. (2005). Incidence of autism spectrum disorders: Changes over time and their meaning. *Acta Paediatrica, 94*, 2–15.

Rydell, R. J., Mackie, D. M., Maitner, A. T., Claypool, H. M., Ryan, M. J., & Smith, E. R. (2008). Arousal, processing, and risk taking: Consequences of intergroup anger. *Personality and Social Psychology Bulletin, 34*, 1141–1152.

Sadler, M. S., Lineberger, M., Correll, J., & Park, B. (2005). Emotions, attributions, and policy endorsement in response to the September 11th terrorist attacks. *Basic and Applied Social Psychology, 27*, 249–258.

Schaffner, B. F., MacWilliams, M., & Nteta, T. (2017, January). *Explaining White polarization in the 2016 vote for President: The sobering role of racism and sexism.* Paper presented at the Conference on The U.S. Presidential Election of 2016: Domestic and International Aspects. IDC Herzliya Campus.

Scherer, K. R. (Ed.). (1988). *Facets of emotion: Recent research.* Hillsdale, NJ: Erlbaum.

Scherer, K. R. (2009). The dynamic architecture of emotion: Evidence for the component process model. *Cognition and Emotion, 23*, 1307–1351.

Scherer, K. R., & Fontaine, J. J. R. (2013). Driving the emotion process: The appraisal component. In J. J. R. Fontaine, K. R. Scherer, & C. Soriano (Eds.), *Components of emotional meaning: A sourcebook* (pp. 186–209). New York, NY: Oxford University Press.

Scherer, K. R., & Wallbott, H. G. (1994). Evidence for universality and cultural variation of differential emotion response patterning. *Journal of Personality and Social Psychology, 66*, 310–328.

Sell, A., Cosmides, L., & Tooby, J. (2014). The human anger face evolved to enhance cues of strength. *Evolution and Human Behavior, 35*(5), 425–429.

Shaver, P. R., Schwartz, J., Kirson, J., & O'Connor, C. (1987). Emotional knowledge: Further explorations of a prototype approach. *Journal of Personality and Social Psychology, 52*, 1061–1086.

Simpson, J. A., & Belsky, J. (2008). Attachment theory within a modern evolutionary framework. In J. Cassidy & P. R. Shaver (Eds.), *Handbook of attachment: Theory, research, and clinical applications* (2nd ed., pp. 131–157). New York, NY: Guilford Press.

Smetana, J. G., Daddis, C., & Chuang, S. S. (2003). "Clean your room!" A longitudinal investigation of adolescent-parent conflict and conflict resolution in middle-class African American families. *Journal of Adolescent Research, 18*, 631–650.

Smith, C. A., & Kirby, L. D. (2009). Putting appraisal in context: Toward a relational model of appraisal and emotion. *Cognition and Emotion, 23*, 1352–1372.

Smith, C. A., & Kirby, L. D. (2011). The role of appraisal and emotion in coping and adaptation. In R. J. Contrada & A. Baum (Eds.), *The handbook of stress science: Biology, psychology, and health* (pp. 195–208). New York, NY: Springer.

Smith, E. R. (1993). Social identity and social emotions: Toward new conceptualizations of prejudice. In D. M. Mackie & D. L. Hamilton (Eds.), *Affect, cognition and stereotyping: Interactive processes in group perception* (pp. 297–315). San Diego, CA: Academic Press.

Solomon, R. C. (1990). *A passion for justice.* Reading, MA: Addison-Wesley.

Spanovic, M., Lickel, B., Denson, T. F., & Petrovic, N. (2010). Fear and anger as predictors of motivation for intergroup aggression: Evidence from Serbia and Republika Srpska. *Group Processes & Intergroup Relations, 13*, 725–739.

Sparks, H. (2015). Mama grizzlies and guardians of the republic: The democratic and intersectional politics of anger in the Tea Party movement. *New Political Science, 37*, 25–47.

Stemmler, G. (2010). Somatovisceral activation during anger. In M. Potegal, G. Stemmler, & C. Spielberger (Eds.), *International handbook of anger* (pp. 103–121). New York, NY: Springer.

Strawhun, J., Adams, N., & Huss, M. T. (2013). The assessment of cyberstalking: An expanded examination including social networking, attachment, jealousy, and anger in relation to violence and abuse. *Violence and Victims, 28*, 715–730.

Stringaris, A., Cohen, P., Pine, D. S., & Leibenluft, E. (2009). Adult outcomes of youth irritability: A 20-year prospective community-based study. *American Journal of Psychiatry, 166*, 1048–1054.

Sukhodolsky, D. G., Golub, A., & Cromwell, E. N. (2001). Development and validation of the anger rumination scale. *Personality and Individual Differences, 31*, 689–700.

Tausch, N., & Becker, J. C. (2013). Emotional reactions to success and failure of collective action as predictors of future action intentions: A longitudinal investigation in the context of student protests in Germany. *British Journal of Social Psychology, 52*, 525–542.

Tausch, N., Becker, J. C., Spears, R., Christ, O., Saab, R., Singh, P., & Siddiqui, R. N. (2011). Explaining radical group behavior: Developing emotion and efficacy routes to normative and nonnormative collective action. *Journal of Personality and Social Psychology, 101*, 129–148.

Taylor, S. (1970). Aggressive behavior as a function of approval motivation and physical attack. *Psychonomic Science, 18*, 195–196.

Tolman, E. C. (1923). A behavioristic account of the emotions. *Psychological Review, 30*, 217–227.

Tomkins, S. S. (1970). Affect as he primary motivational system. In M. B. Arnold (Ed.), Feelings and emotions: The Loyola symposium (pp. 101-110). New York, NY: Academic Press.

Tong, E. M. (2010). The sufficiency and necessity of appraisals for negative emotions. *Cognition and Emotion, 24*, 692–701.

Tooby, J., & Cosmides, L. (2008). The evolutionary psychology of the emotions and their relationship to internal regulatory variables. In M. Lewis, J. Haviland, & L. F. Barrett (Eds.), *Handbook of emotions* (3rd ed., pp. 114–137). New York, NY: Guilford Press.

Valentino, N. A., Gregorowicz, K., & Groenendyk, E. W. (2009). Efficacy, emotions and the habit of participation. *Political Behavior, 31*, 307–330.

Van Stekelenburg, J., & Klandermans, B. (2013). The social psychology of protest. *Current Sociology, 61*, 886–905.

van Zomeren, M., Spears, R., & Leach, C. W. (2008). Exploring psychological mechanisms of collective action: Does relevance of group identity influence how people cope with collective disadvantage? *British Journal of Social Psychology, 47*, 353–372.

Wagner, M. (2014). Fear and anger in great Britain: Blame assignment and emotional reactions to the financial crisis. *Political Behavior, 36*, 683–703.

Waters, E. (2002). Comments on Strange Situation classification. Retrieved from http://www.psychology.sunysb.edu/attachment/measures/content/ss_scoring.pdf.

Webster, S. W. (in press). Anger and declining trust in government in the American electorate. *Political Behavior*. https://doi.org/10.1007/s11109-017-9431-7.

White, S. F., Brislin, S. J., Sinclair, S., & Blair, J. R. (2014). Punishing unfairness: Rewarding or the organization of a reactively aggressive response? *Human Brain Mapping, 35*(5), 2137–2147.

Williams, J. E. (2010). Anger/hostility and cardiovascular disease. In M. Potegal, G. Stemmler, & C. Spielberger (Eds.), *International handbook of anger* (pp. 435–447). New York, NY: Springer.

Wortman, C. B., & Brehm, J. W. (1975). Responses to uncontrollable outcomes: An integration of reactance theory and the learned helplessness model. In L. Berkowitz (Ed.), *Advances in experimental social psychology* (Vol. 8, pp. 277–336). New York, NY: Academic Press.

Zernike, K. (2010). *Boiling mad: Inside Tea Party America*. New York, NY: Times Books.

Chapter 9
Nurturant Love and Caregiving Emotions

Makenzie J. O'Neil, Alexander F. Danvers, and Michelle N. Shiota

Abstract Caregiving for one's offspring and young kin facilitates the evolutionary goal of successful reproduction. In this chapter we define an emotional state of *nurturant love*, elicited by cues of cuteness and helplessness, which activates a suite of physiological, cognitive, and behavioral changes facilitating caregiving toward the eliciting target. We review the literature pertaining to the elicitors and function of nurturant love, compare and contrast this emotion to other affective states that may promote caregiving, discuss empirical evidence regarding the properties and behavioral consequences of nurturant love, and conclude with potential future directions for research in this area.

A mother is watching her children play at a playground. While she is implicitly aware of what each of them is doing, her conscious mind is lost in thoughts of an ongoing crisis at work, the long list of errands she has to run, and worry over medical test results of her own that she is awaiting. Her youngest, a toddler clumsier than the other children, stumbles and falls hard while trying to keep up with his sister. After a moment of shock, tears well in his eyes and he begins to cry. In a flash, the mother's attention snaps away from other thoughts to her son; she instinctively runs to his side, scoops him in her arms, and nuzzles him against her chest while talking to him in a gentle voice and checking for wounds. Not seriously injured, the boy soon smiles and is ready to continue playing.

At the office, a woman suddenly issues a high-pitched and resonant "awww-www!!" while sitting at her desk during a break and begins to laugh. Others join her to see what she is looking at – a video of baby sloths, ineptly playing and making their characteristic squeaks. Shrieks, laughter, and cries of "OMG, SO CUTE!" are heard for a few minutes, after which everyone returns to their own desks feeling a little lighter and more energized.

M. J. O'Neil · M. N. Shiota (✉)
Department of Psychology, Arizona State University, Tempe, AZ, USA
e-mail: lani.shiota@asu.edu

A. F. Danvers
Institute for the Study of Human Flourishing, University of Oklahoma, Norman, OK, USA

© Springer International Publishing AG, part of Springer Nature 2018   175
H. C. Lench (ed.), *The Function of Emotions*,
https://doi.org/10.1007/978-3-319-77619-4_9

For the past year, a middle-aged couple has been fostering a baby girl who came to them soon after she was born, already exposed to several addictive drugs and going through withdrawal. They are anxiously awaiting a final decision by the birth mother and the courts regarding their petition to legally and permanently adopt the child. If the petition is granted, they will be overwhelmed with joy; if not, they know their hearts will break.

A father returns home from work one day to find that his three young children are alone in the house. His wife, who had been increasingly worried about their finances and struggling with anxiety and depression, has abandoned them with a note that says, "I'm sorry, I can't do this anymore. It's all too much."

The mother in the first scenario illustrates a prototype of maternal caregiving, experiencing an instinctive urge to comfort and nurture her child when he was in need. Although her thoughts were initially elsewhere, her attention was automatically redirected toward her child as soon as the need arose. This behavior is easily interpreted through a functional lens; providing care and protection for one's offspring serves the crucial adaptive function of increasing their fitness, and in turn the chance of propagating one's own genes (Hrdy, 1999; Kenrick, Griskevicius, Neuberg, & Schaller, 2010). While parental care is a lifelong and constant commitment, this chapter proposes that a distinct emotion has evolved to facilitate heightened caregiving behavior in response to particular environmental cues. Parents may be instinctually prepared to care for their offspring (Frodi, Lamb, Leavitt, & Donovan, 1978; Hrdy, 1999; Lorenz, 1971), but having one's full attention on them at all times would result in cognitive overload and an inability to pursue resources needed to support both offspring and parents themselves. Several theorists have described an emotional response involving a suite of physiological, cognitive, and motivational changes that can be activated on an as-needed basis, to quickly promote pleasurable bonding, fulfillment of offspring's physical and emotional needs, and protection from environmental threats (e.g., Hrdy, 1999; Lorenz, 1971; Shaver, Morgan, & Wu, 1996). We have called this response *nurturant love* (Shiota et al., 2014, 2017).

A strong theory of parental caregiving, and thus of nurturant love, must strive to account for the other three scenarios as well as the first. Why do humans – and many other mammals – display intense caregiving behavior and associated emotions toward targets that are non-kin, or even of a different species? Under what circumstances, and why, do caregiving responses break down? In this chapter we review the available literature on nurturant love, discussing its elicitors, function, relation to other affective states in close relationships, and motivational, physiological, and cognitive properties. We conclude with ideas about new directions for future research on nurturant love and the caregiving emotions.

Elicitors of Nurturant Love

Nurturant love has been described as a feeling of love and concern for another's well-being, which motivates caregiving behavior (Shiota et al., 2014, 2017). Human infants are distinctive, even among primates, for their extended period of relative helplessness in childhood (Geary & Flinn, 2001; Konner, 2010; Kramer, 2010). Among humans living in traditional hunting and foraging lifestyles, children often consume many more calories than they contribute to a social group until at least their late teens – a gap not seen in other primate species (Kaplan, Hill, Lancaster, & Hurtado, 2000). Providing for children was therefore a major challenge in human evolution. Theorists have suggested that this challenge was met through cooperative breeding, with groups of adults helping to raise each other's offspring (Bogin, Bragg, & Kuzawa, 2014; Hrdy, 2009; Kramer, 2010). Cooperative breeding groups included not only one's biological kin but also larger social groups. This collective caregiving strategy would have created a selection pressure for mechanisms promoting caregiving toward young and helpless others in general, even if they were not one's own biological kin. The human capacity to experience nurturant love toward non-kin thus may be an exaptation of the more ancient, mammalian maternal instinct.

Empirical evidence strongly points to mammalian biological mechanisms that promote bonding with one's own offspring and, in turn, caregiving behavior. In particular, the release of oxytocin during childbirth, nursing, and skin-to-skin touch during infancy appears crucial for facilitating bond formation (Carter, 2014; Galbally, Lewis, IJzendoorn, & Permezel, 2011; Leng, Meddle, & Douglas, 2008; Levine, Zagoory-Sharon, Feldman, & Weller, 2007). The question of what environmental stimuli elicit a nurturant love response in a particular moment, however, is distinct from the question of long-term bonding. In general, nurturant love appears to be elicited by features of an individual that suggest need for care, including youth, weakness, helplessness, and distress (Hrdy, 1999; Trivers, 1974). Across mammalian species, infants have a distinctive set of physical characteristics referred to as *kindchenschema* or more commonly, "cuteness," that are thought to elicit a caregiving response; these include soft, rounded features, small nose and mouth clustered tightly together, high forehead, large cheeks, and large eyes relative to the rest of the face (Lorenz, 1943, as cited in Vicedo, 2009; Trivers, 1974). Mammalian young tend to have short, stubby limbs relative to their bodies as well. Additional physical cues of infancy leading to caregiving responses can also be found in many other primate species. For example, newborns in some species show brightly colored fur that tones down with age. While this might initially seem counteradaptive, as it makes infants more visible to predators, it also makes infancy itself more salient. A characteristic feature of these species is that mothers are less possessive of their children, and infant sharing is common among females (Hrdy, 1999). This suggests that noticeable physical cues of infancy may help facilitate alloparenting, the investment of parental caregiving in youth other than one's own offspring.

Cues of clumsiness and an inability to fully reach one's goals can also elicit caregiving behavior (Lorenz, 1971), signaling to others that the individual needs assistance to thrive. Youthful behaviors that indicate attentiveness and dependence may trigger caregiving as well. Bowlby (1969) argued that reciprocal, mutually satisfying interactions were key to successful attachment and bonding. Notably, both infants and pets can provide unconditional positive regard for their caregivers, and this positive attentiveness is associated with heightened positive affect in stressful situations and increased health and well-being for the caregiver (Archer, 1997).

Because *kindchenschema* features characterize human and mammalian infants generally speaking (Lorenz 1943 as cited in Vicedo, 2009; Lorenz, 1971), individuals presenting childlike appearance and behavior have the potential to elicit others' nurturant response regardless of kinship, species, or even age. Considerable evidence supports this generalization. For example, adults whose facial features are padded with fat ("baby-faced" adults) are judged to have more childlike traits, including naïveté, submissiveness, warmth, and honesty (Berry & McArthur, 1986; Keating, Randall, Kendrick, & Gutshall, 2003; Zebrowitz & Montepare, 2008). Puppies and cats who show high *kindchenschema* features tend to be judged as cuter (Golle, Lisibach, Mast, & Lobmaier, 2013; Little, 2012). Dogs are often spoken to using "motherese," a distinctive type of language typically seen in mothers conversing with infants (Hirsh-Pasek & Treiman, 1982). Certain mammalian species have been known to show nurturing behavior in response to a neotonous stimulus of a different species, as was the case when the gorilla Binti Jua cared for a young boy who had fallen into her cage (Hrdy, 1999), or is the case with humans and their pets (Belk, 1996). This suggests nurturing responses that originally developed in response to infants can be elicited across species (Archer, 1997).

Why Think of Nurturant Love as an Emotion?

Several researchers have proposed that mammalian mothers have caregiving "instincts," such that maternal responses to an eliciting stimulus (e.g., one's own infant or *kindchenschema* features) are automatic and innate (Vicedo, 2009, 2010). Instincts and emotions differ in subtle, yet important ways. In general, instincts are defined as species-typical, automatic, unlearned, mechanically complex yet procedurally inflexible behaviors elicited by clearly defined stimuli, or "releasers" (Hinde, 1982). Konrad Lorenz described instincts as immutable and entirely hardwired, and argued that maternal caregiving must be instinctual because mothers across a wide range of species are able to effectively care for their offspring with no prior training or experience (Vicedo, 2010). For example, despite finding the scent of amniotic fluids unappealing under normal circumstances, rats and sheep find amniotic fluids irresistible immediately after giving birth and proceed to lick their newborns clean, helping to establish the bond between mother and offspring (Hrdy, 1999; Kendrick, Levy, & Keverne, 1992). In response to the presence of their infant or hearing the infant cry, new mothers of all mammalian species can experience a milk letdown response mediated by oxytocin release in the mammary glands, which causes lactation to occur even without suckling (Hrdy, 1999; McNeilly, Robinson, Houston, & Howie, 1983). Many mammalian species – such as sheep, primates, and humans – engage in a type of mutual imprinting between mothers and newborns. Within a day, mothers can distinguish the smell and cry of their own infant from that of others (Formby, 1967; Hrdy, 1999; Porter, 1991; Vicedo, 2010), and shortly after birth, infants imprint on their caregiver (as in Lorenz's own research on ducks). The instinct model of caregiving, first posited by Konrad Lorenz, asserts that mother-child bonding must occur during a critical period shortly after birth to ensure healthy adult functioning in the infant (Vicedo, 2010).

Primate researcher Harry Harlow (1969) initially thought Lorenz's early instinct model would also be appropriate for describing maternal behavior in his monkeys. However, he ultimately came to believe that primate "instincts" were the joint product of genes and experience, and therefore not really instincts at all (Harlow, 1969, as quoted in Vicedo, 2010; Ruppenthal, Arling, Harlow, Sackett, & Suomi, 1976). While rejecting a complete "blank slate" view of the origins of maternal caregiving, Harlow and his colleagues proposed that maternal behavior is driven by a complex interaction among infant signaling, hormonal activity, and the mother's own personal experience. Harlow's idea of maternal responsiveness as part of a prepared learning pattern that requires significant environmental input is more in-line with contemporary theories of emotion, which conceive of emotion as complex and evolved, yet flexible, multimodal responses to stimuli, in which motivations and goals are fixed, but the exact behaviors employed to accomplish those goals are shaped considerably by learning (Colombetti, 2009; Frijda & Parrott, 2011; Griffiths, 2008; Keltner & Gross, 1999; Lazarus, 1991; Tomkins, 1984). Whereas instincts imply a fixed behavioral pattern evoked by a species-typical releaser (e.g., the milk letdown response activated by the sound of a crying infant), emotions are far more malleable in both the situational appraisals/interpreted meaning evoking the emotion and the specific behaviors resulting from experience of the emotion. For example, although smiling infants elicit pleasant feelings in most adults, and a desire to approach (Frodi et al., 1978), adults do not exhibit inflexible, uncontrollable approach behavior toward all smiling infants – one would not automatically pick up and play with a strange infant encountered in an airport, for example, however cute. Instead, the specific form of approach is modulated by learning and context – one might smile at the infant and wave and then see how the parent responds.

Lorenz himself proposed in later writings that interacting with an infant causes an *emotional* motivation to care for it, which then elicits innate caregiving behavioral responses (Lorenz, 1950). Just as humans and other primates are thought to be evolutionarily "prepared" to learn a fear of snakes (Öhman & Mineka, 2003), we may also have an innate preparedness to identify those who need our care in particular and to rely on certain kinds of cues to do so. Infants certainly elicit powerful and distinct affective responses. The sound of an infant crying is physiologically distressing and perceived as aversive; seeing a smiling infant is associated with altered physiological activity, increased positive affect, and approach motivation (Frodi et al., 1978; Out, Pierper, Bakermans-Kranenburg, & Van IJzendoorn, 2010). Among parents and non-parents alike, neural imaging evidence suggests that people respond more strongly to infant cries than adult cries in auditory, emotional, and motor areas of the brain (Young et al., 2016). Both the wide range of human and nonhuman individuals who can elicit caregiving motivation and the wide range of behaviors through which humans express caregiving suggest an emotion, rather than an instinct in the strict meaning of the term.

Relation of Nurturant Love to Other States

This theoretical analysis of nurturant love emphasizes its evolved function (Keltner, Haidt, & Shiota, 2006; Shiota et al., 2014, 2017). In this analysis, nurturant love is thought to activate a suite of mental mechanisms that address a distinct and recurring adaptive problem: caring for an infant, child, or other dependent individual who cannot fully care for him or herself. Nurturant love involves attending to the needs of the other even in situations that are not immediately or intensely distressing. Nurturant love helps caregivers provide a feeling of security to dependents and helps build trusting relationships between caregiver and child. The present definition of nurturant love differentiates it from other affective states involved in care for another's well-being, which we discuss here.

Nurturant love and empathy Empathy is commonly defined as "an affective response that stems from the apprehension or comprehension of another's emotional state or condition, and which is identical or very similar to what the other person is feeling or would be expected to feel" (Eisenberg, Fabes, & Spinrad, 2006, p. 647). It is considered distinct from, while helping to facilitate, many related emotional phenomena including compassion, sympathy, altruistic helping, perspective taking, and emotional contagion (Batson, 2011; Dovidio, Piliavin, Schroeder, & Penner, 2006; de Waal & Preston, 2017). One of the phenomena that empathy is likely to facilitate is the activation of nurturant love. While both empathy and nurturant love are associated with attunement to the affective state of another individual, the prototypical elicitors (e.g. cuteness, neotony) of nurturant love are more specified than empathy generally. Multiple theoretical models have linked nurturance and empathy explicitly, conceptualizing empathy as either an umbrella term that includes nurturance (Batson, Lishner, Cook, & Sawyer, 2005), or as a necessary precursor to nurturing behavior (Preston & de Waal, 2002). Thus, while it is possible that the experience of nurturant love depends in some way on the experience of empathy, it is a distinct experience, and empathy can occur without necessarily leading to nurturant love.

Nurturant love and sympathy Sympathy is another affective state that is thought to be facilitated by empathy (Eisenberg et al., 2006), and also seems to include behavioral features that would be expected in nurturant love. Although empathy and sympathy are often used interchangeably in colloquial speech, sympathy does not necessarily involve feeling what the other person is feeling – a defining characteristic of empathy. Rather, sympathy is best understood as feeling concern or sorrow for a distressed person (Eisenberg et al., 2006). While empathy may lead to sympathy, in that a person who understands the emotional state of a distressed person may then feel more concern for that person, empathy and sympathy are theoretically distinct (Eisenberg et al., 2006).

Although there may be some overlap between sympathy and nurturant love, a conceptual distinction is important. Nurturant love and sympathy both involve concern for another's well-being, as well as a tendency to help the individual toward whom one is feeling the emotion (Batson, 1991; Eisenberg & Fabes, 1990; Zahn-Waxler, Robinson, & Emde, 1992). However, sympathy is experienced specifically as a response toward the target individual's *distress*. In contrast, nurturant love does not require distress and may be evoked by the target individual's positive affect, affiliative or playful behavior, or mere physical appearance. Thus, while the prosocial behavior resulting from sympathy is thought to originate in feelings of empathetic distress (Eisenberg et al., 1989), nurturant love is typically experienced as positive and pleasurable (Shiota et al., 2014).

Nurturant love and compassion Another affective state that falls under the umbrella of caregiving emotions is compassion. Compassion has been defined as "the feeling that arises in witnessing another's suffering and that motivates a subsequent desire to help" (Goetz, Keltner, & Simon-Thomas, 2010, p. 352). While similar to sympathy, compassion is not necessarily characterized by the subjective feeling of distress that is thought to elicit sympathy. Further, although the lay usage of compassion is often associated with tenderness, caring, and a type of love (Fehr & Russell, 1991; Shaver, Schwartz, Kirson, & O'Connor, 1987), evolutionary analyses of compassion suggest that it is functionally distinct from love (Goetz et al., 2010). Goetz et al. (2010) explicitly use antecedent events to distinguish these emotions; compassion occurs in response to suffering and negative events, such as watching an individual receiving a painful electric shock (Batson, O'Quin, Fultz, Vanderplas, & Isen, 1983), whereas love occurs in response to positive events. Consistent with this distinction, nurturant love is thought to be elicited by "cuteness" or cues of vulnerability rather than distress per se (Hinde & Barden, 1985; Lorenz, 1971), although it may also occur in mildly negative events (as in the child falling on the playground in the scenario at the beginning of this chapter).

The content of caregiving is also different in nurturant love from the kind of helping facilitated by compassion or sympathy. The emphasis in nurturant love may often be on providing positive support and affection rather than alleviating distress. Nurturant love may facilitate temporarily providing care or resources that the target (especially if an adult) would typically be expected to provide for him or herself – inviting a kind of "indulgent dependence" (Behrens, 2004). Finally, the implications of compassion and nurturant love for the self-concept, and for the relationship between caregiver and recipient, may differ. Compassion produces a pleasant feeling at the prospect of being able to help humanity generally and may help people transcend their own selfish concerns (Stellar et al., 2017). In contrast, nurturant love may be rooted more closely in a specific relationship. After experiencing nurturant love, an individual is likely to include the recipient of aid in her or his own self-concept (Batson et al., 1997). The self-concept then becomes even more important, because being responsible for oneself involves taking care of two lives.

Despite these distinctions, there may also be some overlap between the elicitors of compassion and nurturant love. For instance, images used to elicit compassion include crying, malnourished, and handicapped children (Eisenberg et al., 1988; Oveis, Horberg, & Keltner, 2010). To the extent that these are states that do not require immediate, "heroic" action, as in the case of malnourished or handicapped children, or that the likely remedy to the situation is comforting behavior, as in the case of the crying child, these may be elicitors of both compassion and nurturant love. Thus, while distinct, nurturant love and compassion might have some overlap in function and elicitors.

Features of Nurturant Love

Though not often published under the relatively new term "nurturant love," a strong and growing body of research addresses the cognitive, motivational, physiological, expressive, and behavioral aspects of our emotional responses to infants and other *kindchenschema* stimuli. This work has been done with human participants as well as nonhuman animals (primarily rats and primates). Importantly, many studies with human participants have used stimuli in which the "cuteness" of the infants is experimentally manipulated, either by comparing responses to infants and adults of the same species or, increasingly, by morphing photographs of human babies to increase or reduce the cuteness of their features. These studies have the advantage of documenting effects of cuteness per se. Moreover, many studies have examined the responses of young adult participants who do not have children of their own to infant stimuli, providing evidence for a nurturant love response that that can occur independent of actually being a parent.

As stimuli, infants exert a powerful pull on our attention. Studies using both dot-probe and eye tracking methods have found that infant human faces draw visual attention more strongly than adult faces (e.g., Brosch, Sander, & Scherer, 2007; Cárdenas, Harris, & Becker, 2013). Magnetoencephalography measures also detect differential neural responding to infant versus adult crying almost immediately, within 100–200 milliseconds of stimulus onset (Young et al., 2016). There is some evidence that the visual attentional bias toward infants is stronger for women than for men. In one study of young adults who had not yet had children of their own, women showed a stronger visual bias toward infants in eye tracking (Cárdenas et al., 2013), and another study found that women's subjective ratings of infant cuteness tracked experimental morphing of *kindchenschema* features more closely than was seen in men (Lobmaier, Sprengelmeyer, Wiffen, & Perrett, 2010). However, another study found that women's and men's ratings of infant attractiveness were influenced by manipulated cuteness to a comparable extent and that both sexes chose to spend more time looking at the cuter baby photos (Parsons, Young, Kumari, Stein, & Kringelbach, 2011). Thus, while the attentional pull of the *kindchenschema* may be somewhat milder for men than for women, it appears to be detected by and motivationally relevant for both sexes.

Neural and physiological measures suggest that infant stimuli also elicit strong approach motivation. In one study of nulliparous women (i.e., those who have not yet given birth), photographs of human babies with experimentally enhanced *kindchenschema* features were not only rated as cuter but also evoked stronger activity in the nucleus accumbens, a crucial structure in the mammalian neural reward circuit facilitating approach behavior (Glocker et al., 2009). This reward response is, not surprisingly, enhanced for one's own infant; multiple fMRI studies have reported stronger reward circuit activation while new mothers viewed photos of their own babies relative to photos of other, control babies (e.g., Bartels & Zeki, 2004; Strathearn, Li, Fonagy, & Montague, 2008). While dopamine serves as the primary neurotransmitter directly facilitating approach behavior in the reward circuit, oxytocin plays an important role in engaging approach motivation in this specific context (Bartels & Zeki, 2004; Skuse & Gallagher, 2009) and may account in part for the enhanced reward responding seen toward one's own child. In both rats and humans, oxytocin released during pregnancy, birth, and nursing facilitates maternal behavior and mother-infant bonding (Levine et al., 2007; Pedersen, Ascher, Monroe, & Prange, 1982). Oxytocin receptor activation in the nucleus accumbens and other reward circuit structures, which facilitates dopaminergic activity, is predictive of stronger "good mother" behavior such as licking and grooming in rats (Francis, Champagne, & Meaney, 2000).

One limitation of the research on reward circuit responding to infant stimuli is the lack of data on male participants. While male rats are understandably excluded from studies of the neural mechanisms of highly sex-typed maternal behavior, men's absence from human fMRI studies is more likely to reflect researchers' choice to focus scarce resources on the "best bet" for showing strong experimental effects. As a result, the extent of sex differences in human reward responding to infant stimuli remains an open question; the dearth of data on men should not be taken as evidence that they do not show such responses.

Evidence from studies of autonomic nervous system responding to cute stimuli is also consistent with heightened approach motivation. Shiota, Neufeld, Yeung, Moser, and Perea (2011) observed more positive changes from baseline in both heart rate and respiration rate while participants viewed photos of cute baby animals than when viewing neutral images. Another study reported a greater increase in heart rate while participants viewed photos of kittens and puppies than when viewing photos of adult animals, although this effect only approached significance (Sherman, Haidt, & Coan, 2009). Some evidence suggests that this increase in arousal is driven by withdrawal of parasympathetic influence on the heart and lungs, rather than an increase in "fight-flight" sympathetic system activation. In the study by Shiota et al. (2011), the increase in heart and respiration rate was not accompanied by corresponding increases in skin conductance or blood pressure, as would be expected from a full-blown sympathetic response. Instead, participants showed a reduction in respiratory sinus arrhythmia (a common measure of parasympathetic influence on the heart) that approached significance. Another study also reported a significant reduction in high-frequency heart rate variability – another common index of parasympathetic influence – while adult participants listened to crying babies (Tkaczyszyn et al., 2013). These studies offer a preliminary picture of visceral responses to cuteness, but more research is needed to fully understand the physiological profile and its autonomic nervous system mechanisms.

Despite the central role that research on facial expressions has played in affective science, little or no attention has been paid to facial expressions of nurturant love. More is known about other nonverbal channels through which this state may be expressed. In chimpanzees, mothers as well as their infants may use a *hoo* sequence – several short, repeated, and musical iterations of this syllable – when they are separated and seeking reunion (Goodall, 1986). Humans have an even more common and distinctive infant-directed speech quality than primates (Falk, 2004). Throughout the world, *motherese* is characterized by high-pitched, musical, prosodic speech directed toward infants and young children (Falk, 2004; Snow, 1972), and a similar speech pattern has been demonstrated in people speaking with their dogs (Hirsh-Pasek & Treiman, 1982).

Touch is another important channel for nonverbal expression of nurturance in mammals. Among rodents infant licking and grooming are distinctive maternal behaviors, and in primates gentle stroking and cuddling are common as well (Champagne, Francis, Mar, & Meaney, 2003; Goodall, 1986). These latter behaviors also communicate nurturance among humans. In studies where young adults were asked to try to express several emotions simply by touching another person's arm, love and sympathy were communicated most often through gentle stroking, patting, and rubbing motions, and these touches were interpreted accurately by touch recipients at rates well above chance (Hertenstein, Keltner, App, Bulleit, & Jaskolka, 2006). One possibility is that nurturant love is expressed more instinctively through touch and tone of voice than through the face, perhaps reflecting the earlier elaboration of the former communication channels among mammals as well as the relatively slow development of visual acuity in humans. However, there appears to be no published research aimed at identifying a facial expression of nurturant love in humans, and it seems premature to declare the nonexistence of such an expression before it has actually been sought.

Finally, although only a few studies have examined the cognitive and behavioral effects of human nurturant love, these offer interesting and theoretically coherent findings. In one study, participants who had recently viewed photos of baby animals identified target letters more quickly when they were used as elements making up a larger whole, versus being the shape of the whole itself, suggesting a bias toward local rather than global visual attention (Nittono, Fukushima, Yano, & Moriya, 2012). The researchers interpret this as an indicator of heightened approach motivation, consistent with findings from other studies linking high approach-motivation emotions to attentional narrowing (Gable & Harmon-Jones, 2008). Especially intriguing are several studies finding that experimentally elicited nurturant love evokes increased caution and care, in both motor and cognitive tasks. For example, in several studies using an "Operation" game as the dependent variable (participants use tweezers to remove plastic organs from small cavities without touching the sides of the cavities), participants who had just viewed photos of cute baby animals performed the task more successfully than those who had viewed photos of adult animals (e.g., Nittono et al., 2012; Sherman et al., 2009). Another pair of studies documented similar effects of high-cuteness stimulus exposure on carefulness in a manual line-tracing task, although this effect was limited to women high on prosocial orientation (Sherman, Haidt, Iyer, & Coan, 2013).

Evidence for increased caution in nurturant love extends to information-processing tasks as well. In two studies, Griskevicius, Shiota, and Neufeld (2010) elicited nurturant love either via relived personal experiences involving pleasurable caregiving or a scenario in which the participant imagines watching a neighbor's small child at a playground. Several other positive emotions and a neutral-affect control were included as additional conditions in each study. After the emotion manipulation, participants read a supposed news article advocating for an unpopular position (requiring comprehensive exams prior to college graduation) with either several high-quality arguments or several poor-quality, superficial arguments. Finally, participants rated their agreement with the article's proposal. Consistent with previously published research on positive mood and persuasive message processing, most positive emotions reduced the effect of argument quality on attitudes toward the proposal, relative to the neutral-affect control. In these conditions, participants were just as easily persuaded by low-quality as by high-quality arguments, suggesting rather careless, heuristic-based processing of the persuasive message. Nurturant love proved a striking exception; however, in this condition the effect of argument quality was *amplified* relative to neutral control, suggesting that nurturant love increased participants' carefulness in evaluating the persuasive message.

Looking Forward

As described above, a growing body of empirical research is examining the physiological, cognitive, and behavioral features associated with nurturant love. However, to gain a more complete understanding of this emotion, future research is needed to closely examine (1) distinct facets of nurturant love responses that theorists have proposed; (2) the extent of overlap with and differentiation from other emotions in intimate relationships, in terms of features and underlying mechanisms; and (3) instances where nurturant love specifically and the caregiving system more broadly fail to function, or function maladaptively.

Multiple facets of nurturant love The role of nurturant love in overall caregiving has been described as including three distinct facets: promoting bonding within the dyad, fulfilling basic needs of the eliciting target, and protecting the target from harm (e.g., Hrdy, 1999; Lorenz, 1971; Shaver et al., 1996; Shiota et al., 2014). While each of these facets serves to facilitate the overarching function of increasing the target's adaptive fitness, there may be distinct cognitive and behavioral mechanisms supporting each aspect of nurturant love behavior. Future research should investigate these mechanisms systematically, assessing which are shared among the facets and which are distinct.

For instance, fulfilling basic needs and protecting the target from harm are both likely to require increased vigilance to the target and its environment. Some preliminary evidence supports heightened vigilance in nurturant love; Griskevicius et al. (2010) found that experiencing nurturant love led to greater responsiveness to argument quality in processing a persuasive message, suggesting an increase in cognitive vigilance and attentiveness. The reduction in parasympathetic nervous system influence on the heart seen in nurturant love (Shiota et al., 2011; Tkaczyszyn et al., 2013) may also suggest that nurturant love promotes alertness and attentiveness. However, many questions about this vigilance remain unaddressed. Does nurturant love lead to a global activation of vigilance across all domains that are related to the infant; or do specific eliciting situations lead to more domain-specific vigilance?

Distinguishing among these three facets of nurturant love suggests another set of questions as well. Although nurturant love is a subjectively pleasant emotion, and is generally thought to facilitate caregiving and nurturance (Shiota et al., 2014), this does not mean that all resulting behaviors will necessarily be desirable or prosocial. In particular, protecting the target from harm may involve heightened tendency to perceive others as potential threats. If the perceived threat is an outgroup member or predator, protecting the target may include discriminatory or aggressive behavior. De Dreu et al. (2010, 2012) found that administration of oxytocin, a neuropeptide associated with caregiving, bonding, and other positive, interpersonal processes, is associated with increased cooperation with ingroup members but increased aggression toward outgroup members, particularly when the outgroup was viewed as a threat to *vulnerable* ingroup members. This suggests that nurturant love may facilitate aggressive, antisocial behavior against those that are viewed as threatening. Future research should examine the possibility that nurturant love leads to more aggressive or discriminatory behavior toward individuals perceived as threatening, or perhaps even outgroups in general.

Caregiving, attachment, and desire To more fully understand bonding as it relates to nurturant love, future research should examine the dynamic relationships among nurturant love and the emotions involved in attachment and (in romantic relationships) sexual desire. Caregiving, attachment, and sex are functionally distinct, yet they share an overarching function of producing offspring and increasing the chance that those offspring will survive to reproductive age (Bowlby, 1969). For example, in a prototypical parent-child relationship, attachment behaviors by the child (e.g., seeking the parent's attention and assistance, crying when distressed or in danger) are likely to evoke caregiving by the parent, in a dyadic pattern that promotes the child's well-being and safety. The emotions associated with the caregiving, attachment, and sex systems may potentially represent branches of "love" with a common origin, sharing important mechanisms (Bowlby, 1969; Shaver et al., 1996; Shiota et al., 2017). Future research should carefully examine the overlap and distinguishing features of these emotion states.

As an example of overlap, oxytocin activity is implicated as a neural mechanism in all three systems (Carter, Williams, Witt, & Insel, 1992). As noted earlier, maternal bonding and caregiving are strongly facilitated by oxytocin and vasopressin release in the central nervous system as well as peripherally (Bick, Dozier, Bernard, Grasso, & Simons, 2013; Preston, 2013; Riem et al., 2011; Strathearn, 2011).

Variations in human oxytocin receptor genes have been associated with childhood pair-bonding and in other attachment relationships (Walum et al., 2012). Oxytocin-dopamine interactions have been linked to sexual arousal and activity (Baskerville & Douglas, 2008; Carter, 1992), and in several mammalian species (including humans) sexual activity causes a release of oxytocin in the brain that promotes pair bonding or attachment between mating partners (Insel & Hulihan, 1995; Young & Wang, 2004). Although the bulk of research on oxytocin in intimate relationships has emphasized this neuropeptide's role in the initial formation of bonds, rather than transient emotion states, the experience of romantic love has been linked to increased peripheral oxytocin release in humans (e.g., Gonzaga, Turner, Keltner, Campos, & Altemus, 2006). It is unclear from this research, however, whether oxytocin release was linked to the nurturant, attachment, or sexual aspect of romantic love, or all three.

As an example of differentiation, studies comparing the emotion states of nurturant love, attachment love, and sexual desire suggest that each of these emotions is activated by distinct elicitors and facilitates different cognitive, motivational, and behavioral profiles. Whereas nurturant love motivates caregiving behavior toward a target in need of care or attention, attachment love can be thought of as the reciprocal emotion, characterized by a feeling of pleasant dependence on another person and facilitates assistance-seeking (Behrens, 2004; Shiota et al., 2014); and sexual desire is an attraction-based response to a potential sexual partner promoting mating behavior (Shiota et al., 2014). Nurturant love seems to promote increased cognitive vigilance, whereas attachment love does not show this effect (Griskevicius et al., 2010). Nurturant love promotes caution; whereas sexual desire promotes risk-taking (Baker & Maner, 2008; Hrdy, 1999; Li, Kenrick, Griskevicius, & Neuberg, 2012). Future research should continue to build on this early evidence to further understand the ways in which these emotions overlap and are distinct.

Caregiving failures   Much of the review above has focused on the function of nurturant love in facilitating effective caregiving. However, there are instances when caregiving fails even toward one's own offspring, sometimes tragically. Closely examining these failures of caregiving may facilitate a richer understanding of the mechanisms supporting nurturant love and the adaptive functions they reflect.

For instance, humans have an unusually high rate of infanticide, especially in many resource-scarce environments where a mother may not feel she has enough resources to care for all of her children (Dorjahn, 1976; McKee, 1984). Understanding when and how mothers decide to continue nurturing some offspring, and not others, can help elucidate the mechanisms of nurturant love. For example, part of the *kindchenschema* involves having short, stubby, limbs with high fat content (Lorenz, 1971). A baby's ability to pad its body with fat stores not only allows it to survive early difficulties but also advertises to caregivers that it is *worthy* of intense parental investment (Hrdy, 1999). Thus, the tendency to find small but chubby infants particularly cute may reflect the information that fat stores provide: that the infant is healthy, sturdy, and likely to survive given adequate parental care.

In the opposite kind of system failure, there are likely instances in which nurturant love is elicited inappropriately or even maladaptively, and future research should examine this more closely. For instance, nurturant love might help explain the "pratfall effect," in which a highly competent person is liked more if she or he commits a clumsy blunder (Aronson, Willerman, & Floyd, 1966). Clumsiness is characteristic of children, still learning to control their motor actions, and seeing a high status person do something clumsy – like accidentally spilling coffee onto himself (as in Aronson et al., 1966) – might momentarily trigger a desire to nurture and bond with that individual. Additionally, people tend to feel warmth toward baby-faced adults (Berry & McArthur, 1986; Keating et al., 2003; Zebrowitz & Montepare, 2008). Empirical work is needed to determine if bonding and the provision of benefits to clumsy or baby-faced people is in part mediated by experiences of nurturant love. Research on the strategic deployment of cute helplessness is also needed to test this hypothesis.

Conclusion

Effectively providing care for one's offspring is foundational to the successful propagation of one's own genes. This chapter described an emotional response originally serving this adaptive goal and exapted to respond to a broader range of eliciting situations that has, until recently, received limited attention from affective science. Elicited by cues of cuteness and behavioral helplessness, nurturant love activates a suite of caregiving behaviors, which includes fulfilling the needs of the eliciting target and protecting it from harm (Hrdy, 1999; Lorenz, 1971). While theorists have long posited the existence of a caregiving emotion, empirical research is just beginning to investigate the physiological, neural, cognitive, and behavioral changes that characterize nurturant love and related states promoting caregiving. A more developed understanding of nurturant love has the potential to enrich our appreciation of the role of emotions in this crucial aspect of human functioning.

References

Archer, J. (1997). Why do people love their pets? *Evolution and Human Behavior, 18*, 237–259.
Aronson, E., Willerman, B., & Floyd, J. (1966). The effect of a pratfall on increasing interpersonal attractiveness. *Psychonomic Science, 4*, 227–228.
Baker, M. D., Jr., & Maner, J. K. (2008). Risk-taking as a situationally sensitive male mating strategy. *Evolution and Human Behavior, 29*, 391–395.
Bartels, A., & Zeki, S. (2004). The neural correlates of maternal and romantic love. *NeuroImage, 21*, 1155–1166.
Baskerville, T. A., & Douglas, A. J. (2008). Interactions between dopamine and oxytocin in the control of sexual behavior. *Progress in Brain Research, 170*, 277–290.
Batson, C. D. (1991). *The altruism question: Toward a social-psychological answer*. Hillsdale, MI: Lawrence Erlbaum.

Batson, C. D. (2011). *Altruism in humans.* New York, NY: Oxford University Press.

Batson, C. D., Lishner, D. A., Cook, J., & Sawyer, S. (2005). Similarity and nurturance: Two possible sources of empathy for strangers. *Basic and Applied Social Psychology, 27*, 15–25.

Batson, C. D., O'Quin, K., Fultz, J., Vanderplas, M., & Isen, A. M. (1983). Influence of self-reported distress and empathy on egoistic versus altruistic motivation to help. *Journal of Personality and Social Psychology, 45*, 706–718.

Batson, C. D., Sager, K., Garst, E., Kang, M., Rubchinsky, K., & Dawson, K. (1997). Is empathy-induced helping due to self-other merging? *Journal of Personality and Social Psychology, 73*, 495–509.

Behrens, K. Y. (2004). A multifaceted view of the concept of amae: Reconsidering the indigenous Japanese concept of relatedness. *Human Development, 47*, 1–27.

Belk, R. W. (1996). Metaphoric relationships with pets. *Society & Animals: Journal of Human-Animal Studies, 4*, 121–145.

Berry, D. S., & McArthur, L. Z. (1986). Perceiving character in faces: The impact of age-related craniofacial changes on social perception. *Psychological Bulletin, 100*, 3–18.

Bick, J., Dozier, M., Bernard, K., Grasso, D., & Simons, R. (2013). Foster mother–infant onding: Associations between foster mothers' oxytocin production, electrophysiological brain activity, feelings of commitment, and caregiving quality. *Child Development, 84*, 826–840.

Bogin, B., Bragg, J., & Kuzawa, C. (2014). Humans are not cooperative breeders but practice biocultural reproduction. *Annals of Human Biology, 41*, 368–380.

Bowlby, J. (1969). *Attachment and loss, Attachment* (Vol. 1). London, England: The Hogarth Press and Institute of Psychoanalysis.

Brosch, T., Sander, D., & Scherer, K. R. (2007). That baby caught my eye... Attention capture by infant faces. *Emotion, 7*, 685–689.

Cárdenas, R. A., Harris, L. J., & Becker, M. W. (2013). Sex differences in visual attention toward infant faces. *Evolution and Human Behavior, 34*, 280–287.

Carter, C. S. (1992). Oxytocin and sexual behavior. *Neuroscience & Biobehavioral Reviews, 16*, 131–144.

Carter, C. S. (2014). Oxytocin pathways and the evolution of human behavior. *Annual Review of Psychology, 65*, 17–39.

Carter, C., Williams, J. R., Witt, D. M., & Insel, T. R. (1992). Oxytocin and social bonding. *Annals of the New York Academy of Sciences, 652*, 204–211.

Champagne, F. A., Francis, D. D., Mar, A., & Meaney, M. J. (2003). Variations in maternal care n the rat as a mediating influence for the effects of environment on development. *Physiology & Behavior, 79*, 359–371.

Colombetti, G. (2009). From affect programs to dynamical discrete emotions. *Philosophical Psychology, 22*, 407–425.

De Dreu, C. K. W., Greer, L. L., Handgraff, M. J. J., Shalvi, S., Van Kleef, G. A., Baas, M., … Feith, S. W. W. (2010). Neuropeptide oxytocin regulates parochial altruism in intergroup conflict among humans. *Science, 328*, 1408–1411.

De Dreu, C. K. W., Shalvi, S., Greer, L. L., Van Kleef, G. A., & Handgraff, M. J. J. (2012). Oxytocin motivates non-cooperation in intergroup conflict to protect vulnerable ingroup members. *PLoS One, 7*, 1–7.

de Waal, F. B. M., & Preston, S. D. (2017). Mammalian empathy: Behavioural manifestations and neural basis. *Nature Reviews Neuroscience, 18*, 498–509.

Dorjahn, V. R. (1976). Rural-urban differences in infant and child mortality among the Temne of Kolifa. *Journal of Anthropological Research, 32*, 74–103.

Dovidio, J. F., Piliavin, J. A., Schroeder, D. A., & Penner, L. (2006). *The social psychology of prosocial behavior.* Mahwah, NJ: Lawrence Erlbaum Associates Publishers.

Eisenberg, N., & Fabes, R. A. (1990). Empathy: Conceptualization, measurement, and relation to prosocial behavior. *Motivation and Emotion, 14*, 131–149.

Eisenberg, N., Fabes, R. A., Bustamante, D., Mathy, R. M., Miller, P. A., & Lindholm, E. (1988). Differentiation of vicariously induced emotional reactions in children. *Developmental Psychology, 24*, 237–246.

Eisenberg, N., Fabes, R. A., Miller, P. A., Fultz, J., Shell, R., Mathy, R. M., & Reno, R. R. (1989). Relation of sympathy and personal distress to prosocial behavior: A multimethod study. *Interpersonal Relations and Group Processes, 57,* 55–66.

Eisenberg, N., Fabes, R. A., & Spinrad, T. L. (2006). Prosocial development. In W. Damon, R. M. Lerner, & N. Eisenberg (Eds.), *Handbook of child psychology, Social, emotional, and personality development* (Vol. 3, 6th ed., pp. 646–718). New York, NY: Wiley.

Falk, D. (2004). Prelinguistic evolution in early hominins: Whence motherese? *Behavioral and Brain Sciences, 27,* 491–503.

Fehr, B., & Russell, J. A. (1991). The concept of love viewed from a prototype perspective. *Journal of Personality and Social Psychology, 60,* 425–438.

Formby, D. (1967). Maternal recognition of infant's cry. *Developmental Medicine and Chile Neurology, 9,* 293–298.

Francis, D. D., Champagne, F. C., & Meaney, M. J. (2000). Variations in maternal behaviour are associated with differences in oxytocin receptor levels in the rat. *Journal of Neuroendocrinology, 12,* 1145–1148.

Frijda, N. H., & Parrott, W. G. (2011). Basic emotions or ur-emotions? *Emotion Review, 3,* 406–415.

Frodi, A. M., Lamb, M. E., Leavitt, L. A., & Donovan, W. L. (1978). Fathers' and mothers' responses to infant smiles and cries. *Infant Behavioral Development, 1,* 187–198.

Gable, P. S., & Harmon-Jones, E. (2008). Approach-motivated positive affect reduces breadth of attention. *Psychological Science, 19,* 476–482.

Galbally, M., Lewis, A. J., Ijzendoorn, M. V., & Permezel, M. (2011). The role of oxytocin in mother-infant relations: A systematic review of human studies. *Harvard Review of Psychiatry, 19,* 1–14.

Geary, D. C., & Flinn, M. V. (2001). Evolution of human parental behavior and the human family. *Parenting, 1,* 5–61.

Glocker, M. L., Langleben, D. D., Ruparel, K., Loughead, J. W., Valdez, J. N., Griffin, M. D., … Gur, R. C. (2009). Baby schema modulates the brain reward system in nulliparous women. *Proceedings of the National Academy of Sciences, 106,* 9115–9119.

Goetz, J. L., Keltner, D., & Simon-Thomas, E. (2010). Compassion: An evolutionary analysis and empirical review. *Psychological Bulletin, 136,* 351–374.

Golle, J., Lisibach, S., Mast, F. W., & Lobmaier, J. S. (2013). Sweet puppies and cute babies: Perceptual adaptation to babyfacedness transfers across species. *PLoS One, 8,* e58248.

Gonzaga, G. C., Turner, R. A., Keltner, D., Campos, B., & Altemus, M. (2006). Romantic love and sexual desire in close relationships. *Emotion, 6,* 163–179.

Goodall, J. (1986). *The chimpanzees of Gombe: Patterns of behavior.* Cambridge, MA: The Belknap Press of Harvard University Press.

Griffiths, P. E. (2008). *What emotions really are: The problem of psychological categories.* Chicago, IL: University of Chicago Press.

Griskevicius, V., Shiota, M. N., & Neufeld, S. L. (2010). Influence of different positive emotions on persuasion processing: A functional evolutionary approach. *Emotion, 10,* 190–206.

Harlow, H. F. (1969). William James and instinct theory. In R. B. MacLeod (Ed.), *William James: Unfinished business* (pp. 21–30). Washington, DC: American Psychological Association.

Hertenstein, M. J., Keltner, D., App, B., Bulleit, B. A., & Jaskolka, A. R. (2006). Touch communicates distinct emotions. *Emotion, 6,* 528–533.

Hinde, R. A. (1982). *Ethology, its nature and relations with other sciences.* Oxford, England: Oxford University Press.

Hinde, R. A., & Barden, L. A. (1985). The evolution of the teddy bear. *Animal Behaviour, 33,* 1371–1373.

Hirsh-Pasek, K., & Treiman, R. (1982). Doggerel: Motherese in a new context. *Journal of Child Language, 9,* 229–237.

Hrdy, S. B. (1999). *Mother nature: Maternal instincts and how they shape the human species.* New York, NY: Ballantine Books.

Hrdy, S. B. (2009). *Mothers and others: The evolutionary origins of mutual understanding.* Cambridge, MA: Harvard University Press.

Insel, T. R., & Hulihan, T. J. (1995). A gender-specific mechanism for pair bonding: Oxytocin and partner preference formation in monogamous voles. *Behavioral Neuroscience, 109*, 782–789.

Kaplan, H., Hill, K., Lancaster, J., & Hurtado, A. M. (2000). A theory of human life history evolution: Diet, intelligence, and longevity. *Evolutionary Anthropology: Issues, News, and Reviews, 9*, 156–185.

Keating, C. F., Randall, D. W., Kendrick, T., & Gutshall, K. A. (2003). Do babyfaced adults receive more help? The (cross-cultural) case of the lost resume. *Journal of Nonverbal Behavior, 27*, 89–109.

Keltner, D., & Gross, J. J. (1999). Functional accounts of emotions. *Cognition and Emotion, 13*, 467–480.

Keltner, D., Haidt, J., & Shiota, M. N. (2006). Social functionalism and the evolution of emotions. In M. Schaller, J. A. Simpson, & D. T. Kenrick (Eds.), *Evolution and social psychology* (pp. 115–142). Madison, CT: Psychosocial Press.

Kendrick, K. M., Levy, F., & Keverne, E. B. (1992). Changes in the sensory processing of olfactory signals induced by birth in sheep. *Science, 256*, 833–836.

Kenrick, D. T., Griskevicius, V., Neuberg, S. L., & Schaller, M. (2010). Renovating the pyramid of needs: Contemporary extensions built upon ancient foundations. *Perspectives on Psychological Science, 5*, 292–314.

Konner, M. (2010). *The evolution of childhood: Relationships, emotion, mind.* Cambridge, MA: Harvard University Press.

Kramer, K. L. (2010). Cooperative breeding and its significance to the demographic success of humans. *Annual Review of Anthropology, 39*, 417–436.

Lazarus, R. S. (1991). *Emotion and adaptation.* New York, NY: Oxford University Press.

Leng, G., Meddle, S. L., & Douglas, A. J. (2008). Oxytocin and the maternal brain. *Current Opinion in Pharmacology, 8*, 731–734.

Levine, A., Zagoory-Sharon, O., Feldman, R., & Weller, A. (2007). Oxytocin during pregnancy and early postpartum: Individual patterns and maternal–fetal attachment. *Peptides, 28*, 1162–1169.

Li, Y. J., Kenrick, D. T., Griskevicius, V., & Neuberg, S. L. (2012). Economic decision biases and fundamental motivations: How mating and self-protection alter loss aversion. *Journal of Personality and Social Psychology, 102*, 550–561.

Little, A. C. (2012). Manipulation of infant-like traits affects perceived cuteness of infant, adult and cat faces. *Ethology, 118*, 775–782.

Lobmaier, J. S., Sprengelmeyer, R., Wiffen, B., & Perrett, D. I. (2010). Female and male responses to cuteness, age and emotion in infant faces. *Evolution and Human Behavior, 31*, 16–21.

Lorenz, K. (1950). The comparative method in studying innate behaviour patterns. *Physiological mechanisms in animal behavior (society's symposium IV)*, Oxford, England: Academic Press. 221–268.

Lorenz, K. (1971). *Studies in animal and human behaviour* (Vol. H), (R. Martin, Trans.). London, England: Methuen.

McKee, L. (1984). Sex differentials in survivorship and the customary treatment of infants and children. *Medical Anthropology, 8*, 91–108.

McNeilly, A. S., Robinson, I., Houston, M. J., & Howie, P. W. (1983). Release of oxytocin and prolactin in response to suckling. *British Medical Journal, 286*, 257–259.

Nittono, H., Fukushima, M., Yano, A., & Moriya, H. (2012). The power of kawaii: Viewing cute images promotes a careful behavior and narrows attentional focus. *PLoS One, 7*, e46362.

Öhman, A., & Mineka, S. (2003). The malicious serpent: Snakes as a prototypical stimulus for an evolved module of fear. *Current Directions in Psychological Science, 12*, 5–9.

Out, D., Pieper, S., Bakermans-Kranenburg, M. J., & Van Ijzendoorn, M. H. (2010). Physiological reactivity to infant crying: A behavioral genetic study. *Genes Brain Behavior, 9*, 868–876.

Oveis, C., Horberg, E. J., & Keltner, D. (2010). Compassion, pride, and social intuitions of self-other similarity. *Journal of Personality and Social Psychology, 98*, 618–630.

Parsons, C. E., Young, K. S., Kumari, N., Stein, A., & Kringelbach, M. L. (2011). The motivational salience of infant faces is similar for men and women. *PLoS One, 6*, e20632.

Pedersen, C. A., Ascher, J. A., Monroe, Y. L., & Prange, A. J. (1982). Oxytocin induces maternal behavior in virgin female rats. *Science, 216*, 648–650.

Porter, R. H. (1991). Mutual mother-infant recognition in infants. In P. G. Hepper (Ed.), *Kin recognition*. Cambridge, England: Cambridge University Press.

Preston, S. D. (2013). The origins of altruism in offspring care. *Psychological Bulletin, 139*, 1305–1341.

Preston, S. D., & de Waal, F. B. M. (2002). Empathy: Its ultimate and proximate bases. *Behavioral and Brain Sciences, 25*, 1–20.

Riem, M. M. E., Bakermans- Kranenburg, M. J., Pieper, S., Tops, M., Boksem, M. A. S., Vermeiren, R. R. J. M., … Rombouts, S. A. R. B. (2011). Oxytocin modulates amygdala, insula and inferior frontal gyrus responses to infant crying: A randomized control trial. *Biological Psychiatry, 70*, 291–297.

Ruppenthal, G. C., Arling, G. L., Harlow, H. F., Sackett, G. P., & Suomi, S. (1976). A 10-year perspective of motherless-mother monkey behavior. *Journal of Abnormal Psychology, 85*, 341–349.

Shaver, P. R., Morgan, H. J., & Wu, S. (1996). Is love a "basic" emotion? *Personal Relationships, 3*, 81–96.

Shaver, P., Schwartz, J., Kirson, D., & O'Connor, C. (1987). Emotion knowledge: Further exploration of a prototype approach. *Journal of Personality and Social Psychology, 52*, 1061–1086.

Sherman, G. D., Haidt, J., & Coan, J. A. (2009). Viewing cute images increases behavioral carefulness. *Emotion, 9*, 282–286.

Sherman, G. D., Haidt, J., Iyer, R., & Coan, J. A. (2013). Individual differences in the physical embodiment of care: Prosocially oriented women respond to cuteness by becoming more physically careful. *Emotion, 13*, 151–158.

Shiota, M. N., Campos, B., Oveis, C., Hertenstein, M. J., Simon-Thomas, E., & Keltner, D. (2017). Beyond happiness: Building a science of discrete positive emotions. *American Psychologist, 72*, 617–643.

Shiota, M. N., Neufeld, S. L., Danvers, A. F., Osborne, E. A., Sng, O., & Yee, C. I. (2014). Positive emotion differentiation: A functional approach. *Social and Personality Psychology Compass, 8*, 104–117.

Shiota, M. N., Neufeld, S. L., Yeung, W. H., Moser, S. E., & Perea, E. F. (2011). Feeling good: Autonomic nervous system responding in five positive emotions. *Emotion, 11*, 1368–1378.

Skuse, D. H., & Gallagher, L. (2009). Dopaminergic-neuropeptide interactions in the social brain. *Trends in Cognitive Sciences, 13*, 27–35.

Snow, C. E. (1972). Mothers' speech to children learning language. *Child Development, 43*, 549–565.

Stellar, J. E., Gordon, A. M., Piff, P. K., Cordaro, D., Anderson, C. L., Bai, Y., … Keltner, D. (2017). Self-transcendent emotions and their social functions: Compassion, gratitude, and awe bind us to others through prosociality. *Emotion Review, 9*, 200–207.

Strathearn, L. (2011). Maternal neglect: Oxytocin, dopamine and the neurobiology of attachment. *Journal of Neuroendocrinology, 23*, 1054–1065.

Strathearn, L., Li, J., Fonagy, P., & Montague, P. R. (2008). What's in a smile? Maternal brain responses to infant facial cues. *Pediatrics, 122*, 40–51.

Tomkins, S. S. (1984). Affect theory. In K. R. Scherer & P. Ekman (Eds.), *Approaches to emotion*. Hillsdale, NJ: Lawrence Erlbaum Associates.

Tkaczyszyn, M., Olbrycht, T., Makowska, A., Soboń, K., Paleczny, B., Rydlewska, A., & Jankowska, E. A. (2013). The influence of the sounds of crying baby and the sounds of violence on haemodynamic parameters and autonomic status in young, healthy adults. *International Journal of Psychophysiology, 87*, 52–59.

Trivers, R. L. (1974). Parent-offspring conflict. *Integrative and Comparative Biology, 14*, 249–264.

Vicedo, M. (2009). The father of ethology and the foster mother of ducks: Konrad Lorenz as expert on motherhood. *Isis, 100*, 263–291.

Vicedo, M. (2010). The evolution of Harry Harlow: From the nature to the nurture of love. *History of Psychiatry, 21*, 190–205.

Walum, H., Lichtenstein, P., Neiderhiser, J. M., Reiss, D., Ganiban, J. M., Spotts, E. L., … Westberg, L. (2012). Variation in the oxytocin receptor gene is associated with pair-bonding and social behavior. *Biological Psychiatry, 71*, 419–426.

Young, K. S., Parsons, C. E., Jegindow, E. M., Woolrich, M. W., van Hartevelt, T. J., Stevner, A. B. A., … Kringelbach, M. L. (2016). Evidence for a caregiving instinct: Rapid differentiation of infant from adult vocalizations using magnetoencephalography. *Cerebral Cortex, 26*, 1309–1321.

Young, L. J., & Wang, Z. (2004). The neurobiology of pair bonding. *Nature Neuroscience, 7*, 1048–1054.

Zahn-Waxler, C., Robinson, J. L., & Emde, R. N. (1992). The development of empathy in twins. Developmental Psychology, *28*, 1038–1047.

Zebrowitz, L. A., & Montepare, J. M. (2008). Social psychological face perception: Why appearance matters. *Social and Personality Psychology Compass, 2*, 1497–1517.

Chapter 10
The Functional and Dysfunctional Aspects of Happiness: Cognitive, Physiological, Behavioral, and Health Considerations

Justin Storbeck and Jordan Wylie

Abstract Research on happiness and the positive effects it has on cognition, physiology, behavior, and health have been on the rise. This chapter seeks to refine these positions through a functionalist approach, arguing that happiness is largely beneficial. However, all is not sanguine as happiness facilitates distraction and mindlessness, seeking happiness can reduce happiness, and excessive happiness can push others away. This chapter reviews the evidence for when happiness is functional and dysfunctional, providing a theoretical framework for knowing when it is favorable to be happy and when it is not.

Defining the function of happiness is challenging, namely, because of diverging notions of what constitutes happiness and the history of how "happiness" has traditionally been studied. The most simple and broad definition of happiness is offered by Ekman and Cordaro (2011); "feelings that are enjoyed, that are sought by the person. There are a number of quite different enjoyable emotions, each triggered by a different event, involving a different signal and likely behavior" (p. 365). Although this definition is broad, it hints at the varied avenues for finding or achieving happiness and that such differences may lead to distinct patterns of eliciting events, behaviors, and physiology. For instance, positive emotions like joy, contentment, and amusement are often considered to be synonymous with happiness, but each has different eliciting events and produces different behaviors and physiological patterns (discussed below). Thus, this broad definition covers multiple aspects of happiness while signaling at a certain duality: the experiencing (i.e., hedonia; "feelings that are enjoyed") versus the seeking of pleasure (i.e., eudaimonic; "are sought by the person").

J. Storbeck (✉)
Queens College, CUNY, Flushing, NY, USA

The Graduate Center, CUNY, New York, NY, USA
e-mail: Justin.Storbeck@qc.cuny.edu

J. Wylie
The Graduate Center, CUNY, New York, NY, USA

© Springer International Publishing AG, part of Springer Nature 2018   195
H. C. Lench (ed.), *The Function of Emotions*,
https://doi.org/10.1007/978-3-319-77619-4_10

Dating all the way back to Aristotle and Plato, philosophers considered two aspects of happiness: hedonic and eudaimonic. This duality is also present in the modern study of happiness and well-being (e.g., Deci & Ryan, 2008; Suardi, Sotgiu, Costa, Cauda, & Rusconi, 2016; Waterman, Schwartz, & Conti, 2006). Hedonic happiness is defined simply as the pursuit of pleasure and the avoidance of pain. Others have expanded this definition to suggest that hedonic happiness refers to positive affect that accompanies obtaining or having desired objects and opportunities one wants to experience (Kraut, 1979; Waterman et al., 2006). Hedonic happiness, though, is often presumed to lack a motivational component beyond enjoyment (Berridge & Kringelbach, 2013) which creates a paradox for its functionality (Ness, 2004), as motivation drives functionality.

Eudaimonic happiness assumes happiness is achieved or maintained by living virtuously, resisting temptation, and achieving personal inner harmony (Suardi et al., 2016) or, more specifically, by achieving goals and self-actualizing experiences (Maslow, 1967). This type of happiness is harder to objectively assess and often relies on subjective reporting of how an individual is achieving their potential and purposes in life (Norton, 1976; Waterman et al., 2006). With that said, self-reported eudaimonic happiness has been linked with well-being (Deci & Ryan, 2008), suggesting such happiness is linked with self-actualization or self-achievement.

Hedonic and eudaimonic happiness are related and yet can be independent. For instance, achieving a personal goal or realizing self-achievement yields both eudaimonic happiness (self-realization) and hedonic happiness (pleasure from goal achievement). Conversely, activities unrelated to personal potentials (i.e., watching a cute cat video) would give rise to hedonic happiness but most likely not eudaimonic happiness. Thus, happiness can consist of both hedonic and eudaimonic happiness, just hedonic happiness, or neither type of happiness (Waterman et al., 2006). It is open for debate whether eudaimonic happiness can exist without hedonic happiness, because achieving goals or self-actualization is itself inherently pleasurable. It is critical to account for these two forms of happiness when identifying the functional utility of happiness as they can have different implications for experience and potentially behavior as we discuss below.

This chapter examines a variety of theories and research to elucidate specific functions of happiness. It is well documented that these functions of happiness are largely positive in nature, conferring many benefits to the individual. Generally, happiness promotes fitness by tuning neurological, physiological, cognitive, and behavioral changes, which facilitate the acquisition and management of resources. This chapter discriminates between prominent descriptive approaches to happiness and then examines the full range of happiness, including the domain-specific instances when it is no longer beneficial. Specifically, this chapter demonstrates how happiness may leave people blind to immediate threats, susceptible to cognitive and memory biases and illusions, diminish intrinsic motivation, and reduce one's social circle. It next demonstrates how happiness has tremendous benefits for health. Finally, the chapter proposes new directions and articulates a functional theory of happiness and executive functioning.

Changes Associated with Happiness

Happiness fosters experiential, behavioral, cognitive, and physiological changes. There is extensive research for understanding the experiential, behavioral, and cognitive changes associated with happiness. However, the research linking happiness and physiology is less studied, leading to greater uncertainty. The other factor that has limited our understanding of happiness is the looseness for how researchers conceptualize happiness and the methods used to induce and measure happiness. For instance, many studies have induced states of amusement, contentment, or joy and labeled the induction as happiness, and yet each of the positive states just mentioned can have slightly different cognitive, behavioral, and physiological outcomes (see Fredrickson, 2013; Kragel & LaBar, 2013). Or researchers may have induced states of happiness or other positive states and only recorded self-reports specific to "positive affect," which limits whether or not the effects were caused by happiness per se or some other positive feelings. Thus, this section reviews findings related to happiness, but the findings may also reflect positive affect more generally.

Experiential Changes Associated with Happiness Experientially, happiness is quite easy to identify as it serves to elicit feelings of pleasure. As mentioned above, Ekman and Cordaro (2011) suggested that happiness elicits "feelings that are enjoyed." Of course, happiness elicits other experiential feelings such as joyfulness, contentment, interest, alertness, curiosity, amusement, fun-loving, silliness, closeness, relief, and calmness (e.g., Ekman & Cordaro, 2011; Fredrickson, 2013). Another aspect that is often associated with happiness is the release from negativity. Namely, feelings of happiness can "undo" feelings of anxiety, worry, sadness, arousal, and other negative feelings (see Fredrickson, 2013; Levenson, 1988), particularly when bonding with others (e.g., Beckes & Coan, 2011; Coan, Schaefer, & Davidson, 2006). At another level, happiness or pleasure can be experienced objectively with a direct link to physiological activity (Berridge & Kringelbach, 2013) or subjectively. Interestingly, the link between both objective and subjective happiness can be tenuous, with one (e.g., subjective) but not the other (e.g., objective), predicting cognitive and behavioral outcomes.

Cognitive and Behavioral Changes Associated with Happiness The cognitive and behavioral phenomena elicited by happiness are relatively well understood. However, one caveat to consider is that the induction of happiness can take many forms, including the elicitation of slight differences in happiness (joy, amusement) or a general positive affective state considered to reflect happiness. Because of the lack of distinction in the literature, there could be neglected heterogeneity of specific positive emotions (e.g., happiness, joy, etc.) that result in subtle differences in cognitive and behavioral effects. The two most prominent findings with respect to happiness are global processing of information and cognitive flexibility. Other cognitive processes that happiness affects includes attention, semantic access, verbal working memory, working memory capacity, and planning, all of which are discussed below.

Global processing of visual information is enhanced when an individual is experiencing a state of happiness (e.g., Gable & Harmon-Jones, 2012; Gasper & Clore, 2002). The benefit of global processing is the ability to focus on the forest as opposed to the trees or to gain a broader, contextual perspective of the surrounding environment when taking in information. For example, one classic approach asks individuals to observe a target shape that consists of a global shape created by the arrangement of a different, local shape (e.g., four triangles—local shape—arranged to create a square, global shape). Next, they are presented with two objects that either represent the global shape (four squares arranged to create a square) or the local shape (three triangles arranged to create a triangle). In this task, global processing represents holistic processing (gestalt) as opposed to focusing on perceptual qualities of the object (local features). Happy individuals often select the shape that matches the global arrangement of the target image (Gasper & Clore, 2002). Neuroimaging studies have further demonstrated that happiness changes the way the brain sees or processes the visual scene. In one study, people induced into a happy, compared to sad, state were presented with faces as target stimuli and houses as distractor stimuli. Activation was observed both in the right fusiform face area (FFA; processes faces) and the left parahippocampal gyrus (general object processing area) for those in a happy compared to sad mood. This finding suggests that the happy individuals took in both stimuli, representing the entire context of the scene (Schmitz, De Rosa, & Anderson, 2009). However, there are still questions concerning the mechanisms that effectively links happiness to global shape processing.

The other cognitive phenomenon most associated with happiness is cognitive flexibility. Cognitive flexibility is the ability to switch from one mind-set to another. Such flexibility is often necessary when solving insight problems with no clear or obvious solutions or solutions that involve forming connections between two distinct concepts. There are a variety of studies that examine the impact of happiness on multiple measures of cognitive flexibility including task switching (Dreisbach & Goschke, 2004), insight problems (Isen, Johnson, Mertz, & Robinson, 1985), and remote associates task (Bolte, Goschke, & Kuhl, 2003). However, these tasks (not including task switching) are often difficult to deconstruct to understand the mechanism through which happiness influences cognitive flexibility. Research by Dreisbach and colleagues finds that happiness reduces cognitive control and facilitates distraction, particularly to novel stimuli. Specifically, they utilized a task that required the prioritization of cognitive demands to try to demonstrate the boundary conditions for when happiness is beneficial and when it is costly with regards to cognitive control (Dreisbach & Goschke, 2004; Dreisbach, Haider, & Kluwe, 2002). Further, tasks such as the remote associates task may involve a combination of cognitive processes, including activation of direct and indirect semantic associates, which may allow for greater associative connections facilitating problem solving. Lastly, the mechanisms related to insight problems are the least understood as happiness may act upon one or many of the elements that would be beneficial for solving these problems. For instance, happiness could increase insight due to increased semantic activation (Bolte et al., 2003; Storbeck & Clore, 2008), verbal working memory (Gray, 2001), working memory capacity (Storbeck & Maswood, 2016;

Yang, Yang, & Isen, 2013), or cognitive flexibility (Ashby, Isen, & Turken, 1999). Overall, the idea that happiness fosters cognitive flexibility and creative insight is consistent with various theories such as the broaden-and-build (B&B) theory (Fredrickson, 2013), the neuropsychological theory of positive affect (Ashby et al., 1999), and Dreisbach's theory of cognitive control (Dreisbach, 2006).

Another cognitive aspect that happiness fosters is that of greater semantic activity. Semantic activity implies that an individual either increases the number of activated semantic concepts in mind (reading "dog" might elicit more semantic related items like *cat, bone, car*) or access to activated concepts (i.e., ease of retrieval). Semantic knowledge is thought to reside within a semantic network for which concepts are stored as nodes and activation of one node results in activation of related nodes or concepts (e.g., Bower, 1981; Neely, 1991). Often such relationships are observed using a semantic or affective priming task (a prime word "dog" precedes a target word "cat" and faster responding to *cat* reflects greater activation caused by *dog*). Storbeck and Clore (2008) observed that happiness facilitated such semantic priming. Semantic activation is also thought to underlie the false memory effect, such that people will falsely recall a non-presented critical lure (i.e., sleep) when presented with a list of words highly associated to the non-presented lure (e.g., bed, pillow, wake, rest). Happiness fostered a greater degree of false memories compared to sadness (Storbeck & Clore, 2005). Presumably, another reason why happiness results in more efficient solving of remote associate problems (i.e., Bolte et al., 2003) is that happiness fosters greater activation of semantic concepts, making it more likely that the solution word comes to mind. Thus, happiness appears to increase semantic activation and/or ease of retrieval, but further research is needed to exactly understand how semantic activity is facilitated.

Other research specific to executive functioning also finds that happiness can be beneficial. For specific domains of executive functioning, happiness facilitates shifting (e.g., cognitive flexibility or task switching), verbal working memory, executive and reactive control, and working memory capacity (Chiew & Braver, 2014; Dreisbach, 2006; Frober & Dreisbach, 2012; Gray, 2001; Kuhl & Kazen, 1999; Storbeck, Davidson, Dahl, Blass, & Yung, 2015; Storbeck & Maswood, 2016; van Wouwe, Band, & Ridderinkhof, 2011; Yang et al., 2013). However, happiness has also been shown to impair proactive control, spatial working memory, and inhibition (Dreisbach, 2006; Frober & Dreisbach, 2012; Gray, 2001; Martin & Kerns, 2011; Phillips, Bull, Adams, & Fraser, 2002; Storbeck & Stewart, 2017). Thus, happiness facilitates many executive functioning processes that benefit broader thinking, maintenance of information, and planning, which are all necessary for achieving long-term oriented goals including the acquisition and maintenance of resources, but the influence on such executive functioning also increases the chance of distraction.

Lastly, happiness fosters behavioral changes that promote social bonding. For instance, happiness promotes touch (Hertenstein, Holmes, McCullough, & Keltner, 2009), fosters attachment (Eisenberger et al., 2011; Panksepp, 2003), encourages cooperation (Baron, Fortin, Frei, Hauver, & Shack, 1990; Barsade, 2002; Forgas, 1998), and promotes trust (Dunn & Schweitzer, 2005) and prosocial behaviors

(Aknin, Dunn, & Norton, 2012; Forest, Clark, Mills, & Isen, 1979). For instance, a classic experiment revealed that greater happiness increased the likelihood of helping a stranger (Forest et al., 1979). Also, happiness is likely to increase empathy, sympathy, and perspective taking, all of which are beneficial for promoting prosocial tendencies (Caprara et al., 2008), as well as social bonding (Campbell, 2010). The cognitive processes that underlie these effects are not well understood, but it is presumed that some of these effects are driven by neurochemical changes with an increase in the release of opioids, dopamine, and oxytocin (e.g., Fredrickson, 2013; Shiota et al., 2017).

Central Nervous System Changes Associated with Happiness One of the most neurobiologically sophisticated models of pleasure comes from Berridge and colleagues. This model proposes that feelings of happiness and enjoyment originate from particular areas of the brain associated with pleasure (Berridge & Kringelbach, 2015; Kringelbach & Berridge, 2009, 2015). Specifically, they have identified areas they refer to as "hot spots" and "cold spots" of pleasure within mostly non-primate populations. These hot and cold spots include the subcortical (nucleus accumbens, ventral pallidum, parabrachial nucleus) and cortical regions (insula, medial, and lateral orbitofrontal cortex) (Berridge & Kringelbach, 2015) and include the amygdala as well (Chemali, Chahine, & Naassan, 2008). Newer translational research with primates is finding continuing support for the model. Neuroimaging studies with humans have identified many overlapping regions but also include aspects of the orbitofrontal cortex, the medial prefrontal cortex, the anterior cingulate cortex, and the basal ganglia (Kringelbach, 2005; Simmons et al., 2014; Suardi et al., 2016). Some notable differences were decreases in the right prefrontal cortex (consistent with frontal asymmetry findings in EEG studies; Coan, Allen, & Harmon-Jones, 2001) and increases in the left amygdala and the hippocampus (Suardi et al., 2016; Urry et al., 2004). Another critical brain area that has been associated with happiness is the basal ganglia, which may facilitate flexibility in navigating complex environments (see Boyd, 2004; Shiota et al., 2017). However, when assessing studies with neuroimaging, it becomes more difficult to identify regions linked directly to pleasure versus those that may support such hedonic evaluations including anticipation, appraisal, and memory regions (Kringelbach & Berridge, 2017). Moreover, the default network, which is thought to reflect resting activity and representations of the self, has also been linked to the experience of hedonic happiness and, in particular, eudaimonic happiness (Kringelbach & Berridge, 2009). The default network may also change over time, reflecting pathological, trait-level changes to the experience of happiness, suggested by findings that individuals with depression often show reduced frontal cortical activity at rest (Drevets et al., 1997; Mayberg, 1997).

A more complex issue is whether dopamine mediates the experience of hedonic happiness or joy (Kringelbach & Berridge, 2017). Studies in non-primates have identified that blocking dopamine impairs the motivation or drive to obtain a rewarding entity (Galistu & D'Aquila, 2012), but if the entity is obtained or experienced, a hedonic response is still elicited (Pecina, Berridge, & Parker, 1997). Reward seeking or motivationally driven behavior is controlled via the mesolimbic system and microcircuits (see Berridge & Kringelbach, 2013; Kringelbach & Berridge, 2017). This system seems to be most correlated with appetitive motivation and the anticipation of pleasure of rewarding stimuli (e.g., sexually attractive people, babies, humor, desirable food; Bartels & Zeki, 2004; Blood & Zatorre, 2001; O'Doherty, 2004) but is not a direct link to the experience of pleasure (Berridge & Kringelbach, 2013; Kringelbach & Berridge, 2015). However, this relationship is complicated. Among evidence that dopamine is related to pleasure (Wickelgren, 1997), other research suggests that the experience of pleasure does not seem directly related to dopamine (Wise, 2008). In other words, hedonic happiness itself is not sufficient to elicit dopamine, but if the hedonic experience has been associated with reward through learning, then those entities that are tied to hedonic experience can become sufficient for releasing dopamine as the hedonic experience is now tied to reward (i.e., dopamine; Berridge & Kringelbach, 2015; Rolls, 1999; Schultz, Dayan, & Montague, 1997). Namely, hedonic experiences can be learned and anticipated, and the anticipation of such hedonic pleasures (even before experiencing them) is now sufficient to elicit a dopamine response.

Opioids are another factor that may be involved in the experience of pleasure. Opioids have been linked with the hedonic happiness hot spots mentioned above (Berridge & Kringelbach, 2013) and seem to be elicited during the experience of pleasure (as opposed to the anticipation of pleasure; Berridge & Kringelbach, 2013; Rolls, 1999). More interestingly, opioids may also be released when touch (Inoue, Burkett, & Young, 2013; Rolls, Grabenhorst, & Parris, 2008) or attachment is involved (Eisenberger et al., 2011; Panksepp, 2003). Thus, the experience of rewarding entities like a tasty snack or the physical contact of another seems to be associated with hedonic pleasure elicited through opioids within brain areas associated with hot spots of pleasure.

Peripheral Nervous System Changes Associated with Happiness   Physiological activation resulting from happiness is not very well understood compared to discrete negative emotions (e.g., sadness, fear, disgust, anger). Early research examined positive affect rather than discrete positive emotions, which may have led to the appearance of a lack of consistent physiological findings across studies (Norman, Berntson, & Cacioppo, 2014). For instance, subtle physiological difference that arise from different positive emotions (e.g., amusement has a different physiological response than joy, but one study may have elicited amusement and another joy, but both studies labeled it "positive affect") may have confounded findings (Norman et al., 2014; Zajonc & McIntosh, 1992). Also, inconsistencies may have arisen due to the selected comparison condition(s) (e.g., happiness to sadness vs. neutral, etc.) and type of mood induction (film vs. pictures vs. autobiographical recall) (Ekman, Levenson, & Friesen, 1983; Levenson, 1992). More recently, there has been a concerted effort to understand how distinct positive emotions influence physiological activity (see Shiota et al., 2017Shiota, Neufeld, Yeung, Moser, & Perea, 2011).

Based on these early physiological studies, initial reviews of the literature found strong evidence that the best predictor of physiological differentiation was based on valence alone (Cacioppo, Berntson, Larsen, Poehlmann, & Ito, 2000; Norman et al.,

2014). Newer research using more multivariate, integrated approaches in both physiological measurements and inductions is allowing for greater predictive utility in how emotions influence physiology system wide. This research has even begun to incorporate machine learning to see if such learning can predict emotions from the physiological patterns, and indeed such studies are finding that emotions, including happiness, can be differentiated. However, the most optimistic study accounted for only 58% predictive utility, though all emotions tested were predicted above chance (see Kragel & LaBar, 2013; Stephens, Christie, & Friedman, 2010). Such models do suggest that with greater effort, more sophisticated measures and assessments, and incorporating multivariate approaches, may be the best way to fully understand physiological changes caused by happiness and other emotions. However, the studies just described did not provide statistical analyses for activation caused by happiness. The other interesting perspective that should be emphasized is that the peripheral nervous system is much more sophisticated than previously assumed. Newer research is finding that each organ and tissue is innervated by distinct sympathetic and parasympathetic pathways, suggesting that each organ and tissue have some functional independence (what happens at one tissue site (e.g., increase activation), might differ from another (e.g., decrease activation); Folkow, 2000; Jänig & Häbler, 2000; Jänig & McLachlan, 1992). This independence is thought to pertain to the sympathoadrenal medullary system for which there is a direct nervous system influence and an adrenomedullary hormonal influence and in most situations have different functional roles (Folkow, 2000). Therefore, more sophisticated assessment, inductions, and analyses may be required to fully develop a comprehensive picture of how discrete emotions influence physiology.

Initial studies and reviews focused specifically on happiness, joy, and amusement are providing some more consistent and specific findings. In general, happiness has consistent ANS effects with a general increase in sympathetic activation (e.g., Tsai, Chentsova-Dutton, Freire-Bebeau, & Przymus, 2002). More specifically, prior research has observed that there is increased cardiac activity due to vagal withdrawal vasodilation, increased electrodermal activity, and increased respiratory activity (see Kreibig, 2010 for a comprehensive review). The sympathetic activation state seems to decrease alpha- and beta-adrenergic influences but increase cholinergic effects (Kreibig, 2010). There is also evidence for decreased heart rate variability and a lengthened period of positive expiratory pressure (PEP), which facilitates breathing and ventilation of the lungs. Though these effects may be induction dependent, in that films or pictures increase heart rate, other types of induction types have found decreased or unchanged physiological activity (see Kreibig, 2010).

For amusement, there appears to be a general increase in sympathetic nervous system activity (e.g., Christie & Friedman, 2004; Demaree, Schmeichel, Robinson, & Everhart, 2004; Guiliani, McRae, & Gross, 2008; Mauss, Levenson, McCarter, Wilhelm, & Gross, 2005; Shiota et al., 2011). Specifically, there is increase in cardiac vagal control, vascular alpha-adrenergic, respiratory and electrodermal activity, and sympathetic cardiac beta-adrenergic deactivation. With that said, heart rate variability seems unreliable, with some studies showing increases, some decreases, and others no influence. Like happiness, there is also a lengthening of PEP (e.g.,

Table 10.1 Influence of distinct positive emotions on the PNS

Positive emotion	Peripheral nervous system influence			
	Cardiac vagal control	Vascular alpha-adrenergic	Respiratory and electrodermal activity	Cardiac beta-adrenergic
Amusement	Increase	Increase	Increase	Decrease
Contentment	Unclear	Decrease	Decrease	Decrease
Happiness	Increase	Decrease	Increase	Decrease
Joy	Increase	Decrease	Increase	Increase

Shiota et al., 2011). Blood pressure remains mostly unchanged. Vasoconstriction is mostly decreased, and some studies do find decreased electrodermal activity (Kreibig, 2010).

Contentment is generally associated with a decrease in sympathetic activation and is associated with decreased cardiovascular, respiratory, and electrodermal activation. This is driven by decreased alpha- and beta-adrenergical and cholinergically mediated sympathetic activation and mild cardiac vagal activation. Contentment may have stronger sympathetic deactivation component compared to amusement (Kreibig, 2010).

Joy typically leads to increased cardiac vagal control, decreased alpha-adrenergic, increased beta-andrenergic, and increased cholinergically mediated sympathetic influence as well as increased respiratory activity. Joy, unlike other positive emotions, shows increased beta-adrenergic sympathetic activation, which is usually associated with motivational engagement (Wright, 1996), co-occurring with increased vagal activation in the response pattern of joy (Kreibig, 2010).

In sum, there is greater support for emotion specific physiological activity; however, the evidence only suggests some degree of specificity (Cacioppo et al., 2000; Cacioppo, Berntson, Klein, & Poehlmann, 1997; Kreibig, 2010; Norman et al., 2014). Table 10.1 outlines the differences in physiological activation across the positive emotions just described.

What Problem Does Happiness Resolve?

As discussed above, happiness has been associated with a variety of cognitive and behavioral outcomes that could increase fitness and the acquisition of resources, specifically by encouraging social bonds and connections and the acquisition and maintenance of resources. Does happiness then facilitate the ability to bond with others and to manage and respond to opportunities producing greater fitness and increased acquisition of resources?

Social Bonding Happiness has long been associated with social bonding, as happiness promotes touch, forming of attachments, cooperation, trust, prosocial behaviors, and inclusion (Hertenstein et al., 2009; Eisenberger et al., 2011; Panksepp,

2003; Baron et al., 1990; Barsade, 2002; Forgas, 1998; Dunn & Schweitzer, 2005; Aknin et al., 2012; Forest et al., 1979). Even just providing an individual with a small amount of money unexpectedly was sufficient to induce that person to help a complete stranger (Forest et al., 1979). Another important study observed an important spiraling aspect between social bonds and happiness. Specifically, happiness increased relationship quality, which in turn increased happiness, which further enhanced the quality of the relationship (Fredrickson & Joiner, 2002). Such findings are important because if two entities are so closely intertwined, it would be expected for them to have a reciprocal relationship (Simon, 1967; Storbeck, 2012; Storbeck & Watson, 2014, and see below for further discussion of this point). Other research finds that people are more attracted to happy individuals and often seek them out (e.g., Bell, 1978; Coyne, 1976), which for the happy individual can maintain levels of happiness through developing relationships and broadening their social networks.

Individual differences in happiness also seem to have important implications for social bonding. Individuals with higher levels of happiness are likely to have more relationships (Benet-Martínez & Karakitapoglu-Aygün, 2003; Kwan, Bond, & Singelis, 1997), marry (De Neve & Cooper, 1998; Lucas, Clark, Georgellis, & Diener, 2003) and marry again after a divorce (Spanier & Furstenberg, 1982). Trait happiness also predicts greater relationship satisfaction (Headey & Veenhoven, 1989), lower levels of loneliness (Benet-Martínez & Karakitapoglu-Aygün, 2003; Cacioppo et al., 2008), higher feelings of self-worth and self-esteem (Cacioppo et al., 2008), increased support-seeking behavior (Cacioppo et al., 2008; Lyubomirsky, Sheldon, & Schkade, 2005), increased intimacy (Cacioppo et al., 2008; Hawkley, Browne, & Cacioppo, 2005), and increased and more diverse social networks. Other factors facilitating social bonding are associations that happiness and well-being have with being more inclusive and having greater empathy and sympathy (Johnson & Fredrickson, 2005), having greater compassion and prospective taking (Nelson, 2009), and showing less bias toward ethnic out-groups (Fredrickson, 2013). Further, research finds that happiness fosters energy (or less fatigue), which is often associated with leisure, play, and social activities further fostering social connections (see Veenhoven, 1990). In sum, happiness, whether a temporary state or a trait, appears to facilitate social bonds and may even have a reciprocal relationship in that as one becomes happier, social behavior is fostered, leading to more involvement in a quality relationship, which in turn increases happiness.

How might happiness be costly to social bonding? Happiness is partly wrapped up in self-esteem and self-worth and environments that foster upward social comparisons can result in a subsequent drop in either self-esteem or self-worth (or both). For instance, an individual attending a block party might notice their neighbor with a new, expensive gadget resulting in a decrease in the individual's self-worth/esteem and such declines can decrease motivation to socialize (Gutierres, Kenrick, & Partch, 1999) or foster competitiveness. Happiness is also linked to narcissism particularly when self-esteem is high (Rose, 2002; Sedikides, Rudich, Gregg,

Kumashiro, & Rusbult, 2004). Narcissism is associated with factors that are not conducive to social bonding; those factors include diminished empathy, gratitude, need for intimacy, as well as heightened competitiveness and hostility (Morf & Rhodewalt, 2001; Rhodewalt, 2001; Sedikides, Campbell, Reeder, & Elliot, 2002). Another downside is that happiness may promote bonding with deviant people, and the bond is maintained with those individuals due to biased memory toward positive rather than negative qualities of the individual (Bower, 1981). Moreover, being friends with "deviant" people may result in divisions to one's social network as non-normative behavior is often rejected (e.g., Schachter, 1951). Lastly, happiness and shared opinions often bolster relationships, but happiness and differing opinions can actually lead to stronger differences and less social bonding (Raghunathan & Corfman, 2006).

Acquisition of Resources Happiness has influences beyond social bonding, including benefits to cognitive abilities that help achieve the goal of managing, maintaining, and responding to opportunities to build current and future resources. As Fredrickson suggests, happiness widens the array of thoughts, action urges, and percepts that come to mind (Fredrickson, 2013). This flexibility is functional for survival because it abbreviates the preparation for specific actions, which are often associated with negative emotions (e.g., withdrawing from a rapidly approaching bear). However, what are the cognitive and behavioral processes that would facilitate such activities? That is an open question, and so far, the answers have been quite general, rather than specific or mechanistically driven with some few exceptions (e.g., Ashby et al., 1999; Dreisbach, 2006). Nethertheless, the cognitive abilities related to happiness are abilities that would appear to help in the acquisition and use of resources. Generally, happiness promotes creativity, cognitive flexibility, and a more flexible cognitive control system; it broadens the scope of attention, shifts attention to novel stimuli, directs attention to rewarding stimuli, increases reliance on heuristics, and increases activation of semantic associates (Bless et al., 1996; Bolte et al., 2003; Carver, 2003; Compton, Wirtz, Pajoumand, Claus, & Heller, 2004; Dreisbach & Goschke, 2004; Fredrickson & Branigan, 2005; Gable & Harmon-Jones, 2012; Isen & Daubman, 1984; Isen, Daubman, & Nowicki, 1987; Johnson & Fredrickson, 2005; Phillips et al., 2002; Rowe, Hirsh, & Anderson, 2007; Storbeck & Clore, 2005, 2008; Tamir & Robinson, 2007). Not only does happiness benefit the described types of cognitive abilities, happiness also fosters intrinsic motivation, energy, interest, learning, and curiosity, which may facilitate engagement of activities to build one's resources (see De Neve, Diener, Tay, & Xuereb, 2013; Fredrickson, 2013). These types of resources can include material, social, or information. Moreover, if this fosters leisure and play, particularly with others, such resources are built through exploration and play with the belief that both enhance success in future social and unknown environments (Boyd, 2004; Fredrickson, 2013; Pellegrini & Smith, 2005; Wyer & Collins, 1992). Happiness also influences judgments by making judgments seem to have more value, such as increasing positive evaluations of political candidates, advertisements, and consumer products (Clore & Huntsinger, 2007; Forgas, 1998; Gorn, Goldberg, & Basu,

1993; Isbell & Wyer, 1999; Murry & Dacin, 1996; Pham, 2007). Happiness also tends to influence judgments by promoting long-term thinking, such that happiness is associated with long-term financial gains by consuming less, saving more, and taking fewer risks with finances (Guven, 2012; Ifcher & Zarghamee, 2011). Lastly, happiness can foster a delay in gratification (De Neve et al., 2013), which may foster better judgments consistent with long-term goals (e.g., avoiding eating sweets to achieve weight loss).

Finally, the last way happiness may manage resources is through preservation of physiological resources. As will be discussed below in the next two sections, happiness, contentment, and joy have the ability to reduce physiological activity elicited by stress (or other negative, arousing events; see Fredrickson, 2013). The argument is that if activating the ANS is costly, particularly for extended periods of time, then happiness can reduce such costs. There is a lot of correlational evidence suggesting that happiness predicts longevity, better health recovery, greater resilience, reduces susceptibility for disease, and can buffer against major life stressors or mood disorders (Fredrickson, Tugade, Waugh, & Larkin, 2003; Ong, Bergeman, Bisconti, & Wallace, 2006; Tugade & Fredrickson, 2004).

Disadvantages of Happiness Although happiness provides a number of advantages, there are clear downsides to happiness. First, happiness is likely to produce memorial errors that are heuristic, gist, or schema consistent (Bless et al., 1996; Storbeck & Clore, 2005, 2011; Forgas, 1998), and although such errors are generally good, they can be problematic for accurate memory. Second, happiness can actually lead to negative social consequences, as happiness can facilitate stereotyping, increase attribution errors, and make individuals more gullible (Bodenhause, Kramer, & Susser, 1994; Forgas, 1998; Forgas & East, 2008). Third, happiness can facilitate and promote attention to positive and/or rewarding stimuli (Tamir & Robinson, 2007) and thus reduce the ability to detect and take action against dangerous stimuli (Ford et al., 2010; Mogg & Bradley, 1999), particularly given that happiness reduces ANS activation (Cacioppo et al., 2008; Cacioppo, Klein, Bernston, & Hartfield, 1993; Kreibig, 2010). Another downside to happiness occurs in those individuals who prioritize the seeking of happiness. Research shows that individuals who are motivated purely by achieving happiness (e.g., "I just want to be happy") often find happiness elusive and report lower levels of happiness compared to their peers, ultimately preventing them from experiencing the positive benefits of happiness (Kesebir & Diener, 2008; Mauss et al., 2012; Schooler, Ariely, & Loewenstein, 2003). Finally, intense levels of happiness have also been associated with less creativity (Davis, 2008) and more behavioral rigidity (Fredrickson & Losada, 2005), both of which predict earlier mortality (Friedman et al., 1993), and engagement in riskier behavior (Cyders & Smith, 2008; Gruber, Johnson, Oveis, & Keltner, 2008).

How Happiness Influences Health-Related Outcomes One of the more popular movements in the field of happiness is the recognition of its positive influence on health. One of the more established models for which happiness (among other positive emotions) enhances health is the broaden-and-build (B&B) theory (Fredrickson,

2001, 2013). This model articulates that positive emotions, including happiness, undo the physiological effects of negative emotions and stressors. Moreover, happiness not only undoes these negative effects but allows for the increase of personal and interpersonal resources to be resilient in future stressful, challenging situations.

The B&B theory serves as a good starting point for understanding the role happiness, and other positive emotions, has in health. The main idea of the B&B theory related to health is the "undo hypothesis" initially proposed by Levenson (1988). The idea is that happiness can undo the arousal activated by negative emotions. Fredrickson and Levenson (1998) tested this idea by showing people a fear clip followed by either a happy, neutral, or sad clip, and they found ANS activity reduced faster in the happiness condition compared to the other conditions. Although this is not related directly to health, it does suggest that happiness can undo physiological consequences associated with negative emotions like anxiety and as a result protect the body and mind from harmful effects of stress. Thus, happiness could have both short- and long-term consequences for health based on this elegant, yet powerful, idea. There is emerging correlational and longitudinal researching supporting this idea and broader theory.

State effects of happiness have been associated with body and brain changes associated with both physical and mental health. Happiness can increase the response to infections (Cohen, Cohen, West, & Aiken, 2003) and can keep the common cold away by the release of secretory immunoglobulin A (S-IgA; Labott, Ahleman, Wolever, & Martin, 1990; Stone, Cox, Valdimarsdottir, Jandorf, & Neale, 1987; Stone et al., 1994). Happiness can even have indirect effects on health in that feeling happy enhances individual's belief that they have the capacity to engage in health promoting behaviors and confidence such behaviors would reduce their illness (Salovey & Birnbaum, 1989). As for mental health, inductions of happiness can increase activity in the left frontal cortex relative to the right (Urry et al., 2004), which can serve as a buffer against depression. Moreover, inductions of happiness can also positively influence vagal tone, which facilitates overcoming emotional stressors and help to reduce negative mental health outcomes (Fredrickson, 2013).

Trait levels of happiness also support positive health outcomes. Happiness associated with long-term meditation practices can broaden people's social connections and influence vagal tone variability (Waugh & Fredrickson, 2006), which is associated with more adaptive regulatory abilities and better health (Thayer, Hansen, Saus-Rose, & Johnsen, 2009). Happiness has also been associated with increased heart rate variability, which is associated with better health outcomes (Bhattacharyya, Whitehead, Rakhit, & Steptoe, 2008). Those with social support and happiness are less vulnerable to ill health and premature death (Cohen, 1988; House, Landis, & Umberson, 1988). One study in particular observed that strong social support, which is associated with happiness (Eisenberger et al., 2011), helped those diagnosed with leukemia and heart disease to have higher survival rates compared to those with less social support (Case, Moss, Case, McDermott, & Eberly, 1992; Colon, Callies, Popkin, & McGlave, 1991). Nuns who reported higher levels of happiness out lived less happy nuns (note that environment was held stable; Danner,

Snowdon, & Friesen, 2001), and these findings have been replicated in a larger sample (Chida & Steptoe, 2008). Other associations have found a correlation between happiness and having more energy and less pain (Cacioppo et al., 2008; Cacioppo, Hughes, Waite, Hawkley, & Thisted, 2006).

Another focal interest is the role of happiness and well-being have on health. One prominent influence stems from eudiamonic happiness, the happiness related to the self and self-actualization. In an aging sample of women, those who reported higher levels of well-being were more likely to have stronger neuroendocrine regulation, lower inflammatory markers, positive relations with others, higher levels of HDL (i.e., "good") cholesterol, and stronger insulin resistance (Ryff & Singer, 2008; Ryff, Singer, & Love, 2004). These findings are correlational and thus should be interpreted cautiously, but the findings are still quite powerful. Finally, longevity and personal maturation is associated with happiness. As people become older, they report higher levels of happiness and a decrease in depression, which may suggest that, as we age, there are natural changes that result in a greater experience of happiness (Cacioppo et al., 2006; Cartensen, Pasupathi, Mayr, & Nesselroade, 2000; Nolen-Hoeksema & Ahrens, 2002).

Happiness, though, does not always lead to better health outcomes. Happiness, as discussed above, can sometimes result in more risky behavior, including unhealthy behaviors (see Gruber, Mauss, & Tamir, 2011). For instance, one study found that people who experience high levels of pleasure during unprotected sex, particularly anal, were less likely to engage in protected sex on future occurrences even for people with high intentions for safer sex (Kelly & Kalichman, 1998). Also, more intense levels of happiness can also have negative consequences for health outcomes. Extreme levels of happiness can be a biomarker for psychopathology (Bentall, 1992; Gruber et al., 2008) and predict an earlier death (Friedman et al., 1993). Lastly, happiness may serve as predictive cues for rewarding behaviors (Berridge & Kringelbach, 2013), but behaviors associated with addictive, negative outcomes (e.g., illicit drug use, gambling), even though rewarding, can cause a host of negative health implications and damage social relationships.

Remaining Questions Concerning Happiness

Physiological Specificity A central question concerning the functional approach is to better understand how happiness, contentment, and joy distinctly influence physiological responding. The study of positive emotions, in general, lags behind the study of discrete negative emotions, and thus more work is required. Moreover, when investigating positive emotions, appropriate conditions must be utilized so that positive emotions are not just compared to negative emotions, but rather comparisons include neutral and other positive emotion conditions (see Shiota et al., 2011). This type of work will be taxing but essential. A diversity of measures and induction techniques should be employed to determine the boundary conditions and distinct impact of situational factors (e.g., music vs. films) and of emotional factors (e.g., arousal, motivational orientation). Such multivariate approaches are the most promising method to better understand physiological specificity (see Kragel & LaBar, 2013; Shiota et al., 2011; Stephens et al., 2010). Clarity should be sought when possible to determine how the ANS activation or deactivation is occurring; namely, is the sympathetic or parasympathetic system actively doing the work, or are the responses due to a withdrawal of one system or the other? As mentioned earlier, there is independence between sympathetic and parasympathetic systems (Folkow, 2000) and care must be taken to fully understand how both systems are independently influencing physiological activity.

Happiness itself is associated with a plethora of cognitive and behavioral scenarios, and each of these cognitive processes and behavioral outcomes may elicit different kinds of physiological activity (see Fredrickson, 2013). Or to put it another way, the context may afford opportunities (Gibson, 1979) for how a person who is happy interacts with the environment and such emotion and affordance interactions may best predict physiological activation (or deactivation). This may be one of the reasons for failing to find clear, convincing evidence for discrete physiological patterns for a specific emotion. Essentially, happiness, depending on cognitive and behavioral goals, may be able to elicit a host of different physiological patterns of activity; meaning we should be open to the possibility of variance but variance that can be predicted based on specific goal-driven behavior. This belief would be supported by propositions of the B&B theory, which articulate that happiness increases action repertoires, and to support the variety of repertoires would require multiple distinct patterns of physiological activity. Unfortunately, few studies focus on such critical goal-driven behavior. Research with paralyzed animals has demonstrated that preparation for action yields similar physiological activation as actual movement (Bandler, Keay, Floyd, & Price, 2000). Therefore, preparation for action may have a large impact in how the physiological system will respond, irrespective of the emotional state induced.

Focus on Mechanisms One of the major issues with much of the emotion and cognition literature has been the focus on phenomena (e.g., affect influences the fundamental attribution error; affect influences the false memory effect), rather than deriving a mechanism for why it influenced such phenomena (Storbeck & Clore, 2005). This focus could be the result of using broad theories that are challenging to falsify. For instance, take the theory that happiness broadens attention and perception (e.g., Gable & Harmon-Jones, 2012; Gasper & Clore, 2000; Rowe et al., 2007). First, is the same mechanism responsible for both attention and perception? For instance, Rowe and colleagues and many others have long interpreted the effects due to a spotlight model of attention; however, more recent work suggests that the effects might be due to a nonspatial attention system (i.e., temporal or flexible attention; Phaf, 2015). Second, are these effects due to more bottom-up driven processes, for instance, we see different patterns of activation in the visual cortex and parietal cortex? Or are these effects driven by top-down processes, and therefore, rely on executive functions like attentional control? Is the mechanism involved in broadening attention/perception the same as that attributed to cognitive flexibility? Further, it is possible that the broadening attention/perception may not even be about attention or perception but rather is directly related to working memory capacity. As mentioned previously, there is strong evidence that happiness may increase working memory capacity compared to neutral and sad emotional states (Storbeck & Maswood, 2016; Yang et al., 2013). If happiness increases working memory capacity, individuals would be able to hold more information in mind to evaluate, process, and ultimately use, enhancing what appears to be global processing, when in fact it could be due to one simple mechanism—increased working memory capacity. Currently, it is hard to extricate one process from the next without specified mechanistic understanding of these distinct cognitive phenomena. Further research needs to critically investigate cognitive and executive functioning tasks that are more process pure, which can facilitate possible mechanisms (see work by Miyake, Friedman and colleagues; Miyake & Friedman, 2012; Miyake et al., 2000).

Some theories are going in this direction to further understand how happiness, and other emotions, directly influences various cognitive and executive processes. One of the groundbreaking approaches was that of Isen and colleagues with the cognitive flexibility model, which beautifully articulated how cognitive flexibility may have been influenced by happiness (Ashby et al., 1999). Unfortunately, the theory, which posits such flexibility is influenced by dopaminergic activity elicited by states of happiness, was hard to test given constraints of present technology. But nonetheless, it tried to apply brain-based mechanisms to the behavioral data observed. Another theory is the cognitive control theory by Dreisbach and colleagues, which argues for a spectrum model of cognitive control with flexibility and maintenance at either end. From this perspective, a state like happiness would be predicted to emphasize cognitive flexibility over maintenance, whereas sadness would emphasize cognitive maintenance over flexibility (see Dreisbach, 2006; Dreisbach & Goschke, 2004). The work is very meticulous and places various conditions on the tasks to identify boundary conditions (novel vs. old stimuli) fosting greater insight into how happiness (or sadness) guides cognitive control. This theory has provided valuable insights into the complex functions of happiness but does not guide specific predictions for other discrete emotions. More research is needed to disentangle the effects of specific emotions on cognition and the role of neurotransmitters in cognitive and executive processing.

The argument presented in the emotion and goal compatibility theory (Storbeck, 2012; Storbeck et al., 2015) has tried to combine the work done by Dreisbach and colleagues and Miyake and colleagues, by trying to understand how emotions, like happiness, directly impact executive functions by examining a host of emotions on well-validated executive function tasks. Albeit the weakness is to downplay non-executive functioning; this is justified because executive control is involved with any judgment and coordination of various cognitive processes, including the robustness of emotions motivating goal-driven behavior (Baddeley, 1996; Perner & Lang, 1999; Pessoa, 2009). The tenets of the model are derived from a functional perspective in that each emotion, like happiness, promotes goal-driven behaviors and by doing so prioritizes specific executive/cognitive processes over other processes to achieve the intended behavior (Bargh, Gollwitzer, Lee-Chai, Barndollar, & Trotschel, 2001; Kruglanski et al., 2002; Simon, 1967). For instance, happiness should promote behaviors related to communication, socialization, conceptual processing, and exploration, and these goals should prioritize the executive functions of verbal working memory, shifting (cognitive flexibility), planning, and executive and attentional control. Functionality is then determined by whether the behavior promoted by the emotion is compatible with situational demands (e.g., being happy and socializing while encountering a pack of hungry wolves is dysfunctional and may lead to imminent death). There also exists a learning component such that situations that are appraised similarly should elicit the same emotion and corresponding behavior (Simon, 1967). Over time, the emotion and behavior (including supporting cognitions and executive functions) become coupled or integrated in a Hebbian-like fashion (Hebb, 1949). Given this integration of emotion and behavior occurs, the emotion and goal compatibility model proposes that emotions become embodied anticipations of the cognitive (and other) requirements of the situations from which they emerge (Simon, 1967; Storbeck, 2012). Such embodiment and fostering of anticipation then also has the advantage of linking hedonic happiness directly with dopamine, avoiding the conundrum discussed earlier with eudaimonic happiness being more strongly linked to dopamine than hedonic happiness (see Kringelbach & Berridge, 2017). Moreover, this goal integration implies less psychological effort is required to maintain high-level performance as correctly anticipating the cognitive requirements of situations conserves psychological resources (e.g., Friston, 2010; Gray, 2004; Gray, Braver, & Raichle, 2002). Thus, part of this theory is derived from the idea that the brain is a predictive machine (Friston, 2010) and emotions can serve as one of many types of cues that help the brain to anticipate situational needs and reduce surprise and minimize psychological effort.

The other interesting aspect of this theory is rooted in a reciprocal relationship between the emotion and the cognitive/executive processes, such that activation should occur in a bi-directional manner. For instance, the authors' lab (Storbeck, 2012; Storbeck et al., 2015) as well as others (Gray, 2001; Gray et al., 2002) has observed that happiness enhances verbal working memory in an efficient manner. Storbeck and Watson (2014) also observed that engaging in a verbal working memory task, compared to a spatial working memory task, fostered greater positivity when evaluating affective images and words. Moreover, when people completed a dot-probe task following a verbal working memory task, those individuals found it harder to disengage from positive images, whereas those individuals completing a spatial working memory task found it more challenging to disengage from negative stimuli. Similar findings have been observed with happiness increasing semantic activation (Bolte et al., 2003; Storbeck & Clore, 2008) and reported feelings of happiness increasing after participants engaged in a task that required greater activation of broad semantic relations (Bar, 2009). Such reciprocal interactions were also discussed earlier in which states of happiness increased social bonding and intense social bonds (like marriage) increased happiness. Thus, models should become more specific toward mechanistic accounts and to be more specific for the role that distinct (positive) emotions, like happiness, will have on cognition, behavior, and physiology; and if the relationship is truly functional then the relationship should also be reciprocal.

Summary

Happiness is associated with both hedonic and eudaimonic pleasure, and both types of pleasure may lead to subtle differences in expression of cognition, physiology, behavior, and outcomes, particularly related to neurobiology. With that said, there is general agreement that happiness facilitates fitness and the acquisition and maintenance of resources with resources being broadly defined (personal, social, capital, etc.). Primarily, it is thought that fitness and accumulation of resources can occur on a more long-term scale, including cognitions that emphasize flexibility, learning, exploration, problem solving, and social bonding. Such cognitions benefit the ability to avoid response-driven behaviors and rather have the flexibility to engage in behaviors that might be free from situational constraints to emphasize long-term outcomes. For instance, receiving a bonus check or salary increase may create an urge or impulse to spend the extra amount, when, in fact, most economic models would suggest that the money be put away for savings/retirement. Engaging in such behaviors may then also lead to greater eudaimonic happiness by increasing ones self-actualization, and the research would suggest this may also lead to a healthier more productive life. Just remember not to strive for happiness, as happiness and their benefits will be difficult to catch.

References

Aknin, L. B., Dunn, E. W., & Norton, M. I. (2012). Happiness runs in a circular motion: Evidence for a positive feedback loop between prosocial spending and happiness. *Journal of Happiness Studies, 13*, 347–355.

Ashby, G., Isen, A., & Turken, A. (1999). A neuropsychological theory of positive affect and its influence on cognition. *Psychological Review, 106*, 529–550.

Baddeley, A. D. (1996). Exploring the central executive. *Quarterly Journal of Experimental Psychology: Human Experimental Psychology, 49A*, 5–28.

Bandler, R., Keay, K. A., Floyd, N., & Price, J. (2000). Central circuits mediating patterned autonomic activity during active vs. passive emotional coping. *Brain Research Bulletin, 53*, 95–104.

Bar, M. (2009). A cognitive neuroscience hypothesis of mood and depression. *Trends in Cognitive Sciences, 13*, 456–463.

Bargh, J., Gollwitzer, P., Lee-Chai, A., Barndollar, K., & Trotschel, R. (2001). The automated will: Nonconscious activation and pursuit of behavioral goals. *Journal of Personality and Social Psychology, 81*, 1014–1027.

Baron, R., Fortin, S., Frei, R., Hauver, L., & Shack, M. (1990). Reducing organizational conflict: The role of socially-induced positive affect. *The International Journal of Conflict Management, 1*, 133–152.

Barsade, S. (2002). The ripple effect: Emotional contagion and its influence on group behavior. *Administrative Science Quarterly, 47*, 644–675.

Bartels, A., & Zeki, S. (2004). The neural correlates of maternal and romantic love. *NeuroImage, 21*, 1155–1166.

Beckes, L., & Coan, J. A. (2011). Social baseline theory: The role of social proximity in emotion and economy of action. *Social and Personality Psychology Compass, 5*, 976–988.

Bell, P. (1978). Affective state, attraction, and affiliation: Misery loves happy company too. *Personality and Social Psychology Bulletin, 4*, 616–619.

Benet-Martínez, V., & Karakitapoglu-Aygün, Z. (2003). The interplay of cultural syndromes and personality in predicting life satisfaction: Comparing Asian Americans and European Americans. *Journal of Cross-Cultural Psychology, 34*, 38–60.

Bentall, R. P. (1992). A proposal to classify happiness as a psychiatric disorder. *Journal of Medical Ethics, 18*, 94–98.

Berridge, K. C., & Kringelbach, M. L. (2013). Neuroscience of affect: Brain mechanisms of pleasure and displeasure. *Current Opinion in Neurobiology, 23*, 294–303.

Berridge, K. C., & Kringelbach, M. L. (2015). Pleasure systems in the brain. *Neuron, 86*, 646–664.

Bhattacharyya, M., Whitehead, D., Rakhit, R., & Steptoe, A. (2008). Depressed mood, positive affect, and heart rate variability in patients with suspected coronary artery disease. *Psychosomatic Medicine, 70*, 1020–1027.

Bless, H., Clore, G. L., Schwarz, N., Golisano, V., Rabe, C., & Wölk, M. (1996). Mood and the use of scripts: Does a happy mood really lead to mindlessness? *Journal of Personality and Social Psychology, 71*, 665–679.

Blood, A. J., & Zatorre, R. J. (2001). Intensely pleasurable responses to music correlate with activity in brain regions implicated in reward and emotion. *Proceedings of the National Academy of Sciences, 98*, 11818–11823.

Bodenhause, G., Kramer, G., & Susser, K. (1994). Happiness and stereotypical thinking in social judgment. *Journal of Personality and Social Psychology, 66*, 621–632.

Bolte, A., Goschke, T., & Kuhl, J. (2003). Emotion and intuition: Effects of positive and negative mood on implicit judgments of semantic coherence. *Psychological Science, 14*, 416–421.

Bower, G. H. (1981). Mood and memory. *American Psychologist, 36*, 129–148.

Boyd, B. (2004). Laughter and literature: A play theory of humor. *Philosophy and Literature, 28*, 1–22.

Cacioppo, J., Berntson, G., Klein, D., & Poehlmann, K. (1997). The psychophysiology of emotion across the lifespan. *Annual Review of Gerontology and Geriatrics, 17*, 27–47.

Cacioppo, J., Hughes, M., Waite, L., Hawkley, L., & Thisted, R. (2006). Loneliness as a specific risk factor for depressive symptoms. *Psychology and Aging, 21*, 140–151.

Cacioppo, J. T., Berntson, G. G., Larsen, J. T., Poehlmann, K. M., & Ito, T. A. (2000). The psychophysiology of emotion. In M. Lewis & J. Haviland-Jones (Eds.), *Handbook of emotions* (2nd ed., pp. 173–191). New York, NY: Guildford Press.

Cacioppo, J. T., Hawkley, L., Kalil, A., Hughes, M., Waite, L., & Thisted, R. (2008). Happiness and the invisible threads of social connection. In M. Eid & R. J. Larsen (Eds.), *The science of subjective well-being* (pp. 195–219). New York, NY: Guilford Press.

Cacioppo, J. T., Klein, D. J., Bernston, G. G., & Hartfield, E. (1993). The psychophysiology of emotion. In M. Lewis & J. Haviland-Jones (Eds.), *Handbook of emotions*. New York, NY: Guildford Press.

Campbell, A. (2010). Oxytocin and human social behavior. *Personality and Social Psychology Review, 14*, 281–295.

Caprara, G. V., Di Giunta, L., Eisenberg, N., Gerbino, M., Pastorelli, C., & Tramontano, C. (2008). Assessing regulatory emotional self-efficacy in three countries. *Psychological Assessment, 20*, 227–237.

Cartensen, L., Pasupathi, M., Mayr, U., & Nesselroade, J. (2000). Emotional experiences of everyday life across the adult life span. *Journal of Personality and Social Psychology, 79*, 644–655.

Carver, C. (2003). Pleasure as a sign you can attend to something else: Placing positive feelings within a general model of affect. *Cognition & Emotion, 17*, 241–261.

Case, R., Moss, A., Case, N., McDermott, M., & Eberly, S. (1992). Living alone after myocardial infraction: Impact on prognosis. *Journal of the American Medical Association, 267*, 515–519.

Chemali, Z., Chahine, L., & Naassan, G. (2008). On happiness: A minimalist perspective on a complex neural circuitry and its psychosocial constructs. *Journal of Happiness Studies, 9*(4), 489–501.

Chida, Y., & Steptoe, A. (2008). Positive psychological well-being and mortality: A quantitative review of prospective observational studies. *Psychosomatic Medicine, 70*, 741–756.

Chiew, K., & Braver, T. (2014). Dissociable influences of reward motivation and positive emotion on cognitive control. *Cognitive, Affective, & Behavioral Neuroscience, 14*, 509–529.

Christie, I. C., & Friedman, B. H. (2004). Autonomic specificity of discrete emotion and dimensions of affective space: A multivariate approach. *International Journal of Psychophysiology, 51*, 143–153.

Clore, G. L., & Huntsinger, J. (2007). Feelings as information for judgment and cognitive processing. *Trends in Cognitive Science, 11*, 393–399.

Coan, J. A., Allen, J. J. B., & Harmon-Jones, E. (2001). Voluntary facial expression and hemispheric asymmetry over the frontal cortex. *Psychophysiology, 38*, 912–925.

Coan, J. A., Schaefer, H. S., & Davidson, R. J. (2006). Lending a hand: Social regulation of the neural response to threat. *Psychological Science, 17*, 1032–1039.

Cohen, J., Cohen, P., West, S., & Aiken, L. (2003). *Applied multiple regression/correlation analysis for the behavioral sciences* (3rd ed.). Hillsdale, NJ: Erlbaum.

Cohen, S. (1988). Psychosocial models of the role of social support in the etiology of physical disease. *Health Psychology, 7*, 269–297.

Colon, E., Callies, A., Popkin, M., & McGlave, P. (1991). Depressed mood and other variables related to bone marrow transplantation survival in acute leukemia. *Psychosomatics, 32*, 420–425.

Compton, R., Wirtz, D., Pajoumand, G., Claus, E., & Heller, W. (2004). Association between positive affect and attentional shifting. *Cognitive Therapy and Research, 28*, 733–744.

Coyne, J. (1976). Depression and the response of others. *Journal of Abnormal Psychology, 85*, 186–193.

Cyders, M. A., & Smith, G. T. (2008). Emotion-based dispositions to rash action: Positive and negative urgency. *Psychological Bulletin, 134*, 807–828.

Danner, D., Snowdon, D., & Friesen, W. (2001). Positive emotions in early life and longevity: Findings from the nun study. *Journal of Personality and Social Psychology, 80*, 804–813.

Davis, M. (2008). Understanding the relationship between mood and creativity: A meta-analysis. *Organizational Behavior and Human Decision Processes, 108*, 25–38.

De Neve, J., Diener, E., Tay, L., & Xuereb, C. (2013). The objective benefits of subjective well-being.. Centre for Economic Performance.

De Neve, K. M., & Cooper, H. (1998). The happy personality: A meta-analysis of 137 personality traits and subjective well-being. *Psychological Bulletin, 124*, 197–229.

Deci, E. L., & Ryan, R. M. (2008). Self-determination theory: A macrotheory of human motivation, development, and health. *Canadian Psychology/Psychologie Canadienne, 49*, 182–185.

Demaree, H., Schmeichel, B., Robinson, J., & Everhart, D. (2004). Behavioural, affective, and physiological effects of negative and positive emotional exaggeration. *Cognition and Emotion, 18*, 1079–1097.

Dreisbach, G. (2006). How positive affect modulates cognitive control: The costs and benefits of reduced maintenance capability. *Brain and Cognition, 60*, 11–19.

Dreisbach, G., & Goschke, T. (2004). How positive affect modulates cognitive control: Reduced perseveration at the cost of increased distractibility. *Journal of Experimental Psychology: Learning, Memory, and Cognition, 30*, 343–353.

Dreisbach, G., Haider, H., & Kluwe, R. H. (2002). Preparatory processes in the task-switching paradigm: Evidence from the use of probability cues. *Journal of Experimental Psychology: Learning, Memory, and Cognition, 28*, 468–483.

Drevets, W. C., Price, J. L., Simpson, J. R., Todd, R. D., Reich, T., Vannier, M., & Raichle, M. E. (1997). Subgenual prefrontal cortex abnormalities in mood disorders. *Nature, 386*, 824–827.

Dunn, J. R., & Schweitzer, M. E. (2005). Feeling and believing: The influence of emotion on trust. *Journal of Personality and Social Psychology, 88*, 736–748.

Eisenberger, N., Master, S., Inagaki, T., Taylor, S., Shirinyan, D., Lieberman, M., & Naliboff, B. (2011). Attachment figures activate a safety signal-related neural region and reduce pain experience. *Proceedings of the National Academy of Sciences, 108*, 11721–11726.

Ekman, P., & Cordaro, D. (2011). What is meant by calling emotions basic. *Emotion Review, 3*, 364–370.

Ekman, P., Levenson, R. W., & Friesen, W. (1983). Autonomic nervous system activity distinguishes among emotions. *Science, 221*, 1208–1210.

Folkow, B. (2000). Perspectives on the integrative functions of the 'sympatho-adrenomedullary system'. *Autonomic Neuroscience, 83*, 101–115.

Ford, B., Tamir, M., Brunye, T., Shirer, W., Mahoney, C., & Taylor, H. (2010). Keeping your eyes on the prize: Anger and visual attention to threats and rewards. *Psychological Science, 21*, 1098–1105.

Forest, D., Clark, M. S., Mills, J., & Isen, A. M. (1979). Helping as a function of feeling state and nature of the helping behavior. *Motivation and Emotion, 3*, 161–169.

Forgas, J. P. (1998). Mood and judgment: The affect infusion model (AIM). *Psychological Bulletin, 117*, 39–66.

Forgas, J. P., & East, R. (2008). On being happy and gullible: Mood effects on skepticism and the detection of deception. *Journal of Experimental Social Psychology, 44*, 1362–1367.

Fredrickson, B. (2013). Positive emotions broaden and build. In P. Devine & A. Plant (Eds.), *Advances in experimental social psychology* (pp. 1–53). Burlington, MA: Academic.

Fredrickson, B., & Levenson, R. W. (1998). Positive emotions speed recovery from the cardiovascular sequelae of negative emotions. *Cognition and Emotion, 12*, 191–220.

Fredrickson, B., Tugade, M., Waugh, C., & Larkin, G. (2003). What good are positive emotions in crises? A prospective study of resilience and emotions following the terrorist attacks on the United States on September 11th, 2001. *Journal of Personality and Social Psychology, 84*, 365–376.

Fredrickson, B. L. (2001). The role of positive emotions in positive psychology: The broaden- and-build theory of positive emotions. *American Psychologist, 56*, 218–226.

Fredrickson, B. L., & Branigan, C. (2005). Positive emotions broaden the scope of attention and thought-action repertoires. *Cognition and Emotion, 19*, 313–332.

Fredrickson, B. L., & Joiner, T. (2002). Positive emotions trigger upward spirals toward emotional well-being. *Psychological Science, 13*, 172–175.

Fredrickson, B. L., & Losada, M. F. (2005). Positive affect and the complex dynamics of human flourishing. *American Psychologist, 60*, 678–686.

Friedman, H., Tucker, J., Tomlinson-Keasey, C., Schwartz, J., Wingard, D., & Criqui, M. (1993). Does childhood personality predict longevity? *Journal of Personality and Social Psychology, 65*, 176–185.

Friston, K. (2010). The free-energy principle: A unified brain theory? *Nature Reviews Neuroscience, 11*, 127–138.

Frober, K., & Dreisbach, G. (2012). How positive affect modulates proactive control: Reduced usage of informative cues under positive affect with low arousal. *Frontiers in Psychology, 3*, 265.

Gable, P. A., & Harmon-Jones, E. (2012). Reducing attentional capture of emotion by broadening attention: Increased global attention reduces early electrophysiological responses to negative stimuli. *Biological Psychology, 90*, 150–153.

Galistu, A., & D'Aquila, P. S. (2012). Effect of the dopamine D1-like receptor antagonist SCH 23390 on the microstructure of ingestive behavior in water-deprived rats licking for water and NaCl solutions. *Physiological Behavior, 105*, 230–233.

Gasper, K., & Clore, G. L. (2000). Do you have to pay attention to your feelings to be influenced by them? *Personality and Social Psychology Bulletin, 26*, 698–711.

Gasper, K., & Clore, G. L. (2002). Attending to the big picture: Mood and global versus local processing of visual information. *Psychological Science, 13*, 34–40.

Gibson, J. J. (1979). *The ecological approach to visual perception*. Boston, MA: Houghton Mifflin.

Gorn, G., Goldberg, M., & Basu, K. (1993). Mood, awareness and product evaluation. *Journal of Consumer Psychology, 2*, 237–256.

Gray, J. (2001). Emotional modulation of cognitive control: Approach-withdrawal states double-dissociate spatial from verbal two-back task performance. *Journal of Experimental Psychology: General, 130*, 436–452.

Gray, J. (2004). Integration of emotion and cognitive control. *Current Directions in Psychological Science, 13*, 46–48.

Gray, J., Braver, T., & Raichle, M. (2002). Integration of emotion and cognition in the lateral prefrontal cortex. *Proceedings of the National Academy of Sciences, 99*, 4115–4120.

Gruber, J., Johnson, S., Oveis, C., & Keltner, D. (2008). Risk for mania and positive emotional responding: Too much of a good thing? *Emotion, 8*, 23–33.

Gruber, J., Mauss, I., & Tamir, M. (2011). A dark side of happiness? How, when, and why happiness is not always good. *Perspectives on Psychological Science, 6*, 222–233.

Guiliani, N., McRae, K., & Gross, J. (2008). The up- and down-regulation of amusement: Experiential, behavioral, and autonomic consequences. *Emotion, 8*, 714–719.

Gutierres, S., Kenrick, D., & Partch, J. (1999). Beauty, dominance, and the mating game: Contrast effects in self-assessment reflect gender differences in mate selection. *Personality and Social Psychology Bulletin, 25*, 1126–1134.

Guven, C. (2012). Reversing the question: Does happiness affect consumption and savings behavior? *Journal of Economic Psychology, 33*, 701–717.

Hawkley, L. C., Browne, M. W., & Cacioppo, J. T. (2005). How can I connect with thee? Let me count the ways. *Psychological Science, 16*, 798–804.

Headey, B., & Veenhoven, R. (1989). Does happiness induce a rosy outlook? In R. Veenhoven (Ed.), *How harmful is happiness? Consequences of enjoying life or not* (pp. 106–127). Amsterdam, The Netherlands: Universitaire Pers Rotterdam.

Hebb, D. O. (1949). *The organization of behavior: A neuropsychological approach*. New York, NY: Wiley.

Hertenstein, M., Holmes, R., McCullough, M., & Keltner, D. (2009). The communication of emotion via touch. *Emotion, 9*, 566–573.

House, J., Landis, K., & Umberson, D. (1988). Social relationships and health. *Science, 241*, 540–545.

Ifcher, J., & Zarghamee, H. (2011). Happiness and time preference: The effect of positive affect in a random-assignment experiment. *The American Economic Review, 101*, 3109–3129.

Inoue, K., Burkett, J., & Young, L. (2013). Neuroanatomical distribution of u-opioid receptor mRNA and binding in monogamous prairie voles (Microtus ochrogaster) and non-monogamous meadow voles (Microtus pennsylvanicus). *Neuroscience, 244*, 122–133.

Isbell, L. M., & Wyer, R. S., Jr. (1999). Correcting for mood-induced bias in the evaluation of political candidates: The roles of intrinsic and extrinsic motivation. *Personality and Social Psychology Bulletin, 25*, 237–249.

Isen, A. M., & Daubman, K. A. (1984). The influence of affect on categorization. *Journal of Personality and Social Psychology, 47*, 1206–1217.

Isen, A. M., Daubman, K. A., & Nowicki, G. P. (1987). Positive affect facilitates creative problem solving. *Journal of Personality and Social Psychology, 52*, 1122–1131.

Isen, A. M., Johnson, M. M., Mertz, E., & Robinson, G. F. (1985). The influence of positive affect on the unusualness of word associations. *Journal of Personality and Social Psychology, 48*, 1413–1426.

Jänig, W., & Häbler, H. J. (2000). Sympathetic nervous system: Contribution to chronic pain. *Progress in Brain Research, 129*, 451–468.

Jänig, W., & McLachlan, E. M. (1992). Characteristics of function-specific pathways in the sympathetic nervous system. *Trends in Neurosciences, 15*, 475–481.

Johnson, K. J., & Fredrickson, B. L. (2005). "We all look the same to me" positive emotions eliminate the own-race bias in face recognition. *Psychological Science, 16*, 875–881.

Kelly, J. A., & Kalichman, S. C. (1998). Reinforcement value of unsafe sex as a predictor of condom use and continued HIV/AIDS risk behavior among gay and bisexual men. *Health Psychology, 17*, 328–335.

Kesebir, P., & Diener, E. (2008). In pursuit of happiness: Empirical answers to philosophical questions. *Perspectives on Psychological Science, 3*, 117–125.

Kragel, P. A., & LaBar, K. S. (2013). Multivariate pattern classification reveals autonomic and experiential representations of discrete emotions. *Emotion, 13*, 681–690.

Kraut, R. (1979). Two conceptions of happiness. *Philosophical Review, 87*, 167–196.

Kreibig, S. (2010). Autonomic nervous system activity in emotion: A review. *Biological Psychology, 84*, 394–421.

Kringelbach, M. L. (2005). The human orbitofrontal cortex: Linking reward to hedonic experience. *Nature Reviews Neuroscience, 6*, 691–702.

Kringelbach, M. L., & Berridge, K. C. (2009). Towards a functional neuroanatomy of pleasure and happiness. *Trends in Cognitive Sciences, 13*, 479–487.

Kringelbach, M. L., & Berridge, K. C. (2015). Motivation and pleasure in the brain. In W. Hofmann & L. F. Nordgren (Eds.), *The psychology of desire* (pp. 129–145). New York, NY: Guildford Press.

Kringelbach, M. L., & Berridge, K. C. (2017). The affective core of emotion: Pleasure, subjective well-being, and optimal metastability in the brain. *Emotion Review, 9*, 191–199.

Kruglanski, A., Shah, J., Fishbach, A., Friedman, R., Chun, W., & Sleeth-Keppler, D. (2002). A theory of goal systems. *Advances in Experimental Social Psychology, 34*, 331–378.

Kuhl, J., & Kazen, M. (1999). Volitional facilitation of difficult intentions: Joint activation of intention memory and positive affect removes Stroop interference. *Journal of Experimental Psychology: General, 128*, 382–399.

Kwan, V. S., Bond, M. H., & Singelis, T. M. (1997). Pancultural explanations for life satisfaction: Adding relationship harmony to self-esteem. *Journal of Personality and Social Psychology, 73*, 1038–1051.

Labott, S., Ahleman, S., Wolever, M., & Martin, R. (1990). The physiological and psychological effects of the expression and inhibition of emotion. *Behavioral Medicine, 16*, 182–189.

Levenson, R. (1988). Emotion and the autonomic nervous system: A prospectus for research on autonomic specificity. In H. Wagner (Ed.), *Social psychophysiology and emotion: Theory and applications* (pp. 17–42). Chichester, England: Wiley.

Levenson, R. W. (1992). Autonomic nervous system differences among emotions. *Psychological Science, 3*, 23–27.

Lucas, R. E., Clark, A. E., Georgellis, Y., & Diener, E. (2003). Reexamining adaptation and the set point model of happiness: Reactions to changes in marital status. *Journal of Personality and Social Psychology, 84*, 527–539.

Lyubomirsky, S., Sheldon, K., & Schkade, D. (2005). Pursuing happiness: The architecture of sustainable change. *Review of General Psychology, 9*, 111–131.

Martin, E., & Kerns, J. (2011). The influence of positive mood on different aspects of cognitive control. *Cognition and Emotion, 25*, 265–279.

Maslow, A. H. (1967). A theory of metamotivation: The biological rooting of the value- life. *Journal of Humanistic Psychology, 7*, 93–127.

Mauss, I. B., Levenson, R. W., McCarter, L., Wilhelm, F. H., & Gross, J. J. (2005). The tie that binds? Coherence among emotion experience, behavior, and physiology. *Emotion, 5*, 175–190.

Mauss, I. B., Savino, N. S., Anderson, C. L., Weisbuch, M., Tamir, M., & Laudenslager, M. L. (2012). The pursuit of happiness can be lonely. *Emotion, 12*, 908–912.

Mayberg, H. S. (1997). Limbic-cortical dysregulation: A proposed model of depression. *The Journal of Neuropsychiatry and Clinical Neurosciences, 9*, 471–481.

Miyake, A., & Friedman, N. P. (2012). The nature and organization of individual differences in executive functions four general conclusions. *Current Directions in Psychological Science, 21*, 8–14.

Miyake, A., Friedman, N. P., Emerson, M., Witzki, A., Howerter, A., & Wagner, T. (2000). The unity and diversity of executive functions and their contributions to complex "frontal lobe" tasks: A latent variable analysis. *Cognitive Psychology, 41*, 49–100.

Mogg, K., & Bradley, B. P. (1999). Selective attention and anxiety: A cognitive-motivational perspective. In T. Dalgleish & M. Power (Eds.), *Handbook of cognition and emotion* (pp. 145–170). Oxford, England: Wiley.

Morf, C. C., & Rhodewalt, F. (2001). Unraveling the paradoxes of narcissism: A dynamic self-regulatory processing model. *Psychological Inquiry, 12*, 177–196.

Murry, J. P., Jr., & Dacin, P. A. (1996). Cognitive moderators of negative-emotion effects: Implications for understanding media context. *Journal of Consumer Research, 22*, 439–447.

Neely, J. H. (1991). Semantic priming effects in visual word recognition: A selective review of current findings and theories. *Basic Processes in Reading: Visual Word Recognition, 11*, 264–336.

Nelson, D. (2009). Feeling good and open-minded: The impact of positive affect on cross cultural empathetic responding. *The Journal of Positive Psychology, 4*, 53–63.

Ness, R. (2004). Natural selection and the elusiveness of happiness. *Philosophical Transactions of the Royal Society of London B, 359*, 1333–1347.

Nolen-Hoeksema, S., & Ahrens, C. (2002). Age differences and similarities in the correlates of depressive symptoms. *Psychology and Aging, 17*, 116–124.

Norman, G. J., Berntson, G. G., & Cacioppo, J. T. (2014). Emotion, somatovisceral afference, and autonomic regulation. *Emotion Review, 6*, 113–123.

Norton, D. (1976). *Personal destinies: A philosophy of ethical individualism.* Princeton, NJ: Princeton University Press.

O'Doherty, J. P. (2004). Reward representations and reward-related learning in the human brain: Insights from neuroimaging. *Current Opinion in Neurobiology, 14*, 769–776.

Ong, A., Bergeman, C., Bisconti, T., & Wallace, K. (2006). Psychological resilience, positive emotions, and successful adaptation to stress in later life. *Journal of Personality and Social Psychology, 91*, 730–749.

Panksepp, J. (2003). Feeling the pain of social loss. *Science, 302*, 237–239.

Pecina, S., Berridge, K., & Parker, L. (1997). Pimozide does not shift palatability: Separation of anhedonia from sensorimotor suppression by taste reactivity. *Pharmacology Biochemistry and Behavior, 58*, 801–811.

Pellegrini, A. D., & Smith, P. K. (2005). *The nature of play: Great apes and humans.* New York, NY: Guilford Press.

Perner, J., & Lang, B. (1999). Development of theory of mind and executive control. *Trends in Cognitive Sciences, 3*, 337–344.

Pessoa, L. (2009). How do emotion and motivation direct executive control? *Trends in Cognitive Sciences, 13*, 160–166.

Phaf, R. H. (2015). Attention and positive affect: Temporal switching or spatial broadening? *Attention, Perception, & Psychophysics, 77*, 713–719.

Pham, M. T. (2007). Emotion and rationality: A critical review and interpretation of empirical evidence. *Review of General Psychology, 11*, 155–178.

Phillips, L., Bull, R., Adams, E., & Fraser, L. (2002). Positive mood and executive function: Evidence from Stroop and fluency tasks. *Emotion, 2*, 12–22.

Raghunathan, R., & Corfman, K. (2006). Is happiness shared doubled and sadness shared halved? Social influence on enjoyment of hedonic experiences. *Journal of Marketing Research, 43*, 386–394.

Rhodewalt, F. (2001). The social mind of the narcissist: Cognitive and motivation aspects of interpersonal self-constructions. In J. P. Forgas, K. Williams, & L. Wheeler (Eds.), *The social mind: Cognitive and motivational aspects of interpersonal behavior* (pp. 177–198). New York, NY: Cambridge University Press.

Rolls, E. T. (1999). *The brain and emotion.* Oxford, England: Oxford University Press.

Rolls, E. T., Grabenhorst, F., & Parris, B. (2008). Warm pleasant feelings in the brain. *NeuroImage, 41*, 1504–1513.

Rose, P. (2002). The happy and unhappy faces of narcissism. *Personality and Individual Differences, 33*, 379–391.

Rowe, G., Hirsh, J., & Anderson, A. (2007). Positive affect increases the breadth of attentional selection. *Proceedings of the National Academy of Sciences, 104*, 383–388.

Ryff, C., & Singer, B. (2008). Know thyself and become what you are: A eudaimonic approach to psychological well-being. *Journal of Happiness Studies, 9*, 13–39.

Ryff, C., Singer, B., & Love, G. (2004). Positive health: Connecting well-being with biology. *Philosophical Transactions of the Royal Society of London B, 359*, 1383–1394.

Salovey, P., & Birnbaum, D. (1989). Influence of mood on health-relevant cognitions. *Journal of Personality and Social Psychology, 57*, 539–551.

Schachter, S. (1951). Deviation, rejection and communication. *Journal of Abnormal and Social Psychology, 46*, 190–207.

Schmitz, T., De Rosa, E., & Anderson, A. (2009). Opposing influences of affective state valence on visual cortical encoding. *The Journal of Neuroscience, 29*, 7199–7207.

Schooler, J., Ariely, D., & Loewenstein, G. (2003). The pursuit and assessment of happiness may be self-defeating. In J. Carrillo & I. Brocas (Eds.), *The psychology of economic decisions* (pp. 41–70). Oxford, England: Oxford University Press.

Schultz, W., Dayan, P., & Montague, P. (1997). A neural substrate of prediction and reward. *Science, 275*, 1593–1599.

Sedikides, C., Campbell, W. K., Reeder, G. D., & Elliot, A. J. (2002). The self in relationships: Whether, how, and when close others put the self "in its place". *European Review of Social Psychology, 12*, 237–265.

Sedikides, C., Rudich, E. A., Gregg, A. P., Kumashiro, M., & Rusbult, C. (2004). Are normal narcissists psychologically healthy?: Self-esteem matters. *Journal of Personality and Social Psychology, 87*, 400–416.

Shiota, M., Campos, B., Oveis, C., Hertenstein, M., Simon-Thomas, E., & Keltner, D. (2017). Beyond happiness: Building a science of discrete positive emotions. *American Psychologist, 72*, 617–643.

Shiota, M., Neufeld, S., Yeung, W., Moser, S., & Perea, E. (2011). Feeling good: Autonomic nervous system responding in five positive emotions. *Emotion, 11*, 1368–1378.

Simmons, W., Rapuano, K., Ingeholm, J., Avery, J., Kallman, S., Hall, K., & Martin, A. (2014). The ventral pallidum and orbitofrontal cortex support food pleasantness inferences. *Brain Structure & Function, 219*, 473–483.

Simon, H. (1967). Motivational and emotional controls of cognition. *Psychological Review, 74*, 29–39.

Spanier, G. B., & Furstenberg, F. F., Jr. (1982). Remarriage after divorce: A longitudinal analysis of well-being. *Journal of Marriage and the Family, 44*, 709–720.

Stephens, C. L., Christie, I. C., & Friedman, B. H. (2010). Autonomic specificity of basic emotions: Evidence from pattern classification and cluster analysis. *Biological Psychology, 84*, 463–473.

Stone, A., Cox, D., Valdimarsdottir, H., Jandorf, L., & Neale, J. (1987). Evidence that secretory IgA antibody is associated with daily mood. *Journal of Personality and Social Psychology, 52*, 988–993.

Stone, A., Neale, J., Cox, D., Napoli, A., Valdimarsdottir, H., & Kennedy-Moore, E. (1994). Daily events are associated with secretory immune response to an oral antigen in men. *Health Psychology, 13*, 440–446.

Storbeck, J. & Clore, G.L. (2011). Affect influences false memories at encoding: Evidence from recognition data. *Emotion, 11*, 981–989.

Storbeck, J. (2012). Performance costs when emotion tunes inappropriate cognitive abilities: Implications for mental resources and behavior. *Journal of Experimental Psychology: General, 141*, 411–416.

Storbeck, J., & Clore, G. L. (2005). With sadness come accuracy, with happiness, false memory: Mood and the false memory effect. *Psychological Science, 16*, 785–791.

Storbeck, J., & Clore, G. L. (2008). The affective regulation of cognitive priming. *Emotion, 8*, 208–215.

Storbeck, J., Davidson, N. A., Dahl, C., Blass, S., & Yung, E. (2015). Emotion, working memory task demands, and individual differences predict behavior, cognitive effort, and negative affect. *Cognition and Emotion, 29*, 95–117.

Storbeck, J., & Maswood, R. (2016). Happiness increases verbal and spatial working memory capacity, sadness does not: Emotion, working memory, and executive control. *Cognition and Emotion, 30*, 925–938.

Storbeck, J., & Stewart, J. L. (2017). *Sadness and fear enhance facets of inhibition: Support for the emotion and goal compatibility theory*. Unpublished manuscript.

Storbeck, J., & Watson, P. (2014). Verbal makes it positive, spatial makes it negative: Working memory biases judgments, attention, and moods. *Emotion, 14*, 1072–1086.

Suardi, A., Sotgiu, I., Costa, T., Cauda, F., & Rusconi, M. (2016). The neural correlates of happiness: A review of PET and fMRI studies using autobiographical recall methods. *Cognitive, Affective, & Behavioral Neuroscience, 16*, 383–392.

Tamir, M., & Robinson, M. D. (2007). The happy spotlight: Positive mood and selective attention to rewarding information. *Personality and Social Psychology Bulletin, 33*, 1124–1136.

Thayer, J. F., Hansen, A. L., Saus-Rose, E., & Johnsen, B. H. (2009). Heart rate variability, prefrontal neural function, and cognitive performance: The neurovisceral integration perspective on self-regulation, adaptation, and health. *Annals of Behavioral Medicine, 37*, 141–153.

Tsai, J. L., Chentsova-Dutton, Y., Freire-Bebeau, L., & Przymus, D. E. (2002). Emotional expression and physiology in European Americans and Hmong Americans. *Emotion, 2*, 380–397.

Tugade, M. M., & Fredrickson, B. L. (2004). Resilient individuals use positive emotions to bounce back from negative emotional experiences. *Journal of Personality and Social Psychology, 86*, 320–333.

Urry, H., Nitschke, J., Dolski, I., Jackson, D., Dalton, K., Mueller, C., et al. (2004). Making a life worth living: Neural correlates of well-being. *Psychological Science, 15*, 367–372.

van Wouwe, N. C., Band, G. P., & Ridderinkhof, K. R. (2011). Positive affect modulates flexibility and evaluative control. *Journal of Cognitive Neuroscience, 23*, 524–539.

Veenhoven, R. (1990). The utility of happiness. *Social Indicators Research, 20*, 333–354.

Waterman, A., Schwartz, S., & Conti, R. (2006). The implications of two conceptions of happiness (hedonic enjoyment and eudaimonia) for the understanding of intrinsic motivation. *Journal of Happiness Studies, 9*, 41–79.

Waugh, C. E., & Fredrickson, B. L. (2006). Nice to know you: Positive emotions, self–other overlap, and complex understanding in the formation of a new relationship. *The Journal of Positive Psychology, 1*, 93–106.

Wickelgren, I. (1997). Getting the brain's attention. *Science, 278*, 35–37.

Wise, R. (2008). Dopamine and reward: The anhedonia hypothesis 30 years on. *Neurotoxicity Research, 14*, 169–183.

Wright, R. (1996). Brehm's theory of motivation as a model of effort and cardiovascular response. In P. M. Gollwitzer & J. Bargh (Eds.), *The psychology of action: Linking cognition and motivation to behavior* (pp. 424–453). New York, NY: Guilford Press.

Wyer, R. S., & Collins, J. E. (1992). A theory of humor elicitation. *Psychological Review, 99*, 663–688.

Yang, H., Yang, S., & Isen, A. (2013). Positive affect improves working memory: Implications for controlled cognitive processing. *Cognitive and Emotion, 27*, 474–482.

Zajonc, R. B., & McIntosh, D. N. (1992). Emotions research: Some promising questions and some questionable promises. *Psychological Science, 3*, 70–74.

Chapter 11
Awe: A Self-Transcendent and Sometimes Transformative Emotion

Alice Chirico and David B. Yaden

Abstract Awe is a complex emotion arising from the perception of literal or figurative vastness. Several subjective components of awe have been identified, including feelings of connectedness and self-diminishment, making it a form of self-transcendent experience. Awe has also been linked to increased well-being and altruistic behavior. This chapter describes recent advances in the experimental literature on awe, reviews some methods of inducing this emotion in the lab, and discusses some theories regarding its functions.

> In the upper reaches of pleasure and on the boundary of fear is a little studied emotion – awe.
>
> –Keltner & Haidt, 2003; p. 297

The view from the top of a mountain, staring up at the dark sky punctuated by stars, and hearing a "mind-blowing" idea clearly articulated – all of these circumstances are capable of inducing a particular emotion: awe. But what is awe? And what are its functions?

Awe's introduction into modern emotion research is largely due to a now classic article by Keltner and Haidt (2003). In this chapter, awe is described from the perspective of various fields, such as philosophy, religion, art, and psychology. Awe is defined as a complex emotion arising from a perception of vastness and a need to accommodate the perception into existing mental schemas. This vastness can come from perceptual or conceptual stimuli (Yaden, Iwry, et al., 2016). Given the paucity of psychological researchers focusing on this phenomenon in 2003, Keltner and Haidt labeled awe as a "little studied emotion" (p. 297). However, since 2003, this once esoteric emotion has captured the attention of a number of psychological researchers. A quick search in a psychology database (PsycINFO) returned 137 articles since 2003.

A. Chirico
Department of Psychology, Catholic University of the Sacred Heart, Milan, Italy

D. B. Yaden (✉)
Department of Psychology, University of Pennsylvania, Philadelphia, PA, USA
e-mail: dyaden@sas.upenn.edu

© Springer International Publishing AG, part of Springer Nature 2018   221
H. C. Lench (ed.), *The Function of Emotions*,
https://doi.org/10.1007/978-3-319-77619-4_11

In Keltner and Haidt's (2003) article, awe is referred to as a "complex" emotion. This label is appropriate, given that several features of awe distinguish it from other emotions. Awe often contains both positive and negative valence (Gordon et al., 2017; Yaden et al., in press). For instance, awe can arise both from beautiful breathtaking panoramas (Keltner & Haidt, 2003) and from dreadful and terrifying natural phenomena, like severe thunderstorms (Piff, Dietze, Feinberg, Stancato, & Keltner, 2015; Gordon et al., 2017). Additionally, awe has several qualities that place it on the border between an emotional state and altered state of consciousness due to its capacity to alter the senses of time, space, and self. For example, the sense of self has been empirically shown to diminish and the sense of connectedness to increase during states of awe (Piff et al., 2015). This finding has led to awe being classed as a self-transcendent experience (STE), temporary mental states characterized by an increased sense of connectedness and/or diminished sense of self (Yaden, Haidt, Hood, Vago, & Newberg, 2017).

This chapter reviews research on awe conducted since Keltner and Haidt's 2003 article. It covers elicitors of awe as well as new means to induce it in the lab, the primary subjective qualities of awe, and outcomes associated with the experience of awe. This chapter concludes by discussing awe from a functionalist perspective (Lench, Bench, Darbor, & Moore, 2015), by reviewing prevailing theories of awe related to social dominance and offering a new speculative perspective that proposes that the emotion of awe may have first arisen from natural rather than social triggers.

What Is Awe?

The perspectives proposed in the Keltner and Haidt (2003) article, introducing awe to mainstream psychological science, grew largely out of the discrete emotion tradition and other preliminary work by Ekman (1992) and Lazarus (1991). Specifically, Lazarus (1991) acknowledged the complex and multifaceted nature of awe, and Ekman identified awe as a potential basic emotion (Ekman, 1992) originating from a blend of wonder and fear. This perspective holds that basic emotions are human universals (Ekman & Cordaro, 2011).

In order to elucidate the nature of awe, Keltner and Haidt (2003) oriented their attention toward the core aspects of this emotion – focusing on "prototypical awe." The approach of analyzing a "prototype" was pioneered by Eleanor Rosch (1983). This prototypical approach draws from the literature around the philosophy of concepts (Margolis & Laurence, 1999). According to Rosch (1983), most commonly used concepts (e.g., animals, toys, means of transport) have "fuzzy" boundaries in that it is difficult to sharply delineate between related concepts using a set of necessary and sufficient conditions. Instead, definitions are organized around the clearest instance of a category, called a "prototype." According to this view, the more a given instance resembles its prototype, the more it can be considered identical to the concept. Furthermore, prototypical members share more common features with the prototype than nonmembers. In terms of emotion, according to this view, emotions are not so much clearly differentiated categories but fuzzy systems in which different emotional nuances should be placed at different distances depending on their degree of similarity with the core element of the category, that is, the prototype. Fehr and Russell (1984) were among the first to propose an implementation of this "proto-typical approach" to emotions. Ekman and Cordaro (2011) similarly support this perspective on emotions as categories, though with poorly defined limits, referring to "emotion families." Specifically, they posited that basic emotions should be con-textualized into groups organized around a *central theme* (i.e., exclusive character-istics of a family), while specific *criteria* would define how much a member belongs to a category.

In terms of awe, Keltner and Haidt (2003) offer a prototypical analysis by defin-ing its core features as well as contextual variations. They developed the so-called *prototypical model of awe*. They relied on the idea of awe as an emotion with fuzzy boundaries but with the stable central core of appraisal dimensions. Specifically, awe is characterized by two appraisal dimensions:

(i) *Vastness*: this appraisal dimension refers to the perception of stimuli as percep-tually and/or conceptually vast. Both sweeping views and understanding a com-plex theory (such as theory of relativity) could be counted as potential elicitors of awe.

(ii) *Need for accommodation*: this appraisal dimension refers to altering mental frames or schemas according to new incoming information. For instance, upon understanding Einstein's theory of relativity, one must alter their understanding of both time and space. However, elements of novelty and surprise are also involved with this dimension, as it appears that not all instances of awe require alterations to existing mental schemas.

Additionally, Keltner and Haidt identified five additional emotional themes – often related to the nature of the elicitor of awe – that can "flavor" the experience of awe, giving rise to different awe-related states:

(i) Threat: a fear component can be added to awe when individuals face some-thing perceived as potentially dangerous. This theme would seem to place awe close to the concept of the *sublime*. According to Kant (1790/1914), a key component of the sublime is facing a danger from a safe position, like safely standing on the edge of the Grand Canyon for the first time. This fearful com-ponent of awe was investigated by psychology only recently, showing that fear can indeed be a component of an experience of awe (Gordon et al., 2017).

(ii) Beauty: aesthetically appealing elicitors can introduce a variation in the core theme of awe, thus providing another theme related to this emotion. An exam-ple of an elicitor of this theme might be viewing the ceiling of the Sistine Chapel or the Pyramids of Giza. This component is considered important to the emerging field of aesthetic psychology (Konecni, 2005; Schindler et al., 2017).

(iii) Ability: when we encounter extraordinary examples of talent and ability, the emotion of awe can be accompanied by a feeling of *admiration* (Onu, Kessler,

& Smith, 2016). For instance, listening to a brilliant singer or watching an athlete play might give rise to this theme.

(iv) Virtue: this theme is related to instances of exceptional morality, turning awe into a feeling of *elevation* (Haidt, 2003). For example, reading about the lives of the saints might, for a Catholic individual, give rise to the theme of virtue from acts of charity and devotion to other people.

 (v) Supernatural: this is the least clearly defined theme offered by Keltner and Haidt (2003). This appraisal theme appears in experiences that are perceived to have a religious or spiritual component (Yaden, Le Nguyen, et al., 2016).

All of these additional themes should be considered cultural variations of this emotion, arising secondarily, only after the prototypical features of awe have been established. It is unclear how consistent this part of Keltner and Haidt's (2003) theory is with mainstream emotion theory, though these themes provide interesting avenues for further empirical research.

Researchers often classify awe in several different emotion categories. For instance, awe has been conceived as belonging to the family of *positive emotions*, since it is most often experienced as positively valenced (Campos, Shiota, Keltner, Gonzaga, & Goetz, 2013; Shiota, Campos, & Keltner, 2003; Shiota, Keltner, & John, 2006; Shiota, Keltner, & Mossman, 2007). For instance, research from Sung and Yih (2015) showed the ability of awe to broaden attentive focus in a task where people were required to complete a global-local visual processing task (Kimchi & Palmer, 1982).

Awe has also been classified as a member of the *aesthetic emotion family*. Indeed, awe is considered as similar to the notion of sublime, which usually arises from somewhat threatening stimuli (Konecni, 2005). Although Shiota et al. (2007) demonstrated that only one out of three experiences of awe has any negative valence, this less common negative variant of awe deserves attention due to its different physiological and behavioral outcomes (Gordon et al., 2017).

Awe has additionally been classified as part of the *epistemological emotion* family (Keltner & Haidt, 2003). These emotions arise as responses to shifts in the comprehension of the world. For this reason, it could be labeled an "epistemic state," in that evaluations of the reality of a given perception are altered (Yaden, Le Nguyen, et al., 2016). In this regard, research from Valdesolo and Graham (2014) provided the first account for this still obscure emotional category, which has been difficult to operationalize (Chirico, Yaden, Riva, & Gaggioli, 2016). Keltner and Haidt (2003) captured one proxy of this component, that is, they found that a sense of uncertainty originates from awe-inducing stimuli.

Furthermore, recent findings confirmed awe as a member of the *prosocial emotion family* (Piff et al., 2015; Prade & Saroglou, 2016; Stellar et al., 2017). Awe often results in decreased aggressive attitudes (Yang, Yang, Bao, Liu, & Passmore, 2016) and an enhanced tendency to attend to others' welfare (Stellar et al., 2017). Recent findings demonstrated that this prosocial function was mediated by a sense of self-diminishment called "the small self" (Stellar et al., 2017). This insight led researchers to study the relationship between awe and the emotion of humility

(Kristjánsson, 2017; Stellar et al., 2017). Specifically, both awe and humility share the same propensity for altruism (Stellar et al., 2017).

In sum, awe is elicited by the need to accommodate a perception of vastness and may have certain themes associated with it, depending on the nature of the elicitor. Awe has several features that make it somewhat unusual. While most emotions are either positively or negatively valenced, and though awe is usually positive, it can contain positive and negative components (Gordon et al., 2017). Lastly, in terms of outcomes, awe has been experimentally shown to increase well-being (Rudd, Vohs, & Aaker, 2012) and enhance prosocial behavior (Piff et al., 2015). These outcomes of awe may be crucial to understanding its functions.

What Are the Functions of Awe?

Keltner and Haidt's (2003) view draws, in part, from the functionalist paradigm, which considers emotions in terms of the role they play in facilitating adaptive behavior (Keltner & Gross, 1999; Plutchik, 1980). According to this approach, emotions are considered a result of the interaction between various psychological and physiological systems in order to facilitate a goal-directed response from the organism to a particular set of circumstances (Keltner & Gross, 1999). Construing emotions as functions allows for researchers to understand the links between their subjective components and outcomes (Lench et al., 2015; Lench, Flores, & Bench, 2011). In other words, according to this approach, emotions should be conceived as ways to adapt to survival problems. Therefore, the question posed by this perspective is: what kind of survival problem does awe address?

This chapter presents two potential answers to this question. The first is described by Keltner and Haidt (2003), who posit that awe initially helped to maintain social hierarchy by being elicited by powerful leaders. According to this view, awe arose from the social function of facilitating a subordinate-leader relationship. From the subordinate's perspective, the reaction of fear and respect combined with wonder in front of someone more powerful would strengthen and maintain social hierarchies. The negative or fearful aspects of awe are particularly relevant to this perspective, though this perspective has been somewhat neglected in the research literature (Chirico et al., 2016). Specifically, this view of awe depends on circumstances in which there is a power gradient in the group (Keltner, Gruenfeld, & Anderson, 2003). According to this view, awe acted as a primordial response to displays of power (Keltner & Haidt, 2003) by gathering people around a central dominant figure, thus reinforcing their shared social identity (Keltner & Haidt, 1999). The emotion then became generalized to any form of vastness (even nonsocial kinds), such as sweeping scenery. That is, according to their view, social triggers came before natural ones.

This chapter provides an additional view that awe was a response to nature, and only later did it become attributed to social circumstances. Natural scenery, one's immediate environmental surroundings, was, it should be noted, often a matter of life or death in hunter-gatherer contexts. That is, finding the right place to seek shelter mattered. A theory called "prospect and refuge" (Appleton, 1996) describes the ideal kind of shelter – a location that provides both safety (at least one side protected from attack) and vantage (the ability to see approaching enemies or predators). These conditions are most often fulfilled by elevated locations with a sweeping view of the surrounding area – and this sweeping view of natural scenery happens to be the stereotypical and most prevalent elicitor of awe in contemporary settings (e.g., the Grand Canyon). This view is given some support from research in the field of aesthetics – a study that tested the prospect and refuge theory found a preference in children for sweeping scenery viewed from an elevated position (Fischer & Shrout, 2006). Furthermore, this view fits well with Kant's classic formulation of the sublime – viewing danger from safety (Kant, 1914).

Awe, then, may have been a signal that one is in a safe environment due to having both safety and a good vantage of potential dangers. Awe's association with prosocial behavior makes some sense in this view, as prosocial behavior may be nonadaptive in unsafe environments but adaptive in safe environments. Therefore, the primordial awe may have been first a response to surprisingly safe shelters that allowed for a good vantage of potential approaching enemies, thus creating an ideal context for prosocial behaviors to take place.

Supporting this view, research from the author's lab shows that physical beauty is a much more prevalent elicitor of awe, despite plenty of opportunities for the emotion to arise from dominant others (e.g., bosses; Yaden et al., in press). The social-first view would have to explain how awe initially served a function related to social hierarchy but is now most often triggered by natural beauty. The nature-first view, on the other hand, would predict that the initial elicitors of awe remain the most prevalent, which is the case.

Furthermore, in hunter-gatherer contexts, groups were small enough that most individuals would know one another and would see one another frequently. This fact would make it difficult for the novelty component of awe to arise. Additionally, awe may be unnecessary to maintain social hierarchies as aggression and submission are already deeply ingrained social responses apparent in other mammalian contexts (Sidanius & Pratto, 2001), in species such as rodents, which seem to lack the emotion of awe. A proto version of awe has been arguably observed in primates, however, in response to waterfalls, gusts of wind, and thunder (Goodall, 2005).

Social triggers also elicit awe in humans, but this seems to occur most often in cases where one does not know the individual who is the object of awe. Being "starstruck" by a famous or powerful person is a contemporary example. It may be the case that awe only later came to be elicited by social stimuli when human groups grew large enough that impressive leaders were less known and more imposing due to their unfamiliarity. It might be that when leaders came to be seen as "forces of nature," as it were, or in cases in which individuals were able to project an exaggerated impression of power, that social circumstances induced intense experiences of awe.

However, the social-first view emphasizes the role that awe may play in learning. According to this view, awe facilitates faster learning due to the social hierarchy that it maintains. The nature-first view does not address this aspect, nor does it make sense of the need for accommodation appraisal dimension. Further analyses on the functions of awe are needed.

The Self-Transcendent and Transformative Aspects of Awe

Regardless of the true *primum movens* of awe, this emotion has important social consequences. In particular, awe has a self-transcendent quality in that it decreases self-salience and increases feelings of connectedness to other people and has been empirically demonstrated to cause increased prosocial behavior (Piff et al., 2015).

More specifically, awe was classed as a "variety of self-transcendent experience" (Yaden, Haidt, et al., 2017), which also includes the constructs of flow (Chirico, Serino, Cipresso, Gaggioli, & Riva, 2015; Csíkszentmihályi, 1990), mindfulness (Kabat-Zinn, 2003), other self-transcendent positive emotions (Van Cappellen, Saroglou, Iweins, Piovesana, & Fredrickson 2013), peak experiences (Maslow & Pi, 1964), and mystical experiences (Hood, 1975; Yaden et al., 2015). Each of these mental states shares a self-transcendent quality (though they are quite different in many other ways), and each of them is associated with well-being (Yaden, Haidt, et al., 2017).

The self-transcendent quality may exist on a spectrum of intensity, referred to as the *unitary continuum* (Yaden, Haidt, et al., 2017). Mystical experiences are at the far end of this spectrum, as these experiences can include feelings of complete oneness with other people and environment. Empirical research on mystical experiences elicited by psychedelic substances, for example, has shown that these experiences are associated with increased well-being that can last for over a year (Griffiths Richards, Johnson, McCann, & Jesse, 2008; Griffiths, Richards, McCann, & Jesse, 2006; Yaden, Le Nguyen, et al., 2017). Furthermore, mystical experiences are sometimes rated among life's most meaningful moments. In the Griffiths et al. (2006) study, two-thirds of the sample rated their experience in the top five most meaningful moments of their life. This raises the possibility that sufficiently intense awe experiences also may result in lasting enhancements to well-being and, in some cases, could even be counted as transformative.

While it is less clear why this would be the case from a functionalist perspective, awe appears capable of being transformative. Transformative changes are deep, radical, and enduring changes (Gaggioli, 2016). In other words, after such an experience, one is never quite the same – or one at least evaluates oneself as forever changed. These experiences affect the way people perceive themselves and the surrounding world, thus acting as potential drivers of a personal transformative change (Gaggioli, 2016; Gaggioli, Chirico, Triberti, & Riva, 2016). The conversion of Saint Paul on the road to Damascus – when Paul, a Christian persecutor, fell down from his horse while hearing the voice of God on him and saw a blinding light – is a paradigmatic case of transformation. A number of researchers have discussed transformative experiences; Schneider dedicated his work to present six stories on personal change (Schneider, 2009). Pearsall (2007) devoted a book to describe his personal experience of transformation occurring after the death of his son. Regarding the transformative nature of awe, Pearsall stated:

> True awe raises more questions than it does answers and challenges faith more than confirms it... Awe is when life grants us the chance to think differently and deeper about itself, so that we are not left squandering its gift by languishing it away. Being in awe can make a real mess of our lives by disrupting our certainty about ourselves and the world, but it also enlivens and invigorates our living and can change how we decide to live. (p. xviii).

Maslow also identified awe as a core moment in the process of change or as the spark to initiate transformation (Chirico et al., 2016; Maslow, 1962). These cases may occur when intense feelings of awe result in a need to accommodate many of one's mental structures or schemas. It may be that under certain circumstances the need for accommodation results in changes to one's sense of self. In other words, the need for accommodation might make the experience of awe extremely pertinent to an individual to the extent that it can affect her or his identity. Therefore, awe's transformative function can, perhaps, trigger a restructuring of individuals' inner world at the most intimate level.

Eliciting Intense Awe Experiences in Experimental Settings

Despite the potential to study self-transcendence and even personal transformations resulting from awe, researchers usually focus on instances of awe that are somewhat more subtle in order to fit the constraints of an experimental setting (Chirico et al., 2016). Silvia, Fayn, Nusbaum, and Beaty (2015) highlighted the difficulty of inducing high-intensity experiences of awe in the lab. Silvia et al. (2015) described the gap between awe captured in qualitative reports and the operationalization of awe in controlled settings. Moreover, they suggested a possible solution to this issue, calling for researchers to look for "Other methods and traditions to place the findings from low-intensity and small-scale lab research in context (Silvia et al., 2015, p. 382).

There are a few popular methods for inducing awe in experimental settings. The first is watching videos that induce awe (e.g., Piff et al., 2015). The next, somewhat less effective method, is to use awe-inspiring images (e.g., Shiota, Neufeld, Yeung, Moser, & Perea, 2011). Other labs have asked participants to recall and write about awe experiences (e.g., Griskevicius, Shiota, & Neufeld, 2010). Keltner's lab has had some success with bringing participants to scenic settings to look at California Oaks (Piff et al., 2015) or to a museum to see dinosaur bones on display (Shiota et al., 2007).

The authors' research groups responded to the call by Silvia et al. (2015) to look beyond conventional methods to induce awe, in order to create a more intense version of it in lab settings. After analyzing the issue, the lab rephrased the issue posed by Silvia. In methodological terms, their call can be viewed as attaining ecological validity. Therefore, attention was oriented toward innovative methods able to ensure a high degree of ecological validity despite the complexity of the target experience of awe. A search of the available emotion-induction methods showed virtual reality (VR) as a new method that is effectively able to induce the multifaceted and intense emotional experience of awe even in highly controlled laboratory settings (Parsons, 2015).

VR is a simulative technology able to generate the feeling of being present within a virtual environment, as if it were real. Specifically, users can have a certain degree of control in the virtual environment by navigating inside it, exploring it, manipulating virtual objects, or interacting with virtual agents (Triberti & Chirico, 2016; Parsons, 2015; North & North, 2016; Riva, 2005; Riva et al., 2016). VR technology makes this possible by integrating different tools such as head tracking, controllers (e.g., joystick), different types of displays (2D, 360° field of view), and stimulations (i.e., visual, auditory, haptic). These features allow VR to reproduce complex instances of emotional experiences while preserving a high degree of experimental control. Moreover, it is possible to change specific aspects of a scenario, analyzing the subsequent impact on users' experience.

Besides these technical aspects, VR can provide additional assets for the study of emotions more generally. VR can enhance the intensity of emotional states through a peculiar experience called "presence," i.e., the sense of "being there" in a virtual or real environment along with the ability to pursue personal intentions within it (Riva & Waterworth, 2003, 2014; Waterworth, Waterworth, Mantovani, & Riva, 2010; Waterworth, Waterworth, Riva, & Mantovani, 2015). Moreover, through VR, it is possible to recreate almost any kind of experience, including those violating laws of physics (e.g., Ritter et al., 2012) and emotionally complex ones (e.g., Chirico, Ferrise, Cordella, & Gaggioli, 2018).

Recent perspectives on the design of emotional experiences (Triberti, Chirico, La Rocca, & Riva, 2017) proposed appraisal themes of complex emotions as design guidelines for the development of both virtual and real environments. A basic implementation of this approach in the field of awe was provided by Chirico et al. (2017), in which the vastness appraisal dimension of awe was manipulated by changing users' field of view in a virtual environment. Users had the possibility to explore a static awe-inspiring (i.e., a view of tall trees) or neutral environment (i.e., hens wandering) either on a 2D or 360° format. In other words, participants could observe emotional scenarios as if they were in a normal cinema with a 2D monitor (i.e., watching tall trees from a distance) or as if they were truly "in" the scene (i.e., in a forest surrounded by tall trees). In this case, the dimension of presence (i.e., "the physical extent of the sensorial information"; Coelho, Tichon, Hine, Wallis, & Riva, 2006, p. 29) was manipulated by means of changing the technological features of the medium. Self-report assessments and psychophysiological measures of awe showed that induced awe was more intense when elicited by 360° virtual scenarios. This approach supports the need to "design" experiences of awe in the lab to simulate natural experiences and suggests that VR is a promising tool to pursue this goal.

Conclusion

Since Keltner and Haidt's (2003) article introducing awe to mainstream emotion research, the emotion of awe has received empirical attention elaborating its triggers, subjective qualities, and outcomes. Awe has been shown to be complex, both in terms of its mix of positive and negative valence and its capacity to alter the senses of time, space, and self. The functions of awe are still unclear but may be most related to its capacity to enhance social connectedness. The theoretical debate of whether awe's function first arose out of social hierarchy dynamics and was later elicited by natural scenery, or whether it was initially a signal of an environment offering safety and a sweeping vantage (i.e., prospect and refuge) and was later triggered by impressive leaders, is worthy of further discussion from the functionalist perspective. Moreover, the self-transcendent and transformational aspects of this emotion deserve more empirical attention. Lastly, new means to elicit awe are becoming available, such as VR. Going forward, more ecologically valid studies will provide answers to the many open questions still surrounding the emotion of awe.

References

Appleton, J. (1996). *The experience of landscape*. Chichester, England: Wiley.

Campos, B., Shiota, M. N., Keltner, D., Gonzaga, G. C., & Goetz, J. L. (2013). What is shared, what is different? Core relational themes and expressive displays of eight positive emotions. *Cognition and Emotion, 27*, 37–52.

Chirico, A., Cipresso, P., Yaden, D. B., Biassoni, F., Riva, G., & Gaggioli, A. (2017). Effectiveness of immersive videos in inducing awe: An experimental study. *Scientific Reports, 7*, 1218. https://doi.org/10.1038/s41598-017-01242-0

Chirico, A., Ferrise, F., Cordella, L., & Gaggioli, A. (2018). Designing awe in virtual reality: An experimental study. *Frontiers in Psycholology, 8*, 2351.

Chirico, A., Serino, S., Cipresso, P., Gaggioli, A., & Riva, G. (2015). When music "flows". State and trait in musical performance, composition and listening: A systematic review. *Frontiers in Psychology, 6*. https://doi.org/10.3389/fpsyg.2015.00906

Chirico, A., Yaden, D., Riva, G., & Gaggioli, A. (2016). The potential of virtual reality for the investigation of awe. *Frontiers in Psychology, 7*. https://doi.org/10.3389/fpsyg.2016.01766

Coelho, C., Tichon, J., Hine, T. J., Wallis, G., & Riva, G. (2006). Media presence and inner presence: The sense of presence in virtual reality technologies. In *From communication to presence: Cognition, emotions and culture towards the ultimate communicative experience* (pp. 25–45). IOS Press, Amsterdam.

Csíkszentmihályi, M. (1990). *Flow: The psychology of optimal experience*. New York, NY: Harper Collins.

Ekman, P. (1992). An argument for basic emotions. *Cognition and Emotion, 6*, 169–200.

Ekman, P., & Cordaro, D. (2011). What is meant by calling emotions basic. *Emotion Review, 3*, 364–370.

Fehr, B., & Russell, J. A. (1984). Concept of emotion viewed from a prototype perspective. *Journal of Experimental Psychology: General, 113*, 464–486.

Fischer, M. A., & Shrout, P. E. (2006). Children's liking of landscape paintings as a function of their perceptions of prospect, refuge, and hazard. *Environment and Behavior, 38*, 373–393.

Gaggioli, A. (2016). Transformative experience design. In A. Gaggioli, A. Ferscha, G. Riva, S. Dunne, & I. Viaud-Delmon (Eds.), *Human computer confluence: Transforming human experience through symbiotic technologies* (pp. 96–121). Berlin: De Gruyter Open.

Gaggioli, A., Chirico, A., Triberti, S., & Riva, G. (2016). Transformative interactions: Designing positive technologies to foster self-transcendence and meaning. *Annual Review of Cybertherapy and Telemedicine, 14*, 169–175.

Griffiths, R. R., Richards, W. A., Johnson, M. W., McCann, U. D., & Jesse, R. (2008). Mystical-type experiences occasioned by psilocybin mediate the attribution of personal meaning and spiritual significance 14 months later. *Journal of Psychopharmacology, 22*, 621–632.

Griffiths, R. R., Richards, W. A., McCann, U., & Jesse, R. (2006). Psilocybin can occasion mystical-type experiences having substantial and sustained personal meaning and spiritual significance. *Psychopharmacology, 187*, 268–283.

Griskevicius, V., Shiota, M. N., & Neufeld, S. L. (2010). Influence of different positive emotions on persuasion processing: A functional evolutionary approach. *Emotion, 10*, 190–206.

Goodall, J. (2005). Primate spirituality. *Encyclopedia of religion and nature* 1303–1306.

Gordon, A. M., Stellar, J. E., Anderson, C. L., McNeil, G. D., Loew, D., & Keltner, D. (2017). The dark side of the sublime: Distinguishing a threat-based variant of awe. *Journal of Personality and Social Psychology, 113*, 310–328.

Haidt, J. (2003). Elevation and the positive psychology of morality. In C. L. Keyes & J. Haidt (Eds.), *Flourishing: Positive psychology and the life well-lived* (pp. 275–289). Washington, DC: American Psychological Association.

Hood, R. W., Jr. (1975). The construction and preliminary validation of a measure of reported mystical experience. *Journal for the Scientific Study of Religion, 14*, 29–41.

Kabat-Zinn, J. (2003). Mindfulness-based interventions in context: Past, present, and future. *Clinical Psychology: Science and Practice, 10*, 144–156.

Kant, I. (1914). *Kant's critique of judgement* (rev. J. H. Bernard, Trans.). New York, NY: Macmillan (Original work published 1790).

Keltner, D., & Gross, J. J. (1999). Functional accounts of emotions. *Cognition and Emotion, 13*, 467–480.

Keltner, D., Gruenfeld, D. H., & Anderson, C. (2003). Power, approach, and inhibition. *Psychological Review, 110*, 265–284.

Keltner, D., & Haidt, J. (1999). Social functions of emotions at four levels of analysis. *Cognition and Emotion, 13*, 505–521.

Keltner, D., & Haidt, J. (2003). Approaching awe, a moral, spiritual, and aesthetic emotion. *Cognition and Emotion, 17*, 297–314.

Kimchi, R., & Palmer, S. E. (1982). Form and texture in hierarchically constructed patterns. *Journal of Experimental Psychology: Human Perception and Performance, 8*, 521–535.

Konecni, V. J. (2005). The aesthetic trinity: Awe, being moved, thrills. *Bulletin of Psychology and the Arts, 5*, 27–44.

Kristjánsson, K. (2017). Awe: An Aristotelian analysis of a non-Aristotelian virtuous emotion. *Philosophia, 45*, 125–142.

Lazarus, R. S. (1991). *Emotion and adaptation.* Oxford, England: Oxford University Press.

Lench, H. C., Bench, S. W., Darbor, K. E., & Moore, M. (2015). A functionalist manifesto: Goal-related emotions from an evolutionary perspective. *Emotion Review, 7*, 90–98.

Lench, H. C., Flores, S. A., & Bench, S. W. (2011). Discrete emotions predict changes in cognition, judgment, experience, behavior, and physiology: A meta-analysis of experimental emotion elicitations. *Psychological Bulletin, 137*, 834–855.

Margolis, E., & Laurence, S. (1999). *Concepts: Core readings.* Cambridge, MA: MIT Press.

Maslow, A. H. (1962). Lessons from the peak-experiences. *Journal of Humanistic Psychology, 2*, 9–18.

Maslow, A. H., & Pi, K. D. (1964). *Religions, values, and peak-experiences.* Columbus, OH: Ohio State University Press. Columbus, Ohio.

North, M. M., & North, S. M. (2016). Virtual reality therapy. In J. Luiselli & A. Fischer (Eds.), *Computer-assisted and web-based innovations in psychology, special education, and health* (pp. 141–156). Oxford, England: Academic.

Onu, D., Kessler, T., & Smith, J. R. (2016). Admiration: A conceptual review. *Emotion Review, 8,* 218–230.

Parsons, T. D. (2015). Virtual reality for enhanced ecological validity and experimental control in the clinical, affective and social neurosciences. *Frontiers in Human Neuroscience, 9.* https:// doi.org/10.3389/fnhum.2015.00660

Pearsall, P. (2007). *Awe: The delights and dangers of our eleventh emotion.* Deerfield Beach, FL: Health Communications, Inc.

Piff, P. K., Dietze, P., Feinberg, M., Stancato, D. M., & Keltner, D. (2015). Awe, the small self, and prosocial behavior. *Journal of Personality and Social Psychology, 108,* 883–899.

Plutchik, R. (1980). A general psychoevolutioanry theory of emotion. In R. Plutchik & H. Kellerman (Eds.), *Emotion: Theory, research, and experience: Theories of emotion* (pp. 3–33). New York, NY: Academic.

Prade, C., & Saroglou, V. (2016). Awe's effects on generosity and helping. *The Journal of Positive Psychology, 11,* 522–530.

Ritter, S. M., Damian, R. I., Simonton, D. K., van Baaren, R. B., Strick, M., Derks, J., & Dijksterhuis, A. (2012). Diversifying experiences enhance cognitive flexibility. *Journal of Experimental Social Psychology, 48,* 961–964.

Riva, G. (2005). Virtual reality in psychotherapy: Review. *Cyberpsychology & Behavior, 8,* 220–230.

Riva, G., Villani, D., Cipresso, P., Repetto, C., Triberti, S., Di Lernia, D., … Gaggioli, A. (2016). Positive and transformative technologies for active ageing. *Studies in Health Technology and Informatics, 220,* 308–315.

Riva, G., & Waterworth, J. A. (2003). Presence and the self: A cognitive neuroscience approach. *Presence Connect, 3*(3.) Retrieved from: http://www8.informatik.umu.se/~jwworth/Riva-Waterworth.htm

Riva, G., & Waterworth, J. A. (2014). Being present in a virtual world. In M. Grinshaw (Ed.), *The oxford handbook of virtuality* (pp. 205–221). Oxford, England: Oxford University Press.

Rosch, E. (1983). Prototype classification and logical classification: The two systems. In E. K. Scholnick (Ed.), *New trends in conceptual representation: Challenges to Piaget's theory* (pp. 73–86). Hillsdale, NJ: Erlbaum.

Rudd, M., Vohs, K. D., & Aaker, J. (2012). Awe expands people's perception of time, alters decision making, and enhances well-being. *Psychological Science, 23,* 1130–1136.

Schindler, I., Hosoya, G., Menninghaus, W., Beermann, U., Wagner, V., Eid, M., & Scherer, K. R. (2017). Measuring aesthetic emotions: A review of the literature and a new assessment tool. *PLoS One, 12,* e0178899.

Schneider, K. J. (2009). *Awakening to awe: Personal stories of profound transformation.* Plymouth, England: Jason Aronson.

Shiota, M. N., Campos, B., & Keltner, D. (2003). The faces of positive emotion. *Annals of the New York Academy of Sciences, 1000,* 296–299.

Shiota, M. N., Keltner, D., & John, O. P. (2006). Positive emotion dispositions differentially associated with Big Five personality and attachment style. *The Journal of Positive Psychology, 1,* 61–71.

Shiota, M. N., Keltner, D., & Mossman, A. (2007). The nature of awe: Elicitors, appraisals, and effects on self-concept. *Cognition and Emotion, 21,* 944–963.

Shiota, M. N., Neufeld, S. L., Yeung, W. H., Moser, S. E., & Perea, E. F. (2011). Feeling good: Autonomic nervous system responding in five positive emotions. *Emotion, 11,* 1368–1378.

Sidanius, J., & Pratto, F. (2001). *Social dominance: An intergroup theory of social hierarchy and oppression.* Cambridge, England: Cambridge University Press.

Silvia, P. J., Fayn, K., Nusbaum, E. C., & Beaty, R. E. (2015). Openness to experience and awe in response to nature and music: Personality and profound aesthetic experiences. *Psychology of Aesthetics, Creativity, and the Arts, 9,* 376–384.

Stellar, J. E., Gordon, A. M., Piff, P. K., Cordaro, D., Anderson, C. L., Bai, Y., … Keltner, D. (2017). Self-transcendent emotions and their social functions: Compassion, gratitude, and awe bind us to others through prosociality. *Emotion Review, 9*, 200–207.

Sung, B., & Yih, J. (2015). Does interest broaden or narrow attentional scope? *Cognition and Emotion, 30*, 1485–1494.

Triberti, S., & Chirico, A. (2016). Healthy avatars, healthy people: Care engagement through. In G. Griffigna (Ed.), *Transformative healthcare practice through patient engagement*, Hershey, PA: IGI Global (pp. 247–275). doi: https://doi.org/10.4018/978-1-5225-0663-8.ch010.

Triberti, S., Chirico, A., La Rocca, G., & Riva, G. (2017). Developing emotional design: Emotions as cognitive processes and their role in the design of interactive technologies. *Frontiers in Psychology, 8*, 1773.

Valdesolo, P., & Graham, J. (2014). Awe, uncertainty, and agency detection. *Psychological Science, 25*, 170–178.

Van Cappellen, P., Saroglou, V., Iweins, C., Piovesana, M., & Fredrickson, B. L. (2013). Self-transcendent positive emotions increase spirituality through basic world assumptions. *Cognition and Emotion, 27*, 1378–1394.

Waterworth, J. A., Waterworth, E. L., Mantovani, F., & Riva, G. (2010). On feeling (the) present. *Journal of Consciousness Studies, 17*, 167–188.

Waterworth, J. A., Waterworth, E. L., Riva, G., & Mantovani, F. (2015). Presence: Form, content and consciousness. In B. F. Lombard, M. Freeman, J. IJsselsteijn, & W. Schaevitz (Eds.), *Immersed in media: Telepresence theory, measurement & technology* (pp. 35–58). Berlin: Springer.

Yaden, D. B., Eichstaedt, J. C., Schwartz, H. A., Kern, M. L., Le Nguyen, K. D., Wintering, N. A., … Newberg, A. B. (2015). The language of ineffability: Linguistic analysis of mystical experiences. *Psychology of Religion and Spirituality, 8*, 244–252.

Yaden, D. B., Haidt, J., Hood, R. W., Jr., Vago, D. R., & Newberg, A. B. (2017). The varieties of self-transcendent experience. *Review of General Psychology, 21*, 143–160.

Yaden, D. B., Iwry, J., Slack, K. J., Eichstaedt, J. C., Zhao, Y., Vaillant, G. E., & Newberg, A. B. (2016). The overview effect: Awe and self-transcendent experience in space flight. *Psychology of Consciousness: Theory, Research, and Practice, 3*, 1.

Yaden, D. B., Kaufman, Hyde, Chirico, Gaggioli, Zhang, & Keltner. (in press). The awe experience scale (AWE-S): A multifactorial measure for a complex emotion.

Yaden, D. B., Le Nguyen, K. D., Kern, M. L., Belser, A. B., Eichstaedt, J. C., Iwry, J., … Newberg, A. B. (2017). Of roots and fruits: A comparison of psychedelic and nonpsychedelic mystical experiences. *Journal of Humanistic Psychology, 57*, 338–353.

Yaden, D. B., Le Nguyen, K. D., Kern, M. L., Wintering, N. A., Eichstaedt, J. C., Schwartz, H. A., … Newberg, A. B. (2016). The noetic quality: A multimethod exploratory study. *Psychology of Consciousness: Theory, Research, and Practice, 4*, 54–62.

Yang, Y., Yang, Z., Bao, T., Liu, Y., & Passmore, H.-A. (2016). Elicited awe decreases aggression. *Journal of Pacific Rim Psychology, 10*, 1–13.

Chapter 12
Emotions of Excellence: Communal and Agentic Functions of Pride, Moral Elevation, and Admiration

Lisa A. Williams

Abstract Excellence is a potent emotional elicitor. When it is oneself that achieves excellence, pride can arise. When another person achieves excellence, moral elevation and admiration can arise. This trio of "emotions of excellence" serves both communal and agentic functions. This chapter reviews these functions as well as how such functions might play out in one example context – the workplace – and concludes by outlining paths for future research, highlighting the need for integrative work across emotions and across functions as well as the application of new technologies to this intriguing area of research.

> Interdependence is and ought to be as much the ideal of man as self-sufficiency. Man is a social being.
>
> –Mahatma Gandhi

Gandhi points out two ways of acting in social life: acting in a way that benefits the self and acting in a way that benefits one's relationships. This delineation echoes a dominant theme in social psychology: individuals must balance needs to "get ahead" (i.e., pursue agentic outcomes) and "get along" (i.e., pursue communal outcomes). Navigating the cooperation and competition between these two motives lies at the heart of adaptive social functioning.

Work in affective science has revealed that emotions provide a mechanism via which individuals might make contextually appropriate choices to pursue getting ahead and/or getting along. This chapter focuses on a key context in which such opportunities arise: excellence of the self or of others. Specifically, it outlines a view of how pride, moral elevation, and admiration serve both communal and agentic functions. In addition to reviewing supportive empirical evidence regarding agentic and communal functions of these three emotions, this chapter highlights how these emotions and their functions might play out in one example context – the workplace.

L. A. Williams (✉)
School of Psychology, University of New South Wales, Sydney, NSW, Australia
e-mail: lwilliams@unsw.edu.au

© Springer International Publishing AG, part of Springer Nature 2018   235
H. C. Lench (ed.), *The Function of Emotions*,
https://doi.org/10.1007/978-3-319-77619-4_12

The chapter concludes by outlining paths for future research, highlighting the need for research that integrates across emotions and across functions, as well as the application of new technologies to this intriguing area of research.

Getting Along and Getting Ahead: Core Demands of Social Life

The emergence of human societal structures required not only meeting basic survival needs but also successfully navigating the social environment. One popular theoretical approach in the study of social needs is to consider drives to get along and to get ahead (Locke, 2015). With its roots in work by Bakan (1966) and Hogan (1982), this delineation has had substantial staying power in social and personality psychology (Abele & Wojciszke, 2014; Fiske, Cuddy, & Glick, 2007; Horowitz et al., 2006; McAdams, 1988; Trapnell & Paulhus, 2012). Emphasizing their ubiquitous nature, this pair of needs has been referred to as "life's recurring challenges" (Ybarra et al., 2008).

Communion lies at the relational core of human sociality. The need to "get along" relates not only to requirements to connect with and be accepted by others (Baumeister & Leary, 1995) but also to behave in ways consistent with social and moral norms (Bicchieri, 2005; Harms & Skyrms, 2008). Reflecting this dual nature, Abele et al. (2016) argue that communion comprises two sub-facets: interpersonal warmth and morality. Ybarra et al. (2008) point out that communion is a persistent need that does not vary according to situation or person, due to the negative consequences of being socially rejected (see DeWall & Bushman, 2011, for a review).

Agency, or the need to "get ahead," is centered around acquisition and demonstration of skills, both of which contribute to status attainment. A sub-facet approach is also relevant here, with agency comprising both competence (serving skill attainment) and assertiveness (serving skill recognition by others; Abele et al., 2016). Ybarra et al. (2008) put forth a compelling case that, while communion can be expected among all group members at all times, agency might be more contextually constrained, limited to those who need or have a skill and to situations in which that skill is relevant.

Adaptive functioning requires a balance between pursuit of getting ahead and getting along. Indeed, pursuing one at the expense of the other (i.e., unmitigated agency or unmitigated communion) brings along a suite of deleterious outcomes (e.g., Helgeson & Fritz, 1999). Moreover, it is of critical import for individuals to recognize when opportunities to get ahead and get along arise. Herein lies an adaptive challenge that emotions might help resolve. In a given context that provides an opportunity to get along or to get ahead, might emotions help cue individuals to those contexts and shape thoughts and behaviors in an adaptive manner (i.e., in a manner that takes advantage of that opportunity)?

This chapter focuses on one particular context in which achieving this balance might be required: the achievement of excellence. Excellence of the self is the prototypical eliciting context of pride. Excellence of others can give rise to admiration (in cases of skill-based excellence) and moral elevation (in cases of morality-based excellence). The chapter advances the argument that excellence contexts provide the opportunity to get along and get ahead – an opportunity that is cued by and indeed realized by the positive emotions of pride, admiration, and moral elevation.

Getting Along and Getting Ahead in the Face of Excellence: The Role of Emotion

Before proceeding, a definition of "excellence" is in order. Psychologists, philosophers, and practitioners might each have their own definitions of excellence. However, the Oxford English Dictionary provides a useful inclusive definition: excellence is "the possession chiefly of good qualities in an eminent or unusual degree; surpassing merit, skill, virtue, worth, etc." This definition aptly highlights both skill and virtue as contributors to excellence. While the definition itself is agnostic with regard to the agent of excellence, it can be useful to identify the agent, especially as it relates to the question of how positive emotions shape functional outcomes in excellence contexts. Specifically, excellence of the self can prompt pride, and excellence of others can prompt moral elevation (for virtue) and admiration (for skill).

It is worth noting that these three emotions fit within the broader class of positive emotions. Fredrickson's (2001, 2013) influential broaden-and-build theory provides a guiding framework for how positive emotions as a class serve adaptive outcomes. Specifically, according to the theory, positive emotions assist individuals to broaden their attention and build resources. The broaden-and-build approach also highlights the role that positive emotions can play in producing an "upward spiral," in which positive emotional experience brings about adaptive outcomes that further the experience of positive emotions (e.g., Fredrickson & Joiner, 2002). Some of these outcomes can be aligned with "getting along," such as garnering social support (Fredrickson, Cohn, Coffey, Pek, & Finkel, 2008) and reduction of group-based biases (Johnson & Fredrickson, 2005), or with "getting ahead," such as goal attainment (Wong, Tschan, Messerli, & Semmer, 2013). However, as revealed below, reflecting on the discrete nature of pride, moral elevation, and admiration affords a careful consideration of how they might cue and function in excellence-based contexts.

Evidence is reviewed below that speaks to how pride, moral elevation, and admiration promote functional outcomes in the service of getting ahead and getting along. Note that the aim of this review is not to be exhaustive, but rather illustrative, highlighting how the communion/agency framework provides a guiding structure for understanding functions of these emotions in social space. Where relevant, the text highlights functions that stem from both experiencing and expressing the emotion in question.

Excellence of the Self: A Context for Pride

Pride is commonly felt upon achievement of a socially valued outcome (Mascolo & Fischer, 1995). Compelling evidence suggests that pride is communicated by a suite of nonverbal behaviors (e.g., a small smile, expanded posture, raised chin; Tracy & Matsumoto, 2008; Tracy & Robins, 2007a). Highlighting its agentic and communal functions, pride has been classed among self-conscious emotions (Tracy, Robins, & Tangney, 2007) as well as moral emotions (Tangney, Stuewig, & Mashek, 2007).

Before proceeding, it is worth noting the theoretical distinction between authentic and hubristic pride (e.g., Tracy & Robins, 2007b; cf. Williams & DeSteno, 2010). For the purposes of this chapter, focus will be placed on social functions of authentic forms of pride, that is, pride that stems from tangible achievement. By and large, authentic pride is held to be the more adaptive of the two forms of pride (Tracy & Robins, 2007c). In the case that reviewed research differentiated between authentic and hubristic pride, findings are noted that relate to authentic forms.

Given its eliciting context, it is clear that the experience of pride might alert an individual to the fact that they have achieved excellence. The functions of this emotion extend beyond this cuing role, however, to shaping behaviors that serve needs to get ahead and get along.

Getting ahead Pride's role in facilitating agentic outcomes is robustly supported by empirical research. Work by Jessica Tracy and colleagues (see Martens, Tracy, & Shariff, 2011, for a review) has underscored the central relationship between pride and high status (see also Weisfeld & Dillon, 2012, for an account linking pride to dominance). For instance, pride and high status are associated conceptually at an implicit level (Shariff & Tracy, 2009; Shariff, Tracy, & Markusoff, 2012). Further, individuals displaying (authentic) pride expressions are rated as higher in prestige-based status than individuals displaying a neutral expression (Williams & Godwin, 2018), though the degree to which pride expressions elicit high explicit status appears to be moderated by culture (Tracy, Shariff, Zhao, & Henrich, 2013).

The link between pride and high status is not surprising in light of goal-related behaviors that are prompted by the experience of this emotion. Put succinctly, pride promotes goal-related action consistent with agentic motives. For instance, in the first empirical study of behavioral outcomes of pride, participants led to feel pride via social acclaim persevered longer in working on a goal-related task than participants in a neutral condition, in a positive mood comparison condition, and a heightened self-efficacy condition (Williams & DeSteno, 2008). Other work links pride with performance boosts (Herrald & Tomaka, 2002). Further underscoring links between pride and goal pursuit, trait-level (authentic) pride is associated with constructs related to goal engagement (Carver, Sinclair, & Johnson, 2010), intrinsic motivation (Damian & Robins, 2013; Mack, Kouali, Gilchrist, & Sabiston, 2015), and self-control (Hofmann & Fisher, 2012; cf. Wilcox, Kramer, & Sen, 2011). Recent research suggests that such links may be moderated by achievement-related appraisals and activation of a self-regulatory goal (Salerno, Laran, & Janiszewski, 2015). In fact, the experience of pride may undermine temporal choice self-control, as has been observed among children engaging in delay of gratification tasks (Shimoni, Asbe, Eyal, & Berger, 2016).

Agentic motives activated by pride carry into the interpersonal domain. For instance, following prior successful performance on a related task, proud individuals demonstrate leadership behaviors (and are subsequently more liked) in a group task (Williams & DeSteno, 2009). Martens and Tracy (2012) established that participants are more likely to copy answers from individuals expressing pride relative to individuals expressing neutrality, happiness, and shame. Further corroborating this link, Horberg, Kraus, and Keltner (2013) demonstrated that perceivers infer pride expressers as more self-interested and oriented toward merit-based resource distributions, which – given a proud individual's prior success – should lead to heightened status via resource attainment.

Getting along Pride can also prompt communal outcomes, at least in terms of morality. The link between pride and morality is sensible, given that achievements that give rise to pride can of course be moral in nature. Indeed, engaging in blood donation (Masser, Smith, & Williams, 2014) and volunteering (Boezeman & Ellemers, 2007, 2008) are known contexts in which pride is experienced. As such, goal-reinforcing functions of pride would serve to increase the likelihood of future prosocial behavior. In line with this, trait-level (authentic) pride positively predicts moral behavior (Bureau, Vallerand, Ntoumanis, & Lafrenière, 2013; Krettenauer & Casey, 2015). State-level (authentic) pride elicits selfless moral behavior but only among those high in moral identity (Sanders, Wisse, Van Yperen, & Rus, 2018). Even thinking about another situation that might elicit pride leads individuals to act more cooperatively in a resource dilemma game (Dorfman, Eyal, & Bereby-Meyer, 2014).

Morality-enforcing aspects of pride appear to be particularly important across childhood development (Hart & Matsuba, 2007). At least one reason that children opt to act morally is in anticipation of resulting pride from doing so (Krettenauer & Jia, 2013; Krettenauer, Jia, & Mosleh, 2011). Further, pride stemming from prior moral action reinforces intentions to behave prosocially in the future among adolescents (Etxebarria, Ortiz, Apodaca, Pascual, & Conejero, 2015). Other work suggests important moderators of moral pride in adolescents, including the degree to which acting morally requires personal effort and/or going against one's group (Etxebarria, Ortiz, Apodaca, Pascual, & Conejero, 2014).

Consistent with these behavioral outcomes, individuals expressing pride are perceived to be more prosocial. For instance, after reading a verbal statement from another player that communicated (authentic) pride, participants inferred that the player had taken fewer resources from a common pool (Wubben, De Cremer, & van Dijk, 2012). Note, however, that felt pride appears to heighten competitiveness and dominance in negotiation settings (Butt & Choi, 2006; Butt, Choi, & Jaeger, 2005), so there may exist a gap between perceived behaviors associated with pride in such settings and those that actually ensue (see also van der Schalk, Kuppens, Bruder, & Manstead, 2015, Study 1, for null results of pride expressions).

Whether pride might promote functional outcomes within the warmth facet of communion is subject to debate. Whereas the experience of pride has been shown to undermine social orienting behaviors, including mimicry (Dickens & DeSteno, 2014), it also appears to reduce prejudice and discrimination, at least in its authentic form (Ashton-James & Tracy, 2012). Other work suggests that affiliation-promoting outcomes of pride may depend on the target: proud individuals perceive more identity overlap with strong individuals but less identity overlap with weak individuals (Oveis, Horberg, & Keltner, 2010). An important caveat of this work is that pride in these studies is not tied to moral excellence. It may very well be the case that pride stemming from prior moral excellence prompts outcomes associated with communal warmth.

Pride: a summary   The weight of evidence for pride's social-functional outcomes rests in promoting agency. Characterization of pride as "the fundamental emotion of success, power, and status" (Tracy, Weidman, Cheng, & Martens, 2012) is fitting. However, as reviewed above, pride also serves to cue individuals to communal opportunities, at least in the moral domain. Thus, pride serves to advance outcomes that resolve both the need to get along and get ahead in contexts of excellence of the self.

Excellence of Others: A Context for Moral Elevation and Admiration

Positive emotions can arise in response to excellence of others. Seminal work in this area highlighted key differences between moral elevation, which arises from witnessing others' excellence in virtue, and admiration, which arises from witnessing others' excellence in skill (Algoe & Haidt, 2009). In the years since, research has provided deep insight into functions of these emotions (see Onu, Kessler, & Smith, 2016; Pohling & Diessner, 2016; Thomson & Siegel, 2017, for reviews).

Before reviewing empirical evidence that speaks to communal and agentic functions of these two emotions, it is worth noting that moral elevation and admiration exist within a network of several related states. For instance, some researchers differentiate admiration from "adoration" (Schindler, Paech, & Löwenbrück, 2015; Schindler, Zink, Windrich, & Menninghaus, 2013), whereas others discuss broader concepts that might subsume these states, such as "reverence" (Ai, Wink, Gall, Dillon, & Tice, 2017) and being "moved" (Schubert, Zickfeld, Seibt, & Fiske, 2018; Seibt, Schubert, Zickfeld, & Fiske, 2017; Zickfeld, Schubert, Seibt, & Fiske, 2017). However, as will be revealed below, differentiating between positive emotion elicited by witnessing skill-based excellence (admiration) and virtue-based excellence (moral elevation) has utility for considering how these experiences influence choices to get along and/or get ahead in a given context.

Getting ahead Of the two emotions that arise in response to excellence of others, admiration is the primary driver of agentic outcomes. One broad function of admiration is emulation: admiration prompts actions aimed at emulating the admired other. Given that admiration arises in contexts of skill-based excellence, emulation takes the form of wanting to improve one's own skills. Support for this stems from self-reported intentions to improve oneself following inductions of state admiration (Algoe & Haidt, 2009; Galliani & Vianello, 2012; Schindler et al., 2015; van de Ven, 2017). Interestingly, when examined in direct upward social comparison contexts (i.e., the excelling other was in fact outperforming the self), admiration fails to predict self-reported or behavioral improvement (van de Ven, Zeelenberg, & Pieters, 2011). Instead, in these cases, the experience of "benign envy" drives efforts for self-improvement. Thus, agency promoting functions of admiration may be limited to situations in which one's own performance is unknown or not relevant. Further, perceived attainability of the admired skill moderates the impact of admiration on motivation (van de Ven et al., 2011).

Admiration also serves functions that maintain status hierarchies. In the intergroup domain, admiration for another group increases deference toward and propensity to learn from that group, leading to the claim that one function of admiration is "regulating social hierarchy" (Sweetman, Spears, Livingstone, & Manstead, 2013). At the trait level, admiration for others' skill is associated with higher levels of respect for others (Sarapin, Christy, Lareau, Krakow, & Jensen, 2015). While not necessarily "getting ahead" per se, it is clear that admiration serves to foment interpersonal orientations that serve the overall social goal of navigating status hierarchies.

A handful of studies have revealed agentic outcomes of moral elevation. After watching videos that elicited moral elevation, participants in one study reported heightened desires to work hard to achieve success (Oliver, Hartmann, & Woolley, 2012). Further, as is the case with trait-level admiration, moral elevation is associated with higher levels of respect for others (Sarapin et al., 2015). Moral elevation may also share with admiration the characteristic of moderation by perceived attainability (Han, Kim, Jeong, & Cohen, 2017).

Getting along Of the two emotions that arise in response to excellence of others, moral elevation is the primary driver of communal outcomes. Emulation is a broad function of moral elevation, as is true also for admiration. However, due to the context of virtue-based excellence, emulation prompted by moral elevation takes the form of prosocial motivation. Inductions of elevation robustly elicit higher self-reported motivations or intentions to engage in prosocial acts (Algoe & Haidt, 2009; Aquino, McFerran, & Laven, 2011; Erickson et al., 2018; Freeman, Aquino, & McFerran, 2009; Janicke & Oliver, 2017; Oliver et al., 2012; Schnall & Roper, 2012; Schnall, Roper, & Fessler, 2010; Thomson, Nakamura, Siegel, & Csikszentmihalyi, 2014; Thomson & Siegel, 2013; Van Cappellen, Saroglou,

Iweins, Piovesana, & Fredrickson, 2013; Van de Vyver & Abrams, 2016). In several studies, such intentions track onto actual prosocial behavior (Aquino et al., 2011; Freeman et al., 2009; Siegel, Thomson, & Navarro, 2014; Silvers & Haidt, 2008; Thomson & Siegel, 2013; Van de Vyver & Abrams, 2015). Such patterns also play out for moral elevation at the trait level (Diessner, Iyer, Smith, & Haidt, 2013; Landis et al., 2009) and among individuals with clinical diagnoses of depression and anxiety (Erickson & Abelson, 2012). Communal functions of moral elevation also extend to judgments of others. The experience of moral elevation lowers tolerance for moral violations of others (Strohminger, Lewis, & Meyer, 2011). Thus, morally elevated individuals not only seek moral excellence but are also less tolerant of others who fail to act with moral excellence.

Another outcome of moral elevation in line with its function to promote "getting along" is more inclusive and positive views of others. For instance, moral elevation experiences are characterized by having positive views of humanity (Aquino et al., 2011; Freeman et al., 2009; Siegel et al., 2014) and elicit a general sense of connectedness with others (Erickson et al., 2018; Janicke & Oliver, 2017). Further, while connectedness outcomes of moral elevation can be directed toward close others (Janicke & Oliver, 2017), they can also extend to out-groups. For instance, induced moral elevation reduces prejudice against sexual minorities (Lai, Haidt, & Nosek, 2013) and increases individuals' sense of connection with members of diverse groups (Oliver et al., 2015). Additionally, moral elevation prompts prosocial behavior that crosses intergroup lines (Freeman et al., 2009). Individuals who are more inclined to experience moral elevation tend to experience higher trust and liking for others (Sarapin et al., 2015).

Research also supports the premise that admiration has communal functions. Several studies support admiration's role in prompting "getting along" with the admired target. Specifically, the experience of admiration is associated with desire to praise and affiliate with the target (Algoe & Haidt, 2009; Van de Vyver & Abrams, 2015, 2016). Communal functions of admiration also take the broader form of benevolence, trust, and liking (Sarapin et al., 2015; Van Cappellen et al., 2013), especially toward ingroup members (Ray, Mackie, Smith, & Terman, 2012). Communal outcomes of admiration also extend to out-group members. Seger, Banerji, Park, Smith, and Mackie (2017) documented that intergroup contact elicits admiration for out-groups, which in turn reduces prejudice. It should be noted, however, that admiration has limited effects on social perception more broadly. Whereas envy prompts better memory of others, admiration does not (Hill, DelPriore, & Vaughan, 2011).

Moral elevation and admiration: a summary Excellence of others may give rise to two positive emotions: admiration in the case of skill-based excellence and moral elevation in the case of virtue-based excellence. The majority of evidence aligns admiration with agentic functions and moral elevation with communal functions. However, there is also support for agentic functions of moral elevation and communal functions of admiration. As such, these two emotions cue individuals to the contextual opportunity to get along and get ahead, prompting behaviors and cognitions that take advantage of that opportunity in an adaptive manner.

Emotions of Excellence: Coda

Excellence clearly is a potent elicitor of emotional experience. When it is oneself that achieves excellence, pride can arise. When another person achieves excellence, moral elevation can arise when that excellence is virtuous in nature, and admiration can arise when that excellence is skill-based. These three emotional experiences, in turn, shape outcomes that serve both communal and agentic outcomes. While the weight of evidence speaks to agentic functions of pride and admiration and communal outcomes of moral elevation, it is also clear that pride and admiration serve communal functions and moral elevation agentic functions.

It is worth noting that one's own excellence does not always elicit pride. For instance, in close relationships, positive emotional responses to one's own achievements relative to the other person can be attenuated or even reversed in light of potential impact on the other person (Pinkus, Lockwood, Marshall, & Yoon, 2012). For instance, an employee may feel less positive about achieving a work promotion if their close colleague had also been up for the promotion. Perhaps for this reason, positive expressions in response to success are sometimes suppressed (Webb et al., 2016), and expressive suppression in such contexts, in turn, carries adaptive social benefit (Greenaway & Kalokerinos, 2017).

In a related vein, excellence of others sometimes fails to elicit moral elevation or admiration. In fact, negative emotions such as resentment (Feather, 2006) and malicious envy (Smith & Kim, 2007; van de Ven, Zeelenberg, & Pieters, 2009) can arise, especially if the attained success is perceived as undeserved. The emergence of such negative emotions is damaging for both agentic outcomes (Hill et al., 2011) and communal outcomes (e.g., van de Ven et al., 2009). Perniciously, others' expressions of pride can elicit envy, though this may be limited to expressions of hubristic pride and malicious forms of envy (Lange & Crusius, 2015).

Contexts of excellence may also produce other positive emotions than pride, moral elevation, and admiration. For instance, recent research in the author's lab suggests that excellence of close others can elicit *vicarious pride* (Williams & Davies, 2018). This variant of pride promotes personal goal pursuit, as does its self-oriented counterpart, but also serves communal functions of prompting support for the other person's goal pursuit as well as relationship maintenance (Davies & Williams, 2017). Relatedly, excellence of a group to which one belongs can be the basis of group-level pride (Delvaux, Meeussen, & Mesquita, 2016; Liu, Lai, Yu, & Chen, 2014; Seger, Smith, & Mackie, 2009), which in turn can prompt both agentic and communal outcomes (Harth, Kessler, & Leach, 2008; Harth, Leach, & Kessler, 2013; Schori-Eyal, Tagar, Saguy, & Halperin, 2015; van Leeuwen, van Dijk, & Kaynak, 2013).

Emotions of Excellence in the Workplace

As revealed in the review above, ample evidence supports the premise that pride, admiration, and moral elevation serve to promote both communal and agentic outcomes in the face of excellence of the self or others. This section provides an overview of how excellence in the workplace can elicit pride, moral elevation, and admiration and how, in turn, agentic and communal outcomes might be facilitated.

The workplace is an emotionally evocative context, both in terms of emotions broadly (Lazarus & Cohen-Charash, 2001) and positive emotions specifically (Fredrickson, 2003; Staw, Sutton, & Pelled, 1994). Further, it is clear that the workplace is a context in which the three emotions of excellence examined in this chapter commonly arise. For example, achieving a promotion can elicit pride (Tzafrir & Hareli, 2009), whereas the success of a colleague can elicit admiration (Ford, Agosta, Huang, & Shannon, 2018). Moreover, employees can experience group-level pride in relation to the organization that employs them (Helm, 2013; Tyler & Blader, 2002). Intriguingly, perceived excellence in the organization's moral virtue contributes to such organizational pride (Ellemers, Kingma, van de Burgt, & Barreto, 2011). For instance, an employee who feels that her employer adheres to ethical values is likely to feel proud of being employed by the organization. Thus, at least in some cases, emotions of excellence are entwined at several levels.

Once such emotions arise, do they promote communal and agentic outcomes? In short, yes. The experience of pride predicts increased effort (an agentic function) as well as organizational citizenship behaviors such as helping colleagues and behaving courteously (a communal function; Verbeke, Belschak, & Bagozzi, 2004; see also Hodson, 1998). Further, admiration in the workplace prompts motivations to praise the target (a communal function) and to emulate the target's achievement (an agentic function) (Ford et al., 2018).

The trio of emotions of excellence has particularly crucial roles within the leader/follower context in hierarchical workplaces. For instance, leaders' self-reported disposition to experience pride correlates with their employee's perceptions of that leader's workplace prosociality (Michie, 2009). Further, admiration elicited by a hypothetical skilled leader heightens employee motivation to achieve, and naturally arising admiration for leaders' skills was associated with higher engagement in organizational citizenship behaviors (Galliani & Vianello, 2012). Turning to moral elevation, ethical actions of leaders elicit moral elevation, which in turn prompts organizational citizenship behaviors as well as commitment to stay with the organization (Vianello, Galliani, & Haidt, 2010). Thus, mirroring patterns that emerge in organizational contexts more broadly, pride, admiration, and moral elevation in workplace leader/follower contexts serve both communal and agentic functions.

This brief review of emotions of excellence in the workplace suggests that such emotions can and do arise and, when they do, they function to promote both agentic and communal outcomes. The coming years will no doubt see increased research examining dynamics of these emotions in workplace settings.

Looking to the Future

A rich body of research speaks to communal and agentic functions of pride, moral elevation, and admiration. The experience of these emotions prompts outcomes that serve to make the most of opportunities that excellence affords, namely, opportunities to get ahead and get along. Building on this understanding, the years ahead will no doubt see increasing work in this area, both in basic science and applied realms. This section outlines potential paths for future research, highlighting the need for integrative work across emotions and across functions as well as the application of new technologies to this intriguing area of research.

Tracking a broader trend in discrete emotion research, the prototypical approach in this area is to examine the impact of one emotion on one outcome (e.g., communal or agentic, or even one single outcome within either of those broad categories). In experimental approaches, comparison conditions can be affective in nature but frequently take the form of affectively neutral control conditions. In cross-sectional approaches, integration of other emotions than the focal emotion is sparse. While such "deep-dive" approaches into a particular emotion yield a rich understanding of that emotion, that understanding can be splintered, lacking integration across emotions and/or across functions. If the field is to attain a comprehensive grasp of social-functional dynamics of emotions that arise from excellence, research must simultaneously investigate several emotions across several functional domains.

Given evidence that all three emotions of excellence serve both communal and agentic functions, it will be of utmost import for future research to examine specific contextual features that might guide relative choice between these drives. For instance, research might assess participants' relative (or even simultaneous) choice to engage in agentic and communal behaviors. By systematically varying other features of the situation (e.g., relational closeness, relative status), a comprehensive understanding will emerge of the moderating factors that determine how pride, admiration, and moral elevation function in a given context.

As noted above, some research adopts a focus on state-level experience of pride, admiration, and moral elevation, while other research examines processes at the trait level. Scant research integrates across these levels of investigation. Mirroring broader person-by-situation approaches in social psychology, it will be fruitful for future research to examine how dispositions to experience these three emotions determine respective in-the-moment experiences and how such dynamics, in turn, shape communal and agentic outcomes.

Future research in this area will also benefit from adoption of recent methodological advances. For instance, leveraging ecological momentary assessment via participants' mobile devices can ease data collection as well as increase the quantity of resulting data (Miller, 2012). Further, such data can be paired with noninvasive measurement techniques such as the electronically activated recorder (EAR; Mehl, 2017), which records short audio snippets of participants' daily lives, or with other continuous information (e.g., location, activity level) gleaned from a mobile device (Intille, 2007). Such approaches will yield a rich understanding of contexts in which processes otherwise examined in the laboratory play out. Social media provides yet another context in which dynamics of pride, moral elevation, and admiration can be examined. Twitter (Murphy, 2017) and Facebook (Kosinski, Matz, Gosling, Popov, & Stillwell, 2015) are platforms via which psychological scientists are increasingly examining social processes. No doubt, applying such methods to the study of emotions of excellence would be a fruitful endeavor.

Conclusion

Former US President Lyndon B. Johnson is credited with saying, "The noblest search is the search for excellence." When excellence is achieved, it is not only a noble occasion but also an occasion that gives rise to potent emotional experiences. Among these are pride, moral elevation, and admiration. All three play a role in prompting agentic and communal outcomes that serve to capitalize on opportunities that excellence contexts provide. These emotions serve the ultimate end of navigating the balance between "getting along" and "getting ahead." That balance, as noted by Gandhi, represents a noble outcome itself.

References

Abele, A. E., Hauke, N., Peters, K., Louvet, E., Szymkow, A., & Duan, Y. (2016). Facets of the fundamental content dimensions: Agency with competence and assertiveness—Communion with warmth and morality. *Frontiers in Psychology, 7*, 1810.

Abele, A. E., & Wojciszke, B. (2014). Communal and agentic content in social cognition: A dual perspective model. *Advances in Experimental Social Psychology, 50*, 195–255.

Ai, A. L., Wink, P., Gall, T. L., Dillon, M., & Tice, T. N. (2017). Assessing reverence in contexts. *Journal of Humanistic Psychology, 57*, 64–97.

Algoe, S. B., & Haidt, J. (2009). Witnessing excellence in action: The "other-praising" emotions of elevation, gratitude, and admiration. *The Journal of Positive Psychology, 4*, 105–127.

Aquino, K., McFerran, B., & Laven, M. (2011). Moral identity and the experience of moral elevation in response to acts of uncommon goodness. *Journal of Personality and Social Psychology, 100*, 703–718.

Ashton-James, C. E., & Tracy, J. L. (2012). Pride and prejudice. *Personality and Social Psychology Bulletin, 38*, 466–476.

Bakan, D. (1966). *The duality of human existence: An essay on psychology and religion*. Chicago, IL: Rand McNally.

Baumeister, R. F., & Leary, M. R. (1995). The need to belong: Desire for interpersonal attachments as a fundamental human motivation. *Psychological Bulletin, 117*, 497–529.

Bicchieri, C. (2005). *The grammar of society: The nature and dynamics of social norms*. New York, NY: Cambridge University Press.

Boezeman, E. J., & Ellemers, N. (2007). Volunteering for charity: Pride, respect, and the commitment of volunteers. *Journal of Applied Psychology, 92*, 771–785.

Boezeman, E. J., & Ellemers, N. (2008). Pride and respect in volunteers' organizational commitment. *European Journal of Social Psychology, 38*, 159–172.

Bureau, J. S., Vallerand, R. J., Ntoumanis, N., & Lafrenière, M.-A. K. (2013). On passion and moral behavior in achievement settings: The mediating role of pride. *Motivation and Emotion, 37*, 121–133.

Butt, A. N., & Choi, J. N. (2006). The effects of cognitive appraisal and emotion on social motive and negotiation behavior: The critical role of agency of negotiator emotion. *Human Performance, 19*, 305–325.

Butt, A. N., Choi, J. N., & Jaeger, A. M. (2005). The effects of self-emotion, counterpart emotion, and counterpart behavior on negotiator behavior: A comparison of individual-level and dyad-level dynamics. *Journal of Organizational Behavior, 26*, 681–704.

Carver, C. S., Sinclair, S., & Johnson, S. L. (2010). Authentic and hubristic pride: Differential relations to aspects of goal regulation, affect, and self-control. *Journal of Research in Personality, 44*, 698–703.

Damian, R. I., & Robins, R. W. (2013). Aristotle's virtue or Dante's deadliest sin? The influence of authentic and hubristic pride on creative achievement. *Learning and Individual Differences, 26*, 156–160.

Davies, J., & Williams, L. A. (2018, in preparation). "I'm Proud of You": Empirical support for three functions of vicarious pride.

Delvaux, E., Meeussen, L., & Mesquita, B. (2016). Emotions are not always contagious: Longitudinal spreading of self-pride and group pride in homogeneous and status-differentiated groups. *Cognition and Emotion, 30*, 101–116.

DeWall, C. N., & Bushman, B. J. (2011). Social acceptance and rejection. *Current Directions in Psychological Science, 20*, 256–260.

Dickens, L., & DeSteno, D. (2014). Pride attenuates nonconscious mimicry. *Emotion, 14*, 7–11.

Diessner, R., Iyer, R., Smith, M. M., & Haidt, J. (2013). Who engages with moral beauty? *Journal of Moral Education, 42*, 139–163.

Dorfman, A., Eyal, T., & Bereby-Meyer, Y. (2014). Proud to cooperate: The consideration of pride promotes cooperation in a social dilemma. *Journal of Experimental Social Psychology, 55*, 105–109.

Ellemers, N., Kingma, L., van de Burgt, J., & Barreto, M. (2011). Corporate social responsibility as a source of organizational morality, employee commitment and satisfaction. *Journal of Organizational Moral Psychology, 1*, 97–124.

Erickson, T. M., & Abelson, J. L. (2012). Even the downhearted may be uplifted: Moral elevation in the daily life of clinically depressed and anxious adults. *Journal of Social and Clinical Psychology, 31*, 707–728.

Erickson, T. M., McGuire, A. P., Scarsella, G. M., Crouch, T. A., Lewis, J. A., Eisenlohr, A. P., & Muresan, T. J. (2018, in press). Viral videos and virtue: Moral elevation inductions shift affect and interpersonal goals in daily life. *The Journal of Positive Psychology*. https://doi.org/10.10 80/17439760.2017.1365163.

Etxebarria, I., Ortiz, M. J., Apodaca, P., Pascual, A., & Conejero, S. (2014). Antecedents of moral pride: The harder the action, the greater the pride? *Spanish Journal of Psychology, 17*, E52.

Etxebarria, I., Ortiz, M.-J., Apodaca, P., Pascual, A., & Conejero, S. (2015). Pride as moral motive: Moral pride and prosocial behaviour. *Infancia Y Aprendizaje, 38*, 746–774.

Feather, N. T. (2006). Deservingness and emotions: Applying the structural model of deservingness to the analysis of affective reactions to outcomes. *European Review of Social Psychology, 17*, 38–73.

Fiske, S. T., Cuddy, A. J. C., & Glick, P. (2007). Universal dimensions of social cognition: Warmth and competence. *Trends in Cognitive Sciences, 11*, 77–83.

Ford, M. T., Agosta, J. P., Huang, J., & Shannon, C. (2018). Moral emotions toward others at work and implications for employee behavior: A qualitative analysis using critical incidents. *Journal of Business and Psychology, 33*, 155–180. https://doi.org/10.1007/s10869-016-9484-3

Fredrickson, B. L. (2001). The role of positive emotions in positive psychology: The broaden-and-build theory of positive emotions. *American Psychologist, 56*, 218–226.

Fredrickson, B. L. (2003). Positive emotions and upward spirals in organizations. In K. S. Cameron, J. E. Dutton, & R. Quinn (Eds.), *Positive organizational scholarship* (pp. 163–175). San Francisco, CA: Berrett-Koehler.

Fredrickson, B. L. (2013). Positive emotions broaden and build. *Advances in Experimental Social Psychology, 47*, 1–53.

Fredrickson, B. L., Cohn, M. A., Coffey, K. A., Pek, J., & Finkel, S. M. (2008). Open hearts build lives: Positive emotions, induced through loving-kindness meditation, build consequential personal resources. *Journal of Personality and Social Psychology, 95*, 1045–1062.

Fredrickson, B. L., & Joiner, T. E. (2002). Positive emotions trigger upward spirals toward emotional well-being. *Psychological Science, 13*, 172–175.

Freeman, D., Aquino, K., & McFerran, B. (2009). Overcoming beneficiary race as an impediment to charitable donations: Social dominance orientation, the experience of moral elevation, and donation behavior. *Personality and Social Psychology Bulletin, 35*, 72–84.

Galliani, E. M., & Vianello, M. (2012). The emotion of admiration improves employees' goal orientations and contextual performance. *International Journal of Applied Psychology, 2*, 43–52.

Greenaway, K. H., & Kalokerinos, E. K. (2017). Suppress for success? Exploring the contexts in which expressing positive emotion can have social costs. *European Review of Social Psychology, 28*, 134–174.

Han, H., Kim, J., Jeong, C., & Cohen, G. L. (2017). Attainable and relevant moral exemplars are more effective than extraordinary exemplars in promoting voluntary service engagement. *Frontiers in Psychology, 8*, 283.

Harms, W., & Skyrms, B. (2008). Evolution of moral norms. In M. Ruse (Ed.), *The oxford handbook of philosophy of biology* (pp. 434–450). New York, NY: Oxford University Press.

Hart, D., & Matsuba, M. K. (2007). The development of pride and moral life. In J. L. Tracy, R. W. Robins, & J. P. Tangney (Eds.), *The self-conscious emotions: Theory and research* (pp. 114–133). New York, NY: Guilford Press.

Harth, N. S., Kessler, T., & Leach, C. W. (2008). Advantaged group's emotional reactions to intergroup inequality: The dynamics of pride, guilt, and sympathy. *Personality and Social Psychology Bulletin, 34*, 115–129.

Harth, N. S., Leach, C. W., & Kessler, T. (2013). Guilt, anger, and pride about in-group environmental behaviour: Different emotions predict distinct intentions. *Journal of Environmental Psychology, 34*, 18–26.

Helgeson, V. S., & Fritz, H. L. (1999). Unmitigated agency and unmitigated communion: Distinctions from agency and communion. *Journal of Research in Personality, 33*, 131–158.

Helm, S. (2013). A matter of reputation and pride: Associations between perceived external reputation, pride in membership, job satisfaction and turnover intentions. *British Journal of Management, 24*, 542–556.

Herrald, M. M., & Tomaka, J. (2002). Patterns of emotion-specific appraisal, coping, and cardiovascular reactivity during an ongoing emotional episode. *Journal of Personality and Social Psychology, 83*, 434–450.

Hill, S. E., DelPriore, D. J., & Vaughan, P. W. (2011). The cognitive consequences of envy: Attention, memory, and self-regulatory depletion. *Journal of Personality and Social Psychology, 101*, 653–666.

Hodson, R. (1998). Pride in task completion and organizational citizenship behaviour: Evidence from the ethnographic literature. *Work & Stress, 12*, 307–321.

Hofmann, W., & Fisher, R. R. (2012). How guilt and pride shape subsequent self-control. *Social Psychological and Personality Science, 3*, 682–690.

Hogan, R. (1982). A socioanalytic theory of personality. In M. Page (Ed.), *1982 Nebraska symposium on motivation: Personality – current theory and research* (pp. 55–89). Lincoln, NE: University of Nebraska Press.

Horberg, E. J., Kraus, M. W., & Keltner, D. J. (2013). Pride displays communicate self-interest and support for meritocracy. *Journal of Personality and Social Psychology, 105*, 24–37.

Horowitz, L. M., Wilson, K. R., Turan, B., Zolotsev, P., Constantino, M. J., & Henderson, L. (2006). How interpersonal motives clarify the meaning of interpersonal behavior: A revised circumplex model. *Personality and Social Psychology Review, 10*, 67–86.

Intille, S. S. (2007). Technological innovations enabling automatic, context-sensitive ecological momentary assessment. In A. Stone, S. Shiffman, A. A. Atienza, & L. Nebeling (Eds.), *The science of real-time data capture: Self reports in health research* (pp. 308–337). New York, NY: Oxford University Press.

Janicke, S. H., & Oliver, M. B. (2017). The relationship between elevation, connectedness, and compassionate love in meaningful films. *Psychology of Popular Media Culture, 6*, 274–289.

Johnson, K. J., & Fredrickson, B. L. (2005). "We all look the same to me": Positive emotions eliminate the own-race in face recognition. *Psychological Science, 16*, 875–881.

Kosinski, M., Matz, S. C., Gosling, S. D., Popov, V., & Stillwell, D. (2015). Facebook as a research tool for the social sciences: Opportunities, challenges, ethical considerations, and practical guidelines. *American Psychologist, 70*, 543–556.

Krettenauer, T., & Casey, V. (2015). Moral identity development and positive moral emotions: Differences involving authentic and hubristic pride. *Identity, 15*, 173–187.

Krettenauer, T., & Jia, F. (2013). Investigating the actor effect in moral emotion expectancies across cultures: A comparison of Chinese and Canadian adolescents. *The British Journal of Developmental Psychology, 31*, 349–362.

Krettenauer, T., Jia, F., & Mosleh, M. (2011). The role of emotion expectancies in adolescents' moral decision making. *Journal of Experimental Child Psychology, 108*, 358–370.

Lai, C. K., Haidt, J., & Nosek, B. A. (2013). Moral elevation reduces prejudice against gay men. *Cognition and Emotion, 28*, 781–794.

Landis, S. K., Sherman, M. F., Piedmont, R. L., Kirkhart, M. W., Rapp, E. M., & Bike, D. H. (2009). The relation between elevation and self-reported prosocial behavior: Incremental validity over the five-factor model of personality. *Journal of Positive Psychology, 4*, 71–84.

Lange, J., & Crusius, J. (2015). The tango of two deadly sins: The social-functional relation of envy and pride. *Journal of Personality and Social Psychology, 109*, 453–472.

Lazarus, R. S., & Cohen-Charash, Y. (2001). Discrete emotions in organizational life. In R. Payne & C. Cooper (Eds.), *Emotions at work: Theory, research and applications for management* (pp. 45–81). West Sussex: Wiley.

Liu, C., Lai, W., Yu, G., & Chen, C. (2014). The individual and collective facets of pride in chinese college students. *Basic and Applied Social Psychology, 36*, 176–189.

Locke, K. D. (2015). Agentic and communal social motives. *Social and Personality Psychology Compass, 9*, 525–538.

Mack, D. E., Kouali, D., Gilchrist, J. D., & Sabiston, C. M. (2015). Pride and physical activity: Behavioural regulations as a motivational mechanism? *Psychology and Health, 30*, 1049–1062.

Martens, J. P., & Tracy, J. L. (2012). The emotional origins of a social learning bias: Does the pride expression cue copying? *Social Psychological and Personality Science, 4*, 492–499.

Martens, J. P., Tracy, J. L., & Shariff, A. F. (2011). Status signals: Adaptive benefits of displaying and observing the nonverbal expressions of pride and shame. *Cognition and Emotion, 26*, 390–406.

Mascolo, M. F., & Fischer, K. W. (1995). Developmental transformations in appraisals for pride, shame, and guilt. In J. P. Tangney & K. W. Fischer (Eds.), *Self-conscious emotions: The psychology of shame, guilt, embarrassment, and pride* (pp. 64–113). New York, NY: Guilford Press.

Masser, B., Smith, G., & Williams, L. A. (2014). Donor research in australia: Challenges and promise. *Transfusion Medicine and Hemotherapy, 41*, 296–301.

McAdams, D. P. (1988). *Power, intimacy, and the life story: Personological inquiries into identity*. New York, NY: Guilford Press.

Mehl, M. R. (2017). The electronically activated recorder (EAR). *Current Directions in Psychological Science, 26*, 184–190.

Michie, S. (2009). Pride and gratitude: How positive emotions influence the prosocial behaviors of organizational leaders. *Journal of Leadership & Organizational Studies, 15*, 393–403.

Miller, G. (2012). The smartphone psychology manifesto. *Perspectives on Psychological Science, 7*, 221–237.

Murphy, S. C. (2017). A hands-on guide to conducting psychological research on twitter. *Social Psychological and Personality Science, 8*, 396–412.

Oliver, M. B., Hartmann, T., & Woolley, J. K. (2012). Elevation in response to entertainment portrayals of moral virtue. *Human Communication Research, 38*, 360–378.

Oliver, M. B., Kim, K., Hoewe, J., Chung, M. Y., Ash, E., Woolley, J. K., & Shade, D. D. (2015). Media-induced elevation as a means of enhancing feelings of intergroup connectedness. *Journal of Social Issues, 71*, 106–122.

Onu, D., Kessler, T., & Smith, J. R. (2016). Admiration: A conceptual review. *Emotion Review, 8*, 218–230.

Oveis, C., Horberg, E. J., & Keltner, D. J. (2010). Compassion, pride, and social intuitions of self-other similarity. *Journal of Personality and Social Psychology, 98*, 618–630.

Pinkus, R. T., Lockwood, P., Marshall, T. C., & Yoon, H. M. (2012). Responses to comparisons in romantic relationships: Empathy, shared fate, and contrast. *Personal Relationships, 19*, 182–201.

Pohling, R., & Diessner, R. (2016). Moral elevation and moral beauty: A review of the empirical literature. *Review of General Psychology, 20*, 412–425.

Ray, D. G., Mackie, D. M., Smith, E. R., & Terman, A. W. (2012). Discrete emotions elucidate the effects of crossed-categorization on prejudice. *Journal of Experimental Social Psychology, 48*, 55–69.

Salerno, A., Laran, J., & Janiszewski, C. (2015). Pride and regulatory behavior: The influence of appraisal information and self-regulatory goals. *Journal of Consumer Research, 42*, 499–514.

Sanders, S., Wisse, B., Van Yperen, N. W., & Rus, D. (2018, in press). On ethically solvent leaders: The roles of pride and moral identity in predicting leader ethical behavior. *Journal of Business Ethics*. https://doi.org/10.1007/s10551-016-3180-0.

Sarapin, S. H., Christy, K., Lareau, L., Krakow, M., & Jensen, J. D. (2015). Identifying admired models to increase emulation. *Measurement and Evaluation in Counseling and Development, 48*, 95–108.

Schindler, I., Paech, J., & Löwenbrück, F. (2015). Linking admiration and adoration to self-expansion: Different ways to enhance one's potential. *Cognition and Emotion, 29*, 292–310.

Schindler, I., Zink, V., Windrich, J., & Menninghaus, W. (2013). Admiration and adoration: Their different ways of showing and shaping who we are. *Cognition and Emotion, 27*, 85–118.

Schnall, S., & Roper, J. (2012). Elevation puts moral values into action. *Social Psychological and Personality Science, 3*, 373–378.

Schnall, S., Roper, J., & Fessler, D. M. T. (2010). Elevation leads to altruistic behavior. *Psychological Science, 21*, 315–320.

Schori-Eyal, N., Tagar, M. R., Saguy, T., & Halperin, E. (2015). The benefits of group-based pride: Pride can motivate guilt in intergroup conflicts among high glorifiers. *Journal of Experimental Social Psychology, 61*, 79–83.

Schubert, T. W., Zickfeld, J. H., Seibt, B., & Fiske, A. P. (2018). Moment-to-moment changes in feeling moved match changes in closeness, tears, goosebumps, and warmth: Time series analyses. *Cognition and Emotion, 32*, 174–184. https://doi.org/10.1080/02699931.2016.1268998

Seger, C. R., Banerji, I., Park, S. H., Smith, E. R., & Mackie, D. M. (2017). Specific emotions as mediators of the effect of intergroup contact on prejudice: Findings across multiple participant and target groups. *Cognition and Emotion, 31*, 923–936.

Seger, C. R., Smith, E. R., & Mackie, D. M. (2009). Subtle activation of a social categorization triggers group-level emotions. *Journal of Experimental Social Psychology, 45*, 460–467.

Seibt, B., Schubert, T. W., Zickfeld, J. H., & Fiske, A. P. (2017). Interpersonal closeness and morality predict feelings of being moved. *Emotion, 17*, 389–394.

Shariff, A. F., & Tracy, J. L. (2009). Knowing who's boss: Implicit perceptions of status from the nonverbal expression of pride. *Emotion, 9*, 631–639.

Shariff, A. F., Tracy, J. L., & Markusoff, J. L. (2012). (Implicitly) judging a book by its cover: The power of pride and shame expressions in shaping judgments of social status. *Personality and Social Psychology Bulletin, 38*, 1178–1193.

Shimoni, E., Asbe, M., Eyal, T., & Berger, A. (2016). Too proud to regulate: The differential effect of pride versus joy on children's ability to delay gratification. *Journal of Experimental Child Psychology, 141*, 275–282.

Siegel, J. T., Thomson, A. L., & Navarro, M. A. (2014). Experimentally distinguishing elevation from gratitude: Oh, the morality. *The Journal of Positive Psychology, 9*, 414–427.

Silvers, J. A., & Haidt, J. (2008). Moral elevation can induce nursing. *Emotion, 8*, 291–295.

Smith, R. H., & Kim, S. H. (2007). Comprehending envy. *Psychological Bulletin, 133*, 46–64.

Staw, B. M., Sutton, R. I., & Pelled, L. H. (1994). Employee positive emotion and favorable outcomes at the workplace. *Organization Science, 5*, 51–71.

Strohminger, N., Lewis, R. L., & Meyer, D. E. (2011). Divergent effects of different positive emotions on moral judgment. *Cognition, 119*, 295–300.

Sweetman, J., Spears, R., Livingstone, A. G., & Manstead, A. S. R. (2013). Admiration regulates social hierarchy: Antecedents, dispositions, and effects on intergroup behavior. *Journal of Experimental Social Psychology, 49*, 534–542.

Tangney, J. P., Stuewig, J., & Mashek, D. J. (2007). Moral emotions and moral behavior. *Annual Review of Psychology, 58*, 345–372.

Thomson, A. L., Nakamura, J., Siegel, J. T., & Csikszentmihalyi, M. (2014). Elevation and mentoring: An experimental assessment of causal relations. *The Journal of Positive Psychology, 9*, 402–413.

Thomson, A. L., & Siegel, J. T. (2013). A moral act, elevation, and prosocial behavior: Moderators of morality. *Journal of Positive Psychology, 8*, 50–64.

Thomson, A. L., & Siegel, J. T. (2017). Elevation: A review of scholarship on a moral and other-praising emotion. *Journal of Positive Psychology, 12*, 628–638.

Tracy, J. L., & Matsumoto, D. (2008). The spontaneous expression of pride and shame: Evidence for biologically innate nonverbal displays. *Proceedings of the National Academy of the Sciences, 105*, 11655–11660.

Tracy, J. L., & Robins, R. W. (2007a). Emerging insights into the nature and function of pride. *Current Directions in Psychological Science, 16*, 147–150.

Tracy, J. L., & Robins, R. W. (2007b). The prototypical pride expression: Development of a nonverbal behavior coding system. *Emotion, 7*, 789–801.

Tracy, J. L., & Robins, R. W. (2007c). The psychological structure of pride: A tale of two facets. *Journal of Personality and Social Psychology, 92*, 506–525.

Tracy, J. L., Robins, R. W., & Tangney, J. P. (2007). *The self-conscious emotions: Theory and research.* New York, NY: Guilford Press.

Tracy, J. L., Shariff, A. F., Zhao, W., & Henrich, J. (2013). Cross-cultural evidence that the nonverbal expression of pride is an automatic status signal. *Journal of Experimental Psychology: General, 142*, 163–180.

Tracy, J. L., Weidman, A. C., Cheng, J. T., & Martens, J. P. (2012). Pride: The fundamental emotion of success, power, and status. In M. M. Tugade, M. N. Shiota, & L. D. Kirby (Eds.), *Handbook of positive emotion* (pp. 294–310). New York, NY: Guilford Press.

Trapnell, P. D., & Paulhus, D. L. (2012). Agentic and communal values: Their scope and measurement. *Journal of Personality Assessment, 94*, 39–52.

Tyler, T. R., & Blader, S. L. (2002). Autonomous vs. comparative status: Must we be better than others to feel good about ourselves? *Organizational Behavior and Human Decision Processes, 89*, 813–838.

Tzafrir, S. S., & Hareli, S. (2009). Employees' emotional reactions to promotion decisions. *Career Development International, 14*, 351–371.

Van Cappellen, P., Saroglou, V., Iweins, C., Piovesana, M., & Fredrickson, B. L. (2013). Self-transcendent positive emotions increase spirituality through basic world assumptions. *Cognition and Emotion, 27*, 1378–1394.

van de Ven, N. (2017). Envy and admiration: Emotion and motivation following upward social comparison. *Cognition and Emotion, 31*, 193–200.

van de Ven, N., Zeelenberg, M., & Pieters, R. (2009). Leveling up and down: The experiences of benign and malicious envy. *Emotion, 9*, 419–429.

van de Ven, N., Zeelenberg, M., & Pieters, R. (2011). Why envy outperforms admiration. *Personality and Social Psychology Bulletin, 37*, 784–795.

Van de Vyver, J., & Abrams, D. (2015). Testing the prosocial effectiveness of the prototypical moral emotions: Elevation increases benevolent behaviors and outrage increases justice behaviors. *Journal of Experimental Social Psychology, 58*, 23–33.

Van de Vyver, J., & Abrams, D. (2016). Is moral elevation an approach-oriented emotion? *The Journal of Positive Psychology, 12*, 178–185.

van der Schalk, J., Kuppens, T., Bruder, M., & Manstead, A. S. R. (2015). The social power of regret: The effect of social appraisal and anticipated emotions on fair and unfair allocations in resource dilemmas. *Journal of Experimental Psychology: General, 144*, 151–157.

van Leeuwen, E., van Dijk, W., & Kaynak, Ü. (2013). Of saints and sinners: How appeals to collective pride and guilt affect outgroup helping. *Group Processes and Intergroup Relations, 16*, 781–796.

Verbeke, W., Belschak, F., & Bagozzi, R. P. (2004). The adaptive consequences of pride in personal selling. *Journal of the Academy of Marketing Science, 32*, 386–402.

Vianello, M., Galliani, E. M., & Haidt, J. (2010). Elevation at work: The effects of leaders' moral excellence. *The Journal of Positive Psychology, 5*, 390–411.

Webb, L., Stegall, S., Mirabile, S., Zeman, J., Shields, A., & Perry-Parrish, C. (2016). The management and expression of pride: Age and gender effects across adolescence. *Journal of Adolescence, 52*, 1–11.

Weisfeld, G. E., & Dillon, L. M. (2012). Applying the dominance hierarchy model to pride and shame, and related behaviors. *Journal of Evolutionary Psychology, 10*, 15–41.

Wilcox, K., Kramer, T., & Sen, S. (2011). Indulgence or self-control: A dual process model of the effect of incidental pride on indulgent choice. *Journal of Consumer Research, 38*, 151–163.

Williams, L. A., & Davies, J. (2017). Beyond the self: Pride felt in relation to others. In A. Carter & E. Gordon (Eds.), *The moral psychology of pride* (pp. 43–68). London, England: Rowman & Littlefield.

Williams, L. A., & DeSteno, D. (2008). Pride and perseverance: The motivational role of pride. *Journal of Personality and Social Psychology, 94*, 1007–1017.

Williams, L. A., & DeSteno, D. (2009). Pride. *Psychological Science, 20*, 284–288.

Williams, L. A., & DeSteno, D. (2010). Pride in parsimony. *Emotion Review, 2*, 180–181.

Williams, L. A., & Godwin, A. (2018, in preparation). The differential impact of authentic and hubristic pride expressions on social inclusion.

Wong, E., Tschan, F., Messerli, L., & Semmer, N. K. (2013). Expressing and amplifying positive emotions facilitate goal attainment in workplace interactions. *Frontiers in Psychology, 4*, 188.

Wubben, M. J. J., De Cremer, D., & van Dijk, E. (2012). Is pride a prosocial emotion? Interpersonal effects of authentic and hubristic pride. *Cognition and Emotion, 26*, 1084–1097.

Ybarra, O., Chan, E., Park, H., Burnstein, E., Monin, B., & Stanik, C. (2008). Life's recurring challenges and the fundamental dimensions: An integration and its implications for cultural differences and similarities. *European Journal of Social Psychology, 38*, 1083–1092.

Zickfeld, J. H., Schubert, T. W., Seibt, B., & Fiske, A. P. (2017). Empathic concern is part of a more general communal emotion. *Frontiers in Psychology, 8*, 723.

Chapter 13
The Emotional Toolkit: Lessons from the Science of Emotion

Heather C. Lench, Cassandra L. Baldwin, Dong An, and Katie E. Garrison

Abstract What do emotions do for people? This chapter presents a framework that emotions function much like a precision toolkit, with particular emotions best used to fix particular problems. This means that emotions are not always functional or always dysfunctional. Instead each emotion prepares people to deal with particular issues. The key to promoting functional emotion in our own lives, then, is to recognize what emotions do and to regulate how we express them. This chapter also brings together perspectives from the science of emotion to identify the next big questions about emotion.

> Virtuous behavior is to experience emotions at the right time, toward the right objects or people, for the right reason, in the right manner in accordance with the mean.
>
> –Aristotle, *Nicomachean Ethics*

Emotions are powerful – they have the ability to overwhelm us and can be intensely painful. Emotions are so powerful that they mark the events that we remember in our lives and, as a consequence, shape who we are as people (Levine, Safer, & Lench, 2006). The impact of emotion is undeniable, but this does not mean that emotions should be considered frightening, dangerous, or irrational. Recent research has revealed that the power of emotion often works for people, protecting social relationships and preparing people to pursue goals and respond to threats. Based on the work presented throughout this book and a functional approach to emotion, this chapter argues that emotions function like a precision toolkit, with particular emotions best used to fix particular problems. As a result of this precision,

H. C. Lench (✉) · C. L. Baldwin · K. E. Garrison
Department of Psychological and Brain Sciences, Texas A&M University,
College Station, TX, USA
e-mail: hlench@tamu.edu

D. An
Department of Philosophy, Texas A&M University, College Station, TX, USA

© Springer International Publishing AG, part of Springer Nature 2018   253
H. C. Lench (ed.), *The Function of Emotions*,
https://doi.org/10.1007/978-3-319-77619-4_13

emotions are not always helpful or always hurtful to people. Instead, each emotion prepares people to deal with specific issues in their lives.

What Emotions Do

Each of the chapters in this book clearly demonstrates that *emotions matter*. Emotions affect people, often changing their physiology, cognition, and behavior in consequential ways. The impact of emotions across systems can range from the seemingly innocuous narrowing of attention experienced during sadness (Huron, 2018; Karnaze & Levine, 2018) to the overwhelming urge to attack experienced during anger (Roseman, 2018). These changes, from a functional perspective, all facilitate the function of the emotion. In other words, each change arose through natural selection to occur in conjunction with the experience of an emotion because it helped to resolve the problem that elicits the emotion. The narrowing of attention experienced during sadness, for example, is thought to promote careful processing of situations when the person is failing (Karnaze & Levine, 2018). This careful processing should result in better responses to failure and, ultimately, greater success. Beyond changing our reactions in the moment of experience, the chapters also demonstrate that emotions significantly matter for the overall course of our lives. Fear and anxiety, for example, can develop into psychiatric disorders that are often debilitating (Parsafar & Davis, 2018). Anger can influence our political responses and our willingness to take action for or against a political system (Roseman, 2018). Emotions of excellence, such as pride and admiration, can push us to new heights and promote our success in the workplace (Williams, 2018). In some cases, the experience of an emotion in the moment, such as awe, can even be self-transformative, fundamentally altering who we are as people and how we see the world around us (Chirico & Yaden, 2018).

Another major point that the chapters in this book make clear is that both *positive and negative emotions can be helpful* to people. Positive emotions, such as happiness and awe, can promote our engagement with the world around us and prompt people to seek out new opportunities or experiences (Chirico & Yaden, 2018; Storbeck & Wylie, 2018). Emotions such as nurturant love keep us connected to social networks and promote caring for children (O'Neil, Danvers, & Shiota, 2018). Negative emotions, such as sadness and jealousy, can promote help from our social network and prompt us to protect our loved ones (Karnaze & Levine, 2018; Yong & Li, 2018). The fact that negative emotions are often helpful can sometimes be surprising because negative emotions feel bad and people usually want to avoid experiencing them (Lench & Carpenter, 2018). However, from a functional perspective, each emotion is the result of selection for its ability to resolve a particular type of problem. Negative emotions might feel bad, but they help us solve problems when things are not going well. Several of the chapters add a caveat to the claim that emotions can be helpful – they demonstrate that the functions of an emotion can be helpful or harmful to our overall goal pursuits and intentions. In other words, emotions are always functional, but that function can be enacted in ways that could help or hurt people's lives, relationships, and overall success. Boredom prompts people to find new and engaging experiences, but some people will choose new experiences that are harmful, such as using drugs (Danckert, Mugon, Struk, & Easterwood, 2018). Similarly, happiness can promote cognitive flexibility, but that flexibility can promote distraction and a focus on short-term goal pursuits that actually reduce our chances of overall life happiness (Storbeck & Wylie, 2018).

What also becomes clear across chapters is that *the functions of emotions are complex*. Multiple functions have been proposed for each emotion, some of which are interpersonal in nature and others intrapersonal. Sadness, for example, is thought to promote the interpersonal function of recruiting help from others through expression and weeping (Huron, 2018), as well as the intrapersonal function of promoting cognitive change (Karnaze & Levine, 2018) and potentially goal disengagement or goal protection (Tibbett & Lench, 2015). The proliferation of proposed functions can sometimes lead to the impression that the function of emotions has not been identified or is controversial, but this does not accurately reflect the state of the literature. One solution to this quandary is to view the functions of an emotion in terms of the adaptive challenge that the emotion is theorized to resolve. Sadness, as an example, is theorized to be a response to situations that involve failure and loss that is beyond the ability of the individual to address. Viewed from this standpoint, the multiple functions of sadness coalesce around this challenge. If the individual cannot address the loss alone, then recruiting help is adaptive in that others might be able to solve the challenge or provide support to the individual. In the case that there is no way to prevent the loss, then cognitive restructuring, which could involve goal disengagement or protection, is adaptive in that it would permit the individual to deal with the failure or loss and its consequences. A focus on the adaptive challenge that is addressed by an emotion thus simplifies the proposed functions for the emotion and also opens avenues for future study. What other functions should be present in the case of sadness, if it is a response to situations that involve failure or loss that the individual cannot address? Are there boundary conditions that would change the function of sadness depending on the specific situation, such as the recruitment of help only when there is a greater-than-zero probability of avoiding the loss?

The Emotional Toolkit

The scientific study of emotion has also revealed that people can control their emotional responses (Gross & Thompson, 2007). Using a functional approach to emotion, this chapter presents a framework to promote the utility of emotion by recognizing what emotions do for us and to us and regulating how we respond to emotion. Like Aristotle, this chapter suggests that people can change how they emotionally respond to situations so that their responses promote their long-term goals and match what is needed in a given situation. In other words, people can change the way that they perceive situations and the actions that they take so that emotions work for them and help them accomplish goals and attain greater well-being.

Functional accounts of emotion posit that specific emotions, such as anger and sadness, arose through natural selection because they resolved challenges faced by our ancestors. To understand the structure of our emotions and their functions, it is helpful to have a perspective on how emotions likely unfolded over time (Lench, Bench, Darbor, & Moore, 2015). Some emotions have been demonstrated to occur across species, and in response to particular stimuli that are biologically significant, such as the joy experienced while eating sweets or the fear experienced while being rushed by an attacking animal. Other emotions appear to be experienced primarily among humans and are based on a cognitive evaluation of goals and situations, such as the joy experienced when people perceive that they have succeeded or the fear experienced when perceiving a threat to the chance to attend college. Given the differences in the degree to which these emotional responses are present across species and require cognitive evaluation, we must think about their potential functions differently.

The key here is that natural selection builds upon what is already present. Gould and Vrba (1982) give the example of bones. It is likely that bones initially evolved because they provided nutrient storage. When animals moved to land, however, bones also became useful for support, and natural selection acted on bones for that purpose, resulting in bone structures that support animals within their specific land environments. Similarly, it is likely that positive and negative responses, which are present even in very simple organisms, evolved because they provided a fast evaluation of beneficial and harmful stimuli and the motivation to move toward or away from those stimuli. More specific emotional responses to specific stimuli likely built upon this preexisting positive/negative emotional response. Joy upon being tickled, for example, likely built upon a general positive response through natural selection acting to promote social bonding (see Panksepp & Burgodorf, 2003, for an analysis of laughing rats). Specific emotional responses to relatively complex evaluations of goals and situations, in turn, likely built upon this preexisting specific structure. The argument here is that people who could link cognitions about goal status to existing emotional systems, and take advantage of the resulting motivation, would have been more successful than humans who lacked that ability (Lench et al., 2015). For example, an early human who linked an evaluation that a goal is blocked to the emotion of anger would likely be better at eliminating whatever is blocking the goal than others. Because of this relative advantage, the tendency to link emotion to specific cognitive evaluations would have become more prevalent in humans over time.

This means we have two types of tools at our disposal in the emotion toolkit. *We have a set of tools that are powerful but difficult to control* (think a jackhammer). From an evolutionary standpoint, these are critically important for our functioning. One of the proposed functions of anger, for example, is to intimidate others and change their behavior (Roseman, 2018) and through this intimidation to remove them as obstacles to our goals. This is effective – others will concede to the demands of people who express anger (Lench, Tibbett, & Bench, 2016; Tamir & Ford, 2012; Van Kleef, De Dreu, & Manstead, 2004). But anger only "works" to intimidate others if there is a real threat that angry people might lose control and attack (Pinker, 1997). If anger never resulted in loss of control, anger would lose its power to affect others because we would all know that there was no actual threat. Similarly, who would reach out to help the sad person if we knew that crying was a strategy to enlist our assistance rather than true hurt (Huron, 2018)? Because of this reality, it is critical that some emotions are difficult to control. This also means that there is limited opportunity for us to shape these tools. People could potentially learn not to feel fear and jump when they see the movement of a snake in the grass, but such learning is likely to require extensive and focused training given how rapidly and automatically these responses occur (Öhman & Mineka, 2001). It would be difficult or impossible to turn these emotional tools on or off, but people do appear to have some control over the direction of these tools through emotion regulation strategies (Ochsner & Gross, 2005). People might not be able to stop their fear at seeing the movement of a snake, but they can rapidly deploy reappraisal strategies to reduce their fear responses (e.g., "Oh, it's just a hose..."). In other words, cognitive reappraisal could help in situations where there is a mismatch between the situation and the emotional response. If there is no mismatch, of course, then the emotional tool will function as intended – fear would promote a rapid response to the actual snake in the grass.

We have another set of tools in the emotion toolkit that are easier to control because they are the result of how we perceive situations. In one study, researchers recorded travelers who had lost luggage on an airline (Scherer & Ceschi, 1997). Travelers varied in the emotion they experienced – anger or anxiety – even though the objective situation was identical. What predicted people's emotional response was how they *perceived* the situation. Studies have repeatedly demonstrated that perception is what matters for these types of emotional responses, not the objective situation (e.g., Moors, Ellsworth, Scherer, & Frijda, 2013; Stein & Hernadez, 2007). Because this type of emotional response depends on perception, changing perception can be used to change the emotion or the intensity of the emotion. There is no evidence that we can eliminate a particular emotional response completely, but there is lots of evidence about how people can change their perception of situations. In fact, this strategy of changing thoughts underlies the most effective therapeutic techniques available for psychiatric disorders such as depression (Butler & Beck, 2000; Butler, Chapman, Forman, & Beck, 2006). The idea that people can shape their thoughts to change their emotions has also entered the public zeitgeist through movements centered on mindfulness training (Carmody & Baer, 2008) and countless self-help programs focused on changing thoughts. The essence of all of these approaches is to learn to control thought patterns over time and builds on the strategy of cognitive reappraisal (Ochsner & Gross, 2005). Imagine, for example, that public speaking is an important part of your career but that you experience intense anxiety before every talk. One approach to reducing this anxiety would be to identify the thought(s) that are creating the anxiety and intentionally changing that cognition (e.g., "how likely is it that the audience will throw things?"). Over time, this cognitive restructuring should become a fairly automated process and require less thought and attention, and emotion intensity should reduce.

Next Big Questions

The chapters in this book raise a number of important questions that remain for the study of emotion. One of these is whether the function of an emotion is dependent upon the cognitive complexity of that emotion. At one point in time, emotions were likely simple approach or avoidance impulses toward or away from relevant stimuli. As organisms evolved and social environments became more complex, our adaptations to the environment also became more complex. People approached stimuli with interest or joy; they approached with a sense of certainty and control. Instead of simply avoiding harm, people learned to withdraw from social rejection or a lost goal. As humans developed higher-order cognitions, they learned to appraise events according to their expectations and past experiences; they learned to be self-conscious and to regulate emotions through cognitive restructuring. An exciting avenue for future research is how these relatively complex emotions operate and function in contemporary life when they are fused with cognitions, social norms, and self-relevance. Researchers have proposed that a function of disgust, for instance, is to avoid harm from contamination. But in today's world, disgust is often tightly connected to issues of morality (Pizarro, Inbar, & Helion, 2011). Do these complex emotions serve the same functions as the less complex emotions from which they stem? How much of an emotional experience is the *essence* of these complex emotions, and how much is a product of cognitions and learned experience? Research across species on the functions of emotion could be particularly useful for evaluating this question.

The chapters in this book focused primarily on the functions of state emotions – emotions that occur within individuals in response to events or circumstances. But, of course, people also vary in the frequency and intensity of their emotional responses. One person might experience anxiety on a daily, even hourly basis, whereas another person might experience anxiety very rarely. An important area for future work is to identify whether trait emotions and state emotions serve the same functions. The chapter by Ein-Dor and Hirschberger (2018) is an excellent example of work in this direction – they present evidence that trait emotion in the form of attachment anxiety appears to serve to protect groups from threats. This is similar to the proposed function of state anxiety, although the proposed function operates at the group rather than the individual level (Parsafar & Davis, 2018). More work is needed to examine the function of trait emotion for other emotional responses and to examine potential functions that are relevant at the group level.

Another important big question to address in emotion science is the importance of different features to emotion and to the function of emotions. As described in each chapter, emotions are characterized by changes in physiology, cognition, and behavior. But the relationships between and among these features are complicated and not yet well understood. As an example, emotions have long been characterized as the causes of actions and action tendencies to behave in a particular way (Frijda, 1987). This conceptualization assumes that emotion and action are separable and independent constructs. Recently, however, theorists have argued that actions are by nature emotional (Nanay, 2017) and that emotions are best characterized as actions related to goal-directed processes (Moors & Boddez, 2017; Moors, Boddez, & De Houwer, 2017). From these perspectives, emotion and action are not separable constructs, and instead one is a quality of the other. Research illuminating the nature of emotions in relation to actions could have implications regarding questions such as the utility of different emotions, why and how emotions are regulated, and how emotions impact other psychological processes. A great deal of empirical work is needed to identify the relationships among emotion experience, physiology, cognition, and emotion.

Conclusions

At the outset, this book invited you to consider the science of emotions and to learn about how and why emotions can be useful for people. The aim was to provide readers with a framework to think about emotions and their effects. The chapters in this book cover a variety of emotions, some positive and some negative, and discuss how they impact our lives. The point of thinking about the functions of emotion, of course, is to improve people's lives. We hope that readers have gained insight into the function of emotion and skills to use their own emotional toolkit.

References

Butler, A. C., & Beck, J. S. (2000). Cognitive therapy outcomes: A review of meta-analysis. *Journal of Norwegian Psychological Association, 37*, 1–9.

Butler, A. C., Chapman, J. E., Forman, E. M., & Beck, A. T. (2006). The empirical status of cognitive behavioral therapy: A review of meta-analyses. *Clinical Psychology Review, 26*, 17–31.

Carmody, J., & Baer, R. A. (2008). Relationships between mindfulness practice and levels of mindfulness, medical and psychological symptoms and well-being in a mindfulness-based stress reduction program. *Journal of Behavioral Medicine, 31*, 23–33.

Chirico, A., & Yaden, D. B. (2018). Awe: A self-transcendent and sometimes-transformative emotion. In H. C. Lench (Ed.), *The functions of emotion: When and why emotions help us*. Cham, Switzerland: Springer.

Danckert, J., Mugon, J., Struk, A., & Easterwood, J. (2018). Boredom – What is it good for? In H. C. Lench (Ed.), *The functions of emotion: When and why emotions help us*. Cham, Switzerland: Springer.

Ein-Dor, T., & Hirschberger, G. (2018). On sentinels and rapid responders: The adaptive function of emotion dysregulation. In H. C. Lench (Ed.), *The functions of emotion: When and why emotions help us*. Cham, Switzerland: Springer.

Frijda, N. H. (1987). Emotion, cognitive structure, and action tendency. *Cognition and Emotion, 1*, 115–143.

Gould, S. J., & Vrba, E. S. (1982). Exaptation – A missing term in the science of form. *Paleobiology, 8*, 4–15.

Gross, J. J., & Thompson, R. A. (2007). Emotion regulation: Conceptual foundations. In J. J. Gross (Ed.), *Handbook of emotion regulation* (pp. 3–24). New York, NY: Guilford Press.

Huron, D. (2018). On the functions of sadness and grief. In H. C. Lench (Ed.), *The functions of emotion: When and why emotions help us*. Cham, Switzerland: Springer.

Karnaze, M. M., & Levine, L. J. (2018). Sadness, the architect of cognitive change. In H. C. Lench (Ed.), *The functions of emotion: When and why emotions help us*. Cham, Switzerland: Springer.

Lench, H. C., Bench, S. W., Darbor, K. E., & Moore, M. (2015). A functionalist manifesto: Goal-related discrete emotions from an evolutionary perspective. *Emotion Review, 7*, 90–98.

Lench, H. C., & Carpenter, Z. K. (2018). What do emotions do for us? In H. C. Lench (Ed.), *The functions of emotion: When and why emotions help us*. Cham, Switzerland: Springer.

Lench, H. C., Tibbett, T. P., & Bench, S. W. (2016). Exploring the toolkit of emotion: What do sadness and anger do for us? *Social and Personality Psychology Compass, 10*, 11–25.

Levine, L. J., Safer, M. A., & Lench, H. C. (2006). Remembering and misremembering emotions. In L. J. Sanna & E. C. Chang (Eds.), *Judgments over time: The interplay of thoughts, feelings, and behaviors* (pp. 271–290). New York, NY: Oxford University Press.

Moors, A., & Boddez, Y. (2017). Author response: Emotional episodes are action episodes. *Emotion Review, 9*, 353–354.

Moors, A., Boddez, Y., & De Houwer, J. (2017). The power of goal-directed processes in the causation of emotional and other actions. *Emotion Review, 9*, 310–318.

Moors, A., Ellsworth, P. C., Scherer, K. R., & Frijda, N. H. (2013). Appraisal theories of emotion: State of the art and future development. *Emotion Review, 5*, 119–124.

Nanay, B. (2017). Comment: Every action is an emotional action. *Emotion Review, 9*, 350–352.

O'Neil, M. J., Danvers, A. F., & Shiota, M. N. (2018). Nurturant love and caregiving emotions. In H. C. Lench (Ed.), *The functions of emotion: When and why emotions help us*. Cham, Switzerland: Springer.

Ochsner, K. N., & Gross, J. J. (2005). The cognitive control of emotion. *Trends in Cognitive Sciences, 9*, 242–249.

Öhman, A., & Mineka, S. (2001). Fears, phobias, and preparedness: Toward an evolved module of fear and fear learning. *Psychological Review, 108*, 483–522.

Panksepp, J., & Burgodorf, J. (2003). "Laughing" rats and the evolutionary antecedents of human joy? *Physiology and Behavior, 79*, 533–547.

Parsafar, P., & Davis, E. L. (2018). Fear and anxiety. In H. C. Lench (Ed.), *The functions of emotion: When and why emotions help us*. Cham, Switzerland: Springer.

Pinker, S. (1997). *How the mind works*. New York, NY: Norton.

Pizarro, D., Inbar, Y., & Helion, C. (2011). On disgust and moral judgment. *Emotion Review, 3*, 267–268.

Roseman, I. (2018). Functions of anger in the emotion system. In H. C. Lench (Ed.), *The functions of emotion: When and why emotions help us*. Cham, Switzerland: Springer.

Scherer, K. R., & Ceschi, G. (1997). Lost luggage: A field study of emotion-antecedent appraisal. *Motivation and Emotion, 21*, 211–235.

Stein, N. L., & Hernadez, M. W. (2007). Assessing understanding and appraisals during emotional experience. In J. A. Coan & J. J. B. Allen (Eds.), *Handbook of emotion elicitation and assessment* (pp. 298–317). Oxford, UK: Oxford University Press.

Storbeck, J., & Wylie, J. (2018). The functional and dysfunctional aspects of happiness: Cognitive, physiological, behavioral, and health considerations. In H. C. Lench (Ed.), *The functions of emotion: When and why emotions help us*. Cham, Switzerland: Springer.

Tamir, M., & Ford, B. Q. (2012). When feeling bad is expected to be good: Emotion regulation and outcome expectances in social conflict. *Emotion, 12*, 807–816.

Tibbett, T. P., & Lench, H. C. (2015). When do feelings help us? The interpersonal function of emotion. In *Advances in Psychology Research* (Vol. 107, pp. 1–10). New York, NY: Nova Science.

van Kleef, G. A., De Dreu, C. K. W., & Manstead, A. S. R. (2004). The interpersonal effects of – Anger and happiness in negotiations. *Journal of Personality and Social Psychology, 86*, 57–76.

Williams, L. A. (2018). Emotions of excellence: Communal and agentic functions of pride, moral elevation, and admiration. In H. C. Lench (Ed.), *The functions of emotion: When and why emotions help us*. Cham, Switzerland: Springer.

Yong, J. C., & Li, N. P. (2018). The adaptive functions of jealousy. In H. C. Lench (Ed.), *The functions of emotion: When and why emotions help us*. Cham, Switzerland: Springer.

Index

© Springer International Publishing AG, part of Springer Nature 2018
H. C. Lench (ed.), *The Function of Emotions*,
https://doi.org/10.1007/978-3-319-77619-4

CPSIA information can be obtained
at www.ICGtesting.com
Printed in the USA
LVHW06*2144130818
586909LV00002B/13/P